Introduction to Sets and Mappings
in Modern Economics

Introduction to Sets and Mappings in Modern Economics

Hukukane Nikaido
Hitotsubashi University, Tokyo, Japan

translated by

Kazuo Sato
United Nations, New York, USA

1970

NORTH-HOLLAND PUBLISHING COMPANY – AMSTERDAM, LONDON

For information address the publisher, North-Holland Publishing Company, 305–311 Keizersgracht, Amsterdam, The Netherlands

This book was originally published in the Japanese language as:

GENDAI KEIZAIGAKU NO SUGAKUTEKI HOHO
By Hukukane Nikaido
Published by Iwanami Shoten, Publishers, Tokyo, 1960

Publishers:

NORTH-HOLLAND PUBLISHING COMPANY – AMSTERDAM
NORTH-HOLLAND PUBLISHING COMPANY, LTD. – LONDON

ISBN 7204 3043 7
Library of Congress Catalog Card Number 69–18376

Printed in The Netherlands

PREFACE

This book is written as an introduction to the modern mathematical approach that is gaining popularity in modern economics, specially directed to students who wish to become familiar with the approach. At the same time, it may also serve as an introduction to elementary topology and its applications. Topology is a field occupying a central position in modern mathematics; it has come to be recognized as a very efficient tool for solving various problems that are posed in economics.

The only mathematical prerequisite for the reader of this book is the college junior's level of differential and integral calculus and the basic theory of determinants. Though complex numbers appear in a few places in Chapter 3 (viz. §16, 17 and 21), they do not require more than a very elementary level of mathematics. As for economic theory, no special prior knowledge is presupposed; whenever necessary, an exposition is given in a form understandable even to the reader specialized in sciences or engineering.

The book proceeds from a mathematical introduction to such problems that can be handled with this preparation. This is repeated by giving another mathematical introduction followed by more advanced problems. Thus, the exposition of basic mathematics and the economic analysis of relevant problems are closely intertwined; this process will gradually elevate the academic standard.

Needless to say, it is impossible in a small volume like this to attempt an exhaustive coverage of problems in modern mathematical economics. Therefore, the book highlights a small number of basic problems and treats them in a detailed manner. The author believes that this is a more effective way of revealing the essentials of the mathematical approach.

The book is arranged as follows: in the first part under the heading of modern static analysis, it discusses the inter-industry analysis, linear programming, the modern analysis of maximum and minimum problems, the activity analysis of production, game theory and saddle point problems, the von Neumann model, and the analysis of consumer behavior. In the second part, it analyzes the existence problem of an equilibrium solution in a Walrasian model. Sprinkled in between, three chapters are devoted to mathematical expositions.

The author has tried to keep expositions elementary. The book, however, does not intend to expound economic doctrines as such. Rather, it aims to show, in a form as palatable as possible to the reader, how economic problems are mathematically studied. In this connection, a special effort has been made to keep the expositions easy and at the same time not to lose mathematical rigor.

The author will be more than happy if this book turns out to be a good study companion not only to economists but also to those students in other disciplines like humanities and sciences who are interested in learning mathematical methods in social sciences.

It should be acknowledged that the second part of this book is based on an earlier booklet written jointly with Professor Yasui in the Iwanami series of *Modern Applied Mathematics.* The author is indebted to Professor Yasui for his kind permission to incorporate its substance in the present book.

Finally, the author wishes to express his hearty gratitude to Professors Shokichi Iyanaga and Takuma Yasui for their generous assistance and encouragement in many respects from suggesting the publication to reading the manuscript.

Winter, 1959 Hukukane Nikaido

PREFACE TO THE ENGLISH EDITION

This book takes a principal aim at introducing the reader to concepts and theorems pertaining to sets and mappings and illustrating, in terms of a few important typical topics, how fruitfully they are applied to the solution of economic problems. In order to achieve this objective, emphasis is placed on a detailed exposition of a very limited number of selected subject matters at the cost of abandoning a broader coverage of material.

Fortunately, since its original publication almost a decade ago, this book seems to have been of some use as a study companion to Japanese students wishing to get acquainted with modern mathematical methods in economic theory. I think an introduction of this kind to modern mathematical methods to be equally helpful to non-Japanese-speaking students and make it worth while removing the language barrier lying between them and the original edition of this book. To my satisfaction, this undertaking is now accomplished by the present translation by Dr. Sato. I hope that English speaking readers will find this book useful as their study companion.

Although I myself find many flaws in this book by reviewing it now some years after the original writing, the book as a whole is almost a living organism to me, which would lose vigor if a drastic revision is made. I therefore desired that the original text remain essentially intact in the present English edition. The translation is based on a slightly revised version of the original edition, prepared by myself by re-examining its entire pages, correcting slips and rewording certain passages on a few pages, to the extent which leaves the essential content and characteristic of the original edition intact. I am extremely happy to note that Dr. Sato's translation transmits the spirit of the original book vividly. I wish to express my most cordial thanks to Dr. Sato for his excellent translation and invaluable co-operation.

The publication of this English edition has only been made possible by the courtesy of the publisher of the original Japanese edition, Iwanami Shoten, Publishers, Tokyo, to whom many thanks are due. I am also very grateful to the North-Holland Publishing Company for undertaking the publication of this English edition of my book.

January, 1970 Hukukane Nikaido

LOGICAL DEVELOPMENTS OF THE BOOK

The diagram below shows how chapters in the book are interrelated.
⟶ represents logical developments in this book
– – – → represents supplementary relations examined in this book
–·—·→ represents relations not taken up in this book

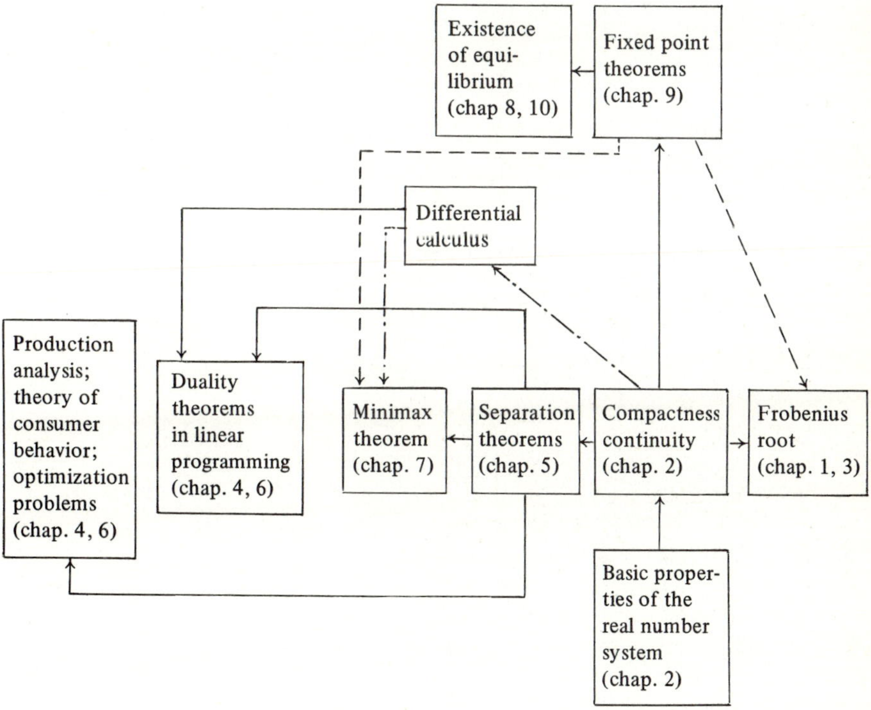

CONTENTS

Preface v
Preface to the English edition vii
Logical developments of the book ix

Introduction 1

Part I. Modern Static Analysis

Chapter 1. Equilibrium in linear economic models. Interindustry analysis 7

1. A broad sketch of a circular flow 7
2. Representation by linear equations 9
3. The Hawkins-Simon condition 13
4. Outputs and prices 19

Chapter 2. Introduction to mathematics (I) Linear algebra and point set theory 24

5. The objective of the chapter 24
6. Sets 25
7. Mappings 32
8. Completeness of the real number system 37
9. Linear spaces 48
10. Matrices and linear mappings 57
11. Convergence in R^n 69
12. A few topological concepts 78

13. Continuous mappings 88
14. Compactness 98

Chapter 3. The Frobenius theorem 107

15. Non-negativity constraints 107
16. The non-negative eigenvalue problem 113
17. The Frobenius root 118
18. Economic significance of the Frobenius root 124
19. C.Neumann series 127
20. Indecomposable matrices 131
21. Indecomposable matrices (continued) 139
22. Relative stability of the balanced growth path 149

Chapter 4. Optimization problems 155

23. The microeconomic approach 155
24. Interior optima and corner optima 158
25. Linear programming problems 163
26. The differential-calculus approach to linear programming 173

Chapter 5. Introduction to mathematics
(II) Properties of convex sets 181

27. Convex sets 181
28. Basic properties of convex sets 193
29. Separation theorems 199
30. Separation theorems in alternative forms 205

Chapter 6. Optimization problems (continued) 211

31. The proof of the duality theorems in linear programming 211
32. Production processes in activity analysis 214
33. Preference ordering and demand functions 221

Chapter 7. Saddle point problems 228

34. The minimax theorem on zero-sum two-person games 228
35. The von Neumann balanced growth model 236
36. Games and linear programming problems 244
37. Optimization problems and saddle point problems 249

Part II. Existence of Equilibrium

Chapter 8. The theory of general equilibrium 265

38. Foundations of equilibrium analysis 265
39. A Walrasian equilibrium model 268
40. Demand and supply functions 275

Chapter 9. Introduction to mathematics
(III) Fixed point theorems 289

41. Simplexes 289
42. Simplicial subdivision 299
43. Brouwer's fixed point theorem 303
44. Kakutani's fixed point theorem 309

Chapter 10. The existence of competitive equilibrium 319

45. The Walras law and economic equilibrium 319
46. The existence of an equilibrium solution 324

Bibliography and references 335

Index 339

INTRODUCTION

As is well known, mathematics has its own intrinsic value quite apart from its practical applications. Even today, many excellent studies are being produced in the field of pure mathematics. It, however, is also true that mathematics has absorbed rich materials and problems from other fields of science in its process of development and given them, in return, fruitful applications. Natural sciences like physics, chemistry and engineering have long been close to mathematics. Now, new fields like biology and economics have come into close contact with mathematics.

The systematic introduction of mathematical methods into economics began with A.A. Cournot (1801–1877). However, it is the epochmaking works of L. Walras (1834–1910) and V. Pareto (1848–1923) late in the nineteenth century and early in the twentieth century that placed firm foundations for mathematical economics. Walras said: "There are today heaven knows how many schools of political economy . . . For my part, I recognize only two: the school of those who do not demonstrate, and the school, which I hope to see founded, of those who do demonstrate their conclusions" *. And as a tool for this demonstration, Walras used mathematics. The active introduction of mathematics into economics, together with the application of mathematical statistics, has by now grown to be one main stream of economic science that nobody can disregard any longer. The mathematical approach has gradually come to receive full recognition though it used to be regarded as a heresy by most economists when it was started at a corner of economics. The efforts of economists themselves as well as the active cooperation of mathematicians

* L. Walras [53], English translation by W. Jaffé, p. 471, cited by courtesy of the translator, George Allen and Unwin, Ltd., and Richard D. Irwin, Inc.

have contributed to making it fully substantive. Broadly speaking, there are two areas in the mathematical approach: one is the theoretical field in the direct footsteps of Cournot and Walras and the other is econometrics, namely empirical studies that place emphasis on statistical treatment of numerical data derived from actual economic life. This book is devoted to the former, leaving the latter to other specialized books. In the theoretical field with which this book is primarily concerned, classical differential and integral calculus has long been the major tool of analysis since Cournot and Walras. Though differential equations, difference equations, linear algebra and the like gradually came to be utilized, the main approach remained to be the mechanical application of differential and integral calculus. It cannot be denied that calculus helped to advance economic theory greatly and gave a high degree of precision to its expressions and formulations. But in spite of its many achievements, the classical method suffered from a great weakness. One of Walras' brilliant attainments is the theory of price formation in multiple markets that he constructed on the basis of equilibrium equations and to which he gave a rigorous mathematical representation. However, because of the primitiveness of his analytical technique, Walras did not succeed in giving a mathematical proof to the existence of a solution for his system of equilibrium equations. This existence problem has only recently been completely solved in the affirmative from a more modern standpoint after nearly half a century of economists' vain search for the solution.

In mathematics of the late nineteenth century and the early twentieth century, the theory of functions of a complex variable more or less established its own system and a wave of new ideas was sweeping the fields of algebra and geometry. Mathematicians became very rigorous and critical at that time as can be witnessed, for instance, in the works of K. Weierstrass (1815–1897). At the same time, as can be seen from the set theory that was established by G. Cantor (1845–1918) and combinatorial topology that was created by H. Poincaré (1854–1912), the keynote was set in that period for elegance, rigor, abstraction and other characteristics inherent in today's mathematics. Calculus with its long history was not an exception. It received the baptism of critical spirits and was being rejuvenated while a sufficiently strong new basis was put in.

In contrast to these trends in mathematics, classical mathematical economics adhered to the traditional mechanical application of calculus in disregard of premises and assumptions and thus often evaded proving central propositions that form the basis of economic theory. This defect must have been due to the isolation of economists from the new contemporary trends in mathematics.

It was the works of two mathematicians, J. von Neumann (1903–1957) and A. Wald (1902–1950) in the nineteen thirties that helped to break up this isolation. Von Neumann created game theory and studied a balanced growth model that now bears his name. Wald studied the existence problem of an equilibrium solution in the Cassel-Wald model. Both solved their problems by applying fresh techniques of modern mathematics and thereby marked a new epoch in mathematical analysis in economics. Unfortunately, their works did not come into immediate reception by economists. However, later the publication of *Theory of Games and Economic Behavior* (first edition, 1944) written jointly by von Neumann and economist O. Morgenstern prompted economists to re-examine the mechanical application of mathematics. They were directed toward such studies that would make full use of the high power of analysis and logical reasoning that is characteristic of mathematics. This type of research is now gaining greater importance in mathematical economics and its further development is anticipated. This is not only because new decorations were added to old, classical studies but more importantly because new studies aim at deeper and more intrinsic mathematical analysis of economic phenomena.

The main achievements in this area so far are the interindustry analysis, linear programming, game theory, and various related problems as well as the aforementioned existence problem of equilibrium solutions and the reformulation of the theory of general equilibrium on the basis of these accomplishments. Of a more recent vintage is the study of the stability problems of equilibrium from the modern point of view. Techniques employed in these studies are not necessarily identical. One should avoid by all means to deprive oneself of analytical flexibility by adhering to any single technique. It is essential to choose a method most appropriate to the kind and nature of a problem under study. Nevertheless, young students should realize how effective it is to have even a smattering of point set theory and a rudiment of topological consideration in solving those problems mentioned above. This book is devoted to the modern mathematical analysis of those aforementioned problmes except the stability problems of equilibrium, namely problems of statics that are most fundamental in mathematical economics.

PART I

MODERN STATIC ANALYSIS

Chapter 1

EQUILIBRIUM IN LINEAR ECONOMIC MODELS. INTERINDUSTRY ANALYSIS

1. A broad sketch of a circular flow

It is the task of economics to study economic aspects of human society. The whirlpool of highly complex economic phenomena that we ourselves experience is the object of our economic study. Subject to a process of ceaseless change, a real economy keeps on growing through periodic cycles alternating between booms and depressions. This reminds us of our human life. Before attempting to approach a fluctuating and growing economy in its full complexities, let us note a basic aspect that underlies all economic phenomena. This is the relation of human beings *versus* nature *via* technology of production and the relation of human beings *versus* human beings constrained by the economic mechanism. In this book, we wish to show how effectively modern techniques of mathematics are to be applied to the analysis of this fundamental problem.

To begin our analysis, let us simplify these economic phenomena. For this purpose, it is important to draw a broad sketch of a stationary flow of exchanges of wealth within a national economy over a given period of time (say, one year). This compares with discussions of an equilibrium in a mechanical system or a stationary fluid flow. Metaphorically speaking, we start from drawing a static, anatomical diagram of the national economy.

When we look at the complex economic working of our society from a certain essential viewpoint, we find a surprisingly simple picture of it. A British physiologist W. Harvey (1578–1657) discovered the mechanics of the circulation of the blood in the human body at the beginning of the seventeenth century. His discovery marks a milestone in the history of physiology. About a century later, F. Quesnay (1694–1774), court physician to the French king Louis XV, conceived of a schema that he called *Tableau Économique* to represent the flow of products through exchange among three classes of society, namely farmers, landowners, and manufacturers *. It is believed that Quesnay arrived at the idea of *Tableau* under the influence of French encyclopedists, J. d'Alembert and V. Mirabeau, who were his friends.

Suppose an agricultural kingdom, whose annual economic life is based on agricultural and mining goods produced from land and a few manufactured goods. The people of this kingdom are divided among the three classes noted above. They produce goods according to their respective functions and share in their distribution. To accomplish the distribution of goods among the members of society, goods are exchanged among these classes through sales and purchases, resulting in a stationary flow of goods that is repeated year after year.

The farmers own some goods like farming implements, cattle and barns (which are called capital goods), rent land from the landowners, and produce foodstuffs and industrial raw materials (mining products in this case). The landowners consist of private landowners and the government (as the tax collector). The manufacturers own some machinery, tools and other facilities (which are also called capital) and process raw materials to produce manufactured goods (including luxurious consumer goods).

Suppose that the farmers produce 40 million dollars of foodstuffs and 10 million dollars of industrial raw materials. They consume \$ 20 millions of foodstuffs by themselves and pay the remaining \$ 20 millions to the landowners as rent. \$ 10 millions of raw materials are sold to the manufacturers in exchange for the repairs and maintenance of implements and barns. Part of self-consumed foodstuffs is fed to cattle. Out of the total of \$ 20 millions of foodstuffs received from the farmers, the landowners consume \$ 10 millions and spend the remaining \$ 10 millions for the purchase of manufactured goods from the manufacturers. The manufacturers produce \$ 30 millions of manufactured goods, out of which \$ 10 millions are used for the repairs and maintenance of their machinery, tools and other facilities, \$ 10 millions for the purchase of food from the landowners and \$ 10 millions for the purchase of raw materials from the farmers. This results in an exact exchange of goods. A stationary annual circular flow of goods emerges. This is the static, anatomical schema of circular flow as exemplified by Quesnay.

We may take another look at these relations. \$ 20 millions of food are ini-

* Quesnay himself called them the productive class, the proprietor class and the sterile class. These names were originated in Quesnay's specifically Physiocrat ideas.

tially sold to the landowners, but \$ 10 millions of it are then re-sold to the manufacturers so that in the final analysis \$ 20 millions of food are handed to the farmers, \$ 10 millions to the landowners, and \$ 10 millions to the manufacturers. The landowners produce no physical goods, but we may assume that they produce \$ 20 millions worth of land services, which they sell to the farmers. As noted by Walras, modern economics considers any "object", be it may tangible or intangible, as social wealth so long as it has a price on it and is exchangeable. We follow this idea and summarize the exchange relationships in an easy-to-see table from a modern viewpoint (table 1).

Table 1

Purchaser Seller	Kind of product	Farmers	Land-owners	Manufac-turers	Total sales	
Farmers	Food	20	10	10	40	50
	Raw materials	0	0	10	10	
Landowners	Land services	20	0	0	20	
Manufacturers	Manufactured goods *	10	10	10	30	
Total purchases		50	20	30		

* (including consumer goods)

This table is read as follows: horizontally, the row of a class or product shows the value of sales by purchaser and the total value of sales. For instance, the row of the manufacturers indicates the sales of 10 to the farmers, 10 to the landowners, and 10 to the manufacturers, totaling at 30. Next, read vertically the column of each class presents the value of purchases by seller and the total value of purchases. For instance, for the manufacturers, the purchases are 10 of food and 10 of raw materials from the farmers, 0 from the landowners, and 10 from the manufacturers with the total purchases of 30. Finally, the total sales and purchases are equal for each class. The table gives a concise representation of the exchange flow of goods which it is difficult to explain verbally

2. Representation by linear equations

Quesnay's work was a precursor to the input-output analysis of interindustry relationships that has been systematically pursued by an American economist, W.W. Leontief (1905–) since the nineteen thirties *. Though K. Marx attempted an analysis of the capitalist reproduction process by means of his celebrated reproduction scheme in a similar vein in the middle of the nineteenth century, the credit should go to Leontief for deepening and developing Quesnay's idea into a powerful tool of economic analysis.

From Quesnay's analysis, the reader must have understood how to deal with commodity flows in an economy. With the aid of this preliminary remark as a clue to deeper study, our next step is to move from our peaceful peasant kingdom to a modern, large-scale industrial economy which produces a multitude of commodities with highly scientific modes and techniques of production.

Let us properly divide agriculture, mining, manufacturing and so on into n sectors, each of which produces a single commodity. For instance, in Quesnay's illustration, the farmers produce foodstuffs and industrial raw materials; we shall divide the farmers into two separate groups, one producing foodstuffs and the other industrial raw materials. If a more detailed analysis is desired, we shall divide the first group into agriculture and fisheries and the second into those producing coal, petroleum, non-ferrous ores and so on.

Let the numbers i and j denote the n sectors and n products. i and j run from 1 to n respectively. Let x_i represent output of the ith commodity produced in the ith sector during a given period, say one year (measured in a suitable unit, e.g., coal in tons). Let x_{ij} be sales from sector i to sector j and c_i be sales from sector i to outside of these sectors. The latter is the sales to the government, exports, household consumption, new plant construction and the like that are not included in the industrial sectors. If the government is distinguished as an industrial sector, sales to the government are included as one of x_{ij}'s and eliminated from c_i's. Sectors which correspond to the n products are called *endogenous sectors*, while all other branches that are included in c_i's constitute *exogenous sectors*.

If output of each sector is exhausted by purchases of the endogenous and exogenous sectors, we have the following equations:

$$
(2.1)\qquad
\begin{array}{ll}
\text{product } 1: & x_1 = x_{11} + x_{12} + \ldots + x_{1n} + c_1 \\
\text{product } 2: & x_2 = x_{21} + x_{22} + \ldots + x_{2n} + c_2 \\
\quad \ldots & \quad \ldots \\
\text{product } i: & x_i = x_{i1} + x_{i2} + \ldots + x_{in} + c_i \\
\quad \ldots & \quad \ldots \\
\text{product } n: & x_n = x_{n1} + x_{n2} + \ldots + x_{nn} + c_n
\end{array}
$$

* W.W. Leontief [19]. (Throughout this book, the number in brackets is the reference number in Bibliography and References at the end of this book.)

(2.1) corresponds to the table given in the preceding section. However, we should note that no economic meaning can be attached to column sums like $x_{11} + x_{21} + ... + x_{n1}$ because $x_{11}, x_{21}, ..., x_{n1}$ are expressed in different units. They are meaningful only when all items are expressed in a common unit like money value as in the preceding table.

Though it is generally meaningless to add numbers columnwise in (2.1), it has an important significance to read numbers along a column. The jth column, $x_{1j}, x_{2j}, ..., x_{nj}$, represents the jth sector's purchases of commodities (like raw materials and semi-finished goods) from all sectors (including itself) in order to produce x_j units of the jth commodity. This sector uses its productive facilities like equipment (i.e. its capital stock), employs workers, and transforms these raw materials and semi-processed goods into its own output x_j. Therefore, we can say that this sector produces output x_j from inputs $x_{1j}, x_{2j}, ..., x_{nj}$. In what follows, we shall examine the technical correspondence between *inputs* and *outputs* in the production process.

How much of inputs does the jth sector require to double its output, provided that it has a slack in its capital equipment and that it can hire additional workers as required? Because of the difficulties of altering modes of production at once in modern industries which use vast amounts of capital equipment embodying modern technology, input combinations are almost invariant. It is realistically justifiable to assume constant proportions between inputs and outputs. Let these constant proportions be denoted by a_{ij}. Then, we have

$$x_{1j} = a_{1j}x_j, x_{2j} = a_{2j}x_j, ..., x_{nj} = a_{nj}x_j \,. \tag{2.2}$$

Inputs required by the jth sector to produce one unit of its product are represented by $a_{1j}, a_{2j}, ..., a_{nj}$ units. a_{ij} is 0 or a positive number by its economic nature and is called an *input coefficient*. If sectors are properly classified, it reflects purely technological relations only.

By using (2.2), x_{ij}'s are eliminated from (2.1) to produce

$$\begin{array}{lllll}(1-a_{11})x_1 & -a_{12}x_2 & - \dots & -a_{1n}x_n & = c_1 \\ -a_{21}x_1 & +(1-a_{22})x_2 & - \dots & -a_{2n}x_n & = c_2 \\ \dots & \dots & \dots & \dots & \\ -a_{n1}x_1 & -a_{n2}x_2 & - \dots & +(1-a_{nn})x_n & = c_n \,. \end{array} \tag{2.3}$$

(2.3) is the basic system of equations of the Leontief inter-industry analysis, which can be used to analyze the current flow of goods in a national economy during a given period of time and to predict the scale of economic activities in a future year.

Out of the total output x_i of the ith commodity $(a_{i1}x_1 + a_{i2}x_2 + ... + a_{in}x_n)$ is consumed as inputs for production. The difference, i.e. the left-hand side of (2.3), is the net output of the ith commodity, which should then be balanced with exogenous demand c_i. Hence, $(c_1, c_2, ..., c_n)$ is called *final demand* and the list of final demand is called the *bill of goods*.

The input coefficient a_{ij} can be obtained from a formula $a_{ij} = x_{ij}/x_j$ where x_j and x_{ij} are actually measured in a certain year. For another year, one can predict final demand or obtain the bill of goods as the government's target (if it has national planning). This determines the right-hand side of (2.3). Solving (2.3) for n unknowns $x_1, x_2, ..., x_n$, one can predict the scale of economic activities in that year. Total output x_j of the jth commodity is an indicator of the level of economic activity in the jth sector. As this sector's employment is determined in proportion to x_j, one can also predict employment in each sector.

Now we must not forget an important point about the restriction placed on signs of most economic variables. The input coefficients a_{ij}'s and final demand c_i's are zero or positive by their economic nature. Likewise, total outputs x_j's must be zero or positive. Then, are we certain that there is always a solution $(x_1, x_2, ..., x_n)$ of (2.3) for any arbitrary nonnegative bill of goods $(c_1, c_2, ..., c_n)$ and that the solution itself is nonnegative? It is self-evident that (2.3) has a nonnegative solution for the particular bill of goods of the base year when the input coefficients are computed because, in this case, (2.3) is merely a rearrangement of (2.1) which is identities holding among the actual observations that are all nonnegative. But our question is concerned with other non-negative numbers arbitrarily given to the bill of goods.

Suppose that the government proposes a certain bill of goods as the target of its national plan. If (2.3) does not have a solution $(x_1, x_2, ..., x_n)$ for this particular bill of goods or if it contains a negative number in it when it has a solution, (2.3) does not hold for whatever non-negative numbers that may be substituted into $x_1, x_2, ..., x_n$ on its left-hand side. There must be at least one good, for which the right-hand side (final demand, i.e. demand) and the left-hand side (net output, i.e. supply) are not equated. Therefore, being in conflict with the technological structure of the economy, this national plan is not feasible. If such an improper situation should arise, the inter-industry analysis would lose most of its significance. Fortunately, this impropriety is ruled out as the next section will show. Consequently, any final demand is feasible. Nevertheless, this property that is extremely convenient to us is not a self-evident truism but a proposition that needs to be demonstrated. Thus, we are led to an important task, namely a mathematical examination of the existence of a solution, that would fortify the foundation of the interindustry analysis.

3. The Hawkins-Simon condition

Making use of our knowledge of determinants, we shall introduce the Hawkins-Simon condition, a condition that equations of type (2.3) satisfy to have non-negative solutions.

Let us consider a system of n linear equations in n unknowns $x_1, x_2, ..., x_n$

$$\begin{array}{l} b_{11}x_1 + b_{12}x_2 + ... + b_{1n}x_n = c_1 \\ b_{21}x_1 + b_{22}x_2 + ... + b_{2n}x_n = c_2 \\ \cdots\cdots\cdots\cdots \\ b_{i1}x_1 + b_{i2}x_2 + ... + b_{in}x_n = c_i \\ \cdots\cdots\cdots\cdots \\ b_{n1}x_1 + b_{n2}x_2 + ... + b_{nn}x_n = c_n \end{array} \tag{3.1}$$

where the coefficients b_{ij}'s are real numbers subject to the sign condition

$$b_{ij} \leqq 0 \quad \text{for} \quad i \neq j\,. \tag{3.2}$$

Therefore, all coefficients except those along the principal diagonal, b_{11}, b_{22}, ..., b_{nn}, are 0 or negative.

In this section, we are interested in the condition that (3.1) satisfies in order to have a non-negative solution. However, we must distinguish the case where (3.1) has a solution when certain specific values are assigned to its right-hand side and the case where (3.1) has a solution for whatever values given its right-hand side. We investigate the relation between these two cases.

(I) *Weak solvability*:
For some $c_i > 0$ ($i = 1, 2, ..., n$), (3.1) has a non-negative solution $x_1, x_2, ..., x_n$.

(II) *Strong solvability*:
For any $c_i \geqq 0$ ($i = 1, 2, ..., n$), (3.1) has a non-negative solution $x_1, x_2, ..., x_n$.

At first sight, (I) may seem to be a condition very much weaker than (II). But, in fact, they have identical content. Two conditions with identical logical content are called equivalent. The Hawkins-Simon condition provides a clue to demonstrating the equivalence of (I) and (II).

(H-S) *The Hawkins-Simon condition* *:

All upper left-corner principal minors of the determinant of the coefficients of (3.1) are positive, i.e.

* D. Hawkins and H.A. Simon [36].

$$b_{11}>0,\quad \begin{vmatrix} b_{11} & b_{12} \\ b_{21} & b_{22} \end{vmatrix}>0,\quad \begin{vmatrix} b_{11} & b_{12} & b_{13} \\ b_{21} & b_{22} & b_{23} \\ b_{31} & b_{32} & b_{33} \end{vmatrix}>0, \ldots, \begin{vmatrix} b_{11} & b_{12} & \ldots & b_{1n} \\ b_{21} & b_{22} & \ldots & b_{2n} \\ \ldots & \ldots & \ldots & \ldots \\ b_{n1} & b_{n2} & \ldots & b_{nn} \end{vmatrix}>0.$$

We shall prove the following very interesting fundamental theorem:

THEOREM 3.1. *The three conditions, (I), (II) and (H-S), are equivalent.*

Proof. When condition B can be derived from condition A, we write A ⇒ B. A demonstration of A ⇒ B ⇒ A suffices as a proof of the equivalence of A and B. In this sense, the equivalence of A and B is denoted by A ⇔ B. We can prove Theorem 3.1 by demonstrating the equivalence between any two of the three conditions (I), (II) and (H-S), but the most orderly presentation will be to show (I) ⇒ (H-S) ⇒ (II) ⇒ (I). With this preliminary observation, let us begin our proof, which is based on mathematical induction on the number of equations.

[A] (I) ⇒ (H-S)

For n=1, (3.1) reduces to $b_{11}x_1 = c_1$. Hence, if there is a solution $x_1 \geqq 0$ for some $c_1 > 0$, we must have $x_1 > 0$ because the product of b_{11} and x_1, i.e. c_1, is not zero. Thus, $b_{11} = c_1/x_1 > 0$. This condition is exactly (H-S) for n=1.

Let us prove (I) ⇒ (H-S), assuming that it has been proved for $n-1$. The proof is based on the reduction of the case of n to that of $n-1$. For this exercise, we find it useful to employ the method of elimination, with which the reader should be familiar in his high-school algebra.

When the number of equations is n, suppose that (3.1) has a solution $x_1 \geqq 0, x_2 \geqq 0, \ldots, x_n \geqq 0$ for some $c_1 > 0, c_2 > 0, \ldots, c_n > 0$. We obtain

$$b_{11}x_1 = c_1 - b_{12}x_2 - b_{13}x_3 - \ldots - b_{1n}x_n \geqq c_1 > 0,$$

by rearranging terms in the first equation of (3.1) because, on the right-hand side, we have $-b_{12}x_2 \geqq 0, -b_{13}x_3 \geqq 0, \ldots, -b_{1n}x_n \geqq 0$ by virtue of the assumption (3.2) and of the non-negativity of the solution. Therefore, $b_{11}x_1 > 0$ and $x_1 \geqq 0$ lead to $b_{11} > 0$ and $x_1 > 0$ just as we have seen for n=1.

x_1 is eliminated from equations 2 to n of (3.1) by forming equation $i - b_{i1}/b_{11} \times$ equation 1 for i=2, 3, ..., n. (Note that as $b_{11} > 0$, we can divide by $b_{11} \neq 0$.) We obtain

$$
\begin{aligned}
b_{11}x_1 + b_{12}x_2 + \ldots + b_{1n}x_n &= c_1 \\
b'_{22}x_2 + \ldots + b'_{2n}x_n &= c'_2 \\
b'_{32}x_2 + \ldots + b'_{3n}x_n &= c'_3 \\
\cdots\cdots\cdots\cdots & \\
b'_{n2}x_2 + \ldots + b'_{nn}x_n &= c'_n \ .
\end{aligned}
\tag{3.3}
$$

Now the new coefficient b'_{ij} is related to the old coefficient b_{ij} according to

$$b'_{ij} = b_{ij} - \frac{b_{i1}b_{1j}}{b_{11}} \qquad (2 \leqq i,\ j \leqq n) \tag{3.4}$$

and the new constant term c'_i to the original constant term c_i according to

$$c'_i = c_i - \frac{b_{i1}c_1}{b_{11}} \qquad (2 \leqq i,\ j \leqq n)\ . \tag{3.5}$$

The second to the nth equations of (3.3) constitute a system of $n-1$ equations in $x_2, x_3, \ldots, x_n$. Let us check the signs of their coefficients and constant terms. For $i,j=2,3,\ldots,n$, we have $b_{i1} \leqq 0$, $b_{1j} \leqq 0$ from the original condition (3.2). Also we have $b_{11} > 0$ as we have already proved. Therefore, $-b_{i1}b_{1j}/b_{11} \leqq 0$, which implies $b'_{ij} \leqq 0$ from (3.4) for $i \neq j$, $2 \leqq i,j \leqq n$. Similarly, $c'_i = c_i - b_{i1}c_1/b_{11} \geqq c_i > 0$ $(2 \leqq i \leqq n)$.

Thus, the coefficients of the new reduced system (equations 2 to n of (3.3)) satisfy (3.2), while its constant terms are all positive. Moreover, we know $x_2 \geqq 0, x_3 \geqq 0, \ldots, x_n \geqq 0$ is the solution of the reduced system. Thus, the new system satisfies the condition (I) and, by the inductive hypothesis, fulfils (H-S) so that we have

$$
\begin{vmatrix}
b'_{22} & b'_{23} & \ldots & b'_{2k} \\
b'_{32} & b'_{33} & \ldots & b'_{3k} \\
\cdots & \cdots & \cdots & \cdots \\
b'_{k2} & b'_{k3} & \ldots & b'_{kk}
\end{vmatrix} > 0 \quad (k = 2, 3, \ldots, n)\ .
\tag{3.6}
$$

Now the steps of elimination that have been followed to derive (3.3) from (3.1) are simply to multiply the first row of the original determinant by certain numbers and to add it to all the other rows. Therefore, the corresponding principal minors are equal in value. Hence, expanding along the first column, we get

$$\begin{vmatrix} b_{11} & b_{12} & \cdots & b_{1k} \\ b_{21} & b_{22} & \cdots & b_{2k} \\ \cdots & \cdots & \cdots & \cdots \\ b_{k1} & b_{k2} & \cdots & b_{kk} \end{vmatrix} = \begin{vmatrix} b_{11} & b_{12} & \cdots & b_{1k} \\ 0 & b'_{22} & \cdots & b'_{2k} \\ \cdots & \cdots & \cdots & \cdots \\ 0 & b'_{k2} & \cdots & b'_{kk} \end{vmatrix} = b_{11} \begin{vmatrix} b'_{22} & \cdots & b'_{2k} \\ \vdots & & \vdots \\ b'_{k2} & \cdots & b'_{kk} \end{vmatrix} > 0$$

$$(k = 2, 3, \ldots, n)$$

by virtue of $b_{11} > 0$ and (3.6). This demonstrates (I) ⇒ (H-S).

[B] (H-S) ⇒ (II)

For n=1, (3.1) reduces to $b_{11}x_1 = c_1$. If it satisfies the (H-S) condition, we have $b_{11} > 0$ and, therefore, this equation has a solution $x_1 = c_1/b_{11} \geqq 0$ for any $c_1 \geqq 0$. Let us now assume that (H-S) ⇒ (II) has been proved for a system of $n-1$ equations.

When the condition (H-S) should hold for the general system (3.1), we get $b_{11} > 0$. Hence, just like in [A], we can transform (3.1) into (3.3) by elimination. Then, the relation between the original and new principal minors yields

$$\begin{vmatrix} b'_{22} & \cdots & b'_{2k} \\ \vdots & & \vdots \\ b'_{k2} & \cdots & b'_{kk} \end{vmatrix} = \frac{1}{b_{11}} \begin{vmatrix} b_{11} & b_{12} & \cdots & b_{1k} \\ b_{21} & b_{22} & \cdots & b_{2k} \\ \cdots & \cdots & \cdots & \cdots \\ b_{k1} & b_{k2} & \cdots & b_{kk} \end{vmatrix} > 0 \quad (2 \leqq k \leqq n).$$

The sign of its right-hand side is determined by the (H-S) condition that we have initially assumed to hold for (3.1). Thus, the determinant composed of the coefficients in the new equation system (equations 2 to n in (3.3)) satisfies the (H-S) condition and, by the inductive hypothesis, the new system has a non-negative solution $x_2, x_3, \ldots, x_n$ for any nonnegative constant terms, in particular c'_i $(i = 2, 3, \ldots, n)$, on its right-hand side.

Let the constant terms $c_1, c_2, \ldots, c_n$ on the right-hand side of (3.1) be arbitrarily given non-negative numbers. Then, (3.5) gives $c'_i \geqq 0$ $(2 \leqq i \leqq n)$, which ensures a non-negative solution $x_2, x_3, \ldots, x_n$ for equations 2 to n of (3.3). Substituting this solution into equation 1, we get

$$x_1 = \frac{1}{b_{11}} (c_1 - b_{12}x_2 - b_{13}x_3 - \ldots - b_{1n}x_n).$$

We have $x_1 \geqq 0$ from the sign condition (3.2) as well as $b_{11} > 0, c_1 \geqq 0$, and $x_i \geqq 0$ $(2 \leqq i \leqq n)$. This shows that (3.3) has a non-negative solution for any $c_i \geqq 0$. Obviously this solution is also a solution for (3.1) because (3.3) can be transformed back into (3.1) through reversing the process of elimination. Thus, we have proved that (H-S) ⇒ (II).

We may add that there is only one solution $x_1, x_2, ..., x_n$ for (3.1) – in other words, the solution is *unique* – as we know from the theory of determinants. Cramer's Rule shows that this solution is $x_j = \Delta_j/\Delta$ ($j = 1, 2, ..., n$), where Δ represents the determinant of the coefficients in (3.1) and Δ_j the determinant in which $(c_1, c_2, ..., c_n)$ replaces the jth column of Δ.

[C] (II) ⇒ (I)

This is evident from what (I) and (II) imply.

This completes our proof of Theorem 3.1.

Let us apply Theorem 3.1 to the basic input-output equations (2.3). We examine the equations (3.7) that are more general than (2.3) in anticipation of what we will discuss in a later chapter:

$$\begin{array}{lllll} (\rho - a_{11})x_1 & - a_{12}x_2 & - \;\cdots & & - a_{1n}x_n = c_1 \\ - a_{21}x_1 & + (\rho - a_{22})x_2 & - \;\cdots & & - a_{2n}x_n = c_2 \\ \cdots\cdots & \cdots\cdots & \cdots\cdots & \cdots & \\ - a_{n1}x_1 & - a_{n2}x_2 & - \;\cdots & & + (\rho - a_{nn})x_n = c_n \end{array} \tag{3.7}$$

where the coefficients are subject to the sign condition $a_{ij} \geqq 0$ $(1 \leqq i, j \leqq n)$ and ρ is a real number. (3.7) reduces to (2.3) when $\rho = 1$.

Put

$$b_{ii} = \rho - a_{ii} \qquad (1 \leqq i \leqq n)$$

and

$$b_{ij} = -a_{ij} \qquad (i \neq j,\ 1 \leqq i,\ j \leqq n)\,.$$

Obviously, $b_{ij} \leqq 0$ $(i \neq j)$. This makes (3.7) a special case of (3.1). Therefore, we have the following theorem:

THEOREM 3.2. *The conditions (I), (II) and (H-S) are all equivalent in (3.7).*

The (H-S) condition in (3.7) is specified as follows:

$$\rho - a_{11} > 0, \quad \begin{vmatrix} \rho - a_{11} & -a_{12} \\ -a_{21} & \rho - a_{22} \end{vmatrix} > 0\,, \tag{3.8a}$$

$$\begin{vmatrix} \rho - a_{11} & -a_{12} & -a_{13} \\ -a_{21} & \rho - a_{22} & -a_{23} \\ -a_{31} & -a_{32} & \rho - a_{33} \end{vmatrix} > 0\,, \tag{3.8b}$$

$$(3.8c)\qquad \ldots,\ \begin{vmatrix} \rho-a_{11} & -a_{12} & \cdots & -a_{1n} \\ -a_{21} & \rho-a_{22} & \cdots & -a_{2n} \\ \cdots & \cdots & \cdots & \cdots \\ -a_{n1} & -a_{n2} & \cdots & \rho-a_{nn} \end{vmatrix} > 0 .$$

This theorem is extremely important for the interindustry analysis. As (I) is equivalent to (II) in (3.7), it follows that (2.3) always has a unique, non-negative solution for any non-negative final demand, provided that (2.3) has a non-negative solution for a positive bill of goods in a certain year. Thus, the question posed at the end of section 2 has been completely answered.

Before closing this section, we give a corollary. With respect to the coefficients a_{ij} of (3.7), we define the ith *row sum*

$$r_i = \sum_{j=1}^{n} a_{ij} = a_{i1} + a_{i2} + \ldots + a_{in} \quad (i = 1, 2, \ldots, n)$$

and the jth *column sum*

$$s_j = \sum_{i=1}^{n} a_{ij} = a_{1j} + a_{2j} + \ldots + a_{nj} \quad (j = 1, 2, \ldots, n) .$$

COROLLARY

(i) *If $\rho > r_i$ $(i = 1, 2, \ldots, n)$, then (I), (II) and (H-S) hold for (3.7).*
(ii) *If $\rho > s_j$ $(j = 1, 2, \ldots, n)$, then (I), (II) and (H-S) hold for (3.7).*

These conditions are called the *Brauer-Solow row sum and column sum criteria.*

Proof. These results follow directly from Theorem 3.2.

(i) Let $c_i = \rho - r_i > 0$ $(i = 1, 2, \ldots, n)$ as $\rho > r_i$. Then, for these specific constant terms, we have a solution $x_1=1, x_2=1, \ldots, x_n=1$. Namely, the condition (I) holds in this case. Therefore, Theorem 3.2 ensures that the conditions (II) and (H-S) also hold.

(ii) Transposing the coefficients of (3.7) across the principal diagonal, we form a system of new equations in unknowns $p_1, p_2, \ldots, p_n$ as follows:

$$(3.9)\qquad \begin{array}{l} (\rho-a_{11})p_1 - a_{21}p_2 - \ldots - a_{n1}p_n = v_1 \\ -a_{12}p_1 + (\rho-a_{22})p_2 - \ldots - a_{n2}p_n = v_2 \\ \cdots\cdots\cdots\cdots\cdots\cdots\cdots\cdots \\ -a_{1n}p_1 - a_{2n}p_2 - \ldots + (\rho-a_{nn})p_n = v_n \end{array}$$

(3.9) is identical to (3.7) in form. The column sum of a_{ij} in (3.7) is the row sum of a_{ij} in (3.9). Therefore, it follows from (i) that, if $\rho > s_j$ ($j = 1, 2, ..., n$), (3.9) satisfies (I), (II) and (H-S). The principal minors of the determinant of the coefficients of (3.9) are all positive because of (H-S). The principal minors of (3.7), which are their transposes, have the same positive values as those. This proves that (H-S) holds for (3.7) in this case. Theorem 3.2, then, proves that (I) and (II) also hold.

It is thus clear that the Brauer-Solow criteria are nothing but a specific case of (I). In the next section, we shall discuss what the column sum implies in economic terms.

4. Outputs and prices

As the determinants of the coefficients of (3.7) and (3.9) are transposes of each other, (3.7) and (3.9) are called *dual* to each other. The proof of the corollary given in the preceding section indicates that if one of them satisfies either of (I), (II) and (H-S), both systems satisfy all of the three conditions. We now proceed further on the assumption that these conditions for the existence of a solution are satisfied.

(3.7) has a unique, non-negative solution $x_1, x_2, ..., x_n$ for any nonnegative values of c_i ($i = 1, 2, ..., n$) independently of its dual (3.9). In other words, the solution of (3.7) is determined not in conjunction with (3.9) but by itself. The same applies to the solution of (3.9). In spite of this apparent independence, the two systems stand in a special relation to each other with respect to their coefficients and there exists an interesting interconnection between their solutions.

THEOREM 4.1. *Let the solution of (3.7) be $x_1, x_2, ..., x_n$ and that of (3.9) $p_1, p_2, ..., p_n$. Then,*

$$\sum_{i=1}^{n} c_i p_i = \sum_{j=1}^{n} v_j x_j \tag{4.1}$$

always holds. This relation is called duality.

Proof. So far we have avoided as deliberately as possible the use of $\sum$, a symbol indicating summation. From now on, we shall try to familiarize ourselves with this notation. For those who are not used to it, let us add a simple remark.

Three types of summation, expressed with $\sum$, over a number of quantities

a_{ij} with double subscripts or suffixes i and j

$$\sum_{i=1}^{m}\sum_{j=1}^{n} a_{ij}\,, \quad \sum_{j=1}^{n}\sum_{i=1}^{m} a_{ij}\,, \quad \sum_{i,\,j=1}^{m,\,n} a_{ij}$$

turn out to be identical. i runs from 1 to m and j from 1 to n, where m and n can be different from each other. The total number of a_{ij} is mn. The first summation is obtained by making m subtotals over j and then by adding them together over i. The second summation is obtained in reverse order, i.e. by making n subtotals over i and then adding them together over j. The third summation is a direct sum of all a_{ij}'s. It is obvious that these three summations are identical.

Keeping this remark about $\sum$ in mind, we can complete the proof of the duality by merely rewriting equations.

The solution of (3.7), $x_1, x_2, ..., x_n$, satisfies

$$\rho x_i - \sum_{j=1}^{n} a_{ij} x_j = c_i \quad (i = 1, 2, ..., n)\,, \tag{4.2}$$

while that of (3.9), $p_1, p_2, ..., p_n$, satisfies

$$\rho p_j - \sum_{i=1}^{n} a_{ij} p_i = v_j \quad (j = 1, 2, ..., n)\,. \tag{4.3}$$

Hence, we have

$$\sum_{i=1}^{n} c_i p_i = \sum_{i=1}^{n} (\rho x_i - \sum_{j=1}^{n} a_{ij} x_j) p_i = \sum_{i=1}^{n} \rho p_i x_i - \sum_{i=1}^{n} p_i \sum_{j=1}^{n} a_{ij} x_j$$

$$= \sum_{j=1}^{n} \rho p_j x_j - \sum_{j=1}^{n} x_j \sum_{i=1}^{n} a_{ij} p_i$$

$$= \sum_{j=1}^{n} (\rho p_j - \sum_{i=1}^{n} a_{ij} p_i) x_j = \sum_{j=1}^{n} v_j x_j\,.$$

Next, let us explore the implication of the duality (4.1) for the special case of $\rho = 1$ in (3.7) or (4.2), i.e. the basic interindustry equations (2.3). We must first clarify the economic meaning of the dual equations. Our basic and dual equations are given as follows:

$$\text{basic equations:} \quad x_i - \sum_{j=1}^{n} a_{ij}x_j = c_i \qquad (i = 1, 2, ..., n)$$

$$\text{dual equations:} \quad p_j - \sum_{i=1}^{n} a_{ij}p_i = v_j \qquad (j = 1, 2, ..., n)\,.$$

The jth sector produces a unit of the jth commodity with $a_{1j}, a_{2j}, ..., a_{nj}$ units of inputs. Let p_j be the *price* of a unit of the jth commodity. Then, one unit of the jth commodity is sold for $p_j \times 1 = p_j$, for which the jth sector must pay $\sum_{i=1}^{n} a_{ij}\, p_i$ to all sectors (including itself). Therefore, v_j as the sum of capitalists' share, *profits*, and workers' share, *wage bill*, should be equal to $p_j - \sum_{i=1}^{n} a_{ij}p_i$. This is what the dual equations imply. v_j is the *average value added* in the jth sector. The condition (II) for the existence of the solution in the dual equations implies that there exists a price system $p_1 \geqq 0, p_2 \geqq 0, ..., p_n \geqq 0$ that makes any non-negative values added $v_1, v_2, ..., v_n$ feasible. Theorem 3.2 has made it clear how interrelated the three existence conditions are for the dual equations, and the non-negativity of prices reinforces the importance of this theorem.

c_i on the right-hand side of the basic equations represents the net output of the ith commodity. Hence, c_ip_i is the net value output and the left-hand side of (4.1) is the total net value output for the economy as a whole and is called *national product*. On the other hand, value added per unit of output in the jth sector is given by v_j and, therefore, the sum of profits and wages in this sector is v_jx_j when the level of output is x_j. This indicates that the right-hand side of (4.1) is the sum total of profits and wages in this national economy. This is called *national income.* The duality expresses the equality of national product and national income.

Employment. Let l_j be the volume of employment required to produce one unit of the jth commodity. Then, the jth sector employs l_jx_j of labor. For the economy as a whole, the total employment is $\sum_{j=1}^{n} l_jx_j$. Given the *wage rate* (unit price of labor) w, the working class receives $w\sum_{j=1}^{n} l_j x_j$ out of national income. The capitalist class obtains the remainder.

So far, the households of workers are treated as an exogenous sector. We may include them as one of the n endogenous sectors. In this treatment, we suppose that the workers' households produce a commodity called labor with inputs of various (consumption) goods. In other words, these (consumption) goods are consumed by workers to reproduce labor services. Let this sector be the nth sector. Then, its inputs per unit of labor are $a_{1n}, a_{2n}, ..., a_{nn}$ of goods. Of course, $a_{in} = 0$ for any good i that does not enter the household's consumption. Looked at this way, the reproduced labor is given by x_n. We can set the net output of labor c_n to be zero or to be positive (corresponding to, say, population expansion). However we shall not proceed any further in this direction as this sort of a problem is beyond the scope of this book. It is, of course, possible to include two or more household sectors in the endogenous sectors.

Dollar's worth unit. In connection with the economic implication of the column sum that appeared in the corollary of Sect. 3, a remark may be given here on a technical term, *dollar's worth unit.* We stated in Sect. 2 that the input coefficient a_{ij} is computed from actual observations of x_{ij} and x_j, which are measured in physical units. However, it is the intersectoral transaction $p_i x_{ij}$ and total production $p_j x_j$, both in value terms, that are measured in actual statistical practices. Then, $a_{ij}^* = p_i x_{ij}/p_j x_j$ is used as the input coefficient. There is a relation

$$(4.4) \qquad a_{ij}^* = \frac{p_i a_{ij}}{p_j} \quad (1 \leqq i,\ j \leqq n)$$

between the two input coefficients a_{ij} and a_{ij}^*. The input coefficient a_{ij} is computed from physical magnitudes x_{ij} and x_j which are expressed in physical units like tons, kilowatts and so on. Theoretically speaking, there is nothing wrong in changing units of measurement since we are free to select any kind of units. Of course, such changes entail changes in the input coefficients. Then, what about a_{ij}^*? In what sort of a unit is it computed? x_j physical units of the jth commodity are expressed in dollar value as \$ $p_j x_j$. If we adopt, as the new unit of measurement, the volume of the jth commodity that can be bought by one dollar (a unit of money), x_j physical units of the jth commodity are equal to $p_j x_j$ new money units. This unit is called the *dollar's worth unit.* Thus, a_{ij}^* is the input coefficient when all goods are expressed in the dollar's worth unit.

If we compute the difference between 1 and the column sum of a^*_{ij}, we get

$$
\begin{aligned}
1-\sum_{i=1}^{n} a^*_{ij} &= 1-\frac{1}{p_j}\sum_{i=1}^{n} a_{ij}p_i \\
&= \frac{1}{p_j}\left(p_j-\sum_{i=1}^{n} a_{ij}p_i\right) \\
&= v_j/p_j \qquad (j=1, 2, \ldots, n)
\end{aligned}
$$

because of (4.4). In terms of the dollar's worth unit, all prices are expressed as 1 so that the left-hand side of the equation above is the average value added in the jth sector.

Chapter 2

INTRODUCTION TO MATHEMATICS
(I) LINEAR ALGEBRA AND POINT SET THEORY

5. The objective of the chapter

Chapter 1 discussed the existence conditions of solutions for the basic input-output equations through the effective use of fundamental properties of determinants. The present chapter is devoted to an introduction to mathematics in order to prepare ourselves for deeper analysis, leaving the economic world for the time being. The exposition in this chapter provides the basis necessary for analytical developments in this book. The reader, therefore, is requested to secure a clear-cut understanding of what various concepts and theorems mean and how mathematical reasoning works.

The reader who studied classical calculus must be more or less familiar with what limits are all about. The first step into topological considerations is to understand clearly the concept of limits and to push the analysis further on the basis of this concept. Therefore, we begin this chapter with re-examining how to look at numbers and other mathematical entities from the viewpoint of limits. The reader is asked to spend some time to enhance his understanding of this concept. This would help him to improve his familiarity with modern mathematical techniques. New wine must be stored in new bottles. Modern mathematics expresses itself through many novel concepts and newfangled symbols. This might have diminished would-be students' enthusiasm and even repelled them from modern mathematics. But this particular inclination of modern mathematics is not due to mathematicians' love of flashy ornaments or pedantism. It has its own reason in discarding old bottles. Modern mathematics is devoid of useless decorations; it is functional, easy to use, and yet elegant in its façade. Such features are quite appealing to our modern sense of beauty. However, mathematicians did not create new wine bottles at one sitting. While handed down from generation to generation of mathematicians, their master hands removed useless ornaments one after another from the old and reshaped them to be fit to keep the essence of mathematics. Indeed, modern mathematics did not emerge in alienation of orthodox, traditional mathematics but evolved as an extension of the latter.

Most basic in modern mathematics both as an expressive term and as an analytical tool is the concept of sets. A set is a collection of "entities" that have certain properties. Modern mathematics employs sets to represent properties and conditions; it analyzes the latter by studying the structure of sets. Broadly speaking, this is one of the characteristics of modern mathematics.

There are a number of ways of examining the structure of sets, depending on the conditions that determine sets. However, quite important from the modern point of view is an analysis of the structure of sets based on the concept of limits. This constitutes the crux of the matter in topolygy, may it be at the elementary or advanced level.

This chapter will provide basic background information at the common-sense level by introducing the reader to the concept of sets, basic properties of real numbers, elementary topological considerations of finite-dimensional spaces and a few important, though elementary, theorems.

6. Sets

In the preceding section, we defined a set as a collection of "entities" with certain properties. To begin with, let us give some concrete examples of sets in order to sharpen our understanding of this new concept.

Example 6.1. All human beings living on earth. This is a group whose members are all human beings. It is specified by two properties: (1) living on earth and (2) human beings. As it is a collection of "entities" called human beings, it forms a set. Since sets are conceptual and logical, it is not necessary to conduct an exhaustive census all over the earth in order to consider the set of all human beings. It is enough if we can visualize a collection of this sort in our mind. Any missing person whose whereabouts are unknown can be a member of this set so long as he is alive somewhere on earth. A question may be raised as to whether the Abominable Snowman of the Himalayas can be a member of this set. It depends on what is meant by the second of the two conditions that define this set. It may be an important issue in anthropology to determine whether the Snowman is human or not, but for our present purpose, we need only to give neat logical content to the condition (2) that enables us to classify any entity as a human or a non-human being. Moreover, it does not matter at all if this content of the condition is so complex that we are not only unable to pass an instant judgment to whether a certain entity satisfies the condition or not but also we may have to spend millions of years before coming to a final judgment.

A logical condition is such as, by its very nature, can be determined to be either true or false for any given "entity" *. The time required to determine this is not essential in defining a set. To help us to come to grips with the concept of sets, let us imagine an idealized logical machine that would perform instantaneously all logical judgments. Given a certain (possibly infinite) number of conditions, this machine would inspect all "entities" in no time and produce a complete list of "entities" that satisfy these conditions. This list is our set.

Let $P(x)$, $Q(x)$, ... denote the conditions about "entity" x. A is a set of those entities that satisfy the conditions and is notationally represented as

$$A = \{x | P(x), Q(x), \ldots\}.$$

In our present example,

$$A = \{x | x \text{ lives on earth}; x \text{ is a human being}\}.$$

Let us give some other examples of sets.

Example 6.2. A set of all natural numbers 1, 2, 3, ...; a set of all real numbers larger than 2; a set of all solutions of an equation.

Example 6.3. A geometrical figure. This is a set of entities called points.

Example 6.4. A set of all means of travel from Tokyo to Paris.

A member of the set is called an *element*. When x is a member of the set A, it is said that "x is an element of A", "x is contained in A", "x belongs to A", or "A contains x". In notation, we write

$$x \in A \quad \text{or} \quad A \ni x .$$

$x \notin A$ means that x does not belong to A.

Elements of a set need not be physical entities that actually exist. In the examples cited above, elements of a set are (1) human beings, (2) numbers, (3) points on a plane, and (4) means of travel.

* For a missing person, we can always decide at least in principle either that he is "alive" on earth or that he is "not alive" on earth.

When a set has a finite number of elements, it is called a *finite set;* when it contains an infinite number of elements, it is called an *infinite set.*

Operations on sets

Equality. When two sets A and B consist of identical elements, they are said to be equal. This is expressed as $A = B$. When A and B are not equal, we write $A \neq B$. This is a negation of $A = B$. It implies that members of A and those of B are not completely identical with each other, but it does not exclude the possibility that A and B have some common members. It should be noted that a negation in logical operations compares with what we term a partial negation in grammar. Furthermore, even if the conditions defining A may look different from those defining B, it is possible that $A = B$.

Consider two sets $A = \{x | P(x)\}$ and $B = \{x | Q(x)\}$. Suppose that the conditions $P(x)$ and $Q(x)$ are equivalent, i.e. $P(x) \Leftrightarrow Q(x)$. This equivalence implies that $Q(x)$ follows from $P(x)$ and that $P(x)$ follows from $Q(x)$ *. For any element x of A (i.e. $x \in A$), $P(x)$ holds by definition. Then, we have $P(x) \Rightarrow Q(x)$ by assumption. Hence, x is also an element of B (i.e. $x \in B$). Similarly, we can show that $Q(x) \Rightarrow P(x)$ implies that $x \in A$ if $x \in B$. Thus, we get $A = B$. By the same token, the equivalence of $P(x)$ and $Q(x)$ immediately follows from $A = B$. Thus, $A = B$ is perfectly identical with $P(x) \Leftrightarrow Q(x)$. This correspondence is one of the important functions that the concept of sets performs.

From the description given above, the reader may have understood the following basic fact that can be used in proofs involving sets. In order to prove $A = B$ for two sets A and B, it suffices to prove two logical propositions, (1) "$x \in A \Rightarrow x \in B$" and (2) "$x \in B \Rightarrow x \in A$".

Inclusion. When $x \in B$ for $x \in A$, it is said that "A is a *subset* of B", "A is included in B", or "B includes A". In notation, this is written as $A \subset B$ or $B \supset A$. Our notation indicates that A is a part of B. Fig. 6.1 is a conceptual figure that illustrates this relation. As conceptual figures provide intuitive visual aids to various relations of sets, they are frequently used to supplement our expositions. However, graphical illustrations do not serve as proofs and cannot be substituted for them. Moreover, we are not always able to represent sets graphically.

If we use the concept of subsets, we can replace $A = B$ with equivalent relations $A \subset B$ and $B \subset A$. We may regard a set A as its own subset. When $A \subset B$ and $A \neq B$ at the same time, A is termed a *proper subset* of B. The fact that A is a proper subset of B implies that $A \subset B$ and that its converse does not hold (i.e. $A \not\supset B$). In order to prove this, therefore, it suffices to prove two

* See Section 3.

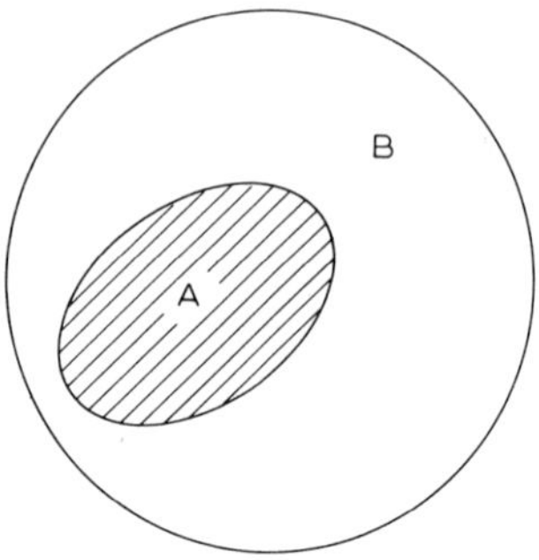

Fig. 6.1.

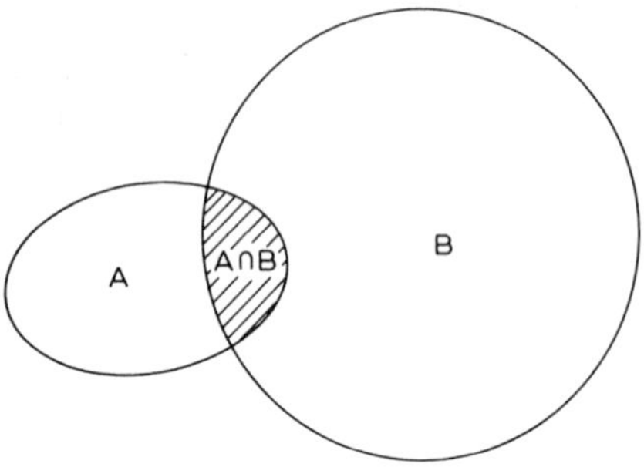

Fig. 6.2.

propositions: (1) "$x \in B$ for *any* $x \in A$" and (2) "$x \notin A$ for *some* $x \in B$".

Intersection. The set of elements that are contained in both A and B is called the *intersection* of A and B. It is the shaded part in fig. 6.2. In notation, it is written as

$$A \cap B .$$

Therefore, we have $A \cap B = \{x | x \in A, x \in B\}$. Let $P(x)$ and $Q(x)$ be the conditions specifying sets A and B respectively. Then, $A \cap B$ is a set of elements that satisfy both $P(x)$ and $Q(x)$. Hence, the operation on sets, $A \cap B$, corresponds to a logical operation of having $P(x)$ *and* $Q(x)$ for the conditions. Conditions are now made more stringent so that $A \cap B \subset A, B$.

If the two conditions $P(x)$ and $Q(x)$ are in contradiction with each other, there might be no element that satisfies both conditions. Then, $A \cap B$ becomes a meaningless symbol. However, to make things more convenient, we think of a special set that contains no element in itself. This is called *an empty set* and expressed in notation by ϕ. We say in this case that "$A \cap B$ is an empty set" and write $A \cap B = \phi$. The empty set is a very convenient concept just like 0 in the case of numbers. We adopt a convention that the empty set ϕ satisfies $\phi \subset A$ for any set A.

Just as we have defined the intersection of two sets, we can define the intersection of three or more (possibly an infinite number of) sets. The intersection of n sets A_i $(i = 1, 2, ..., n)$ is shown by

$$A_1 \cap A_2 \cap ... \cap A_n \quad \text{or} \quad \bigcap_{i=1}^{n} A_i$$

in notation. It is a set of elements common to all sets $A_1, A_2, ..., A_n$; fig. 6.3 illustrates the intersection of these sets.

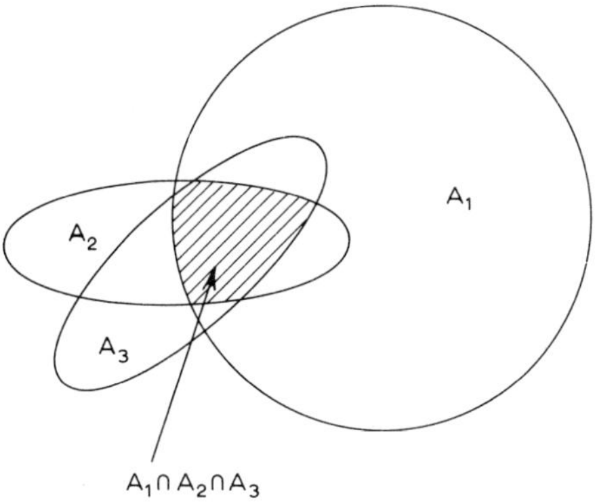

Fig. 6.3.

When we have an infinite number of sets from which the intersection is derived, we cannot employ the usual method of numbering to distinguish them. In this case, numbers are generalized into *indexes* as follows: Take a set Λ, which may be in general an infinite set *. Individual elements λ of Λ are used in place of numbers and suffixed to those sets from which the intersection must be obtained. Thus, we write A_λ and express the intersection of sets $A_\lambda, A_{\lambda'}, \ldots$ (more precisely, A_λ $(\lambda \in \Lambda)$) as

$$\bigcap_{\lambda \in \Lambda} A_\lambda .$$

When λ ranges within Λ, A_λ represents all sets that should produce the intersection. When $\Lambda = \{1, 2, \ldots, n\}$, we have

$$\bigcap_{\lambda \in \Lambda} A_\lambda = \bigcap_{i=1} A_i .$$

When Λ is the set of all natural numbers, i.e. $\Lambda = \{1, 2, 3, \ldots\}$, we may represent $\bigcap_{\lambda \in \Lambda} A_\lambda$ as

$$\bigcap_{i=1}^{\infty} A_i .$$

Union. The *union* of sets A and B is the set of elements that are contained at least in one of the two sets. In notation, we write

$$A \cup B .$$

* Λ is a capital letter of Greek alphabet λ.

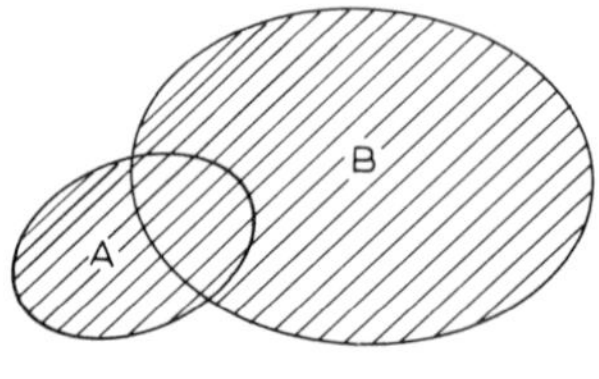

Fig. 6.4.

Fig. 6.4 represents this relation. Let $P(x)$ and $Q(x)$ be the conditions defining A and B respectively. Then,

$$A \cup B = \{x \mid P(x) \text{ or } Q(x)\}.$$

Notice that the operation on the conditions is not "$P(x)$ *and* $Q(x)$" but "$P(x)$ *or* $Q(x)$". Though it is shown graphically as A and B combined, one should not be misled about the true relation.

"$P(x)$ or $Q(x)$" is less stringent than the original conditions $P(x)$ and $Q(x)$ taken separately. Hence, it follows that

$$A \cup B \supset A \quad \text{and} \quad A \cup B \supset B.$$

It does not matter whether A and B overlap each other or not (i.e. whether $A \cap B \neq \phi$ or $A \cap B = \phi$) to form $A \cup B$. Fig. 6.4 is the case of $A \cap B \neq \phi$.

As is the case with intersections, we can think of the union of three or more sets:

$$\bigcup_{i=1}^{n} A_i, \quad \bigcup_{i=1}^{\infty} A_i, \quad \bigcup_{\lambda \in \Lambda} A_\lambda.$$

They are sets composed of elements contained at least in one of the given sets A_λ.

Complement. Let B be a subset of A. Then, those elements of A that are not contained in B form a set, which is called the *complement* of B in A. Whenever it is evident, the phrase "in A" is omitted. Confusions are not likely because in many cases operations are performed to form intersections, unions, and complements of $B, C, \ldots$ which are all subsets of a basic set A (that is called the *embracing set*).

The complement of B is written as B^c. With $Q(x)$ specifying B, we have $B = \{x \mid x \in A, Q(x)\}$ and, hence, $B^c = \{x \mid x \in A, \overline{Q(x)}\}$, where $\overline{Q(x)}$ is a negation of $Q(x)$. As A is taken for the embracing set in this case, $x \in A$ holds both in B and B^c. Therefore, the operation of making a complement corresponds to a logical operation of negation with respect to the essential condition $Q(x)$. Consult fig. 6.5.

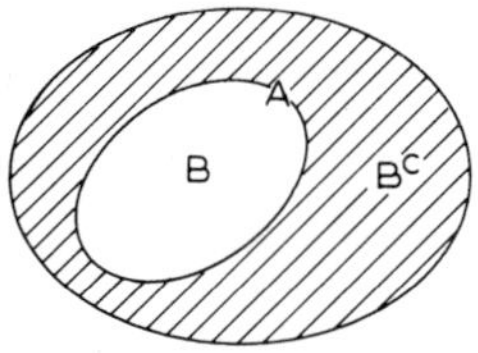

Fig. 6.5.

Relations of set operations

The following formulas hold with respect to the operations $\cap$, $\cup$, ^{c}, ...

(6.1) if $A \supset B, C$, then $A \supset B \cap C,\ B \cup C$;

(6.2) if $A \subset B, C$, then $A \subset B \cap C,\ B \cup C$;

(6.3) $A \cap B = B \cap A \subset A, B$. If $A \subset B$, then $A \cap B = A$;

(6.4) $A \cup B = B \cup A \supset A, B$. If $A \supset B$, then $A \cup B = A$;

(6.5) $(A \cap B) \cap C = A \cap B \cap C$;

(6.6) $(A \cup B) \cup C = A \cup B \cup C$;

(6.7) $(A \cap B) \cup C = (A \cup C) \cap (B \cup C)$;

(6.8) $(A \cup B) \cap C = (A \cap C) \cup (B \cap C)$;

(6.9) $(A \cap B)^c = A^c \cup B^c$ (De Morgan's Rule);

(6.10) $(A \cup B)^c = A^c \cap B^c$ (De Morgan's Rule);

(6.11) $(A^c)^c = A$.

Their proofs are all easy. However, we show the proof of (6.9) for the reader who is not familiar with how to do it.

Proof of (6.9). It suffices to show that elements contained in the sets on both sides of the equation are identical.

1) Let $x \in (A \cap B)^c$. By definition of the complement, $x \notin A \cap B$. Now the fact that an element is contained in $A \cap B$ implies that it is contained in both A and B. Therefore, either $x \notin A$ or $x \notin B$ holds. In the former case, $x \in A^c$ and in the latter case, $x \in B^c$. Hence, x is contained in either A^c or B^c. By definition of the union, we have $x \in A^c \cup B^c$. This proves that $(A \cap B)^c \subset A^c \cup B^c$.

2) Following the same procedure, we can prove $A^c \cup B^c \subset (A \cap B)^c$. This completes the proof of (6.9).

These rules can be extended to a larger number of sets in a straightforward manner.

7. Mappings

The concept of a function which classical calculus taught us is a great help in understanding the concept of a mapping. This is the subject of this section. Consider, for instance, a familiar specific function like $f(x) = x^2$. This formula means that its value at $x = a$ is $f(a) = a^2$. In other words, a real number is associated with any arbitrary real number according to a particular rule, specified by this function, that x^2 corresponds to x. Consider another specific example, $f(x) = 1/x$. We cannot take any arbitrary real number in this example if we are to use this formula as a rule to associate a real number with some real number. For $1/x$ is not calculable at $x = 0$. But for any other real number we can always find its reciprocal and therefore make one definite real number correspond to the original number.

In the two examples that we have studied, the so-called independent variable or argument x and its functional value $f(x)$ are both real numbers. However, the domain within which the independent variable ranges is not the same in the two examples. We can now readily use the concept of sets. Let us abbreviate the expression, "the domain within which the independent variable ranges", to the "domain of definition" of the function. It is a certain definite set of real numbers, to which is applied the rule of correspondence specific to the function under study. In short, it is a set of real numbers for which the value of the function is defined. In the first example, the domain of definition of $f(x) = x^2$ is the set of all real numbers R, whereas that of the second example $f(x) = 1/x$ is the set X of all real numbers except 0 (i.e., a certain proper subset of R). As beginning students of calculus, we used to devote ourselves to exercises like differentiating and integrating functions so that we tended to pay more attention to specific formulas like x^2 or $1/x$. However, after graduating from such a stage, we now find it important to define the concept of a function in a general way. A real-valued function is said to be given on the domain X if a real number $f(x)$ corresponds to each number x of X by a certain rule where X is a given subset of the set of all real numbers R. Here it is necessary to clarify the following two points:

1) The domain of definition X may be any subset of R. It need not be a special set like those in the two examples above.

2) The rule of correspondence need not be expressed in a mathematical formula. It need not be represented in a simple way by a formula or other

means if neat logical content can be given to it, as is the case with the properties or conditions of sets considered in the preceding section.

In any case, we must always think of a function as a correspondence defined on a certain domain of definition.

The square of a rational number is also a rational number. Therefore, we can consider a function that associates a rational number with a rational number by means of a formula $f(x) = x^2$. The domain of definition of this function is the set of all rational numbers. Even though its correspondence rule has the same mathematical expression, this function is considered to be different from the function we examined earlier. This suggests that it is important to pay attention to the relevant domain of definition in considering a functional correspondence or mapping.

These preliminary observations have brought us almost to the summit in our exploration of the very general concept of mappings. The last stretch is very easy for us to climb.

We can easily establish the concept of mappings by looking at sets in general, once we get rid of the strait jacket of confining the domain of definition to a set of real numbers or restricting functional values to real numbers.

Let X and Y be two sets. When to each element x of X an element $f(x)$ of Y corresponds by a certain rule, this correspondence is called a *mapping from X into Y* or a *function on X with values in Y*. X is the *domain* and Y is the *range* *. The notation that has recently been in vogue expresses the mapping of X into Y as $f(x)$: $X \to Y$ or f: $X \to Y$.

Technical terms of mappings. Let us introduce a few technical terms relevant to a maping f: $X \to Y$.

Images. $f(x)$, the element of Y, that corresponds to x, an element of X, is called the image of x. The mapping is just like a camera taking a likeness of a real object on a film. X is the object to be photographed and Y is the film. A good camera, of course, must produce a closest possible likeness of the object, but the mapping or mathematical image-taking may project a deformed picture – however deformed it may be – of X on the film Y.

We have considered the image of an element x. We can also define the image of a subset A of the domain X. Every element x of A has its image $f(x)$ in Y. The collection of all elements of Y that are images of the elements of A constitutes a subset of Y. This is called the image of A under the mapping f and denoted by $f(A)$. Namely, $f(A) = \{f(x) | x \in A\}$. It is nothing but the picture of A projected on the film Y. We have given it a precise definition as a set. See fig. 7.1.

* The term, range, is used in this book in a way somewhat different from the convention in mathematical literature that calls $f(X)$ (the image of the domain X) the range.

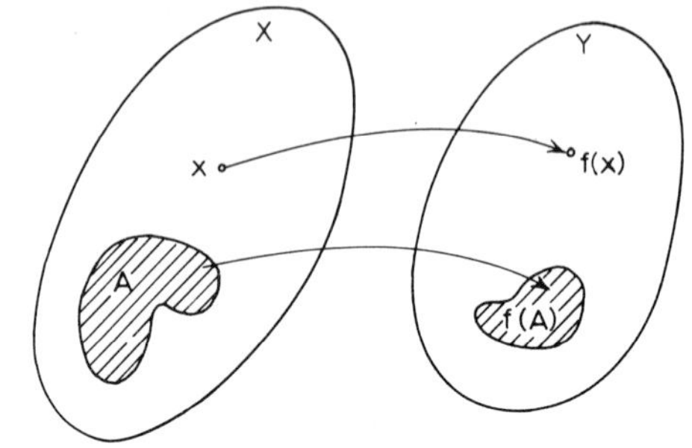

Fig. 7.1.

Inverse images. So far we have examined the mapping under f of an element or a set contained in the domain into the range. We now start from an element or a set in the range.

If we can find, for an element y of Y, an element x of X that has y as its image, such x's form a subset in X. It is called the *inverse image* of y and denoted by $f^{-1}(y)$. If we can find no element x of X that has y as its image, we may write $f^{-1}(y) = \phi$. In either cases, we can establish a subset in X, which can be denoted in the notation of the preceding section by $f^{-1}(y) = \{x | x \in X, f(x) = y\}$. Moreover, we can take a subset B in the range Y and similarly determine the inverse image $f^{-1}(B)$ of B under f, i.e.

$$f^{-1}(B) = \{x | x \in X, f(x) \in B\}.$$

$f^{-1}(B)$ represents a set of x whose image $f(x)$ is contained in the set B.

Example 7.1. Let R be a set of all real numbers. In the aforementioned function $f(x) = x^2 : R \to R$, we have the following:

(1) The image of the element 2 of the domain R is $f(2) = 4$.
(2) The image of the domain R is $f(R) = \{y | y \in R, y \geqq 0\}$.
(3) The inverse image of the element 4 of the range R is $f^{-1}(4) = \{2, -2\}$.
(4) The inverse image of the element -5 of the range R is $f^{-1}(-5) = \phi$.
(5) Subsets B and C in the range, defined by $B = \{y | y \in R, -6 \leqq y < 4\}$ and $C = \{y | y \in R, 0 \leqq y < 4\}$, have an identical inverse image, which is $f^{-1}(B) = f^{-1}(C) = \{x | x \in R, -2 < x < 2\}$.

One-to-one mappings. In the example above, $f^{-1}(4) = \{2, -2\}$, indicating that the inverse image of 4 is a set of two elements. The mapping f, therefore, projects two distinct elements of the domain into a single element of the range. A camera with a lense that is poor in resolving power cannot distinguish two separate points. It is convenient to give a name to a mapping that is perfect in resolving power. A mapping f: $X \to Y$ is called *one-to-one* if any two distinct elements of the domain have distinct images, i.e. if "$x, x' \in X$, $x \neq x' \Rightarrow f(x) \neq f(x')$". This implies that "for x, $x' \in X$, $f(x) = f(x') \Rightarrow x = x'$". We may also state that "for any element y of the range Y, its inverse image $f^{-1}(y)$ contains at most one element" (i.e. $f^{-1}(y)$ is an empty set or a set consisting of one single element). For instance, $f(x) = 1/x$: $X \to R$ is a one-to-one mapping, where R is the set of all real numbers and X is the set obtained by deleting 0 from R.

"Onto" mappings. When the image of a domain X coincides with its range, i.e. when $f(X) = Y$, f is called a mapping from X *onto* Y. If we replace the range Y in any mapping f: $X \to Y$ by $f(X)$, we have f: $X \to f(X)$. This new mapping obviously maps X onto $f(X)$.

If a mapping f: $X \to Y$ is a one-to-one mapping from X onto Y, the lense f projects perfectly resolved images of elements of X on the entire film Y. In this case, the inverse image $f^{-1}(y)$ of any element y of Y is a non-empty set consisting of one single element (of X). If this element is represented as $f^{-1}(y)$, the correspondence $y \to f^{-1}(y)$ gives a mapping from Y onto X. This is called the *inverse mapping* of f. For instance, the mapping by a linear equation $f(x) = 2x + 3$: $R \to R$ is a one-to-one mapping of R onto R; its inverse mapping is given by $f^{-1}(y) = \frac{1}{2}y - \frac{3}{2}$: $R \to R$.

Composition of mappings. Let us have two mappings f: $X \to Y$ and g: $Y \to Z$. Notice that the range of f and the domain of g coincide. For any $x \in X$, we have the image $f(x)$. As $f(x) \in Y$, which is the domain of g, we can determine $g(f(x))$. This shows that there is a mapping from X into Z according to a rule that associates an element of Z with any $x \in X$ by means of the two mappings f and g. The new mapping is called the *composite* or *product* of f and g and denoted by gf *. More specifically, gf: $X \to Z$ and the rule of correspondence is $(gf)(x) = g(f(x))$.

The order of composition is important in making a composed mapping. In the case mentioned above, we may be able to define gf but not necessarily fg. To define fg, the image $g(Y)$ of Y under g must be contained in the domain of f.

If the two mappings are both mappings from X into X itself, i.e. f: $X \to X$ and g: $X \to X$, we can unambiguously define fg and gf. But it does not necessarily follow that $fg = gf$. The following example may be used to make this point clear.

* As noted below, this is gf, not fg.

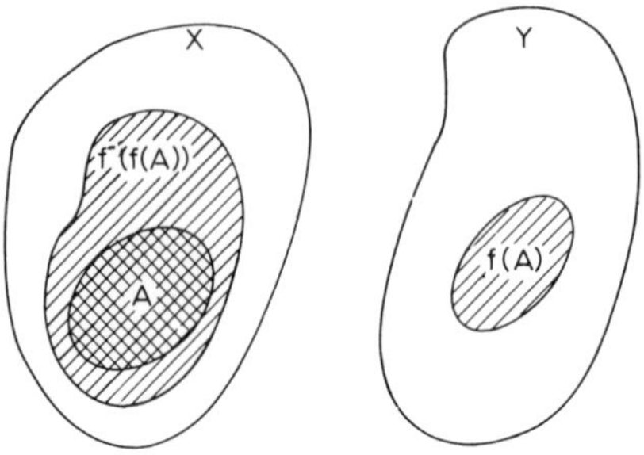

Fig. 7.2.

Example 7.2. Let $f(x) = x^2$: $R \to R$ and $g(x) = x + 1$: $R \to R$. Then, $(fg)(x) = f(g(x)) = (x + 1)^2$ and $(gf)(x) = g(f(x)) = x^2 + 1$. Therefore, for $x \neq 0$, $(fg)(x) \neq (gf)(x)$ so that $fg \neq gf$.

We may also note that two mappings, defined on the same domain, differ from each other if some element of the domain has different images under the two mappings. This should not be confused with a more stringent condition that every element of the domain has different images under the two mappings. Let us note once more that a negation is generally a partial negation.

We can easily ascertain a rule

$$h(gf) = (hg)f \qquad \text{(associative law)}$$

for three or more mappings, e.g. f: $X \to Y$, g: $Y \to Z$, and h: $Z \to W$. The proof of this proposition is left to the reader.

Some rules of mappings. To close this section, we give a number of basic rules describing the relations between set-theoretic operations and mappings.

For a mapping f: $X \to Y$, we have the following:

(7.1) If $A \subset X$, then $A \subset f^{-1}(f(A))$.

(7.2) If $B \subset f(X)$, then $B = f(f^{-1}(B))$.

(7.3) If $A_\lambda \subset X$, then $f(\bigcup_{\lambda \in \Lambda} A_\lambda) = \bigcup_{\lambda \in \Lambda} f(A_\lambda)$

(7.4) and $f(\bigcap_{\lambda \in \Lambda} A_\lambda) \subset \bigcap_{\lambda \in \Lambda} f(A_\lambda)$.

(7.5) If $B_\lambda \subset Y$, then $f^{-1}(\bigcup_{\lambda \in \Lambda} B_\lambda) = \bigcup_{\lambda \in \Lambda} f^{-1}(B_\lambda)$

(7.6) and $f^{-1}(\bigcap_{\lambda \in \Lambda} B_\lambda) = \bigcap_{\lambda \in \Lambda} f^{-1}(B_\lambda)$.

(7.7) If f is a mapping from X onto Y and if $A \subset X$, then $f(A^c) \supset (f(A))^c$.

(7.8) If $B \subset Y$, then $f^{-1}(B^c) = (f^{-1}(B))^c$.

Let g: $Y \to Z$.

(7.9) If $C \subset Z$, then $(gf)^{-1}(C) = f^{-1}(g^{-1}(C))$.

As these rules can be easily proved, the reader is invited to try his hand at proving them in the same way as he proved the rules on sets. The proof of (7.4) is given below for the reader's reference

The proof of (7.4). Take any element y of the set on the left-hand side of the relation, i.e. $y \in f(\bigcap_{\lambda \in \Lambda} A_\lambda)$. y is an element of the image of the set $\bigcap_{\lambda \in \Lambda} A_\lambda$. Hence, by the definition of the image of a set, we can write $y = f(x)$ where x is some $x \in \bigcap_{\lambda \in \Lambda} A_\lambda$. As $x \in \bigcap_{\lambda \in \Lambda} A_\lambda$, x belongs to every A_λ so that $y \in f(A_\lambda)$. As this holds for any $\lambda \in \Lambda$, we have $y \in \bigcap_{\lambda \in \Lambda} f(A_\lambda)$. [Q.E.D.].

We may note that the set on the right-hand side in (7.4) is generally larger than the one on the left-hand side. For instance, in the function $f(x) = x^2$: $R \to R$ (see Example 7.1), let

$$A_1 = \{x \mid x \in R, -2 \leqq x \leqq 0\}$$

and

$$A_2 = \{x \mid x \in R, 0 \leqq x \leqq 3\}.$$

Then, $A_1 \cap A_2 = \{0\}$. $\therefore f(A_1 \cap A_2) = \{0\}$.
On the other hand, $f(A_1) = \{y \mid y \in R, 0 \leqq y \leqq 4\}$, $f(A_2) = \{y \mid y \in R, 0 \leqq y \leqq 9\}$.
$\therefore f(A_1) \cap f(A_2) = f(A_1) \neq f(A_1 \cap A_2)$.

8. Completeness of the real number system

This section is devoted to a recapitulation of what we know about real numbers with special emphasis placed on their important properties pertaining to the concept of limits. The central topic of this discussion is the completeness of the real number system.

Ordering of real numbers. Real numbers contain integers like ..., $-2, -1, 0, 1, 2, \ldots$, rational numbers like $-\frac{1}{3}$, $\frac{2}{5}$, etc., and irrational numbers like $\sqrt{2}$, π (the ratio of the circumference of a circle to its diameter), and e (the base of natural logarithms). The real number system is a set R composed of all those real numbers. As is well known, the four arithmetical operations, namely addition, subtraction, multiplication, and division, are possible within R. Henceforth, $x \in R$ means that x is a real number.

It is always possible to order real numbers. For any $x, y \in R$, one of the following three conditions holds:

(1) $x > y$ (x is larger than y),

(2) $x = y$ (x is equal to y),

(3) $x < y$ (x is smaller than y).

When (1) or (2) holds (i.e. (3) does not hold), we write $x \geqq y$; when (2) or (3) holds (i.e. (1) does not hold), we write $x \leqq y$ *. Then, for $x, y, z \in R$,

(4) if $x \geqq y$ and $y \geqq z$, we have $x \geqq z$.

If we further assume $x > y$ or $y > z$, we naturally get $x > z$ in (4).

The ordering and the four arithmetical operations of real numbers satisfy the following well-known formulas: For any $x, y, z \in R$,

(8.1) $x > y \Rightarrow x + z > y + z$ (similarly, $x \geqq y \Rightarrow x + z \geqq y + z$),

(8.2) $x > y,\ z > 0 \Rightarrow xz > yz$ (similarly, $x \geqq y,\ z \geqq 0 \Rightarrow xz \geqq yz$),

(8.4) $x^2 \geqq 0$; moreover, $x^2 = 0 \Leftrightarrow x = 0$.

Note that $-1 \cdot x = -x$.

Completeness of the real number system. Between two different numbers, $x, y \in R$ ($x > y$), there is always a third real number $z \in R$ such that $x > z > y$ (e.g. $z = (x + y)/2$). It immediately follows that there are real numbers between x and z and between z and y. Repeating this process *ad infinitum,* we can find that real numbers are infinitely jampacked between x and y. This fact is described as "real numbers are *densely* distributed". The same observation applies to the rational number system, too. Therefore, the denseness does not describe exactly the fact that real numbers are continuously distributed.

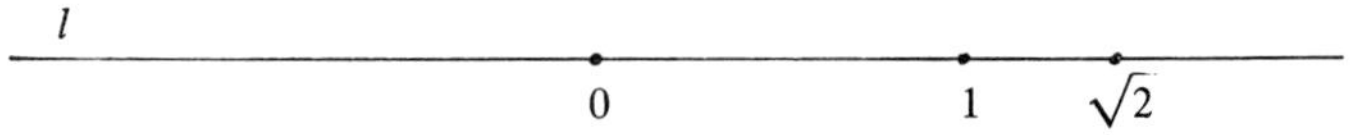

Fig. 8.1.

Plot the origin O and the unit point 1 on a straight line l and measure all numbers on it. We have one-to-one correspondence between points on the line and real numbers (as measured on the line). If real numbers x and y in R are such that $x > y$, the point corresponding to x lies on the right of the point

* The notation $\geqq$ was already used in Chapter 1.

corresponding to y. However, points corresponding to rational numbers (rational points) alone cannot completely fill out the line l. For there are many other points on the line l like $\sqrt{2}$ (the length of the diagonal in a unit square) that are not rational points. It is only when these other numbers are added to rational numbers that points are continuously distributed along the line. What then is exactly meant by a continuous distribution of points? We must now go a little deeper and examine our intuitive idea of a straight line. This enables us to give a clear, mathematical expression to the continuity or completeness of the real number system.

Cut the line l into two parts l_1 and l_2 and assume the following conditions:

(i) $l = l_1 \cup l_2$, $l_1 \cap l_2 = \phi$. I.e. the line l is a union of two non-empty subsets l_1 and l_2 with no intersection between them.

(ii) Any point on l_1 lies on the left of any point on l_2.

As we have cut the line, there must be one cut-off point on it. On the right of this point, there are no points of l_1; on its left, there are no points of l_2. Our intuition tells us that this is what a line should be as a set. We cannot give a mathematical proof to our intuition, but we can create a mathematical concept out of this intuition, which then can serve as a basis of analysis. This is an important routine rule of mathematical analysis and we follow it below.

Let the cut-off point be a. Because of (i), we must have either $a \in l_1$ or $a \in l_2$. If $a \in l_1$, a is the rightmost point of l_1; if $a \in l_2$, it is the leftmost point of l_2.

We find an end point in one of the subsets whenever we separate a line into two subsets subject to (i) and (ii). This gives a precise expression to our intuition about the distribution of points along a line.

We can restate this fact about real numbers as follows:

The axiom of continuity. Separate the set of real numbers, R, into two non-empty subsets R_1 and R_2, subject to

(I) $R = R_1 \cup R_2$ and $R_1 \cap R_2 = \phi$ and

(II) $x < y$ for any $x \in R_1$ and any $y \in R_2$.

Then, there exists the largest number, or maximum, in R_1 or the smallest number, or minimum, in R_2. The system of rational numbers does not satisfy this axiom. Consider the set of all rational numbers and a subset $R_2 = \{x \mid x > 0, x^2 > 2\}$ within it. Let R_1 be the complement of R_2. Then, R_1 and R_2 are subject to (I) and (II). But there is neither a maximum in R_1 nor a minimum in R_2.

The real number system is rigorously constructed out of the rational number system and it is proved that the axiom of continuity holds for the real number system obtained in this way. The reader can consult textbooks of pure mathematics on this point. We shall take this axiom for granted and proceed to describe a number of facts about the concept of limits.

Supremum and infimum. Let $X \neq \phi$ be a subset of R. If there is a real number b such that $x \leqq b$ for any $x \in X$, X is said to be *bounded from above* and b is called an *upper bound* of X. Similarly, if there is a real number a such that $x \geqq a$ for any $x \in X$, X is said to be *bounded from below* and a is called a *lower bound* of X.

It does not necessarily follow that X contains the maximum, namely $\max_{x \in X} x$, even if X is bounded from above, provided that X is not a finite set. For instance, $X = \{x \mid x < 1\}$ does not contain the maximum in itself; nevertheless, 1 is an upper bound of this set and the minimum of all (apparently infinitely many) possible upper bounds.

THEOREM 8.1. *Let* $\phi \neq X \subset R$.

(a) *If X is bounded from above, there is a minimum among all upper bounds of X.*

(b) *If X is bounded from below, there is a maximum among all lower bounds of X.*

Proof. (a) Denote the set of upper bounds of X by $R_2 = \{b \mid x \leqq b$ (for any $x \in X)\}$, and let R_1 be the complement of R_2. Then, the real number system is separated into two non-empty subsets R_1 and R_2. We have $R = R_1 \cup R_2$ and $R_1 \cap R_2 = \phi$ so that (I) holds. Also, for $a \in R_1$ and $b \in R_2$, we have always $a < b$. In fact, if $a \nless b$, then $a \geqq b$. As b is an upper bound, a which is not less than b is also an upper bound so that $a \in R_2$. Hence, $R_1 \cap R_2 \ni a$, which contradicts $R_1 \cap R_2 = \phi$. Then, (II) also holds. The axiom of continuity states either (A) that R_1 contains a maximum α or (B) that R_2 contains a minimum β. We now show that (A) does not hold in this case. If (A) is assumed to hold, $\alpha \in R_1$ and, hence, $\alpha \notin R_2$, indicating that α is not an upper bound of X. It follows that there is an x in X such that $\alpha < x$. Then, α' such that $\alpha < \alpha' < x$ cannot be an upper bound of X so that $\alpha' \in R_1$. It shows that R_1 contains a real number greater than α, a contradiction with the assumption of α being the maximum in R_1. In other words, if (A) is assumed to hold, there follows a contradiction. Hence, we have proved that (B) holds.

(b) can be proved in exactly the same way as above [Q.E.D.].

The least upper bound β of X in Theorem 8.1 is called the *supremum* of X and denoted by $\sup_{x \in X} x = \beta$. The greatest lower bound α of X is called the *infimum* of X and denoted by $\inf_{x \in X} x = \alpha$.

The supremum and infimum are very important concepts. They coincide with the maximum or minimum, if X contains the latter. Where there are no maximum or minimum, they serve as substitutes. We rewrite the conditions of supremum and infimum for the reader's reference:

$\beta = \sup_{x \in X} x$ means

(8.5) that β is one of the upper bounds of X, i.e. $x \leqq \beta$ (for any $x \in X$) and

(8.6) that β is the least upper bound of X so that a real number β' less than β is not an upper bound of X and that there is a real number $x \in X$ such that $\beta' < x$.

$\alpha = \inf_{x \in X} x$ means

(8.7) that α is one of the lower bounds of X, i.e. $\alpha \leqq x$ (for any $x \in X$) and

(8.8) that α is the greatest lower bound of X so that a real number α' greater than α is not a lower bound of X and that there is a real number $x \in X$ such that $\alpha' > x$.

If X is not bounded from above, "for whatever large real number a there is a real number x in X such that $x > a$" *. This situation is conveniently denoted by $\sup_{x \in X} x = +\infty$. Correspondingly, if X is bounded from above, we may write $\sup_{x \in X} x < +\infty$. Similarly, we write $\inf_{x \in X} x = -\infty$ and $\inf_{x \in X} x > -\infty$.

Convergence of a sequence. When a real number x_n is associated with each n in numbers 1, 2, 3, ..., n, ..., this is called a sequence of such numbers or simply a *sequence*, denoted by $\{x_n\}$. x_n is the nth term of the sequence. In contrast to the sequence $\{x_n\}$, $\{x_n \mid n = 1, 2, \ldots\}$ merely represents a set, which is nothing but the collection of all real numbers appearing as terms in the sequence. The sequence takes an account of the order of appearance of real numbers $x_1, x_2, x_3, \ldots$ when n moves over 1, 2, 3, ...

* This is a logical negation of a proposition that "X is bounded from above".

Example 8.1. $\{x_n = (-1)^n\}$ and $\{y_n = (-1)^{n+1}\}$ are different sequences. But their terms form an identical set $\{1, -1\}$.

We can now give a precise definition to the property that a sequence $\{x_n\}$ *converges* to a real number a.

For any real number $\epsilon > 0$, an integer $n(\epsilon)$ can be chosen such that the inequality

$$(8.9) \qquad a - \epsilon < x_n < a + \epsilon ,$$

holds for $n \geqq n(\epsilon)$. a is called the *limit* of the sequence $\{x_n\}$. It is denoted by $\lim_{n\to\infty} x_n = a$ or $x_n \to a \ (n \to \infty)$.

$\lim_{n\to\infty} x_n = +\infty$ means that for any real number a, an integer $n(a)$ can be chosen such that the inequality

$$(8.10) \qquad a < x_n$$

holds for $n \geqq n(a)$.

$\lim_{n\to\infty} x_n = -\infty$ can be similarly interpreted.

The theorem below is useful in determining whether a sequence converges or not. The sequence $\{x_n\}$ is said to be *increasing* if $x_{n+1} \geqq x_n$ $(n = 1, 2, 3, ...)$ and *strictly increasing* if $x_{n+1} > x_n$ $(n = 1, 2, 3, ...)$. When the inequalities are reversed, it is said to be *decreasing* and *strictly decreasing* respectively.

THEOREM 8.2

(a) *With respect to an increasing sequence* $\{x_n\}$,

(a.1) *if it is bounded from above,* $\lim_{n\to\infty} x_n = \sup_n x_n$ *and*

(a.2) *if it is not bounded from above,* $\lim_{n\to\infty} x_n = +\infty$.

(b) *With respect to a decreasing sequence* $\{x_n\}$,

(b.1) *if it is bounded from below,* $\lim_{n\to\infty} x_n = \inf_n x_n$ *and*

(b.2) *if it is not bounded from below,* $\lim_{n\to\infty} x_n = -\infty$.

Proof. We present the proof of (a), as (b) can be proved in exactly the same manner.

(a.1) Let $\sup_n x_n = \beta$. By virtue of (8.5), we have $x_n \leqq \beta \ (n \geqq 1)$ for any number n. On the other hand, $\beta - \epsilon$ is less than β for any $\epsilon > 0$ and, by virtue of (8.6), $\beta - \epsilon < x_{n(\epsilon)}$ for some number $n(\epsilon)$. As the sequence is increasing,

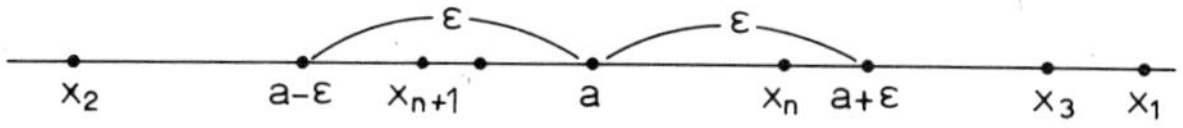

Fig. 8.2.

$\beta - \epsilon < x_{n(\epsilon)} \leqq x_n$ (for $n \geqq n(\epsilon)$). Considering these inequalities together, we get

$$\beta - \epsilon < x_n \leqq \beta < \beta + \epsilon \qquad (\text{for } n \geqq n(\epsilon)) . \quad [\text{Q.E.D.}]$$

(a.2) As $\sup_n x_n = +\infty$, we have for any real number a, $a < x_{n(a)}$ at some number $n(a)$. Following the same steps taken in the latter half of (a.1), we get $a < x_n$ (for $n \geqq n(a)$). [Q.E.D.]

Example 8.2. For $a > 0$, (1) $\lim_{n\to\infty} na = +\infty$ and (2) $\lim_{n\to\infty} a/n = 0$.

Proof of (1). This proposition follows from (a.2) of Theorem 8.2 if the sequence $\{na\}$ which is increasing is shown to be not bounded from above. Suppose that $\sup_n na = \beta < +\infty$. Then, (8.6) shows that, for $\beta' = \beta - a$, we have $\beta - a < na$ at some number n so that $\beta < (n+1)a$, which contradicts (8.5). Hence, $\beta = +\infty$ and $\{na\}$ is not bounded from above.

Proof of (2). For any $\epsilon > 0$, we have $\lim_{n\to\infty} n\epsilon = +\infty$ because of (1). Therefore, there exists a number $n(a, \epsilon)$ such that $a < n\epsilon$ (for $n \geqq n(a, \epsilon)$). Rewriting it, we get $0 \leqq a/n < \epsilon$ (for $n \geqq n(a, \epsilon)$). $\therefore \lim_{n\to\infty} a/n = 0$.

Example 8.3. (1) If $a > 1$, then $\lim_{n\to\infty} a^n = +\infty$; (2) if $1 > a > 0$, then $\lim_{n\to\infty} a^n = 0$.

Proof of (1). Let $a = 1 + \delta$ where $\delta > 0$. Observe that $a^n = (1+\delta)^n \geqq 1 + n\delta$. Example 8.2 shows that $\lim_{n\to\infty} n\delta = +\infty$. Hence, there is a number $n(M)$ for any positive number M such that $n\delta > M - 1$ (for $n \geqq n(M)$). Thus, $a^n \geqq 1 + n\delta > M$ (for $n \geqq n(M)$).

Proof of (2). As $1/a > 1$, we have $\lim_{n\to\infty} 1/a^n = +\infty$ by virtue of (1) of this example. Therefore, we can find a number $n(\epsilon)$ for $\epsilon > 0$ such that $1/a^n > 1/\epsilon$ (for $n \geqq n(\epsilon)$). Then, $0 < a^n < \epsilon$ (for $n \geqq n(\epsilon)$).

Convergence in absolute value. Inequality (8.9) is used to define the convergence of a sequence. We can rewrite it in a more convenient form by introducing the concept of absolute value.

When a real number x is compared with 0, we have either $x > 0, x = 0$ or $x < 0$. x is said to be positive if $x > 0$ and negative if $x < 0$ as the reader knows well. A real number $x \neq 0$ is either positive or, if not, $-x$ is positive. Taking note of this fact, we define the absolute value of x, i.e. $|x|$ as follows:

$$(8.11) \qquad |x| = \begin{cases} x & (\text{for } x \geqq 0) \\ -x & (\text{for } x < 0) \end{cases}$$

or

$$(8.12) \qquad |x| = \max(x, -x)\,.$$

The absolute value satisfies the following important relations:

$$(8.13) \qquad |x| \geqq 0; \text{ moreover, } |x| = 0 \Leftrightarrow x = 0.$$

$$(8.14) \qquad |x| = |-x| \geqq x\,.$$

$$(8.15) \qquad |xy| = |x|\,|y|\,.$$

$$(8.16) \qquad ||x| - |y|| \leqq |x \pm y| \leqq |x| + |y|\,.$$

As the proof is easy, it is left to the reader.

Inequality (8.9) can be rewritten in terms of absolute value as follows: For any real number $\epsilon > 0$, some number $n(\epsilon)$ can be chosen such that the inequality

$$(8.17) \qquad |x_n - a| < \epsilon$$

holds for $n \geqq n(\epsilon)$. As $|x_n - a| < \epsilon$ can be rewritten as $-\epsilon < |x_n - a| < \epsilon$, we can see that $\lim_{n\to\infty} x_n = a$ is equivalent to $\lim_{n\to\infty} |x_n - a| = 0$.

Basic properties of the convergence of sequences.

(1) If $\lim_{n\to\infty} x_n = a$, then $\lim_{n\to\infty} |x_n| = |a|$.

(2) If $x_n = a$ $(n = 1, 2, 3, \ldots)$, then $\lim_{n\to\infty} x_n = a$.

(3) If $\lim_{n\to\infty} x_n = a$, then $\{x_n\}$ does not converge to b $(\neq a)$ (uniqueness of the limit).

If $\lim_{n\to\infty} x_n = a$ and $\lim_{n\to\infty} y_n = b$, one gets

(4) $\lim_{n\to\infty} cx_n = c \lim_{n\to\infty} x_n$ for any real number c;

(5) $\lim_{n\to\infty} (x_n \pm y_n) = \lim_{n\to\infty} x_n \pm \lim_{n\to\infty} y_n$;

(6) $\lim_{n\to\infty} (x_n y_n) = \lim_{n\to\infty} x_n \lim_{n\to\infty} y_n$;

(7) $\lim_{n\to\infty} x_n/y_n = \lim_{n\to\infty} x_n / \lim_{n\to\infty} y_n$, provided that $b \neq 0$;

(8) $\lim_{n\to\infty} x_n \geqq 0$, provided that $x_n \geqq 0$ $(n = 1, 2, 3, \ldots)$;

(9) $\lim_{n\to\infty} x_n = 0$, provided that $|x_n| \leqq \epsilon_n$ $(n = 1, 2, 3, \ldots)$ and that $\lim_{n\to\infty} \epsilon_n = 0$.

Proof

(1) (8.16) shows that $||x_n| - |a|| \leqq |x_n - a|$. The right-hand side converges to 0, as we have already noted. Hence, there is a number $n(\epsilon)$ for any $\epsilon > 0$ such that $||x_n| - |a|| \leqq |x_n - a| < \epsilon$ for $n \geqq n(\epsilon)$.

(2) It is self-evident.

(3) Suppose that $\lim_{n\to\infty} x_n = b (\neq a)$ at the same time. Then, it follows from (8.16) that

$$|a - b| = |a - x_n + x_n - b| \leqq |a - x_n| + |x_n - b| .$$

As $a \neq b$, we have $|a - b| > 0$. In addition, both terms on the right-hand side of the equation above converge to 0. Therefore, there are numbers n' and n'' such that

$$|a - x_n| < \tfrac{1}{3}|a - b| \text{ for } n \geqq n'$$

and

$$|b - x_n| < \tfrac{1}{3}|a - b| \text{ for } n \geqq n'' .$$

For $n \geqq \max(n', n'')$, it follows from the inequality that $|a - b| < \frac{2}{3}|a - b|$, i.e. $1 < \frac{2}{3}$, which is a contradiction. Thus, $\lim_{n\to\infty} x_n = b$ does not hold.

(4) When $c = 0$, it reduces to (2) where $a = 0$. Therefore, let $c \neq 0$. As $\lim_{n\to\infty} |x_n - a| = 0$, there is a number $n(\epsilon/|c|)$ for any $\epsilon > 0$ such that $|x_n - a| < \epsilon/|c|$ (for $n \geqq n(\epsilon/|c|)$). $\therefore$ $|cx_n - ca| = |c(x_n - a)| = |c||x_n - a| < \epsilon$ (for $n \geqq n(\epsilon/|c|)$).

(5) $$|(x_n \pm y_n) - (a \pm b)| = |(x_n - a) \pm (y_n - b)| \leqq |x_n - a| + |y_n - b| .$$

Both terms on the right-hand side converge to 0. Hence, the left-hand side converges to 0 in the same way as in the proofs we have given above. The reader may try the formal procedure using ϵ and n.

(6) $$\begin{aligned} |x_n y_n - ab| &= |x_n y_n - a y_n + a y_n - ab| \leqq |x_n y_n - a y_n| + |a y_n - ab| \\ &= |(x_n - a) y_n| + |a(y_n - b)| = |x_n - a||y_n| + |a||y_n - b| . \end{aligned}$$

As $\lim_{n\to\infty} |y_n| = |b|$ by virtue of (1), we get $|y_n| < \delta$ for all terms beyond the mth (i.e. for $n \geqq m$) if a positive number δ is given such that $\delta > |b|$. Hence, $|x_n y_n - ab| \leqq \delta |x_n - a| + |a||y_n - b|$ (for $n \geqq m$). Its right-hand side converges to 0 by virtue of (4) and (5). So does its left-hand side.

(7) This follows from (6) if we prove $\lim_{n\to\infty} 1/y_n = 1/b$. Before proceeding, however, we may note that $1/y_n$ is indeterminate for n such that $y_n = 0$, if this possibility is not ruled out. But because of $\lim_{n\to\infty} |y_n| = |b| > 0$, we get a certain number m such that $0 < |b|/2 < |y_n|$ for all $n \geqq m$. In other words, $|y_n| \neq 0$ for $n \geqq m$. This insures that $1/y_n$ is determinate for all numbers n not less than m. For $n \geqq m$, we have

$$|1/y_n - 1/b| = \left| \frac{b - y_n}{b y_n} \right| = \frac{|b - y_n|}{|b||y_n|} \leqq \frac{2|b - y_n|}{|b|^2} .$$

The last inequality is obtained by replacing $|y_n|$ on the denominator by $|b|/2$ that is smaller than it. Its right-hand side converges to 0 by virtue of (4). So does its left-hand side.

(8) If $a < 0$, we have $3a/2 < x_n < a/2 < 0$ for sufficiently large $n \geqq n(a)$. This contradicts the assumption.

(9) This has already frequently been employed in the proofs above. The reader may try the formal proof with ϵ and n.

Example 8.4. A sequence $\{x_n\}$, given by $x_{n+1} = \sqrt{x_n} + 1$ $(n = 1, 2, \ldots)$, $x_1 = 1$, is convergent and $\lim_{n\to\infty} x_n = (3 + \sqrt{5})/2$.

Proof. (i) This sequence is bounded from above. This will be proved by induction. First, we show that $x_1 = 1 < 3$. If $x_n < 3$,

$$3 - x_{n+1} = 3 - (\sqrt{x_n} + 1) = 2 - \sqrt{x_n} = \frac{4 - x_n}{2 + \sqrt{x_n}} > 0 .$$

Hence, $x_{n+1} < 3$. This proves that $x_n < 3$ $(n = 1, 2, \ldots)$ and that $\{x_n\}$ is bounded from above. (3 is one of the upper bounds.)

(ii) This sequence is increasing. This is proved also by induction. Note that $x_2 - x_1 = \sqrt{x_1} + 1 - x_1 = 2 - 1 > 0$. Suppose that $x_n \geqq x_{n-1}$. Then, x_{n-1}, $x_n > 0$ and

$$x_{n+1} - x_n = \sqrt{x_n} - \sqrt{x_{n-1}} = \frac{x_n - x_{n-1}}{\sqrt{x_n} + \sqrt{x_{n-1}}} \geqq 0.$$

This proves that the sequence is increasing.

It follows from (i) and (ii) above that this sequence is convergent by virtue of (a.1) of Theorem 8.2. Let $\lim_{n\to\infty} x_n = a$. From the relation $x_{n+1} = \sqrt{x_n} + 1$, we have $(x_{n+1} - 1)^2 = x_n$. Its left-hand side converges to $(a-1)^2$ as shown by (2), (5) and (6) above. Its right-hand side, of course, converges to a. Because of the uniqueness of the limit (see (3) above), we have $(a-1)^2 = a$. Solving this quadratic equation, we get $a = (3 \pm \sqrt{5})/2$. As $\sqrt{5} > 1$, we have $2 > 3 - \sqrt{5}$, i.e. $1 > (3 - \sqrt{5})/2$. On the other hand, x_n is increasing from $x_1 = 1$ to $\lim_{n\to\infty} x_n = a$ so that $a \geqq 1$. Hence, $a = (3 + \sqrt{5})/2$.

Subsequences. Extract numbers from the sequence $1, 2, 3, \ldots, n, \ldots$ to get a sequence $n_1, n_2, n_3, \ldots, n_\nu, \ldots$ This is called a subsequence. n_ν is the νth term of this sequence. By extracting corresponding terms from a sequence $\{x_n\}$, we get a subsequence $\{x_{n_\nu}\}$, i.e.

$$x_{n_1}, x_{n_2}, \ldots, x_{n_\nu}, \ldots ,$$

which is a sequence by itself if ν is considered as a number. Therefore, we can discuss the limit of x_{n_ν} for $\nu \to \infty$, i.e. $\lim_{\nu\to\infty} x_{n_\nu}$.

We can now add another property to (1)–(9) above:

(10) If $\lim_{n\to\infty} x_n = a$, then $\lim_{\nu\to\infty} x_{n_\nu} = a$ for any subsequence $\{x_{n_\nu}\}$ of $\{x_n\}$.

As its proof is very easy, it is omitted.

A sequence converging to a supremum (or infimum). Let $\sup_{x \in X} x = \beta \ (< +\infty)$ for a non-empty set X of real numbers. Then, there is a sequence $\{x_n\}$ such that

$$x_n \in X \quad (n = 1, 2, 3, \ldots) \text{ and}$$

$$\lim_{n\to\infty} x_n = \beta .$$

The existence of such a sequence will be effectively and frequently employed for the analytical purpose in this book. It is easy to prove its existence. It suffices to determine terms of the sequence by making use of the properties of the supremum (8.5) and (8.6).

(8.6) shows that there is $x \in X$ such that $\beta - 1/n < x$ for $\beta' = \beta - 1/n$. Pick one of these x's and call it x_n. This process determines a sequence $\{x_n\}$. It is easy to prove that this sequence converges to β.

$$|x_n - \beta| \leqq 1/n \quad (n = 1, 2, 3, \ldots) .$$

Its right-hand side converges to 0 as shown in Example 8.2. Therefore, its left-hand side also converges to 0 so that $\lim_{n\to\infty} x_n = \beta$.

We can show in exactly the same way that there is a sequence $\{x_n\}$ of X that converges to $\inf_{x \in X} x = \alpha\ (> -\infty)$. Similarly, there exists a sequence $\{x_n\}$ of X such that $\lim_{n \to \infty} x_n = +\infty$ or $\lim_{n \to \infty} x_n = -\infty$ when $\sup_{x \in X} x = +\infty$ or $\inf_{x \in X} x = -\infty$. The reader is invited to try the proofs.

9. Linear spaces

In economic analysis, we very often deal with magnitudes composed of n real numbers. For instance, final demands for goods c_i, sectoral levels of output x_j, and their prices p_j are represented by groups of n numbers like $c_1, c_2, \ldots, c_n$; $x_1, x_2, \ldots, x_n$; and $p_1, p_2, \ldots, p_n$. Economic analysis can be carried out efficiently if a collection of such homogeneous numbers is taken as a mathematical entity. The linear space that we shall discuss in this section is, so to speak, a canvass on which we can paint economic magnitudes in a concise and clear fashion.

Real linear spaces. All n-tuples of real numbers $x_1, x_2, \ldots, x_n$ or

$$(9.1) \qquad x = \begin{bmatrix} x_1 \\ x_2 \\ \cdot \\ \cdot \\ \cdot \\ x_n \end{bmatrix}$$

compose a *linear space* over the real number system. It is also called a *vector space* and denoted by R^n. An element of R^n is called a *vector* *.

Linear operations on vectors, i.e. addition, subtraction and scalar multiplication of vectors, can be performed in R^n. R^n is called a linear space because of this property.

We shall define each of these operations below. Let

$$x = \begin{bmatrix} x_1 \\ x_2 \\ \cdot \\ \cdot \\ \cdot \\ x_n \end{bmatrix} \quad \text{and} \quad y = \begin{bmatrix} y_1 \\ y_2 \\ \cdot \\ \cdot \\ \cdot \\ y_n \end{bmatrix} \in R^n .$$

* An element of R^n is often called a point instead of a vector in this book.

Then, linear operations are defined by the following rules:

(9.2) $$x \pm y = \begin{bmatrix} x_1 \pm y_1 \\ x_2 \pm y_2 \\ \cdot \\ \cdot \\ x_n \pm y_n \end{bmatrix} \quad \text{(addition and subtraction)}$$

and

(9.3) $$\alpha x = \begin{bmatrix} \alpha x_1 \\ \alpha x_2 \\ \cdot \\ \cdot \\ \cdot \\ \alpha x_n \end{bmatrix} \quad \text{for a real number } \alpha \text{ (scalar multiplication).}$$

Two vectors are defined to be *equal*, namely

$$x = y$$

if $x_j = y_j$ $(j = 1, 2, ..., n)$.

It is easy to prove that these vector operations satisfy the following rules just like operations on real numbers:

Let $x, y, z \in R^n$ and α and β real numbers. Then,

(i) $x + y = y + x$;

(ii) $(x + y) + z = x + (y + z)$;

(iii) $x + 0 = x$, where 0 is the zero vector $0 = \begin{bmatrix} 0 \\ 0 \\ \cdot \\ \cdot \\ 0 \end{bmatrix}$;

(iv) $\alpha(x + y) = \alpha x + \alpha y$;

(v) $(\alpha + \beta)x = \alpha x + \beta x$;

(vi) $\alpha(\beta x) = (\alpha\beta)x$;

(vii) $0 \cdot x = 0$; $\alpha \cdot 0 = 0$;

(viii) $1 \cdot x = x$.

x_j is called the jth *component* of a vector. In this book, we use a subscript to indicate the component number. On the other hand, to number vectors, we use superscripts like $x^1, x^2, \ldots, x^k$.

k vectors $x^1, x^2, \ldots, x^k$ are said to be *linearly independent* if they are such that

$$\sum_{i=1}^{k} \alpha_i x^i = 0$$

implies $\alpha_1 = \alpha_2 = \ldots = \alpha_k = 0$ (α's are real numbers). In other words, the linear independence of vectors implies that they satisfy no homogeneous linear relation unless all its coefficients are zero.

When the vectors are not linearly independent, they are said to be *linearly dependent.* In this case, we have

$$\sum_{i=1}^{k} \alpha_i x^i = 0$$

for some specific values of coefficients, not all of which are 0.

Example 9.1. n unit vectors in R^n

$$e^1 = \begin{bmatrix} 1 \\ 0 \\ 0 \\ \cdot \\ \cdot \\ 0 \end{bmatrix}, \quad e^2 = \begin{bmatrix} 0 \\ 1 \\ 0 \\ \cdot \\ \cdot \\ 0 \end{bmatrix}, \ldots, \quad e^i = \begin{bmatrix} 0 \\ \cdot \\ \cdot \\ 0 \\ 1 \\ 0 \\ \cdot \\ \cdot \\ 0 \end{bmatrix} \left.\vphantom{\begin{matrix} 0 \\ \cdot \\ \cdot \\ 0 \\ 1 \end{matrix}}\right\} i, \ldots, \quad e^n = \begin{bmatrix} 0 \\ 0 \\ 0 \\ \cdot \\ \cdot \\ 1 \end{bmatrix}$$

are linearly independent.

Proof.

$$\sum_{i=1}^{k} \alpha_i e^i = \begin{bmatrix} \alpha_1 \\ \alpha_2 \\ \cdot \\ \cdot \\ \alpha_n \end{bmatrix} = 0 \ \text{ implies } \ \alpha_1 = \alpha_2 = \ldots = \alpha_n = 0.$$

Example 9.2. If $x^1, x^2, \ldots, x^k$ are linearly independent, any m vectors $(1 \leqq m \leqq k)$ chosen from these k vectors are also linearly independent.

Proof. Take any subset J from the set of indexes $I = \{1, 2, \ldots, k\}$. The proposition to be proved here is the linear independence of the set of vectors $\{x^i | i \in J\}$. Suppose that $\sum_{i \in J} \alpha_i x^i = 0$. For numbers not contained in J, let

$\alpha_i = 0\ (i \notin J)$. Then, for the k coefficients, $\alpha_1, \alpha_2, ..., \alpha_k$, we have

$$\sum_{i=1}^{k} \alpha_i x^i = \sum_{i \in J} \alpha_i x^i + \sum_{i \notin J} \alpha_i x^i = 0 + 0 = 0 .$$

As $x^1, x^2, ..., x^k$ are linearly independent, $\alpha_1 = \alpha_2 = ... = \alpha_k = 0$. $\therefore \alpha_i = 0$ $(i \in J)$. Therefore, $\{x^i |\ i \in J\}$ is linearly independent.

THEOREM 9.1. *If $x^j \in R^n$ $(j = 1, 2, ..., k)$ are linearly independent, then $k \leqq n$.*

Proof. We shall prove by induction on n that a set of k vectors $(k > n)$ is linearly dependent.

(i) When $n = 1$, R^1 is the set of all real numbers R. Consider a set of $k (> 1)$ real numbers $x^1, x^2, ..., x^k$. When they are all 0, we have

$$\sum_{i=1}^{k} 1 \cdot x^i = 0$$

where the coefficients are all set at unity. Hence, they are linearly dependent. On the other hand, when at least one of them is not 0, let $x^1 \neq 0$ *. Put the coefficients to be $\alpha_1 = -x^2/x^1$, $\alpha_2 = 1$, $\alpha_3 = \alpha_4 = ... = \alpha_k = 0$. Then,

$$\sum_{i=1}^{k} \alpha_i x^i = -x^1 (x^2/x^1) + x^2 = 0 .$$

As $\alpha_2 \neq 0$, they are linearly dependent.

(ii) Assume that the theorem holds for R^{n-1}. Let k vectors $x^j \in R^n$ $(k > n)$ be

$$x^j = \begin{bmatrix} x_{1j} \\ x_{2j} \\ \cdot \\ \cdot \\ \cdot \\ x_{n-1\, j} \\ x_{nj} \end{bmatrix} \quad (j = 1, 2, ..., k). \tag{9.4}$$

* Renumber the superscripts if necessary. This procedure is admissible when the renumbering does not affect the substance of the arguments in any essential manner. We shall make frequent use of this procedure in this book.

When $x^j = 0$ $(j = 1, 2, ..., k)$, they are obviously linearly dependent (see the first half of (i)).

Assume now that there is a non-zero vector and that the vectors are so numbered that $x^k \neq 0$. As further renumbering of components does not affect our argument here in any essential way, let the last component of x^k be $x_{nk} \neq 0$.

Putting $\beta_j = x_{nj}/x_{nk}$ $(1 \leqq j \leqq k-1)$. we get

$$(9.5) \qquad y^j = x^j - \beta_j x^k = \begin{bmatrix} y_{1j} \\ y_{2j} \\ \vdots \\ y_{n-1\,j} \\ 0 \end{bmatrix} \qquad (1 \leqq j \leqq k-1),$$

indicating that the nth components of the $k-1$ vectors y^j are all zero. We may consider the first n – 1 components of each vector in (9.5) to define a vector in R^{n-1}. Then, as we have a total of $k-1$ $(> n-1)$ such vectors, we have by the inductive hypothesis real numbers $\alpha_1, \alpha_2, ..., \alpha_{k-1}$ (not all of which are 0) such that

$$\sum_{j=1}^{k-1} \alpha_j \begin{bmatrix} y_{1j} \\ y_{2j} \\ \vdots \\ y_{n-1j} \end{bmatrix} = 0 .$$

As the nth component is zero in all vectors in (9.5), we also have

$$\sum_{j=1}^{k-1} \alpha_j y^j = 0$$

for the same set of coefficients. Hence, putting the kth coefficient as

$$\alpha_k = -\sum_{j=1}^{k-1} \alpha_j \beta_j ,$$

we get

$$\sum_{j=1}^{k} \alpha_j x^j = \sum_{j=1}^{k-1} \alpha_j x^j - \left(\sum_{j=1}^{k-1} \alpha_j \beta_j\right) x^k$$

$$= \sum_{j=1}^{k-1} \alpha_j (x^j - \beta_j x^k) = \sum_{j=1}^{k-1} \alpha_j y^j = 0 .$$

Moreover, not all of $\alpha_1, \alpha_2, ..., \alpha_k$ are 0. Thus, the k vectors are linearly dependent. [Q.E.D.]

We also have the following theorem:

THEOREM 9.2. *Let k vectors $x^j \in R^n$ $(1 \leqq j \leqq k < n)$ be linearly independent. The adjunction of some suitable $n - k$ vectors $x^j \in R^n$ $(k + 1 \leqq j \leqq n)$ to them can make $x^1, x^2, ..., x^k, x^{k+1}, ..., x^n$ linearly independent.*

Proof. It suffices to show that by adjuncting x^{k+1} to $x^1, x^2, ..., x^k$, we can make the enlarged set of vectors linearly independent. When this is possible, we can reach a linearly independent set of n vectors by adjuncting one vector after another.

(i) Assume that the theorem holds for R^{n-1}. Let the given linearly independent k vectors $x^j \in R^n$ be (9.4). Because of the linear independence, each $x^j \neq 0$ and in particular $x^k \neq 0$. As usual, let the nth component of x^k be non-zero, i.e. $x_{nk} \neq 0$, for the sake of what follows. Form $k - 1$ vectors (9.5) as in the proof of Theorem 9.1. They are linearly independent. Indeed, if

$$\sum_{j=1}^{k-1} \alpha_j y^j = 0 ,$$

we have

$$\sum_{j=1}^{k-1} \alpha_j x^j - \Big(\sum_{j=1}^{k-1} \alpha_j \beta_j\Big) x^k = 0$$

and, hence,

$$\alpha_1 = \alpha_2 = ... = \alpha_{k-1} = \sum_{j=1}^{k-1} \alpha_j \beta_j = 0$$

due to the linear independence of x^j $(1 \leqq j \leqq k)$. As vectors of (9.5) can be treated as vectors in R^{n-1}, we can adjunct a vector of the form

$$x^{k+1} = \begin{bmatrix} x_{1\ k+1} \\ x_{2\ k+1} \\ \vdots \\ x_{n-1\ k+1} \\ 0 \end{bmatrix}$$

and make $y^1, y^2, ..., y^{k-1}, x^{k+1}$ linearly independent by the inductive hypothesis. Then, $x^1, x^2, \ldots, x^k, x^{k+1}$ are linearly independent.

In fact, putting

$$0 = \sum_{j=1}^{k+1} \alpha_j x^j$$

and substituting (9.5) into it, we get

$$0 = \sum_{j=1}^{k-1} \alpha_j (y^j + \beta_j x^k) + \alpha_k x^k + \alpha_{k+1} x^{k+1}$$

$$= \sum_{j=1}^{k-1} \alpha_j y^j + \alpha_{k+1} x^{k+1} + (\alpha_k + \sum_{j=1}^{k-1} \alpha_j \beta_j) x^k .$$

With respect to the nth component, we can see that it is 0 in y^j and in x^{k+1} but not so in x^k. Hence, the coefficient of x^k is 0, i.e.

$$\alpha_k + \sum_{j=1}^{k-1} \alpha_j \beta_j = 0. \tag{9.7}$$

Hence,

$$\sum_{j=1}^{k-1} \alpha_j y^j + \alpha_{k+1} x^{k+1} = 0.$$

By virtue of the linear independence of y^j and x^{k+1}, we get $\alpha_1 = \alpha_2 = \ldots = \alpha_{k-1} = \alpha_{k+1} = 0$. Finally, $\alpha_k = 0$ from (9.7).

(ii) $n = 2$ is the smallest n for which the statement of the theorem makes sense. In this case, assume that a non-zero vector

$$x = \begin{bmatrix} x_1 \\ x_2 \end{bmatrix} \in R^2$$

is given. If $x_1 \neq 0$, we can easily verify that

$$\begin{bmatrix} x_1 \\ x_2 \end{bmatrix} \text{ and } \begin{bmatrix} 0 \\ 1 \end{bmatrix}$$

are linearly independent. [Q.E.D.]

Suppose that x^i $(1 \leqq i \leqq k)$ are linearly independent but that x and x^i $(1 \leqq i \leqq k)$ are linearly dependent. Then, because of the latter assumption, there are $k + 1$ real numbers α and α_i $(1 \leqq i \leqq k)$ (not all of them zero), such that

$$\alpha x + \sum_{i=1}^{k} \alpha_i x^i = 0. \tag{9.8}$$

If $\alpha = 0$, we have

$$\sum_{i=1}^{k} \alpha_i x^i = 0$$

and, by the first assumption, $\alpha_1 = \alpha_2 = \ldots = \alpha_k = 0$. This is a contradiction. Hence, $\alpha \neq 0$. Putting $\beta_i = -\alpha_i/\alpha$ $(1 \leqq i \leqq k)$, we can rewrite (9.8) as

$$x = \sum_{i=1}^{k} \beta_i x^i . \tag{9.9}$$

In other words, x is a *linear combination* of $x^1, x^2, \ldots, x^k$.

Furthermore, the expansion coefficients β_i are uniquely determined. We can see this as follows: If

$$x = \sum_{i=1}^{k} \gamma_i x^i ,$$

we have

$$\sum_{i=1}^{k} \beta_i x^i = \sum_{i=1}^{k} \gamma_i x^i \quad \text{or} \quad \sum_{i=1}^{k} (\beta_i - \gamma_i) x^i = 0 .$$

It follows from the linear independence of x^i $(1 \leqq i \leqq k)$ that $\beta_i - \gamma_i = 0$ $(i = 1, 2, \ldots, k)$ i.e. $\beta_i = \gamma_i$ $(i = 1, 2, \ldots, k)$.

For n linearly independent $x^j \in R^n$ $(1 \leqq j \leqq n)$, we find that for any $x \in R^n$, x and x^j $(1 \leqq j \leqq n)$ are linearly dependent because of Theorem 9.1. This is the case of $k = n$ in (9.9). To paraphrase, any $x \in R^n$ can be uniquely expanded into a linear combination of $x^1, x^2, \ldots, x^n$. In this sense, $x^1, x^2, \ldots, x^n$ are said to form a *basis* of R^n. e^i $(1 \leqq i \leqq n)$ in Example 9.1 form one of the bases of R^n.

From these theorems, we can see that the maximum number of vectors that form a linearly independent set is n. This is called the *dimension* of R^n (as a linear space).

THEOREM 9.3. *n vectors*

$$x^j = \begin{bmatrix} x_{1j} \\ x_{2j} \\ \vdots \\ x_{nj} \end{bmatrix} \quad (j = 1, 2, \ldots, n) \tag{9.10}$$

are linearly independent if and only if the determinant composed of these vectors is non-zero, i.e.

$$\Delta = \begin{vmatrix} x_{11} & x_{12} & \cdots & x_{1n} \\ x_{21} & x_{22} & \cdots & x_{2n} \\ \cdots & \cdots & \cdots & \cdots \\ x_{n1} & x_{n2} & \cdots & x_{nn} \end{vmatrix} \neq 0\,.$$

Proof. (i) *Necessity.* Let us assume as usual that $x_{nn} \neq 0$. The assumption can be still satisfied even if we rearrange the vector indexes and component indexes when necessary. It corresponds to renumbering rows and columns in the determinant under examination. It affects the sign of the determinant but not its nonvanishingness. Following the procedure employed in the proof of Theorem 9.1, we set up (9.5) for $k = n$. Then, as before, we can show that

$$\begin{bmatrix} y_{1j} \\ y_{2j} \\ \vdots \\ y_{n-1\,j} \end{bmatrix} \qquad (j = 1, 2, \ldots, n-1)$$

are linearly independent. Therefore, assuming that the theorem holds for R^{n-1}, we have

$$\Gamma = \begin{vmatrix} y_{11} & y_{12} & \cdots & y_{1\,n-1} \\ y_{21} & y_{22} & \cdots & y_{2\,n-1} \\ \cdots & \cdots & \cdots & \cdots \\ y_{n-1\,1} & y_{n-1\,2} & \cdots & y_{n-1\,n-1} \end{vmatrix} \neq 0\,.$$

We can now get

$$\Delta' = \begin{vmatrix} y_{11} & y_{12} & \cdots & y_{1\,n-1} & x_{1n} \\ y_{21} & y_{22} & \cdots & y_{2\,n-1} & x_{2n} \\ \cdots & \cdots & \cdots & \cdots & \cdots \\ y_{n-1\,1} & y_{n-1\,2} & \cdots & y_{n-1\,n-1} & x_{n-1\,n} \\ 0 & 0 & \cdots & 0 & x_{nn} \end{vmatrix} = x_{nn}\Gamma \neq 0$$

by expanding Δ' along the nth row. By relation (9.5), we can see that Δ' is a determinant that is obtained by replacing the jth column of Δ $(1 \leqq j \leqq n-1)$ by the jth column of $\Delta - \beta_j \times$ the nth column of Δ. $\therefore\ \Delta = \Delta' \neq 0$. It is obvious that the theorem holds for $n = 1$.

(ii) *Sufficiency.* Let

$$\sum_{j=1}^{k} \alpha_j x^j = 0\,.$$

In an expanded form, this is expressed as the following linear equations in $\alpha_1, \alpha_2, \ldots, \alpha_n$:

$$\begin{aligned} x_{11}\alpha_1 + x_{12}\alpha_2 + \ldots + x_{1n}\alpha_n &= 0\,, \\ x_{21}\alpha_1 + x_{22}\alpha_2 + \ldots + x_{2n}\alpha_n &= 0\,, \\ \cdots\cdots\cdots\cdots\cdots\cdots\cdots\cdots\cdots \\ x_{n1}\alpha_1 + x_{n2}\alpha_2 + \ldots + x_{nn}\alpha_n &= 0\,. \end{aligned}$$

The determinant of the coefficients of this equation system is given by $\Delta \neq 0$, while the constant terms on the right-hand side are all zero. By Cramer's Rule, we see

$$\alpha_j = \Delta_j/\Delta = 0 \quad (j = 1, 2, \ldots, n)\,,$$

where Δ_j is a determinant which replaces the jth column of Δ by 0. Hence, $\Delta_j = 0$ and the conclusion above follows. This proves that, if $\Delta \neq 0$, x^j ($j = 1, 2, \ldots, n$) are linearly independent. [Q.E.D.]

So far, we have arranged an n-tuple of real numbers columnwise as in (9.1). Vector operations given by (9.2) and (9.3) are, in essence, componentwise operations on real numbers. When components are arranged rowwise as in

$$(9.11) \qquad x = (x_1, x_2, \ldots, x_n)\,,$$

there should be no essential change in operational procedures and the foregoing exposition for vectors of type (9.1) is also valid for vectors of type (9.11) *mutatis mutandis*. In this case, Δ in Theorem 9.3 is a determinant composed of n vectors of type (9.11) as its rows.

To distinguish vectors expressed by (9.1) and (9.11), we call them a *column vector* and a *row vector* respectively.

10. Matrices and linear mappings

Matrices. In the preceding section, we examined an n-tuple of real numbers as a mathematical entity called a vector. Then, for a system of equations

$$(10.1) \qquad \begin{aligned} a_{11}x_1 + a_{12}x_2 + \ldots + a_{1n}x_n &= b_1\,, \\ a_{21}x_2 + a_{22}x_2 + \ldots + a_{2n}x_n &= b_2\,, \\ \ldots \quad \ldots \quad \ldots \quad \ldots \quad &\ldots \\ a_{n1}x_1 + a_{n2}x_2 + \ldots + a_{nn}x_n &= b_n\,, \end{aligned}$$

which was discussed in Chapter 1, this enables us to treat the solution

$x_1, x_2, ..., x_n$, the constant terms $b_1, b_2, ..., b_n$, etc. as column vectors

$$(10.2) \qquad x = \begin{bmatrix} x_1 \\ x_2 \\ \vdots \\ x_n \end{bmatrix}, \quad b = \begin{bmatrix} b_1 \\ b_2 \\ \vdots \\ b_n \end{bmatrix}, \quad \text{etc.}$$

in a summary form. Similarly, (10.1) can be expressed in a more concise manner if we define a new mathematical entity for the system of n^2 coefficients a_{ij}.

Keep the unknowns x_j, constant terms b_i, and all operational symbols like + and = out of (10.1) and write out the coefficients a_{ij} in a tabular form

$$(10.3) \qquad A = \begin{bmatrix} a_{11} & a_{12} & \cdots & a_{1n} \\ a_{21} & a_{22} & \cdots & a_{2n} \\ \cdots & \cdots & \cdots & \cdots \\ a_{n1} & a_{n2} & \cdots & a_{nn} \end{bmatrix}.$$

We specify the multiplication of this array A and the vector x in (10.2) in such a way that Ax, the product of A and x, is a vector in R^n, keeping in mind that x is a vector in R^n. For this purpose, we define the components of Ax according to

$$(10.4) \qquad \text{the } i\text{th component of } Ax = a_{i1}x_1 + a_{i2}x_2 + \ldots + a_{in}x_n \,.$$

Then, (10.1) can be expressed concisely by

$$(10.5) \qquad Ax = b \,,$$

which is a relation between vectors x and b in R^n.

A table of n^2 real numbers arrayed in a square is called a *matrix*. Just as in determinants, a_{ij} is called the (i, j) *element*, the ith horizontal line from above

$$a_{i1}, a_{i2}, ..., a_{in}$$

the ith *row*, and the jth vertical line from left

$$\begin{matrix} a_{1j} \\ a_{2j} \\ \vdots \\ a_{nj} \end{matrix}$$

the jth *column*.

We must note that a matrix and a determinant are qualitatively different as mathematical concepts. While a matrix represents a table of numbers, a determinant indicates a numerical value like

$$\begin{vmatrix} 1 & 2 \\ 2 & 5 \end{vmatrix} = 1.$$

However, there is an important connection between the two. For instance, the value of the determinant that is obtained from the matrix (10.3) without altering its arrangement

$$\text{(10.6)} \qquad \det A = \begin{vmatrix} a_{11} & a_{12} & \dots & a_{1n} \\ a_{21} & a_{22} & \dots & a_{2n} \\ \dots & \dots & \dots & \dots \\ a_{n1} & a_{n2} & \dots & a_{nn} \end{vmatrix}$$

is closely related to the properties of A as a matrix. (10.6) is called the *determinant of the matrix A*. It may be represented alternatively by a symbol $|A|$ instead of $\det A$.

Example 10.1. The determinant of the matrix $A = \begin{bmatrix} 1 & 2 & 3 \\ 4 & 5 & 6 \\ 7 & 8 & 9 \end{bmatrix}$ is

$$\det A = \begin{vmatrix} 1 & 2 & 3 \\ 4 & 5 & 6 \\ 7 & 8 & 9 \end{vmatrix} = 0\,.$$

(10.3) defines the matrix A as a square array of n^2 real numbers. We extend this idea and define a matrix in general

$$\text{(10.7)} \qquad A = \begin{bmatrix} a_{11} & a_{12} & \dots & a_{1n} \\ a_{21} & a_{22} & \dots & a_{2n} \\ \dots & \dots & \dots & \dots \\ a_{m1} & a_{m2} & \dots & a_{mn} \end{bmatrix}$$

which arranges mn real numbers in a rectangular form. The multiplication of A and a vector $x \in R^n$ is defined by (10.4), just as in (10.3), so that Ax is a vector. In this general case, as i ranges from 1 to m, we have $Ax \in R^m$.

It is obvious that the rectangular matrix (10.7) corresponds to a system of m equations in n unknowns:

$$\text{(10.8)} \qquad \begin{array}{l} a_{11}x_1 + a_{12}x_2 + \dots + a_{1n}x_n = b_1\,, \\ a_{21}x_1 + a_{22}x_2 + \dots + a_{2n}x_n = b_2\,, \\ \dots \qquad \dots \qquad \dots \qquad \dots \\ a_{m1}x_1 + a_{m2}x_2 + \dots + a_{mn}x_n = b_m\,. \end{array}$$

(10.7) is called an *(m, n) matrix* or *$m \times n$ matrix*. It reduces to a square matrix of (10.3) when $m = n$. In this sense, (10.3) is called a *square matrix of the nth order.*

Linear mappings. When (10.7) is multiplied into an element x of R^n, Ax becomes an element of R^m. Therefore, a mapping $f(x) = Ax$: $R^n \to R^m$ induced by the matrix A is obtained, for which R^n is the domain and R^m the range.

Recalling the vector operations, (9.2) and (9.3), and the multiplication of A and x, (10.4), we see that this mapping has the following properties:

Let $x, y \in R^n$ and α a real number. Then,

(i) $f(x \pm y) = f(x) \pm f(y)$ and

(ii) $f(\alpha x) = \alpha f(x)$.

Notice that $x \pm y$ and αx on the left-hand side are operations in the domain R^n, while $f(x) \pm f(y)$ and $\alpha f(x)$ on the right-hand side are operations in the range R^m. Thus, to the addition, subtraction and scalar multiplication in the domain correspond the same types of operations between images in the range. A mapping that satisfies (i) and (ii) is called a *linear mapping.*

If f is a linear mapping, finite applications of (i) and (ii) lead to

$$f\left(\sum_{j=1}^{k} \alpha_j x^j\right) = \sum_{j=1}^{k} \alpha_j f(x^j) \tag{10.9}$$

for $x^j \in R^n$ $(j = 1, 2, ..., k)$ and real numbers α_j $(j = 1, 2, ..., k)$.

The discussion above has shown that there is a linear mapping f: $R^n \to R^m$ induced by the matrix A. Next, let us show that any linear mapping can be expressed as matrix operations.

Let f: $R^n \to R^m$ satisfy (i) and (ii) and, hence, (10.9). For $x \in R^n$, $f(x)$ is an element of R^m, namely a vector. Denote its ith component by $f_i(x)$. Then,

$$f(x) = \begin{bmatrix} f_1(x) \\ f_2(x) \\ \vdots \\ f_m(x) \end{bmatrix} . \tag{10.10}$$

n unit vectors e^j $(j = 1, 2, ..., n)$ in R^n, as given in Example 9.1, form a basis of R^n. For $x \in R^n$, an expansion into a linear combination

$$x = \sum_{j=1}^{n} x_j e^j , \qquad x = \begin{bmatrix} x_1 \\ x_2 \\ \vdots \\ x_n \end{bmatrix} \tag{10.11}$$

holds. It follows from (10.9) that

$$f(x) = f\left(\sum_{j=1}^{n} x_j e^j\right) = \sum_{j=1}^{n} x_j f(e^j)$$

so that the ith component of $f(x)$ is given by

$$(10.12) \qquad f_i(x) = \sum_{j=1}^{n} f_i(e^j)\, x_j \,.$$

As x ranges over the domain R^n, its components x_j are altered, but $f_i(e^j)$ are invariant constants determined uniquely by the mapping f. Denote mn real numbers $f_i(e^j)$ to be $f_i(e^j) = a_{ij}$. Then, (10.10) and (10.12) may be written out as

$$(10.13) \qquad \begin{bmatrix} f_1(x) \\ f_2(x) \\ \vdots \\ f_m(x) \end{bmatrix} = \begin{bmatrix} a_{11} & a_{12} & \cdots & a_{1n} \\ a_{21} & a_{22} & \cdots & a_{2n} \\ \cdots & \cdots & \cdots & \cdots \\ \cdots & \cdots & \cdots & \cdots \\ a_{m1} & a_{m2} & \cdots & a_{mn} \end{bmatrix} \begin{bmatrix} x_1 \\ x_2 \\ \vdots \\ x_n \end{bmatrix} .$$

Denoting the matrix in (10.13) by A, we may express it as

$$(10.14) \qquad f(x) = Ax \,.$$

We may sum up this observation in the theorem below.

THEOREM 10.1. *By multiplying a matrix A into a vector $x \in R^n$, a linear mapping $f\colon R^n \to R^m$ is obtained. Conversely, any linear mapping can be written in the form of (10.14).*

Operations on matrices

Equality. (m, n) matrices

$$(10.15) \qquad A = \begin{bmatrix} a_{11} & a_{12} & \cdots & a_{1n} \\ a_{21} & a_{22} & \cdots & a_{2n} \\ \cdots & \cdots & \cdots & \cdots \\ a_{m1} & a_{m2} & \cdots & a_{mn} \end{bmatrix} \text{ and } B = \begin{bmatrix} b_{11} & b_{12} & \cdots & b_{1n} \\ b_{21} & b_{22} & \cdots & b_{2n} \\ \cdots & \cdots & \cdots & \cdots \\ b_{m1} & b_{m2} & \cdots & b_{mn} \end{bmatrix}$$

are defined to be equal to each other, i.e. $A = B$, when all corresponding elements are equal, namely $a_{ij} = b_{ij}$ ($i = 1, 2, \ldots, m$; $j = 1, 2, \ldots, n$). So defined, it can be shown that $Ax = Bx$ (for any $x \in R^n$) is equivalent to $A = B$.

Addition and subtraction. The sum and difference of A and B are defined by

$$(10.16) \qquad A \pm B = \begin{bmatrix} a_{11} \pm b_{11} & a_{12} \pm b_{12} & \cdots & a_{1n} \pm b_{1n} \\ a_{21} \pm b_{21} & a_{22} \pm b_{22} & \cdots & a_{2n} \pm b_{2n} \\ \cdots & \cdots & \cdots & \cdots \\ a_{m1} \pm b_{m1} & a_{m2} \pm b_{m2} & \cdots & a_{mn} \pm b_{mn} \end{bmatrix}.$$

For linear mappings $f\colon R^n \to R^m$ and $g\colon R^n \to R^m$, their sum $f+g$ and difference $f-g$ are defined by $(f \pm g)(x) = f(x) \pm g(x)$, which are also linear mappings from R^n into R^m and may be expressed as

$$(f \pm g)(x) = (A \pm B)x$$

like (10.14) where A and B are the coefficient matrices of f and g in the notation of (10.14).

Scalar multiplication. This is defined as follows: The scalar multiplication of α and A (where α is a real number) is given by

$$(10.17) \qquad \alpha A = \begin{bmatrix} \alpha a_{11} & \alpha a_{12} & \cdots & \alpha a_{1n} \\ \alpha a_{21} & \alpha a_{22} & \cdots & \alpha a_{2n} \\ \cdots & \cdots & \cdots & \cdots \\ \alpha a_{m1} & \alpha a_{m2} & \cdots & \alpha a_{mn} \end{bmatrix}.$$

By multiplying a real number α into a linear mapping $f\colon R^n \to R^m$, we get another linear mapping $\alpha f\colon R^n \to R^m$ (where we define $(\alpha f)(x) = \alpha \cdot f(x)$). (10.17) is a coefficient matrix of αf expressed in the notation of (10.14).

Example 10.2. For $A = \begin{bmatrix} 2 & 3 & 5 \\ 7 & 1 & 4 \end{bmatrix}$ and $B = \begin{bmatrix} 1 & 6 & 2 \\ 3 & 8 & 5 \end{bmatrix}$, we have

$$A + B = \begin{bmatrix} 3 & 9 & 7 \\ 10 & 9 & 9 \end{bmatrix} \quad \text{and} \quad 2A = \begin{bmatrix} 4 & 6 & 10 \\ 14 & 2 & 8 \end{bmatrix}.$$

Multiplication. Given linear mappings $f\colon R^n \to R^m$ and $g\colon R^m \to R^l$, we can make a composed mapping $gf\colon R^n \to R^l$ according to the procedure shown in Section 7 because the range of f = the domain of $g = R^m$. Now, as f and g are linear, we have the following for $x, y \in R^n$ and a real number α:

$$(gf)(x \pm y) = g(f(x \pm y)) = g(f(x) \pm f(y))$$
$$= g(f(x)) \pm g(f(y)) = (gf)(x) \pm (gf)(y)$$

and

$$(gf)(\alpha x) = g(f(\alpha x)) = g(\alpha f(x))$$
$$= \alpha g(f(x)) = \alpha (gf)(x)\,.$$

As (i) and (ii) are satisfied, gf is a linear mapping so that gf can be expressed like (10.14) as

$$(gf)(x) = Cx$$

where C is an (l, n) matrix.

Let A and B be the coefficient matrices of f and g in the notation of (10.14). A is an (m, n) matrix and B an (l, m) matrix:

$$A = \begin{bmatrix} a_{11} & \cdots & a_{1n} \\ \vdots & & \vdots \\ a_{m1} & \cdots & a_{mn} \end{bmatrix} \quad \text{and} \quad B = \begin{bmatrix} b_{11} & \cdots & b_{1m} \\ \vdots & & \vdots \\ b_{l1} & \cdots & b_{lm} \end{bmatrix}.$$

We can now express c_{ij}, elements of C, in terms of a_{kj}, elements of A, and b_{ik}, elements of B. c_{ij} is the value of $(gf)_i(e^j)$, i.e. the ith component of the image in R^l of the unit vector e^j in R^n under gf. As we have

$$e^j = \begin{bmatrix} 0 \\ \vdots \\ 0 \\ 1 \\ 0 \\ \vdots \\ 0 \end{bmatrix} \Big\} j \quad \text{and} \quad f(e^j) = Ae^j = \begin{bmatrix} a_{11} & a_{12} & \dots & a_{1n} \\ a_{21} & a_{22} & \dots & a_{2n} \\ \dots & \dots & \dots & \dots \\ \dots & \dots & \dots & \dots \\ \dots & \dots & \dots & \dots \\ \dots & \dots & \dots & \dots \\ a_{m1} & a_{m2} & \dots & a_{mn} \end{bmatrix} \begin{bmatrix} 0 \\ \vdots \\ 0 \\ 1 \\ 0 \\ \vdots \\ 0 \end{bmatrix} = \begin{bmatrix} a_{1j} \\ a_{2j} \\ \cdot \\ \cdot \\ \cdot \\ \cdot \\ a_{mj} \end{bmatrix},$$

we get

$$(gf)(e^j) = g(f(e^j)) = Bf(e^j) = \begin{bmatrix} b_{11} & b_{12} & \dots & b_{1m} \\ b_{21} & b_{22} & \dots & b_{2m} \\ \dots & \dots & \dots & \dots \\ b_{l1} & b_{l2} & \dots & b_{lm} \end{bmatrix} \begin{bmatrix} a_{1j} \\ a_{2j} \\ \dots \\ a_{mj} \end{bmatrix}$$

so that

$$(10.18) \qquad c_{ij} = (gf)_i (e^j) = \sum_{k=1}^{m} b_{ik} a_{kj} \, .$$

A row of B and a column of A are composed of the same number (namely, m) of elements so that we can multiply elements of the ith row of B, $b_{i1}, b_{i2}, \dots, b_{im}$ and elements of the jth column of A

$$\begin{matrix} a_{1j} \\ a_{2j} \\ \vdots \\ a_{mj} \end{matrix}$$

in their standing order to yield $b_{i1}a_{1j}$, $b_{i2}a_{2j}$, ... down to $b_{im}a_{mj}$, which then can be summed up into (10.18).

Given A and B, all elements of the new matrix C are determined by (10.18). C is called the product of B and A and denoted by $C = BA$. It is important to remember that matrices can be multiplied together if and only if

the number of columns of the matrix on the left
= the number of rows of the matrix on the right.

If A and B are both square matrices of the nth order, AB and BA are both feasible. However, not necessarily $AB = BA$.

Example 10.3. If

$$A = \begin{bmatrix} 1 & 2 & 3 & -1 \\ -1 & 1 & 2 & 1 \end{bmatrix} \quad \text{and} \quad B = \begin{bmatrix} -1 & 1 & 2 \\ 1 & -1 & 3 \\ 0 & 4 & 1 \\ -3 & 2 & -1 \end{bmatrix},$$

we have

$$AB = \begin{bmatrix} 4 & 9 & 12 \\ -1 & 8 & 2 \end{bmatrix}$$

but BA not possible.

Example 10.4. If

$$A = \begin{bmatrix} 0 & 1 \\ 0 & 0 \end{bmatrix} \quad \text{and} \quad B = \begin{bmatrix} 0 & 0 \\ 1 & 0 \end{bmatrix},$$

we have

$$AB = \begin{bmatrix} 1 & 0 \\ 0 & 0 \end{bmatrix} \quad \text{and} \quad BA = \begin{bmatrix} 0 & 0 \\ 0 & 1 \end{bmatrix}. \quad \therefore AB \neq BA .$$

Remark. As is clear from the exposition above, the matrix multiplication is a natural extension of the multiplication of a matrix and a vector. Henceforth, we may if necessary regard a column vector x in R^n as an $(n, 1)$ matrix and the product of a matrix A and a vector x, namely Ax, as the product of an (m, n) matrix A and an $(n, 1)$ matrix x.

We can readily see from this remark that a row vector in R^m, $x = (x_1, x_2, ..., x_m)$ which may be regarded as a $(1, m)$ matrix, can be pre-multiplied (i.e. from the left) into an (m, n) matrix A to yield a $(1, n)$ matrix of a row vector in R^n $(f_1(x), f_2(x), ..., f_n(x))$, namely

$$(x_1, x_2, ..., x_m) \begin{bmatrix} a_{11} & a_{12} & \cdots & a_{1n} \\ \cdots & \cdots & \cdots & \cdots \\ a_{m1} & a_{m2} & \cdots & a_{mn} \end{bmatrix} = (f_1(x), f_2(x), ..., f_n(x)).$$

Its jth component $f_j(x)$ is given by

$$(10.19) \qquad f_j(x) = \sum_{i=1}^{m} a_{ij} x_i \,.$$

We may now regard (10.19) as a relation describing how components are transformed by a linear mapping of a column vector in R^m into a column vector in R^n. Then, this new mapping may be expressed by

$$(10.20) \qquad \begin{bmatrix} f_1(x) \\ f_2(x) \\ \vdots \\ f_n(x) \end{bmatrix} = \begin{bmatrix} a_{11} & a_{21} & \cdots & a_{m1} \\ a_{12} & a_{22} & \cdots & a_{m2} \\ \vdots & \vdots & & \vdots \\ a_{1n} & a_{2n} & \cdots & a_{mn} \end{bmatrix} \begin{bmatrix} x_1 \\ x_2 \\ \vdots \\ x_m \end{bmatrix}$$

in the form of (10.13). The coefficient matrix (10.20) is an (n, m) matrix, whose (j, i) element is equal to the (i, j) element of the given (m, n) matrix. This matrix is called the *transposed matrix* of A and denoted by A', namely

$$m\left\{\overbrace{\begin{bmatrix} a_{11} & a_{12} & \cdots & a_{1n} \\ a_{21} & a_{22} & \cdots & a_{2n} \\ \vdots & \vdots & & \vdots \\ a_{m1} & a_{m2} & \cdots & a_{mn} \end{bmatrix}}^{n}\right.' = \left.\overbrace{\begin{bmatrix} a_{11} & a_{21} & \cdots & a_{m1} \\ a_{12} & a_{22} & \cdots & a_{m2} \\ \vdots & \vdots & & \vdots \\ a_{1n} & a_{2n} & \cdots & a_{mn} \end{bmatrix}}^{m}\right\} n \,.$$

Rules of matrix operations. We have introduced most of matrix operations. We may note many similarities of these operations to numerical operations. We now list some basic rules of matrix operations. It should be noted that, to be meaningful, addition and subtraction are performed on matrices of the same form and multiplication on matrices with one's row size equal to the other's column size. In what follows, $A, B, C, ...$ represent matrices and $\alpha, \beta, \gamma, ...$ real numbers.

$$(10.21) \qquad A + B = B + A \,;$$

$$(10.22) \qquad (A + B) + C = A + (B + C) \,;$$

$$(10.23) \qquad A + 0 = A \,,$$

where 0 is a matrix whose form is the same as A and with all elements zero.

(10.24) $(AB)C = A(BC)$;

(10.25) $AI_n = I_m A = A$, where A is an arbitrary (m, n) matrix,

$$I_m = \underbrace{\begin{bmatrix} 1 & 0 & \cdots & & 0 \\ 0 & 1 & 0 & \cdots & 0 \\ \cdot & 0 & \ddots & \ddots & \cdot \\ \cdot & & \ddots & \ddots & 0 \\ 0 & \cdots & & 0 & 1 \end{bmatrix}}_{m} \Bigg\} m \quad \text{and} \quad I_n = \underbrace{\begin{bmatrix} 1 & 0 & \cdots & & 0 \\ 0 & 1 & 0 & \cdots & 0 \\ \cdot & 0 & \ddots & \ddots & \cdot \\ \cdot & & \ddots & \ddots & 0 \\ 0 & \cdots & & 0 & 1 \end{bmatrix}}_{n} \Bigg\} n ,$$

in other words, I_m and I_n are square matrices of the orders m and n respectively, with 1 along the principal diagonal and 0 for all other elements. They play the role of unity in numerical multiplications.

(10.26) $\alpha(A+B) = \alpha A + \alpha B$;

(10.27) $(\alpha+\beta)A = \alpha A + \beta A$;

(10.28) $o \cdot A = 0$; $\alpha \cdot 0 = 0$;

(10.29) $1 \cdot A = A$;

(10.30) $\alpha\beta \cdot A = \alpha(\beta A)$;

(10.31) $(A')' = A$;

(10.32) $(AB)' = B'A'$.

The verification of these rules is left to the reader.

Let $A, B, C, \ldots$ be square matrices of the nth order. Then, $A \pm B$, AB and BA are always meaningful, all being of the nth order. In these matrix operations, I_n plays exactly the same role as unity in numerical operations. I_n is denoted simply by I whenever its order is evident and is called an *identity matrix*.

If A is a square matrix of the nth order, we obtain a square matrix of the nth order by multiplying A k times. This is denoted by A^k, namely

$$A^k = \underbrace{A \cdot A \cdot A \ldots A}_{k} .$$

Then, we have the exponential law

$$A^{l+k} = A^l A^k$$

just as in numerical operations.

Inverse matrices. We have shown that addition, subtraction and multiplication are possible among square matrices of the nth order. Can we also perform division? In the world of real numbers, we can always divide a real number γ by a real number $\alpha \neq 0$; its quotient γ/α is determined as a real number. As γ/α is the product of γ and $1/\alpha$, the feasibility of division depends in the final analysis on the existence of the reciprocal of α, i.e. $1/\alpha$. Now, the reciprocal of α is a real number β such that $\beta\alpha = \alpha\beta = 1$. This relation, when applied to matrices, leads to the following definition (all matrices in this discussion are taken to be square matrices of the nth order unless otherwise noted):

The *inverse matrix* B of a matrix A is a matrix for which we have *

$$AB = BA = I$$

where

$$I = \begin{bmatrix} 1 & 0 & \cdots & 0 \\ 0 & 1 & \ddots & 0 \\ \vdots & \ddots & \ddots & \vdots \\ \cdot & & \ddots & 0 \\ 0 & 0 & \cdots\, 0 & 1 \end{bmatrix}.$$

Example 10.5. The inverse of

$$A = \begin{bmatrix} 1/\sqrt{2} & -1/\sqrt{2} \\ 1/\sqrt{2} & 1/\sqrt{2} \end{bmatrix}$$

is

$$B - \begin{bmatrix} 1/\sqrt{2} & 1/\sqrt{2} \\ -1/\sqrt{2} & 1/\sqrt{2} \end{bmatrix},$$

which the reader can verify.

Example 10.6. Even though $A \neq 0$, it may have no inverse matrix unlike in numbers. For instance, post-multiply (i.e. from the right)

$$B = \begin{bmatrix} b_{11} & b_{12} \\ b_{21} & b_{22} \end{bmatrix} \quad \text{into} \quad A = \begin{bmatrix} 1 & 2 \\ 2 & 4 \end{bmatrix},$$

to yield

$$AB = \begin{bmatrix} b_{11} + 2b_{21} & b_{12} + 2b_{22} \\ 2b_{11} + 4b_{21} & 2b_{12} + 4b_{22} \end{bmatrix}.$$

* It readily follows from the definition that A is an inverse matrix of B.

We can see that the second row is exactly twice as much as the first row in AB. Hence, whatever values the elements b_{11}, b_{12}, b_{21} and b_{22} may be given, the equality

$$AB = \begin{bmatrix} 1 & 0 \\ 0 & 1 \end{bmatrix}$$

cannot hold. In other words, A has no inverse matrix. Yet $A \neq 0$.

THEOREM 10.2. *A has an inverse matrix if and only if the determinant of A is not zero, i.e. $\det A \neq 0$.*

Proof. (i) *Necessity.* Regard each of the columns of A as a column vector a^j. If the n vectors $a^1, a^2, \ldots, a^n$ are shown to be linearly independent, $\det A \neq 0$ by virtue of Theorem 9.3.

Let

$$\sum_{j=1}^{n} \alpha_j a^j = 0.$$

Then, it suffices to prove $\alpha_1 = \alpha_2 = \ldots = \alpha_n = 0$. Writing out the equations above in matrix notation, we have

$$A \begin{bmatrix} \alpha_1 \\ \alpha_2 \\ \vdots \\ \alpha_n \end{bmatrix} = \begin{bmatrix} 0 \\ 0 \\ \vdots \\ 0 \end{bmatrix} .$$

By assumption, A has an inverse matrix B. Pre-multiplying the above equation by B, we get

$$BA \begin{bmatrix} \alpha_1 \\ \alpha_2 \\ \vdots \\ \alpha_n \end{bmatrix} = B \begin{bmatrix} 0 \\ 0 \\ \vdots \\ 0 \end{bmatrix} = \begin{bmatrix} 0 \\ 0 \\ \vdots \\ 0 \end{bmatrix} .$$

As $BA = I$, we see

$$\begin{bmatrix} \alpha_1 \\ \alpha_2 \\ \vdots \\ \alpha_n \end{bmatrix} = I \begin{bmatrix} \alpha_1 \\ \alpha_2 \\ \vdots \\ \alpha_n \end{bmatrix} = BA \begin{bmatrix} \alpha_1 \\ \alpha_2 \\ \vdots \\ \alpha_n \end{bmatrix} = \begin{bmatrix} 0 \\ 0 \\ \vdots \\ 0 \end{bmatrix} .$$

$\therefore \alpha_1 = \alpha_2 = \ldots = \alpha_n = 0$.

(ii) *Sufficiency.* The main idea of proof is as follows: First, prove that there are B and C such that $AB = I$ and $CA = I$. Next demonstrate that $B = C$. This proves that there is B such that $AB = BA = I$.

As $\det A \neq 0$, a system of linear equations in the unknown vector x

$$(10.33) \qquad Ax = e^j$$

(e^j is a unit vector in R^n) has a unique solution b^j according to Cramer's Rule. By substituting n unit vectors $e^1, e^2, ..., e^n$ one by one into the constant term e^j in (10.33), we get n solution vectors b^j $(j = 1, 2, ..., n)$. Then, the matrix $B = (b^1, b^2, ..., b^n)$, whose jth column is b^j, satisfies $AB = I$ because $I = (e^1, e^2, ..., e^n)$. As $\det A' = \det A \neq 0$, we can show in exactly the same way that there is a matrix D such that $A'D = I$. By transposing both sides of it according to (10.32), we get $D'A = (A'D)' = I' = I$. Hence, $CA = I$ where $C = D'$. Next, $B = C$ can be proved as follows:

$$(10.34) \qquad C = CI = C(AB) = (CA)B = IB = B\ .$$

Finally, to demonstrate the uniqueness of the inverse matrix, let us note that $CA = AB = I$ where B and C are inverse matrices of A. B and C need not be those matrices that were specified in the proof of sufficiency but any inverse matrices of A. When we perform operation (10.34) in an identical manner with respect to B and C, we see that $B = C$ *.

The inverse matrix of A is henceforth denoted by A^{-1}. We can obtain the inverse matrix by solving the equation system of (10.33) and by determining the columns of A^{-1}. The (i, j) element b_{ij} of A^{-1} can be computed by Cramer's Rule as

$$b_{ij} = \Delta_{ji}/\det A$$

where Δ_{ji} is the cofactor of the (j, i) element of $\det A$.

11. Convergence in R^n

We discussed the convergence of real number sequences in Section 8 and introduced the concept of limits into the real number system R. We had a

* Select one of C's that satisfy $CA = I$ as the frame of reference, with which we compare any B such that $AB = I$ and obtain $C = B$. As all B's are equal to the specific matrix C, it follows that B is unique. Finally, compare any C such that $CA = I$ with this unique B to find $C = B$.

specific objective in mind in doing this. We intended to make use of this concept as an incisive instrument to explore the structures and properties of subsets of R. One of the important motives that prompted us to move from the realm of real numbers R to that of vectors R^n was to use the latter as a canvas on which to describe economic phenomena in a more appropriate manner. Our next step is to introduce the concept of limits into R^n, following faithfully the case of the real number system, and to use it to shed light on the properties of subsets of R^n. Topological properties of sets, when thus clarified and effectively utilized, will help us to solve many problems raised in mathematical economics.

Distance in R^n. In the most standard form as shown in (8.17), the convergence of a real number sequence was formulated in terms of absolute value. Notice now that the absolute value of the difference of two real numbers α and β, i.e. $|\alpha - \beta|$, is the distance between them on a line of real numbers. By analogy, we now introduce the concepts corresponding to those of absolute value and distance into the linear space R^n in order to consider the convergence of a sequence of vectors in R^n.

Let $x \in R^n$ and its ith component be x_i. Then,

$$(11.1) \qquad \|x\| = \sqrt{\sum_{i=1}^{n} x_i^2}$$

is called the *norm* or *Euclidean norm* of x.

(11.1) extends the concept of the absolute value of a real number to R^n. They coincide when $n = 1$.

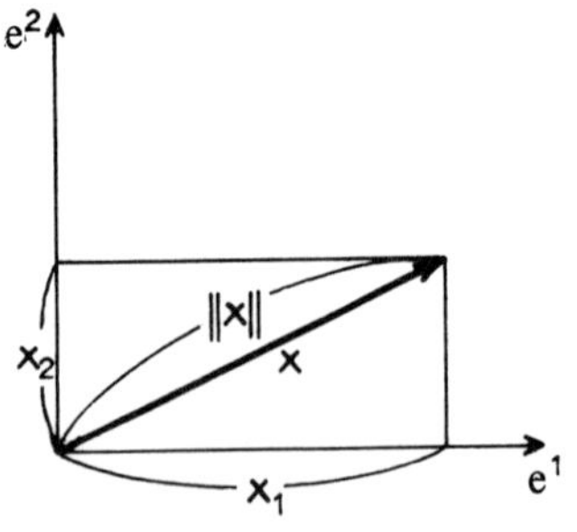

Fig. 11.1.

We may recall that basic properties of absolute values, (8.13) ~ (8.16), played an important role in our discussion of the convergence of real number sequences. We shall list analogous basic properties concerning (11.1).

Let $x, y \in R^n$ and α a real number. Then,

(11.2) $\quad \|x\| \geqq 0;$ moreover, $\|x\| = 0 \Leftrightarrow x = 0\,;$

(11.3) $\quad \|\alpha x\| = |\alpha|\ \|x\|\,;$

(11.4) $\quad \|x \pm y\| \leqq \|x\| + \|y\|\,.$

Proof. We omit the proofs of (11.2) and (11.3), which are easy. To prove (11.4), we define an *inner product* of $x, y \in R^n$ by

(11.5) $$(x, y) = \sum_{i=1}^{n} x_i y_i$$

where x_i and y_i are the components of x and y respectively.

We have an important relation between the inner product and the norm, namely Schwarz's inequality:

(11.6) $\quad |(x, y)| \leqq \|x\|\ \|y\|\,.$

We shall first prove (11.6) and, then, (11.4) from this.

For $y = 0$, both sides of (11.6) reduce to 0 so that the inequality under examination certainly holds in this case.

For $y \neq 0$, i.e. $\|y\| > 0$ by (11.2), consider a quadratic function of a real variable ρ

(11.7) $\quad f(\rho) = \|x - \rho y\|^2 = \|x\|^2 - 2\rho(x, y) + \rho^2\|y\|^2\,.$ *

For any real number ρ, we have $\|x - \rho y\|^2 \geqq 0$. Hence, the discriminant of $f(\rho) = (x, y)^2 - \|x\|^2\|y\|^2 \leqq 0$, from which we get (11.6).

Substituting $\rho = \mp 1$ into (11.7) and considering that $\mp(x, y) \leqq |(x, y)| \leqq \|x\|\ \|y\|$, we get

$$\|x \pm y\|^2 = \|x\|^2 \pm 2(x, y) + \|y\|^2 \leqq \|x\|^2 + 2\|x\|\,\|y\| + \|y\|^2 = (\|x\| + \|y\|)^2\,.$$

* The right-hand side of (11.7) is derived by expanding $\|x - \rho y\|^2$ according to the definition (11.1).

Because of the non-negativity of the norm, it reduces to $||x \pm y|| \leqq ||x|| + ||y||$.

Remark 1. When x and y are both column vectors, their inner product may be expressed as

$$(x, y) = x'y = (x_1, x_2, ..., x_n)\begin{bmatrix} y_1 \\ y_2 \\ \vdots \\ y_n \end{bmatrix} .$$

Remark 2. Let $x \in R^n$ and $y \in R^m$ be column vectors and A an (m, n) matrix. Then,

$$(Ax, y) = (x, A'y) .$$

$\because (Ax, y) = (Ax)' y = (x'A')y = x'(A'y) = (x, A'y)$.

We define the distance between two points * x and y in R^n to be the norm of their difference, i.e.

(11.8) $\quad d(x, y) = ||x - y||$.

It follows immediately from (11.2) ~ (11.4) that

(11.9) $\quad d(x, y) \geqq 0$; moreover, $d(x, y) = 0 \Leftrightarrow x = y$;

(11.10) $\quad d(x, y) = d(y, x)$

and

(11.11) $\quad d(x, y) \leqq d(x, z) + d(z, y)$.

(11.8) renders a precise definition to the concept of distance between two points as we use it in our everyday life. (11.9) ~ (11.11) seem to be intrinsic properties of distance. In particular, (11.11) presents a clear mathematical expression of the familiar property, as shown in fig. 11.2, that the sum of two sides of a triangle is not shorter than the third side.

Convergence of a sequence of points. Let us consider $\{x^\nu\}$, a sequence of points in R^n, and examine its convergence. ν is a superscript indicating indexes **. The νth term x^ν is a point in R^n. Following and relying on the definition of the convergence of a numerical sequence, we are led naturally to the definition below.

* We already noted that the term, point, is used to denote a vector.

** We may write it as $\{x^n\}$. However, ν is substituted for n to avoid confusion with n appearing in R^n.

A sequence of points $\{x^\nu\}$ is said to *converge* to a in R^n when

$$\lim_{\nu\to\infty} d(x^\nu, a) = 0 \qquad (11.12)$$

for $a, x^\nu \in R^n$ ($\nu = 1, 2, \ldots$). It is also expressed by

$$\lim_{\nu\to\infty} x^\nu = a \quad \text{or} \quad x^\nu \to a\ (\nu \to \infty)\,.$$

We have defined the convergence of a sequence of points of $\{x^\nu\}$ with the aid of the convergence of the real number sequence $\{d(x^\nu, a)\}$ to 0. (See fig. 11.3.)

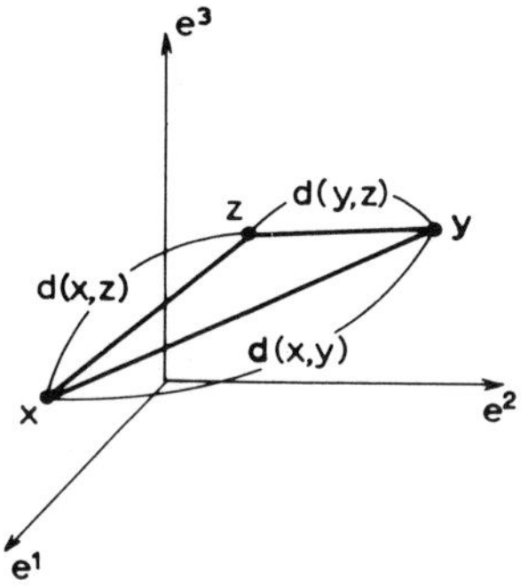

Fig. 11.2.

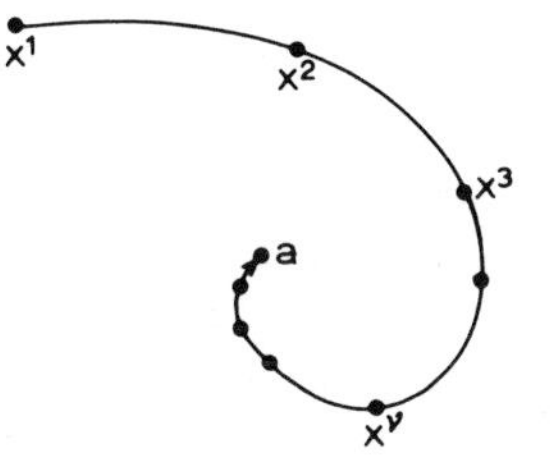

Fig. 11.3.

Remark 3. The convergence of a sequence of points has been defined in terms of the distance (11.8). Before proceeding further, however, it is better to interpose a remark about distance here. Our intuition reveals the distance (11.8) as a plausible concept. But we can introduce other equally plausible definitions of distance in R^n if we are allowed to consider as distance anything that satisfies (11.9) ~ (11.11). For instance, consider the following norms:

$$\|x\|_1 = \sum_{i=1}^{n} |x_i| \qquad (11.13)$$

and

$$\|x\|_2 = \max_{1 \leqq i \leqq n} |x_i|\,. \qquad (11.14)$$

We may regard them as defining distance. It is easy to see that these norms satisfy (11.2) ~ (11.4) due to the properties associated with the absolute values of real numbers. Therefore, both

$$(11.15) \qquad d_1(x, y) = \|x - y\|_1$$

and

$$(11.16) \qquad d_2(x, y) = \|x - y\|_2$$

satisfy the properties of distance (11.9) ~ (11.11).

Just as we defined $\lim_{\nu \to \infty} x^\nu = a$ in terms of $d(x, y)$ in (11.12), we may as well define the convergence of $\{x^\nu\}$ in terms of $d_1(x, y)$ or $d_2(x, y)$. One may rightly wonder whether the concept of convergence may substantially differ in the three cases since they are based on different definitions of distance. To paraphrase, even if $\lim_{\nu \to \infty} x^\nu = a$ in terms of $d(x, y)$, we might find that $\{x^\nu\}$ does not converge to a in terms of $d_1(x, y)$. Fortunately, it can be shown that the three concepts of convergence given above are equivalent. This property ensures that the convergence of a sequence of points can be determined in terms of any of the three definitions of distance. There is an advantage in this because we can use the most convenient one of the three alternative definitions of distance, depending on the problem under study.

THEOREM 11.1. *For $a, x^\nu \in R^n$ ($\nu = 1, 2, \ldots$),*

(i) *the convergence of $\{x^\nu\}$ in terms of any of the three definitions of distance is equivalent to that in terms of the other two;*

(ii) $\lim_{\nu \to \infty} x^\nu = a$ *if and only if the real number sequence $\{x^\nu\}$, consisting of the ith component of x^ν, satisfies* $\lim_{\nu \to \infty} x_i^\nu = a_i$ $(i = 1, 2, \ldots, n)$.

Proof. (i) Let us prove first the following two inequalities holding among the three types of norms:

$$(11.17) \qquad \frac{1}{\sqrt{n}}\|x\|_1 \leqq \|x\| \leqq \|x\|_1$$

and

$$(11.18) \qquad \|x\|_2 \leqq \|x\|_1 \leqq n\|x\|_2 .$$

Then, we get

$$\frac{1}{\sqrt{n}} d_2(x^\nu, a) \leqq \frac{1}{\sqrt{n}} d_1(x^\nu, a) \leqq d(x^\nu, a)$$

$$\leqq d_1(x^\nu, a) \leqq n d_2(x^\nu, a)\,,$$

from which it follows that if one of the sequences $\{d(x^\nu, a)\}$, $\{d_1(x^\nu, a)\}$ and $\{d_2(x^\nu, a)\}$ converges to zero, the other two also converge to 0.

Proof of (11.17). As regards the right-hand inequality, we find

$$||x||_1^2 = (\sum_{i=1}^n |x_i|)^2$$

$$= \sum_{i=1}^n |x_i|^2 + 2\sum_{i>j} |x_i|\,|x_j| \geqq \sum_{i=1}^n |x_i|^2 = ||x||^2\,.$$

$$\therefore ||x|| \leqq ||x||_1\,.$$

As regards the left-hand inequality, we have

$$0 \leqq \sum_{i=1}^n \left(|x_i| - \frac{||x||}{\sqrt{n}}\right)^2 = \sum_{i=1}^n |x_i|^2 - \frac{2||x||}{\sqrt{n}} \sum_{i=1}^n |x_i| + ||x||^2$$

$$= 2||x||^2 - \frac{2||x||}{\sqrt{n}} ||x||_1 = 2||x|| \left(||x|| - \frac{||x||_1}{\sqrt{n}}\right).$$

$$\therefore \frac{||x||_1}{\sqrt{n}} \leqq ||x||\,.$$

Proof of (11.18). The left-hand inequality follows from

$$||x||_2 = \max_{1 \leqq i \leqq n} |x_i| \leqq \sum_{i=1}^n |x_i| = ||x||_1\,,$$

while the right-hand inequality is easily obtained from

$$n||x||_2 - ||x||_1 = n \max_{1 \leqq i \leqq n} |x_i| - \sum_{i=1}^n |x_i|$$

$$= \sum_{i=1}^n (\max_{1 \leqq j \leqq n} |x_j| - |x_i|) \geqq 0\,.$$

(ii) *Necessity.* Let $\lim_{\nu\to\infty} x^\nu = a$. Then, we have

$$|x_i^\nu - a_i| \leqq \max_{1\leqq i\leqq n} |x_i^\nu - a_i| = d_2(x^\nu, a) \to 0 \quad (\nu\to\infty)$$

and, therefore, $\lim_{\nu\to\infty} x_i^\nu = a_i$.

Sufficiency. Let $\lim_{\nu\to\infty} x_i^\nu = a_i$ for each i. Then,

$$d_1(x^\nu, a) = \sum_{i=1}^{n} |x_i^\nu - a_i| \to 0 \quad (\nu\to\infty)$$

because the right-hand side is the sum of a finite number of sequences, each of which converges to 0.

Properties of convergence. In Section 8, we demonstrated properties (1) ~ (10) holding for the convergence of real number sequences. What can we say about the convergence of sequences of points in R^n? As multiplication and division between vectors are not defined, the earlier properties (6) and (7) have no meaning with respect to sequences of points. However, the other properties can be extended to sequences of points. Properties shown below present basic relationships between linear operations and convergence and will frequently be utilized henceforth.

(1) If $\lim_{\nu\to\infty} x^\nu = a$, then $\lim_{\nu\to\infty} ||x^\nu|| = ||a||$;

(2) If $x^\nu = a$ $(\nu = 1, 2, \ldots)$, then $\lim_{\nu\to\infty} x^\nu = a$;

(3) If $\lim_{\nu\to\infty} x^\nu = a$ and $a \neq b$, then $\{x^\nu\}$ does not converge to b (uniqueness of the limit).

For $\lim_{\nu\to\infty} x^\nu = a$ and $\lim_{\nu\to\infty} y^\nu = b$,

(4) If $\{\alpha_\nu\}$ is a real number sequence and $\lim_{\nu\to\infty} \alpha_\nu = \alpha$, then $\lim_{\nu\to\infty} \alpha_\nu x^\nu = \lim_{\nu\to\infty} \alpha_\nu \times \lim_{\nu\to\infty} x^\nu$;

(5) $\lim_{\nu\to\infty} (x^\nu \pm y^\nu) = \lim_{\nu\to\infty} x^\nu \pm \lim_{\nu\to\infty} y^\nu$;

(6) $\lim_{\nu\to\infty} (x^\nu, y^\nu) = (\lim_{\nu\to\infty} x^\nu, \lim_{\nu\to\infty} y^\nu)$;

(7) if $\{x^{\nu_\lambda}\}$ is any subsequence of $\{x^\nu\}$, then $\lim_{\lambda\to\infty} x^{\nu_\lambda} = \lim_{\nu\to\infty} x^\nu$.

The proofs of these properties (1) ~ (7) follow essentially the same procedures as those in Section 8 with regard to real number sequences. In place of the properties (8.13) ~ (8.16) of the absolute value | |, we can make use of the analogous properties (11.2) ~ (11.4) of the norm || ||. We give the proofs of (1) and (6) for the reader's reference, leaving those of the remaining properties to him as exercise problems.

Proof of (1). As $x = x - y + y$ for any $x, y \in R^n$, we get

$$\|x\| = \|x - y + y\| \leqq \|x - y\| + \|y\|$$

(see (11.4)), from which we have $\|x\| - \|y\| \leqq \|x - y\|$. Hence, $|\|x\| - \|y\|| \leqq \|x - y\|$. Thus, if $\lim_{\nu\to\infty} x^\nu = a$, then $|\|x^\nu\| - \|a\|| \leqq \|x^\nu - a\| \to 0$ $(\nu \to \infty)$. $\therefore \lim_{\nu\to\infty} \|x^\nu\| = \|a\|$.

Proof of (6). The inner product (x, y) is a function of two points x and y in R^n. By fixing y, it may be considered as a function of x alone. Then, we have

(11.19) $(\alpha x, y) = \alpha(x, y)$ (where α is a real number)

and

(11.20) $(x^1 + x^2, y) = (x^1, y) + (x^2, y)$.

Similarly, when it is considered as a function of y only with x fixed, we have

(11.21) $(x, \beta y) = \beta(x, y)$ (where β is a real number)

and

(11.22) $(x, y^1 + y^2) = (x, y^1) + (x, y^2)$.

This property is called the *bilinearity* of the inner product. It should be evident from the definition (11.5) that (11.19) ~ (11.22) hold.

Now for the proof of (6), let $\lim_{\nu\to\infty} x^\nu = a$ and $\lim_{\nu\to\infty} y^\nu = b$. Following the proof of (6) in Section 8, we perform a necessary rearrangement of equations concerned, utilizing the bilinearity of the inner product, to get

$$|(x^\nu, y^\nu) - (a, b)| = |(x^\nu, y^\nu) - (a, y^\nu) + (a, y^\nu) - (a, b)|$$

$$\leqq |(x^\nu - a, y^\nu) + (a, y^\nu - b)|$$

$$\leqq \|x^\nu - a\| \, \|y^\nu\| + \|a\| \, \|y^\nu - b\|$$

(by virtue of Schwarz's inequality). On the right-hand side, we see $\lim_{\nu\to\infty} \|x^\nu - a\| = \lim_{\nu\to\infty} \|y^\nu - b\| = 0$. Also we have $\lim_{\nu\to\infty} \|y^\nu\| = \|b\|$ because of (1). Thus, the left-hand side of the inequality converges to 0 by virtue of (5) and (6) in Section 8. $\therefore \lim_{\nu\to\infty} (x^\nu, y^\nu) = (a, b)$.

Metric spaces. We introduced distance $d(x, y)$ in R^n in terms of the norm and then on the basis of distance we defined the concept of convergence. We may note that R^n not only admits distance but also provides a stage for linear operations like addition, subtraction, scalar multiplication, and inner product. However, the convergence of sequences can be discussed even if these operations are absent. If a distance $d(x, y)$ is defined between any two elements x and y in a set A subject to (11.9) ~ (11.11), then we can discuss the convergence of a sequence of points in A. A set A, in which a distance is given subject to (11.9) ~ (11.11), is called a *metric space*. R^n is an example of metric spaces that is most familiar to us. Similarly, any subset A of R^n is a good example of metric spaces. The distance in A is defined to be exactly the same as that in R^n.

12. A few topological concepts

On the basis of our preliminary observations, let us now plunge a scalpel into the structures of sets with the aid of the concept of limits.

Closed sets. Let X be a set in R^n. Consider a sequence of points $\{x^\nu\}$ in X. If $\{x^\nu\}$ does not converge in R^n, it does not converge in X either. Now assume that $\{x^\nu\}$ converges to a in R^n. The uniqueness of limits assures us that $\{x^\nu\}$ converges to no point other than a. Hence, if $a \notin X$, $\{x^\nu\}$ converges to a point a lying not inside but outside of X. When this sort of a phenomenon does not take place, X is called a *closed set.* In other words, X is a closed set if any sequence of points $\{x^\nu\}$ where $x^\nu \in X$ ($\nu = 1, 2, \ldots$) converges to no point outside of X, namely if the operation of deriving a limit is closed within X. To paraphrase this definition *,

$$\text{if } \lim_{\nu\to\infty} x^\nu = a \text{ (in } R^n) \text{ for } x^\nu \in X \ (\nu = 1, 2, \ldots), \text{ then } a \in X.$$

Example 12.1. R^n itself is a closed set. An empty set is also a closed set. A set consisting of a single point is a closed set.

These follow readily from the definition of a closed set. It may sound un-

* This is a contraposition.

natural in the case of an empty set. But as no sequence of points can be chosen in ϕ, it fits in well with the definition. Finally, for the set X consisting of a single point a, we have only one sequence of points $x^\nu = a$ ($\nu = 1, 2, \ldots$), which converges to no point other than a.

Example 12.2. A unit sphere in R^n (i.e. a sphere whose center is at 0 and whose radius is one), $\{x \mid \|x\| = 1\}$, is a closed set.

Proof. Let $x^\nu \in \{x \mid \|x\| = 1\}$ and $\lim_{\nu\to\infty} x^\nu = a$. Then, because of (1) in Section 11, we have $\lim_{\nu\to\infty} \|x^\nu\| = \|a\|$. As $\|x^\nu\| = 1$ ($\nu = 1, 2, \ldots$), we get $\lim_{\nu\to\infty} \|x^\nu\| = 1$. $\therefore \|a\| = 1$ and $a \in \{x \mid \|x\| = 1\}$.

Example 12.3. The inside of the sphere defined in the example above, i.e. $\{x \mid \|x\| < 1\}$, is not a closed set.

We can see this as follows: Take a point a such that $\|a\| = 1$ (e.g., a point whose ith component is $a_i = 1/\sqrt{n}$ ($i = 1, 2, \ldots, n$)) and let $\alpha_\nu = 1 - 1/\nu$ and $x^\nu = \alpha_\nu \cdot a$ ($\nu = 1, 2, \ldots$). Then, $\|x^\nu\| = \|\alpha_\nu a\| = |\alpha_\nu| \, \|a\| = 1 - 1/\nu < 1$. Therefore, $x^\nu \in \{x \mid \|x\| < 1\}$ ($\nu = 1, 2, \ldots$). However, as $\lim_{\nu\to\infty} \alpha_\nu = 1$, we have $\lim_{\nu\to\infty} x^\nu = (\lim_{\nu\to\infty} \alpha_\nu) a = a \notin \{x \mid \|x\| < 1\}$. This proves that the given set is not closed.

Example 12.4. Intervals in R^1, i.e. the real number system R, such as $[a, b] = \{x \mid a \leqq x \leqq b\}$, $[a, +\infty) = \{x \mid a \leqq x\}$, and $(-\infty, a] = \{x \mid x \leqq a\}$ are all closed sets of R.

Proof. Let $x_\nu \in [a, b]$ and $\lim_{\nu\to\infty} x_\nu = \alpha$. As $a \leqq x_\nu \leqq b$ ($\nu = 1, 2, \ldots$), we have $a \leqq \lim_{\nu\to\infty} x_\nu \leqq b$ so that $a \leqq \alpha \leqq b$. $\therefore \alpha \in [a, b]$ according to the formula (8) in Section 8. Proofs are similar for the other intervals.

There are many illustrations of closed sets, which we shall discuss in the next section. Here we shall examine whether a set obtained from a number of closed sets according to the operations on sets, described in Section 6, is a closed set or not.

THEOREM 12.1.

(i) *The intersection of a number* * *of closed sets* X_λ ($\lambda \in \Lambda$), *i.e.* $X = \bigcap_{\lambda\in\Lambda} X_\lambda$, *is also a closed set.*

* The number can be infinite.

(ii) *The union of a finite number of closed sets* X_k $(k = 1, 2, ..., s)$, *i.e.*

$$X = \bigcup_{k=1}^{s} X_k ,$$

is also a closed set.

Proof of (i). Let $\lim_{\nu\to\infty} x^\nu = a$ and $x^\nu \in X$ $(\nu = 1, 2, ...)$. For any $\lambda \in \Lambda$, we have $X \subset X_\lambda$ so that $\{x^\nu\}$ is a sequence of points in X_λ. As X_λ is a closed set and as $\{x^\nu\}$ converges to a, we have $a \in X_\lambda$. As λ is any member in Λ, we get $a \in \bigcap_{\lambda\in\Lambda} X_\lambda = X$. Hence, X is a closed set.

Proof of (ii). Let $\lim_{\nu\to\infty} x^\nu = a$ and $x^\nu \in X$ $(\nu = 1, 2, ...)$. For any number ν, we have

$$x^\nu \in \bigcup_{k=1}^{s} X_k ;$$

at least one X_k of the s sets X_k's $(k = 1, 2, ..., s)$ contains x^ν. Denote the index of this set by $k(\nu)$. There are only a finite number of integers, 1 to s, that can be taken by $k(\nu)$. As ν moves over 1, 2, 3, ..., $k(\nu)$ takes on a common value an infinite number of times. Denote this value by i. Then, by extracting an appropriate subsequence $\nu_1, \nu_2, \nu_3, ..., \nu_\lambda, ...,$ we can make $k(\nu_\lambda) = i$ $(\lambda = 1, 2, 3, ...)$ so that $x^{\nu_\lambda} \in X_i$ $(\lambda = 1, 2, 3, ...)$. On the other hand, $\lim_{\nu\to\infty} x^\nu = a$. Thus, for the subsequence, we also have $\lim_{\lambda\to\infty} x^{\nu_\lambda} = a$. As X_i is a closed set, we have $a \in X_i$ and, hence,

$$a \in \bigcup_{k=1}^{s} X_k .$$

Therefore, X is a closed set.

Open sets. If the complement X^c (in R^n) of a set X in R^n is a closed set, X is called an *open set*. Open and closed sets are dual concepts, closely interconnected through the operation of deriving complements. However, a set X is not automatically made an open set simply because it is not a closed set. The reader is asked to understand clearly what the definition really means to avoid such a misunderstanding.

Example 12.5. $X = \{x \mid \|x\| < 1\}$, the set in Example 12.3, is an open set.

Proof. The complement $X^c = \{x \mid \|x\| \geqq 1\}$ is a closed set. (The reader should check this himself).

Example 12.6. R^n itself and ϕ (empty set) are both open sets.

Proof. The complement of R^n is ϕ and the complement of ϕ is R^n. As these complements are closed sets (see Example 12.1), they are open sets.

Example 12.7. An interval $(a, b) = \{x | a < x < b\}$ in R is an open set in R.

Proof. The complement of (a, b) in R is

$$\begin{aligned}(a, b)^c &= \{x | x \leqq a \text{ or } x \geqq b\} \\ &= \{x | x \leqq a\} \cup \{x | x \geqq b\} \\ &= (-\infty, a] \cup [b, +\infty) .\end{aligned}$$

The latter two intervals are closed sets (see Example 12.4) so that the right-hand side, a union of the two closed sets, is a closed set because of (ii) of Theorem 12.1.

The following theorem is a dual of Theorem 12.1.

THEOREM 12.2.

(i) *The union of a number * of open sets* X_λ $(\lambda \in \Lambda)$, *i.e.* $X = \bigcup_{\lambda \in \Lambda} X_\lambda$, *is also an open set.*

(ii) *The intersection of a finite number of open sets* X_k $(k = 1, 2, ..., s)$, *i.e.*

$$X = \bigcap_{k=1}^{s} X_k ,$$

is also an open set.

Proof of (i). An extension of the formula (6.10) to any arbitrary number of sets leads to $X^c = (\bigcup_{\lambda \in \Lambda} X_\lambda)^c = \bigcap_{\lambda \in \Lambda} X_\lambda^c$ where X_λ's are all open sets. X_λ^c is, therefore, a closed set so that $\bigcap_{\lambda \in \Lambda} X_\lambda^c$ is also a closed set according to (i) of Theorem 12.1. This makes X^c a closed set and X an open set.

Proof of (ii). An extension of the formula (6.9) to a finite number of sets leads to

$$X^c = (\bigcap_{k=1}^{s} X_k)^c = \bigcup_{k=1}^{s} X_k^c .$$

* The number can be infinite.

As X_k^c's are all closed sets,

$$\bigcup_{k=1}^{s} X_k^c$$

is also a closed set because of (ii) of Theorem 12.1. This makes X^c a closed set and X an open set.

Closures. A set X in R^n may not necessarily be a closed set. Consider the possibility of augmenting X into a closed set by adding the fewest possible points to X. If this is accomplished, the resulting set is the smallest closed set that contains X. We show that there actually is a closed set with this property. We can make use of (i) of Theorem 12.1.

Let all closed sets containing X be denoted by X_λ ($\lambda \in \Lambda$). Then, $\bigcap_{\lambda \in \Lambda} X_\lambda$ is also a closed set by virtue of (i) of Theorem 12.1. Any closed set containing X is already considered as one of X_λ. Moreover, $\bigcap_{\lambda \in \Lambda} X_\lambda \subset X_\lambda$. Hence, this $\bigcap_{\lambda \in \Lambda} X_\lambda$ is the smallest closed set containing X. The reader should realize that he is liable to commit a serious mistake if he considers that this completes the proof. For this proof lacks one essential point. We have first let all closed subsets containing X to be X_λ ($\lambda \in \Lambda$), but we have not demonstrated that there actually is at least one closed set containing X. We need to add this point to the proof. It suffices to show a special closed set containing X. We can do this by pointing out that, as is clear from Example 12.1, R^n itself is a closed set including any of its subsets, *a fortiori, X*.

The smallest closed set containing X is called the closure of X and denoted by $\bar{X}$. The definition leads us to $\bar{X} \supset X$ for any X. It is also obvious that X is a closed set if and only if $\bar{X} = X$. It readily follows that $\bar{X} \supset \bar{Y}$ if $X \supset Y$.

We now introduce the concept of distance between a point and a set, which will be useful in expressing the definition of a closure in a form easier to handle.

Distance between a point and a set. The distance between a point a and a set X is defined by

$$(12.1) \qquad d(a, X) = \inf_{x \in X} d(a, x).$$

$d(a, x)$, the distance between the point a and any point x in X, changes as x varies. When we choose x so as to make the distance $d(a, x)$ as short as possible, we have $d(a, x) = \min_{x \in X} d(a, x)$, provided that X contains the point x that is closest to a. However, this is possible only for a special type of sets.

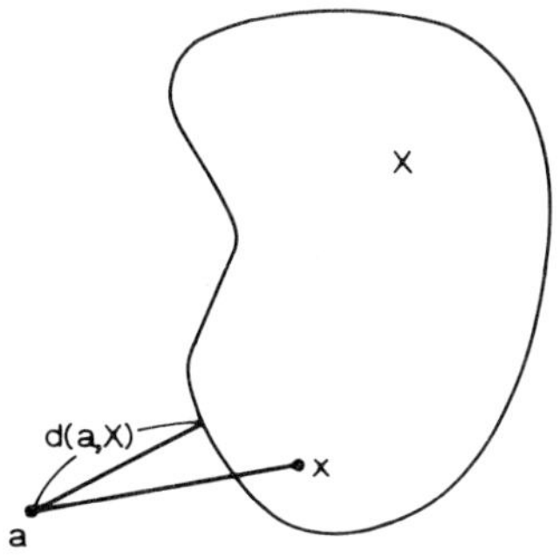

Fig. 12.1.

Therefore, (12.1) is defined in terms of the infimum * of $d(a, x)$. It follows readily from (12.1) that $d(a,X) \geqq 0$ (cf. fig. 12.1).

By using this concept of distance between a point and a set, the closure $\bar{X}$ of a set X can be expressed as follows:

THEOREM 12.3. $\bar{X} = \{a|\ d(a, X) = 0\}$.

Proof. $\bar{X}$ is defined as the smallest closed set that contains X. Therefore, it suffices to show that $A = \{y|d(y, X) = 0\}$ satisfies the three conditions: 1) $A \supset X$, 2) A is a closed set, 3) a closed set Y containing X always contains A.

Proof of 1). For any $x \in X$, we have $d(x, x) = 0$. $\therefore x \in A$, i.e. $X \subset A$.

Proof of 2). Let $\lim_{\nu\to\infty} a^\nu = b$, $a^\nu \in A$ ($\nu = 1, 2, ...$). For each a^ν, $d(a^\nu, X) = 0$; we see from condition (8.8) for the infimum that for any small positive number $\epsilon > 0$ there is $x \in X$ such that $d(a^\nu, x) < \epsilon$. Letting $\epsilon = 1/\nu$ for a^ν and denoting the corresponding x by x^ν, we get

(12.2) $$d(a^\nu, x^\nu) < 1/\nu \quad (\nu = 1, 2, ...)\,,$$

which obviously leads to

(12.3) $$\lim_{\nu\to\infty} d(a^\nu, x^\nu) = 0\,.$$

* See Section 8 for its definition.

The distance between b and x^ν is subject to

$$d(b, x^\nu) \leqq d(b, a^\nu) + d(a^\nu, x^\nu) \qquad (\nu = 1, 2, \ldots)$$

because of condition (11.11) for the distance. The first term of the right-hand side converges to 0 by assumption, while the second term converges to 0 because of (12.3). Hence. $\lim_{\nu\to\infty} d(b, x^\nu) = 0$. As $x^\nu \in X$, we get $d(b, X) \leqq d(b, x^\nu)$ $(\nu = 1, 2, \ldots)$ and $0 \leqq d(b,X) \leqq \lim_{\nu\to\infty} d(b, x^\nu) = 0$ so that $d(b,X) = 0$. $\therefore b \in A$, i.e. A is a closed set.

Proof of 3). Let Y be any closed set containing X. If $a \in A$, then $d(a, X) = 0$. This enables us to choose a sequence of points $\{x^\nu\}$ such that $\lim_{\nu\to\infty} d(a, x^\nu) = d(a, X) = 0$, $x^\nu \in X$ $(\nu = 1, 2, \ldots)$ (see the Remark in Section 8 on a numerical sequence converging to the infimum). This is nothing but $\lim_{\nu\to\infty} x^\nu = a$. As $X \subset Y$, $\{x^\nu\}$ is also a sequence of points in Y. As this sequence of points converges to a and as Y is a closed set by assumption, we must have $a \in Y$. Hence, $A \subset Y$. [Q.E.D.]

It is clear from our proof that "$\overline{X}$ is a collection of all points that are limits of some sequences of points in X".

Example 12.8. Let X be a set of all points in R^n whose components are rational numbers. Then, $\overline{X} = R^n$.

How can we then characterize open sets in terms of the concept of distance? This question is answered by the theorem below.

THEOREM 12.4. *A necessary and sufficient condition for X to be an open set is that*

$$(12.4) \qquad X = \{x \mid d(x, X^c) > 0\}\,.$$

Proof. X is defined to be an open set when its complement X^c is a closed set. X^c is a closed set if and only if $\overline{X^c} = X^c$. On the other hand, Theorem 12.3 shows that $\overline{X^c} = \{a \mid d(a, X^c) = 0\}$. Thus, the fact that X is an open set implies $X^c = \{a \mid d(a, X^c) = 0\}$. Whence the conclusion of this theorem follows.

Let X be an open set. Theorem 12.4 states that $d(a, X^c) > 0$ if $a \in X$. Take a sufficiently small positive number $\epsilon > 0$ satisfying $\epsilon < d(a, X^c)$. The inside of a sphere whose center is at a and whose radius is ϵ, i.e.

$$(12.5) \qquad U(a, \epsilon) = \{x \mid d(a, x) < \epsilon\}$$

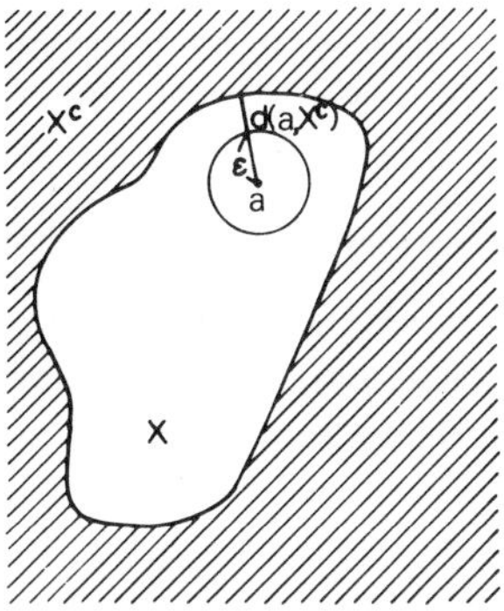

Fig. 12.2.

is a set. Any point x in this set has a distance from a less than $d(a, X^c)$ so that $x \notin X^c$. $\therefore x \in X$ and $U(a, \epsilon) \subset X$. In other words, if X is an open set, the inside of a sphere with its center at each point a of X and with a sufficiently small radius is completely contained in X *. (Cf. fig. 12.2.) (12.5) represents a *spherical* ϵ*-neighborhood* of a. Conversely, if an appropriate spherical neighborhood of any point a in X is contained in X, X is an open set. We can see this as follows: Let a spherical ϵ-neighborhood of a given by (12.5) be contained in X where $\epsilon > 0$ is appropriately chosen. Any $x \in X^c$ implies $x \notin X$ and, in particular, $x \notin U(a, \epsilon)$. Hence, $d(a, x) \geqq \epsilon$ and $d(a, X^c) = \inf_{x \in X^c} d(a, x) \geqq \epsilon > 0$. $\therefore X \subset \{a \mid d(a, X^c) > 0\}$. On the other hand, it is evident that $X \supset \{a \mid d(a, X^c) > 0\}$. Thus, $X = \{a \mid d(a, X^c) > 0\}$. We see from Theorem 12.4 that X is an open set.

Example 12.9. The ϵ-neighborhood (12.5) is an open set.

Proof. Let $x \in U(a, \epsilon)$. Then, for $0 < \delta < \epsilon - d(a, x)$, we have $U(x, \delta) \subset U(a, \epsilon)$. From our remark above, we obtain this conclusion.

Remark. We have used the Euclidean distance (11.5) as our standard concept in order to define the distance between a point and a set and to characterize closed and open sets. We take note that exactly the same formal arguments follow from the alternative concepts of distance (11.15) and (11.16). As the three definitions of distance lead to an identical concept of convergence, closed and open sets are characterized essentially in the same way, whichever definition of distance we may take for defining the distance be-

* How to choose ϵ depends on a.

tween a point and a set. Nevertheless, the ϵ-neighborhood is different in geometric structure, depending on which kind of distance we employ.

Topological spaces. We have explained the concepts of closed and open sets and neighborhoods in R^n. As these concepts have been defined exclusively on the basis of distance and convergence of sequences of points, our discussion can be applied *in toto* to any metric space. Let A be a metric space and $d(x, y)$ a distance function in A. We define the convergence of a sequence of points *via* (11.12) on the basis of this distance. We then determine the closedness of a set through the convergence of sequences. Then, an open set is defined as its complement. Theorems 12.1 ~ 12.4 hold in A without revision. The ϵ-neighborhood is also introduced into A. We say in general that "A has a topology" or "A is a topological space" when some of subsets X in a set A are designated as closed (or open) sets *, the collection of which contains A and ϕ and for which Theorem 12.1 (or Theorem 12.2) holds. A metric space is a special case of topological spaces. R^n, which occupies our major attention in this book, is a case of metric spaces and, as such, is a very special type of a topological space.

It is not an exaggeration to say that all modern mathematics emanates from topological considerations. This is to say that mathematical entities are examined from the viewpoint of "topology". We are going to sail down this main stream of modern mathematics. But an elementary introduction to topological considerations is all we need for solving problems in mathematical economics and the reader need not abhor at the expectation of a steep and long mountain climb toward the summit of modern topology. After all, he is not going to conquer a Himalayan mountain; he is merely asked to climb a small hill a few hundred meters high at most.

Now let us come back to R^n. We have said that any subset A of R^n may be considered as a metric space if the concepts of distance and convergence in R^n are retained in A. In other words, A can be given a topology in the most natural manner on the basis of the topology of R^n. This is called a *relative topology* of A. A subset X of A is also a subset of R^n. It is known to us whether X is a closed set in R^n or not in the proper sense. However, at the same time, it should also be known whether X is a closed set in A or not in the sense of the relative topology of A. But these two properties of X may not necessarily coincide with each other.

* It is sufficient if closed (open) sets are given in an appropriate manner even without having the concepts of distance and convergence of sequences of points introduced in A.

Example 12.10. Let A represent the set of all points whose components are rational numbers (see Example 12.8). A itself is a closed set in the topological space A. However, as we have noted in Example 12.8, $\bar{A} = R^n \neq A$ so that A is not a closed set in R^n.

As this example shows, the relative topology of A, which is a subset of R^n, gives its subset X ($\subset A$) topological properties that are generally different from those it has in R^n. Therefore, if it is necessary to specify, we employ an expression like "X is a closed set *in* (or *of*) A". When we say that "X is a closed set", it should be understood, unless otherwise stated, to mean that X is a closed set in R^n. The same applies to other topological concepts. We may spell out the ϵ-neighborhood (in A) of a point a in A:

$$(12.6) \qquad U(a, \epsilon) = \{x \mid x \in A, d(a, x) < \epsilon\} .$$

As shown in fig. 12.3, when A may be composed of two separate parts, the ϵ-neighborhood (in A) of a is the shaded area in the figure.

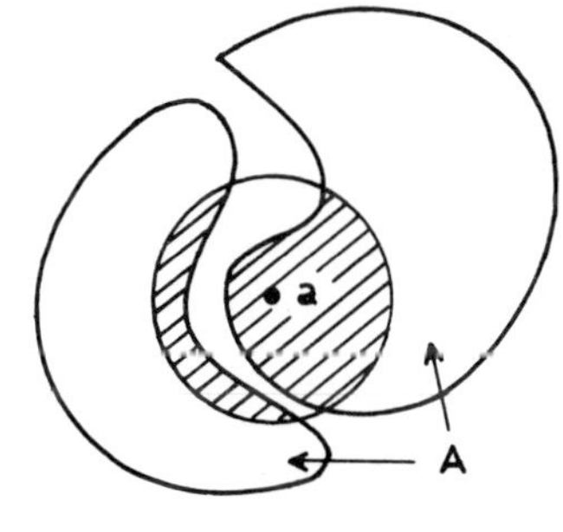

Fig. 12.3.

There are a number of theorems on the relationships between the original and relative topologies. As space does not permit us to make a systematic survey of these, we mention only one proposition in passing:

THEOREM 12.5. *Let $X \subset A \subset B$, X a closed set in A and A a closed set in B. Then, X is a closed set in B. If open sets are substituted for closed sets where the latter appear above, the resulting proposition is also true.*

Proof. (i) The case of closed sets. The simplest proof is based on the original definition of a closed set in terms of the convergence of a sequence of points. It suffices to show that $a \in X$ if $x^\nu \in X$ $(\nu = 1, 2, \ldots)$, $\lim_{\nu\to\infty} x^\nu = a$, $a \in B$. Now, $\{x^\nu\}$ is also a sequence of points in A and A is a closed set in B. Therefore, the limit a is contained in A. Thus, the sequence of points converges to a in A. As X is a closed set in A by assumption, this limit a is contained in X.

(ii) The case of open sets. We shall work out the proof by arguing in terms of neighborhoods. It suffices to show that the appropriate neighborhood (in B) of any point $a \in X$ is contained in X. Note first that a is a point in A. As A is an open set in B, an appropriate neighborhood (in B) of a, $V(a, \delta_1) = \{x \mid x \in B, d(a, x) < \delta_1\}$, is contained in A. Next, as X is an open set in A, an appropriate neighborhood (in A) of a, $V(a, \delta_2) = \{x \mid x \in A, d(a, x) < \delta_2\}$, is contained in X. Let $\epsilon = \min(\delta_1, \delta_2)$. Of course, $\epsilon > 0$. Take the ϵ-neighborhood (in B) of a, $U(a, \epsilon) = \{x \mid x \in B, d(a, x) < \epsilon\}$. This is the neighborhood that we have been looking for because of the following: as $\epsilon \leqq \delta_1$, we have $U(a, \epsilon) \subset V(a, \delta_1) \subset A$. Hence, $U(a, \epsilon) = \{x \mid x \in A, d(a, x) < \epsilon\}$. Recalling $\epsilon \leqq \delta_2$, we have $U(a, \epsilon) \subset V(a, \delta_2) \subset X$. [Q.E.D.]

13. Continuous mappings

In studying the general properties of continuous mappings, we do not find the specific properties of R^n particularly essential. Therefore, we may consider metric spaces X and Y in general and examine mappings from X into Y.

Continuous mappings. In Section 10, we studied mappings between two linear spaces; highlights were given to those mappings that preserve linear operations which are basic in the domain and the range. On the other hand, in these mappings that will be studied in this section, the domains and the ranges are both metric spaces where the convergence of sequences of points, i.e. a limiting process, is defined. It is, therefore, quite natural for us to pay particular attention to those mappings that preserve the limiting process.

Take any sequence of points $\{x^\nu\}$, $(x^\nu \in X)$, that converges to a point a in the domain X of a mapping $f\colon X \to Y$. If its image $\{f(x^\nu)\}$ converges to the image of a, $f(a)$, the mapping f is said to be *continuous* at a. If f is continuous at every point in X, f is said to be *continuous in X*. (Cf. fig. 13.1.)

$\lim_{\nu\to\infty} x^\nu = a$ (in X) is a limiting or topological relation in X. A continuous mapping maintains this relation and projects it as a topological relation in Y, $\lim_{\nu\to\infty} f(x^\nu) = f(a)$.

An ordinary real-valued continuous function is a special example of a con-

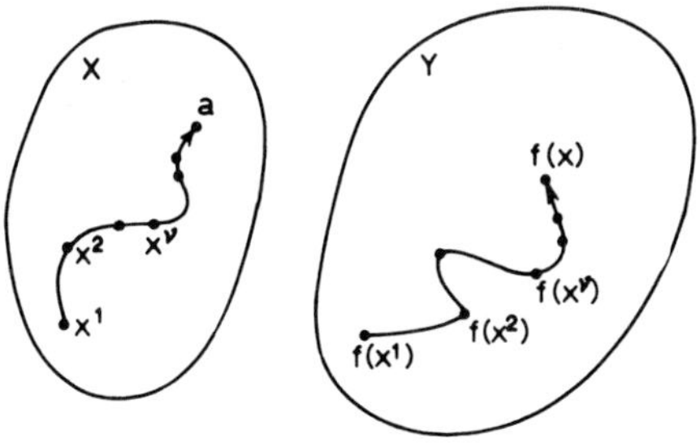

Fig. 13.1.

tinuous mapping. The domain and the range are both sets of real numbers. $f(x) = x^2$ and $f(x) = 1/x$ (both of which are the examples given in Section 7) are continuous in their respective domains. This immediately follows from the basic properties of the convergence of sequences of points given in Section 8.

Now we give a very important example of a continuous mapping.

Example 13.1. Let A be an (m, n) matrix and $x \in R^n$. For any subset X in R^n, the mapping $f(x) = Ax$: $X \to R^m$ is continuous.

Proof. Let a_{ij} be an element of A and $M = \max_{i,j} |a_{ij}|$. We noted in Section 11 that any one of the distance formulas, d, d_1, and d_2, can be employed to examine the convergence in R^n and R^m. In the present example, we employ d_1. Then, for $x, y \in X$, we have

$$\begin{aligned} d_1(f(x), f(y)) &= \sum_{i=1}^{m} |f_i(x) - f_i(y)| = \sum_{i=1}^{m} \left| \sum_{j=1}^{n} a_{ij}x_j - \sum_{j=1}^{n} a_{ij}y_j \right| \\ &\leqq \sum_{i=1}^{m} \sum_{j=1}^{n} |a_{ij}|\, |x_j - y_j| \leqq mM \sum_{j=1}^{n} |x_j - y_j| \\ &= mM\, d_1(x, y) . \end{aligned}$$

Let $\lim_{\nu \to \infty} x^\nu = a$ (in X). Then, putting $x = x^\nu$ and $y = a$ in the above result, we get

$$d_1(f(x^\nu), f(a)) \leqq mM\, d_1(x^\nu, a) \to 0 \quad (\nu \to \infty) .$$

Hence, the mapping is continuous at any point $a \in X$.

Example 13.2. When a mapping $f\colon X \to Y$ makes a single common point b correspond to every and each $x \in X$, f is called a *constant mapping*. It readily follows from the definition of continuity that this mapping is continuous.

Example 13.3. As an example of a mapping that is not continuous, we may cite the following discontinuous function. Consider a real-valued function defined in the interval $[0, 1/\pi]$ (where π is the ratio of the circumference of the circle to the diameter), namely

$$\begin{cases} f(0) = 0\,, \\ f(x) = \sin 1/x \qquad (\text{for } 0 < x \leqq 1/\pi)\,. \end{cases}$$

It can be shown that this function is discontinuous at $x = 0$. For instance, let $x_\nu = 1/(2\nu + \frac{1}{2})\pi$ $(\nu = 1, 2, \ldots)$. Then, $x_\nu \in (0, 1/\pi]$ and $\lim_{\nu\to\infty} x_\nu = 0$. On the other hand, $\sin 1/x_\nu = \sin(2\nu + \frac{1}{2})\pi = 1$ $(\nu = 1, 2, \ldots)$ so that $\lim_{\nu\to\infty} f(x_\nu) = 1 \neq 0 = f(0)$. Hence, the function is discontinuous at $x = 0$ (cf. fig. 13.2).

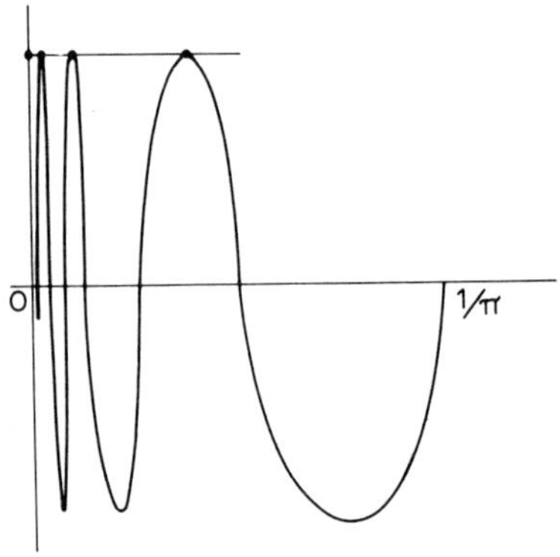

Fig. 13.2

We have started from the definition of continuity in terms of the convergence of a sequence of points. Now we can look at it from another viewpoint. It is very important to rewrite the condition for continuity in an alternative form in order to make the best use of the special properties of continuous mappings.

THEOREM 13.1. *The continuity of $f\colon X \to Y$ at a is equivalent to the following Cauchy criterion of continuity: For any neighborhood $U(f(a), \epsilon)$ of the* *image $f(a)$ of a, one gets*

$$f(V(a,\delta)) \subset U(f(a),\epsilon)$$

by choosing an appropriate neighborhood $V(a,\delta)$ of a.

Proof. (i) *Sufficiency.* Let $\lim_{\nu\to\infty} x^\nu = a$ (in X). We show that $\lim_{\nu\to\infty} f(x^\nu) = f(a)$. For any given $\epsilon > 0$, we have an ϵ-neighborhood $U(f(a),\epsilon)$ of $f(a)$. Then, we take a δ-neighborhood $V(a,\delta)$ of a that satisfies the Cauchy criterion. Select a number $n(\delta)$, according to the definition of convergence, such that $d(x^\nu, a) < \delta$ (for $n \geqq n(\delta)$), i.e. $x^\nu \in V(a,\delta)$ (for $n \geqq n(\delta)$). Now that $f(V(a,\delta)) \subset U(f(a),\epsilon)$, we get $f(x^\nu) \in U(f(a),\epsilon)$ (for $n \geqq n(\delta)$). Rewriting it, we have $d(f(x^\nu), f(a)) < \epsilon$ (for $n \geqq n(\delta)$). [Q.E.D.]

In this proof, ϵ is given to begin with; δ is chosen for this value of ϵ and then $n(\delta)$ is determined for δ. Thus, in the final analysis, $n(\delta)$ is determined for ϵ (cf. fig. 13.3).

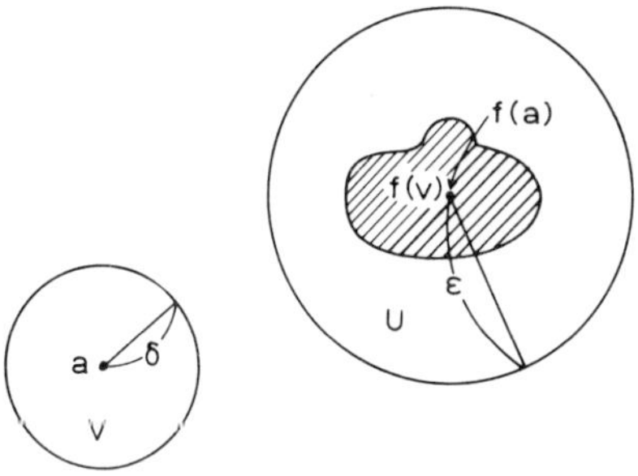

Fig. 13.3.

(ii) *Necessity.* When an ϵ-neighborhood $U(f(a),\epsilon)$ of $f(a)$ is given, we show that an assumption that $f(V(a,\delta))$ is not contained in $U(f(a),\epsilon)$ for any δ-neighborhood $V(a,\delta)$ of a leads to a contradiction. For any δ, as $f(V(a,\delta)) \not\subset U(f(a),\epsilon)$, there exists x such that $x \in V(a,\delta)$ and $f(x) \notin U(f(a),\epsilon)$ for δ. Let $\delta = 1/\nu$ ($\nu = 1, 2, \ldots$) and denote x of the above nature that corresponds to this δ by x^ν. Then, because $x^\nu \in V(a, 1/\nu)$, we have

$$(13.1) \qquad d(x^\nu, a) < 1/\nu \quad (\nu = 1, 2, \ldots)\,.$$

At the same time, as $f(x^\nu) \notin U(f(a),\epsilon)$, we have

$$(13.2) \qquad d(f(x^\nu), f(a)) \geqq \epsilon > 0 \quad (\nu = 1, 2, \ldots)\,.$$

(13.1) leads to $\lim_{\nu\to\infty} x^\nu = a$. Hence, we should get $\lim_{\nu\to\infty} f(x^\nu) = f(a)$ by virtue of continuity, which contradicts (13.2). Hence, for some $\delta > 0$, we must have $f(V(a, \delta)) \subset U(a, \epsilon)$. [Q.E.D.]

We said that a continuous mapping projects a topological relation in the domain as another topological relation in the range. Then, can we say that the image $f(S)$ of an open set S in the domain X is an open set in the range Y? We can see immediately that this conjecture is false. A constant mapping is a simple counterexample. Take a constant mapping $f: R^n \to R^m$ that maps R^n into a point $b \in R^m$. R^n itself is an open set in R^n, but $f(R^n)$ is a set consisting of a single point that is, of course, not open in R^m. Similarly, if S is a closed set in X, $f(S)$ is not necessarily a closed set in Y. In order to characterize continuity correctly in terms of open (closed) sets, we must trace the transition of properties of sets not from the domain to the range but from the range to the domain.

THEOREM 13.2. *$f: X \to Y$ is continuous if and only if the inverse image $f^{-1}(T)$ of any open set T in the range Y is an open set in the domain X.*

Proof. (i) *Necessity.* Assume that f is continuous. Take any point a in $f^{-1}(T)$, the inverse image of an open set T in Y. Then, as $f(a) \in T$ and as T is an open set, an appropriate neighborhood $U(f(a), \epsilon)$ of $f(a)$ is contained in T. By virtue of Theorem 13.1 (Cauchy criterion), we have $f(V(a, \delta)) \subset U(f(a), \epsilon)$ if a neighborhood $V(a, \delta)$ of a is properly chosen. As its right-hand side is contained in T, we get $f(V(a, \delta)) \subset T$, viz. $V(a, \delta) \subset f^{-1}(T)$. It is thus found that $f^{-1}(T)$ contains an appropriate neighborhood of any point $a \in f^{-1}(T)$. This implies that $f^{-1}(T)$ is an open set. (See the remark following Theorem 12.4.)

(ii) *Sufficiency.* It can be proved in almost the same way as (i), but we give the proof for the sake of completeness. Any ϵ-neighborhood $U(f(a), \epsilon)$ of the image $f(a)$ of any $a \in X$ is an open set in Y *. Hence, by assumption, $f^{-1}(U(f(a), \epsilon))$ is an open set in X. As $a \in f^{-1}(U(f(a), \epsilon))$, we get $V(a, \delta) \subset f^{-1}(U(f(a), \epsilon))$ by choosing an appropriate δ-neighborhood $V(a, \delta)$ of a. $\therefore f(V(a, \delta)) \subset U(f(a), \epsilon)$. As the Cauchy criterion holds, f is continuous at a. [Q.E.D.]

The theorem below is a dual of Theorem 13.2.

THEOREM 13.3. *$f: X \to Y$ is continuous if and only if the inverse image $f^{-1}(T)$ of any closed set T in the range Y is a closed set in the domain X.*

* See Example 12.9.

Proof. It follows readily from Theorem 13.2. The mapping rule (7.8) shows the relation $f^{-1}(T^c) = (f^{-1}(T))^c$ holding among four sets T, its complement (in Y) T^c, $f^{-1}(T)$, and its complement (in X) $(f^{-1}(T))^c$. Now if T is a closed set in Y, T^c is an open set in Y. Theorem 13.2 states that the continuity of f is equivalent to the openness of $f^{-1}(T^c)$ in X for any closed set T in Y. As noted above, this set is equal to $(f^{-1}(T))^c$. Hence, the continuity of f is equivalent to the closedness of $f^{-1}(T)$ in X for any closed set T in Y.

Example 13.4. If f: $X \to Y$ is a continuous mapping, the inverse image $f^{-1}(b)$ of any point b in Y is a closed set in X.

This is due to Theorem 13.3 as well as due to the fact that a set $\{b\}$ consisting of a single point is a closed set.

Example 13.5. Let f: $X \to R$ be a real-valued continuous function on X. α and β are constant numbers. Then, the sets $A = \{x \mid x \in X, f(x) \geqq \alpha\}$, $B = \{x \mid x \in X, f(x) \leqq \beta\}$, and $C = \{x \mid x \in X, \alpha \leqq f(x) \leqq \beta\}$ are all closed sets in X, while the sets $O = \{x \mid x \in X, f(x) > \alpha\}$, $P = \{x \mid x \in X, f(x) < \beta\}$, and $Q = \{x \mid x \in X, \alpha < f(x) < \beta\}$ are all open sets in X.

Proof. These sets are given by $A = f^{-1}([\alpha, +\infty))$, $B = f^{-1}((-\infty, \beta])$, $C = f^{-1}([\alpha, \beta])$, $O = f^{-1}((\alpha, +\infty))$, $P = f^{-1}((-\infty, \beta))$, and $Q = f^{-1}((\alpha, \beta))$. The intervals $[\alpha, +\infty)$, $(-\infty, \beta]$, and $[\alpha, \beta]$ are closed sets and $(\alpha, +\infty)$, $(-\infty, \beta)$, and (α, β) are open sets. Hence, Theorems 13.2 and 13.3 yield the conclusion.

Example 13.6. Let Y be a metric space and X its subset. An *identity mapping*, $f(x) = x$: $X \to Y$, that associates with x in X, x itself is continuous. In this case, the topology of X is to be considered relative to Y.

Its proof is obvious. An important fact follows from this: if T is an open (closed) set in Y, $f^{-1}(T) = X \cap T$ is an open (closed) set in X by virtue of Theorems 13.2 and 13.3. In particular, if $T \subset X$ is an open (closed) set in Y, it is also an open (closed) set in X.

Continuity of a composed mapping

THEOREM 13.4. *If f: $X \to Y$ and g: $Y \to Z$ are both continuous, its composed mapping gf: $X \to Z$ is also continuous.*

Proof. Let T be any open set in Z. We have $(gf)^{-1}(T) = f^{-1}(g^{-1}(T))$ *.

* See the mapping rule (7.9).

As g is continuous, $g^{-1}(T)$ is an open set in Y by virtue of Theorem 13.2. Moreover, as f is continuous, $f^{-1}(g^{-1}(T))$ is an open set in X again by virtue of Theorem 13.2. Hence, gf is continuous by Theorem 13.2. [Q.E.D.]

Theorem 13.4 can easily be extended to a mapping composed of a finite number of continuous mappings. The proof is carried out in terms of induction.

Homeomorphisms. Let a mapping $f: X \to Y$ be a one-to-one mapping from X onto Y. Denote the inverse mapping of f by f^{-1}. Then, if the mappings $f: X \to Y$ and $f^{-1}: Y \to X$ are both continuous, f is called a *topological mapping* or *homeomorphism.* It is also said that X and Y are *homeomorphic.* When X and Y are homeomorphic, they have an identical topological structure. One of the objectives of topology is noted to be the study of properties of sets – in particular, those properties that would be kept intact by one-to-one mappings which are continuous both ways from X onto Y and from Y onto X, like the one mentioned above.

Remark 1. Even if $f: X \to Y$ is a continuous, one-to-one mapping from X onto Y, its inverse mapping $f^{-1}: Y \to X$ is not necessarily continuous. However, there is a convenient property in this regard. If X is compact (as we shall discuss it in the next section), f^{-1} is automatically continuous and f is a homeomorphism.

Our general discussion of continuity can be applied to any metric spaces X and Y. We are now to discuss certain relations between linear operations and continuity in R^n.

(1) Let X be a metric space. Given a finite number of continuous mappings $f^j: X \to R^n$ and the same number of real-valued continuous functions $\alpha_j: X \to R$ $(j = 1, 2, ..., s)$, a mapping $f: X \to R^n$ is continuous where

$$f(x) = \sum_{j=1}^{s} \alpha_j(x) f^j(x) .$$

Proof. Let $\lim_{\nu\to\infty} x^\nu = a$ (in X). Then, from the properties (4) and (5) in Section 11,

$$\lim_{\nu\to\infty} f(x^\nu) = \lim_{\nu\to\infty} \sum_{j=1}^{s} \alpha_j(x^\nu) f^j(x^\nu) = \sum_{j=1}^{s} \alpha_j(a) f^j(a) = f(a) .$$

Hence, it is continuous at a.

(2) Let a^j $(j = 1, 2, ..., n)$ be a basis of R^n and X a metric space. Given a mapping $f: X \to R^n$, the image $f(x)$ of a point x in X can be uniquely ex-

panded as a linear combination of a^j's. Their coefficients are determined by x, i.e. they are real-valued functions $\alpha_j(x)$ of x. $f\colon X \to R^n$ is continuous if and only if the n functions $\alpha_j\colon X \to R$ are continuous. As a special case of this finding, we may note that the expansion of a point x in R^n in terms of a linear combination of a^j's has coefficients that are continous functions of x.

Proof. It is evident from (1) above that this condition is sufficient. It is a special case of (1) that sets $s = n$ and $f^j(x) = a^j$ (constant mappings).

Necessity. Denote by A a matrix with a^j on its jth column. Because of the linear independence of a^j ($j = 1, 2, ..., n$), there exists its inverse matrix A^{-1} *. Denote by $g(x)$ a point in R^n with $\alpha_j(x)$ as its jth component. Then, $g(x) = A^{-1}f(x)$. Now the mapping $g\colon X \to R^n$ is composed of the mapping $f\colon X \to R^n$ and a linear mapping $y \to A^{-1}y\colon R^n \to R^n$. Of the two, the former is continuous by assumption and so is the latter by Example 13.1. Hence, g is also continuous by virtue of Theorem 13.4. Taking d_2 as distance in R^n **, we find that $\lim_{\nu\to\infty} x^\nu = a$ (in X) implies

$$|\alpha_j(x^\nu) - \alpha_j(a)| \leqq d_2(g(x^\nu), g(a)) \to 0 \quad (\nu \to \infty) . \qquad \text{[Q.E.D.]}$$

(3) Let A be a square matrix of the order n. Consider a continuous mapping $f\colon R^n \to R^n, f(x) = Ax$. If $\det A \neq 0$, f is a homeomorphism.

Proof. (a) f is one-to-one. ∵ If $f(x) = f(y)$, then $Ax = Ay$. Pre-multiplying A^{-1}, we get $x = y$ so that it is one-to-one.

(b) f is a mapping from R^n onto R^n. ∵ For any $y \in R^n, f(A^{-1}y) = AA^{-1}y = y$ so that $f(R^n) = R^n$.

(c) f and its inverse mapping $f^{-1}\colon R^n \to R^n, f^{-1}(y) = A^{-1}y$ are continuous by virtue of Example 13.1.

(4) Let X be a metric space. If $f^j(x)\colon X \to R$ ($j = 1, 2, ..., s$) is a real-valued continuous function, $f\colon X \to R, f(x) = f^1(x) \cdot f^2(x) ... f^s(x)$ is also continuous.

Proof. If $\lim_{\nu\to\infty} x^\nu = a$ (in X), then $\lim_{\nu\to\infty} f^j(x^\nu) = f^j(a)$ for each j because of the assumption of continuity. Hence, using the formula (6) in Section 8 in the general case with a finite number of sequences, we get

$$\lim_{\nu\to\infty} f(x^\nu) = \lim_{\nu\to\infty} f^1(x^\nu) ... f^s(x^\nu) = f^1(a)f^2(a) ... f^s(a) .$$

* See Theorems 9.3 and 10.2.

** See the distance formula (11.16).

(5) * A polynomial

$$f(x) = \sum_{j=0}^{s} \alpha_j x^j$$

is continuous when it represents a mapping f: $R \to R$.

Proof. Each monomial $f^j(x) = x^j$ is continuous because of (4). Hence, f is a special case of (1) where $n = 1$ and $\alpha_j(x) = \alpha_j$ (constant) so that it is continuous.

(6) A polynomial of n variables,

$$f(x_1, x_2, \ldots, x_n) = \sum \alpha_{\rho_1 \rho_2 \ldots \rho_n} x_1^{\rho_1} x_2^{\rho_2} \ldots x_n^{\rho_n}$$

defines a continuous mapping f: $R^n \to R$ when x_j is considered as the jth component of a point x in R^n.

Proof. We see from (2) that $x \to x_j$ is continuous. $x_j \to x_j^{\rho_j}$ is continuous because of (5). Hence, by (4), $x \to x_1^{\rho_1} x_2^{\rho_2} \ldots x_n^{\rho_n}$ is continuous.

$$x \to \sum \alpha_{\rho_1 \rho_2 \ldots \rho_n} x_1^{\rho_1} x_2^{\rho_2} \ldots x_n^{\rho_n}$$

as the sum of a finite number of constant multiples of continuous functions is a special case of (1) and, therefore, continuous.

(7) If $f_i(x)$ $(i = 1, 2, \ldots, s)$ are real-valued continuous functions in a metric space X, the functions $\max_{1 \leqq i \leqq s} f_i(x)$ and $\min_{1 \leqq i \leqq s} f_i(x)$ are also continuous.

Proof. Let $g(x) = \max_{1 \leqq i \leqq s} f_i(x)$. We prove its continuity at any point a in X. For this, we need only to demonstrate that the inverse image

$$g^{-1}(U(g(a), \epsilon)) = \{x \,|\, |g(x) - g(a)| < \epsilon\}$$

of any ϵ-neighborhood $U(g(a), \epsilon)$ of $g(a)$ is an open set in X. The condition $|g(x) - g(a)| < \epsilon$ implies $\max_{1 \leqq i \leqq s} f_i(x) < g(a) + \epsilon$ and $\max_{1 \leqq i \leqq s} f_i(x) > g(a) - \epsilon$ both at the same time. Of the two inequalities, the former is equivalent to

$$f_i(x) < g(a) + \epsilon \qquad (i = 1, 2, \ldots, s)$$

and the latter to

$$f_i(x) > g(a) - \epsilon \qquad (\text{for some } i)\ .$$

* Superscripts are exponents in x^i, $x_1^{\rho_i}$, etc. in (5) and (6).

Letting

$$A_i = \{x \mid f_i(x) < g(a) + \epsilon\} \quad (i = 1, 2, ..., s)$$

and

$$B_i = \{x \mid f_i(x) > g(a) - \epsilon\} \quad (i = 1, 2, ..., s) \ ,$$

we get

$$g^{-1}(U(g(a), \epsilon)) = (\bigcap_{i=1}^{s} A_i) \cap (\bigcup_{i=1}^{s} B_i) \ .$$

A_i and B_i are open sets in X (see Example 13.5). The right-hand side of this equation is a combination of a finite number of open sets derived by operations $\cap$ and $\cup$; it is an open set by Theorem 12.2. The same procedure can be followed in the proof of the continuity of $\min_{1 \leqq i \leqq s} f_i(x)$.

(8) *The theorem of intermediate values.* Define a continuous function $f(x)$ in the interval $[a, b]$ subject to (i) $f(a) < 0$ and (ii) $f(b) > 0$. Then, $f(c) = 0$ at an appropriate point c in the interval $[a, b]$.

The set $G_f = \{(x, f(x)) \mid a \leqq x \leqq b\}$ in R^2 is called the *graph* of the function. Geometrically interpreted, the theorem states that G_f crosses the segment $\overline{ab}$ at least once (see fig. 13.4). Though this may seem to be a self-evident condition, a proof is really necessary. In fact, we shall prove it on the basis of the basic properties of the real number system and the continuity of mappings that we have discussed above. This theorem is famous and has many applications. It will see effective use in this book, too.

Proof. Let $F = \{x \mid a \leqq x \leqq b, f(x) \geqq 0\}$. F is a subset of the interval $[a, b]$. By assumption, the mapping f: $[a, b] \to R$ is continuous so that F is a closed set in $[a, b]$ as we noted in Example 13.5. F is not empty because $b \in F$ by assumption (ii) *. Now let $c = \inf_{x \in F} x$. An appropriate numerical sequence in F

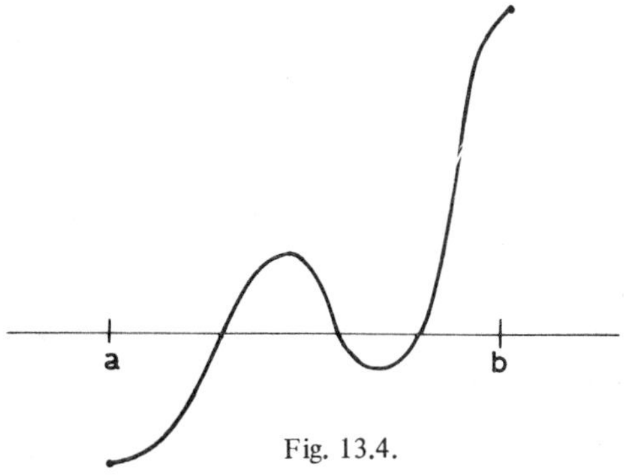

Fig. 13.4.

* We shall miss an important step in our existence proof unless it is explicitly shown.

converges to c (see the Remark in Section 8 on a sequence that converges to an infimum). As F is a closed set in [a, b] while $c \in [a, b]$, we must have $c \in F$. In other words, $c = \min_{x \in F} x$. On the other hand, as $a \notin F$ by assumption (i), we have $a < c$.

On the basis of these preliminaries, we prove now $f(c) = 0$. Let

$$y_\nu = a/\nu + (1 - 1/\nu)\, c \qquad (\nu = 1, 2, \ldots)\,.$$

Then, for any ν, we have

$$a \leqq y_\nu < c$$

because of $a < c$. It follows from the definition of c that $y_\nu \notin F$ ($\nu = 1, 2, \ldots$), whence

$$(13.3) \qquad f(y_\nu) < 0 \qquad (\nu = 1, 2, \ldots)\,.$$

On the other hand, obviously $\lim_{\nu \to \infty} y_\nu = c$ so that $\lim_{\nu \to \infty} f(y_\nu) = f(c)$ due to the continuity of f. (13.3) leads, therefore, to the limit result $f(c) \leqq 0$. In view of $f(c) \geqq 0$, we obtain $f(c) = 0$.

Remark 2. The theorem of intermediate values also holds when the inequality signs in (i) and (ii) are reversed as well as when an equality sign is added to either or both of (i) and (ii) like (i) $f(a) \leqq 0$ and (ii) $f(b) > 0$, in which case we have $c = a$ or $a < c < b$.

14. Compactness

This section is devoted to an exposition of the concept of compactness, which is an important tool constantly employed in topological studies. This concept served as a basis on which many existence theorems were built. It will play an important role in the present book, too.

To facilitate our understanding of this concept, let us note a famous theorem on the maximum and minimum of a continuous function that can be found in any orthodox textbooks of classical calculus *. The theorem is stated as follows: "A real-valued continuous function $f(x)$, defined in a closed interval $[a, b]$, takes a maximum and a minimum in this interval".

The theorem does not necessarily hold if the interval $[a, b]$ is replaced by an open interval (a, b). We may cite one such example.

* See, e.g., R.Courant, *Differential and Integral Calculus*, vol. I (Interscience Publishers, 2nd ed., 1937) p. 63.

Example 14.1. A linear function, $f(x) = x$, defined in the interval (0, 1), is continuous but takes on neither a maximum nor a minimum in this interval.

This example suggests that a certain topological property of the closed interval $[a, b]$ that contains both end points has something to do with the existence of a maximum and a minimum. The theorem given below formalizes this "property".

THEOREM 14.1. *A convergent subsequence can be extracted from any sequence $\{x^{\nu}\}$in the interval $[a, b]$.*

Needless to mention, any given sequence in $[a, b]$ is not necessarily convergent. What the theorem really means is that "a subsequence that is extracted from this sequence in an appropriate manner converges to a limit that belongs to $[a, b]$". Before undertaking a proof of the theorem, let us see how the existence of a maximum and a minimum can be derived from this theorem.

Let $f(x)$ be a real-valued continuous function defined in $[a, b]$. We prove that it in fact reaches a maximum in $[a, b]$. For this purpose, put $\sup_{a \leqq x \leqq b} f(x) = \beta$. β may be a real number ($\beta < +\infty$) or $\beta = +\infty$. In either case, there is a sequence of numbers $\{x_{\nu}\}$ such that $\lim_{\nu \to \infty} f(x_{\nu}) = \beta$, $a \leqq x_{\nu} \leqq b$ (see the Remark in Section 8 on the convergence of a sequence to its supremum). It is not certain whether the sequence $\{x_{\nu}\}$ itself is convergent or not, but an appropriate subsequence $\{x_{\nu_{\lambda}}\}$ can be chosen from it so as to converge to a real number c in $[a, b]$ by virtue of Theorem 14.1. As $\{f(x_{\nu_{\lambda}})\}$ is a subsequence of $\{f(x_{\nu})\}$, the limiting relation $\lim_{\nu \to \infty} f(x_{\nu}) = \beta$ applies to its subsequence as well so that we get $\lim_{\lambda \to \infty} f(x_{\nu_{\lambda}}) = \beta$ *. We now make use of the assumption, so far unutilized, of the continuity of f. It follows from $\lim_{\lambda \to \infty} x_{\nu_{\lambda}} = c$ that $\lim_{\lambda \to \infty} f(x_{\nu_{\lambda}}) = f(c)$. Due to the uniqueness of the limit, we have $f(c) = \beta$. This proves that $\max_{a \leqq x \leqq b} f(x) = f(c)$. At the same time, it rules out the possibility that $\beta = +\infty$.

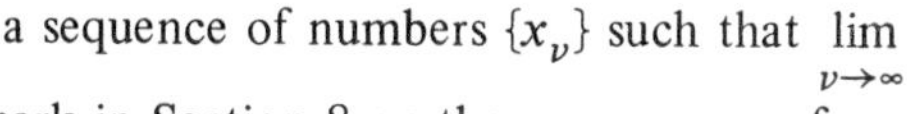

Fig. 14.1.

* Formula (10) in Section 8.

Proof of Theorem 14.1. Let $\{x_\nu\}$ be any arbitrarily given numerical sequence in $[a, b]$. Divide the interval $[a, b]$ at c into two intervals of equal length, $[a, c]$ and $[c, b]$. Then, at least one of these intervals must contain an infinite number of terms of the sequence $\{x_\nu\}$. In other words, at least one interval contains a certain subsequence of $\{x_\nu\}$. To make our exposition more systematic, put $a_1 = a$ and $b_1 = b$ and denote the original sequence $\{x_\nu\}$ by $\{x_{1\nu}\}$. Take one of the intervals, $[a, c]$ and $[c, b]$, that contains a subsequence of $\{x_{1\nu}\}$ * and denote it by $[a_2, b_2]$; let one of the subsequences contained in $[a_2, b_2]$ be $\{x_{2\nu}\}$. Following exactly the same procedure, we divide the interval $[a_2, b_2]$ into two subintervals of equal length. Take one of them that contains an appropriate subsequence $\{x_{3\nu}\}$ of $\{x_{2\nu}\}$ and call it $[a_3, b_3]$. Repeating this procedure, we obtain the following sequences of intervals and subsequences:

(14.1) $$[a_1, b_1] \supset [a_2, b_2] \supset \dots \supset [a_\mu, b_\mu] \supset \dots,$$

(14.2) $$a_1 \leqq a_2 \leqq \dots \leqq a_\mu \leqq a_{\mu+1} \leqq \dots \leqq b_{\mu+1} \leqq b_\mu \leqq \dots \leqq b_2 \leqq b_1,$$

(14.3) $$|a_\mu - b_\mu| = \frac{1}{2^{\mu-1}} |a_1 - b_1| \quad (\mu = 1, 2, \dots)$$

(14.4) $$\begin{array}{l} x_{11}, x_{12}, x_{13}, \dots, x_{1\nu}, \dots \\ x_{21}, x_{22}, x_{23}, \dots, x_{2\nu}, \dots \\ \dots\dots\dots\dots\dots\dots \\ x_{\mu 1}, x_{\mu 2}, x_{\mu 3}, \dots, x_{\mu\nu}, \dots \\ \dots\dots\dots\dots\dots\dots \end{array}$$

(14.5) $\{x_{\mu+1\,\nu}\}$ is a subsequence of $\{x_{\mu\nu}\}$ $(\nu = 1, 2, \dots)$

(14.6) $\{x_{\mu\nu}\}$ is a sequence in the interval $[a_\mu, b_\mu]$ $(\mu = 1, 2, \dots)$.

Let the νth term $x_{\mu\nu}$ of the subsequence $\{x_{\mu\nu}\}$ be the $n(x_{\mu\nu})$th term in the original sequence. Then, $n(x_{\mu+1\,\nu}) \geqq n(x_{\mu\nu})$ from (14.5). This can be seen as follows: Extract a subsequence from $\{x_{\mu\nu}\}$ and renumber its terms consecutively. Then, $x_{\mu+1\,\nu}$ is the νth term in the new subsequence. A comparison of their term numbers in the original sequence reveals that $n(x_{\mu+1\,\nu}) \geqq n(x_{\mu\nu})$ at the least. Hence, we always have $n(x_{\mu+1\,\nu+1}) > n(x_{\mu\nu})$ and in particular $n(x_{\mu+1\,\mu+1}) > n(x_{\mu\mu})$ $(\mu = 1, 2, \dots)$ so that the sequence $\{x_{\mu\mu}\}$ consisting of real numbers along the principal diagonal of (14.4) is a subsequence of the original sequence.

* If both are eligible for the selection, we may take the interval on the left.

Next we examine this subsequence and show that it converges to a real number in $[a, b]$.

From (14.6), we have $a_\mu \leqq x_{\mu\nu} \leqq b_\mu$ so that the μth term $x_{\mu\mu}$ of the sequence in question $\{x_{\mu\mu}\}$ satisfies the inequality

$$(14.7) \qquad a_\mu \leqq x_{\mu\mu} \leqq b_\mu \quad (\mu = 1, 2, ...).$$

By (14.2) the sequence $\{a_\mu\}$ is increasing and bounded from above and $\{b_\mu\}$ is decreasing and bounded from below. Hence, they are both convergent by virtue of Theorem 8.2. Let their limits be $\lim_{\mu\to\infty} a_\mu = \alpha$ and $\lim_{\mu\to\infty} b_\mu = \beta$. Then, by (14.3), $|\alpha - \beta| = \lim_{\mu\to\infty} |a_\mu - b_\mu| = 0$ *. Therefore, $\alpha = \beta$. By (14.7), $\{x_{\mu\mu}\}$ also converges to the same limit. [Q.E.D.]

Compact spaces. Let X be a metric space. X is said to be *compact,* when a convergent subsequence $\{x^{\nu_\lambda}\}$ can be appropriately extracted from any sequence of points $\{x^\nu\}$ in X.

Theorem 14.1 indicates that the interval $[a, b]$ is compact. The closedness or openness of a set is a property of the set relative to a larger set that embraces it. In contrast, the compactness of a set is an inherent and intrinsic property of the set that can be stated without reference to any other set. Dictionaries explain "compact" (kəm'pækt) as "closely and firmly united, condensed, packed into a small space", etc., as against a "compact" ('kɔmpækt), i.e. a small cosmetic case with a built-in mirror. The last ot the definitions seems to be the most appropriate meaning that can be given to the word "compact" as a mathematical term. When an infinite number of different values appear among terms of the sequence $[x^\nu]$ in a compact space X, an infinite number of terms of this sequence are clustered densely around some point of X.

We now describe compact spaces in general and then characterize compact sets in R^n on the basis of Theorem 14.1.

Properties of a compact set. Let X be a metric space. A subset A of X is said to be *bounded* if A is contained in a neighborhood $U(a, \epsilon)$ of an appropriate size where its center a and radius ϵ are arbitrary so long as there is at least one such neighborhood. If $X = R^n$, it is very easy to see that the boundedness of $A \subset R^n$ is equivalent to the boundedness of the norm $\|x\|$ from above in A.

* $1/2^{\mu-1} \to 0$ $(\mu \to \infty)$ by Example 8.3.

THEOREM 14.2. *(The existence of a maximum and a minimum). A real-valued continuous function $f: X \to R$, defined in a compact metric space X, takes on a maximum and a minimum in X.*

Its proof is formally the same as the one presented above by means of Theorem 14.1 for the existence of a maximum and a minimum where $X = [a, b]$. Therefore, we wish to avoid repeating it here.

COROLLARY. *Let A be a compact set in a metric space X. A is a compact set in the relative topology * induced into A in a natural way via the topology of X. Then, we have*

(i) A is bounded.

(ii) A is a closed set in X.

Proof. (i) Let the distance function in X be given by $d(x, a)$. Fixing a point a in X, we can derive an inequality

$$(14.8) \qquad |d(x,a) - d(y,a)| \leqq d(x,y) \quad (x, y \in X)$$

from the basic axiom of distance (11.11). Therefore, the real-valued function $f(x) = d(x, a)$ is continuous in X and also in A in the sense of the relative topology. Thus, by virtue of Theorem 14.2, this function actually takes on a maximum. Let $\max_{x \in A} f(x) = M$ and choose a positive number ϵ such that $\epsilon > M$. Then, $d(x, a) < \epsilon$ (for $x \in A$). I.e. $A \subset U(a, \epsilon)$. Therefore, A is bounded.

(ii) By fixing any point a in X, $f(x) = d(x, a)$ is shown in (i) to be continuous in A. Suppose that a sequence of points $\{x^\nu\}$ in A converges to a point a in X. If we show $a \in A$ on this assumption, we have proved that A is a closed set in X. In fact, as $\lim_{\nu \to \infty} x^\nu = a$, we have $\lim_{\nu \to \infty} d(x^\nu, a) = 0$ by the definition of convergence. Hence, $\inf_{x \in A} f(x) = 0$ and $f(x)$ reaches the minimum 0 at a point b in A. $\therefore$ $f(b) = 0$ and $d(b, a) = f(b) = 0$. From the latter half of the basic axiom of distance (11.9), we obtain $a = b$. As $b \in A$, we get $a \in A$. [Q.E.D.]

THEOREM 14.3. *Let X be a compact metric space and A a closed set in X. Then, A is compact.*

* See Section 12.

Proof. Any sequence of points $\{x^\nu\}$ in A is also a sequence of points in X. As X is compact, a certain subsequence $\{x^{\nu_\lambda}\}$ of this sequence converges to a point a in X. But $\{x^{\nu_\lambda}\}$, a sequence in A, converges to a in X. By assumption, A is a closed set in X so that the limit of $\{x^{\nu_\lambda}\}$, i.e. a, must belong to A. This shows that a subsequence $\{x^{\nu_\lambda}\}$ of the original sequence converges within A. Hence, A is compact.

THEOREM 14.4. *Let X and Y be metric spaces. A continuous mapping f: $X \to Y$ is given. If X is compact, its image $f(X)$ is also compact. I.e., a continuous image of a compact space is also compact.*

Proof. Let $\{y^\nu\}$ be any sequence of points in $f(X)$. Then, by the definition of $f(X)$, each y^ν is given by $y^\nu = f(x^\nu)$, $x^\nu \in X$. Then, because X is compact, some subsequence $\{x^{\nu_\lambda}\}$ of the sequence $\{x^\nu\}$ converges to a limit which is denoted here by a. Hence, $\lim_{\lambda\to\infty} x^{\nu_\lambda} = a$. By the assumed continuity of f, $\lim_{\lambda\to\infty} f(x^{\nu_\lambda}) = f(a) \in f(X)$. Thus, we have extracted a convergent subsequence $\{f(x^{\nu_\lambda})\}$ from the sequence $\{f(x^\nu)\}$. [Q.E.D.]

We noted in Section 13 that a continuous one-to-one mapping of X onto Y is not necessarily a homeomorphism. Nevertheless, when the domain is compact, the inverse mapping is also continuous. This is the theorem below.

THEOREM 14.5. *Let X and Y be metric spaces and X compact. If f: $X \to Y$ is a continuous one-to-one mapping from X onto Y, then its inverse mapping f^{-1}: $Y \to X$ is continuous.*

Proof. In order to prove that f^{-1} is continuous, it suffices to show that the inverse image $(f^{-1})^{-1}(T)$ of a closed set T in the range X is a closed set in the domain Y because of Theorem 13.3. Since $(f^{-1})^{-1}(T) = f(T)$, it amounts to showing that the image $f(T)$ of a closed set T in X under the mapping f is a closed set in Y. As T is a closed set in a compact space X, it is also compact by Theorem 14.3. The mapping f: $T \to Y$ which restricts the domain of f to T is also continuous. Hence, the continuous image $f(T)$ is compact by Theorem 14.4 and is a closed set in Y by the corollary of Theorem 14.2. [Q.E.D.]

If a metric space is compact, it satisfies the conditions (i) and (ii) of the corollary of Theorem 14.2. However, its converse is not true. Compactness is not ensured in a metric space in general even if (i) and (ii) are satisfied. In

R^n, however, compactness follows from these two conditions. Compact sets that will appear in this book belong to R^n. In this sense, the theorem to be given below is important.

THEOREM 14.6. *A subset A in R^n is compact if and only if it satisfies the conditions (i) and (ii) (in the corollary of Theorem 14.2).*

Proof. Its necessity was proved in the corollary of Theorem 14.2. Its sufficiency is to be proved on the basis of Theorem 14.1.

Sufficiency. As A is a bounded set in R^n, the jth component of a point x in A is bounded both from above and below. Denote the upper and lower bounds of x_j by a_j and b_j respectively. Then, putting

$$X = \{x \mid x \in R^n,\ a_j \leqq x_j \leqq b_j \ \ (j = 1, 2, \ldots, n)\}, \tag{14.9}$$

we get $A \subset X$. (Cf. fig. 14.2.) A is a closed set in R^n by assumption, which makes it a closed set in X as noted in Example 13.6. Therefore, by making use of Theorem 14.3, the crux of the proof amounts to showing that X is compact.

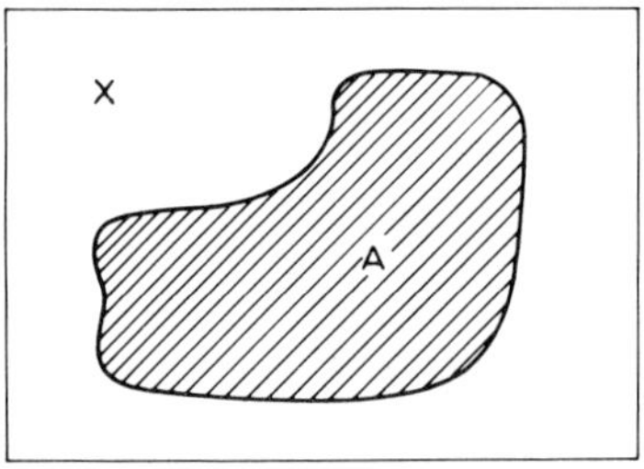

Fig. 14.2.

The numerical sequence $\{x_1^\nu\}$ consisting of the first components of the terms of any sequence of points $\{x^\nu\}$ in X of (14.9) is a sequence of numbers in the interval $[a_1, b_1]$. Therefore, by virtue of Theorem 14.1, an appropriate subsequence $\{x_1^{1\nu}\}$ of $\{x_1^\nu\}$ converges to a real number c_1 in $[a_1, b_1]$. The numerical sequence $\{x_2^{1\nu}\}$ consisting of the second components of the sequence of points $\{x^{1\nu}\}$ is a sequence in the interval $[a_2, b_2]$. Again by Theorem 14.1, a certain subsequence $\{x_2^{2\nu}\}$ converges to a real number c_2 in

$[a_2, b_2]$. Thus, in the subsequence $\{x^{2\nu}\}$, its first component converges to c_1 and the second to c_2 because of the basic property (10) in Section 8 which states that, if a sequence converges to a limit, its subsequence converges to the same limit. Now making repeated use of this property of subsequences and the compactness of $[a_j, b_j]$ for finite times, we apply the same procedure to the rest of the components. Having extracted subsequences $\{x^{3\nu}\}$, $\{x^{4\nu}\}$, ..., $\{x^{n\nu}\}$ step by step, we see the jth component of the last sequence $\{x^{n\nu}\}$ converges to a real number c_j in $[a_j, b_j]$. Let c be a point in R^n whose jth component is c_j. Then, $c \in X$ and, by (ii) of Theorem 11.1, $\lim_{\nu\to\infty} x^{n\nu} = c$. [Q.E.D.]

Example 14.2. The real number system R, intervals $(-\infty, a)$, $(-\infty, a]$, $[b, +\infty)$, $(b, +\infty)$, etc. are not compact because they are not bounded.

Example 14.3. Intervals (a, b), $(a, b]$, $[a, b)$, etc. are bounded. But as they are not closed sets in R, they are not compact either.

Example 14.4. A subset

$$S_n = \{x \mid \sum_{j=1}^{n} x_j = 1,\ x_j \geqq 0\ (j = 1, 2, ..., n)\}$$

in R^n is compact. (See figs. 14.3 and 14.4.)

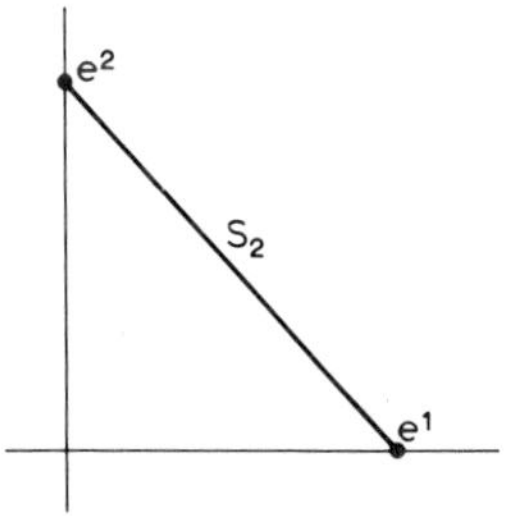

Fig. 14.3.

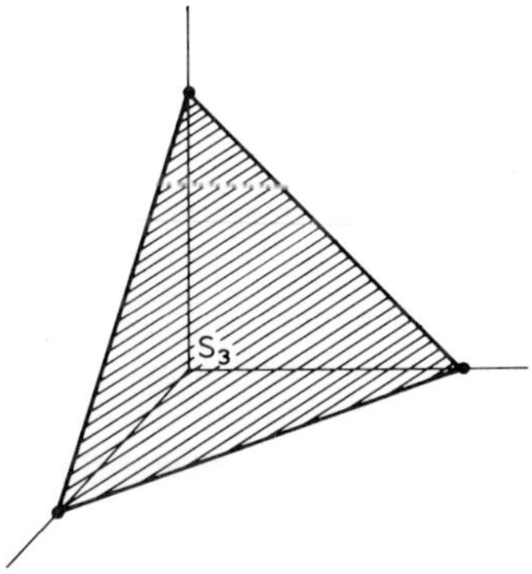

Fig. 14.4.

Proof. (i) S_n is bounded. This is evident because the norm

$$\|x\|_1 = \sum_{j=1}^{n} |x_j| = \sum_{j=1}^{n} x_j = 1$$

for $x \in S_n$.

(ii) S_n is a closed set in R^n. To show this, let $n + 1$ continuous functions f_j defined in R^n be

$$f_0(x) = \sum_{j=1}^{n} x_j, \; f_j(x) = x_j \quad (j = 1, 2, ..., n) .$$

Correspondingly, define $n + 1$ subsets F_j in R^n to be

$$F_0 = \{x \mid f_0(x) = 1\}$$

and

$$F_j = \{x \mid f_j(x) \geqq 0\} \qquad (j = 1, 2, ..., n) .$$

As f_j are continuous, F_j are closed sets in R^n. As

$$S_n = \bigcap_{j=0}^{n} F_j ,$$

whose right-hand side is an intersection of several closed sets, S_n is a closed set by Theorem 12.1. [Q.E.D.]

The compactness of S_n will prove very important in this book. We shall have its immediate application, e.g. to the existence proof of the Frobenius latent root in the next chapter.

Example 14.5. A sphere $\{x \mid d(x, a) = \epsilon\}$ and a closed spherical ϵ-neighborhood $\bar{U}(a, \epsilon) = \{x \mid d(x, a) \leqq \epsilon\}$ in R^n (where $\epsilon > 0$) are both compact.

This example can be proved in the same way as Example 14.4. The reader should try it as an exercise. It is also convenient to verify that $\bar{U}(a, \epsilon)$ is the closure of the spherical neighborhood $U(a, \epsilon)$.

We now close our first mathematical introduction. Though we have devoted more space than originally intended, this chapter contains basic materials that will be used in our later discussions. The reader is urged to examine them carefully and to understand them well. It would not only facilitate his understanding of the rest of the book but also prove useful in many ways as the contemporary intellectual's mathematical common sense.

Chapter 3

THE FROBENIUS THEOREM

15. Non-negativity constraints

Chapter 1 started from the interindustry analysis and examined systems of linear equations of the forms (4.2) and (4.3). We shall now make good use of what we have learned in Chapter 2 and push the analysis of the characteristics of these equation systems to a more advanced level.

We first express these systems in a concise vector and matrix form. Let x be a vector in R^n with x_j as its jth component, c a vector in R^n with c_i as its ith component, A an nth order square matrix with the coefficient a_{ij} as its (i, j) element, and I an nth order identity matrix. Then, the equation system (4.2) is expressed as

(15.1) $$(\rho I - A)x = c\ .$$

Similarly, let p and v be vectors in R^n with p_i and v_j as their respective components. Then, (4.3) is written as

(15.2) $$(\rho I - A')p = v\ .$$

Notice that elements of the matrices A and I appearing in these systems are all 0 or positive real numbers, namely non-negative real numbers. Also the solutions x and p and the constant terms c and v have non-negative real numbers as their components. Unlike in physical sciences and engineering, there are many economic variables that must be represented by non-negative real numbers by their own nature. The equilibrium analysis aims to discover economic laws by expressing an economic system in a mathematical model and by examining the properties of the solutions obtained from the corresponding equation system. As such, it is the most important theoretical construct in modern economics. However, in its early stage of development following Walras, the equilibrium analysis did not go so far as to examining the non-negativity of economic variables. Nevertheless, the non-negativity is an important characteristic of economic phenomena that cannot be neglected. One may suspect that an analysis of this property is necessary for making a deep incision into economic phenomena. Non-negativity is not a mere accessory of equation systems in the equilibrium analysis, but it gives them a unique structural characteristic, differentiating them from those discussed in physical sciences and engineering. Discussion of this characteristic would belong to a proper field of study in mathematical economics. That is why modern mathematical economists not only apply orthodox findings of mathematics to the solution of their unique problems but also keep on trying to invent their own devices. The interindustry analysis, outlined in Chapter 1, is the simplest example of an approach along this line. It analyzes a simple model expressed by a system of linear equations. Non-negative constraints play a key role in all the problems that will be analyzed in this book; Part II that discusses the existence of non-negative solutions in a sophisticated Walrasian equilibrium model will be a climax in this type of analysis.

Following the general view expressed above, we shall apply a deeper analysis to the equations introduced in Chapter 1. Earlier, we noted an important characteristic of (15.1) and (15.2), in which a vital role is played by matrices and vectors with non-negative elements and components. Therefore, we are naturally led to studying matrices and vectors of this type.

When all components of a vector $x \in R^n$ are non-negative, i.e. $x_i \geqq 0$ $(i = 1, 2, \ldots, n)$, x is called a *non-negative vector.* For simplicity, it is denoted by $x \geqq 0$. When $x \geqq 0$ and $x \neq 0$, i.e. at least one component is positive, we write $x \geq 0$. In addition, when all components of x are positive, we write $x > 0$. These are standard notations now adopted in mathematical economics. Analogously, we introduce the concept and notation of non-negativity in an nth order square matrix A. When all elements of A are non-negative, A is called a *non-negative matrix* and denoted by $A \geqq 0$. When $A \geqq 0$ and at least one element is positive, we write $A \geq 0$. When all elements of A are positive, we write $A > 0$ *.

It is easy to prove the following relations:
For vectors $x \geqq 0$ and $y \geqq 0$ and matrices $A \geqq 0$ and $B \geqq 0$,

(15.3) $\lambda x \geqq 0$ and $\lambda A \geqq 0$ when x and A are multiplied by a real number $\lambda \geqq 0$;

(15.4) $x + y \geqq 0, \quad A + B \geqq 0;$

* In these inequalities, 0 on the right-hand side stands for the vector 0 or the matrix 0 when the case may be.

(15.5) $Ax \geqq 0, \quad AB \geqq 0$;

(15.6) the inner product $(x, y) \geqq 0$.

There are a number of relations involving $\geq$ and $>$, like "if $x > 0$ and $y \geq 0$, then $x + y > 0$". But it would be rather cumbersome to list all of them here. Since such relations can be easily derived from the definitions, it would be sufficient for us to pay attention to them only when an occasion arises for their use.

The inequality signs can also be applied between two vectors x and y or two matrices A and B. We define them as *

$$x \geqq y \quad \text{when} \quad x - y \geqq 0 ,$$

$$x \geq y \quad \text{when} \quad x - y \geq 0 ,$$

$$x > y \quad \text{when} \quad x - y > 0 ,$$

$$A \geqq B \quad \text{when} \quad A - B \geqq 0 ,$$

$$A \geq B \quad \text{when} \quad A - B \geq 0 ,$$

$$A > B \quad \text{when} \quad A - B > 0 .$$

These definitions induce a semi-ordering $\geqq$ in R^n and in the set of nth order square matrices. When $n = 1$, it coincides with the ordering of real numbers. When $n \geqq 2$, it shows properties quite analogous to those of the familiar ordering for real numbers. To list some of the important properties, we have

(15.7) $x \geqq y, y \geqq x \Rightarrow x = y; \quad A \geqq B, B \geqq A \Rightarrow A = B.$

(15.8) $x \geqq y, y \geqq z \Rightarrow x \geqq z; \quad A \geqq B, B \geqq C \Rightarrow A \geqq C.$

(15.9) $x^1 \geqq y^1, x^2 \geqq y^2 \Rightarrow x^1 + x^2 \geqq y^1 + y^2; \quad A_1 \geqq B_1, A_2 \geqq B_2 \Rightarrow$
$A_1 + A_2 \geqq B_1 + B_2$.

(15.10) $\lambda \geqq 0, x \geqq y \Rightarrow \lambda x \geqq \lambda y; \quad \lambda \geqq 0, A \geqq B \Rightarrow \lambda A \geqq \lambda B.$

All of them can be easily verified.

However, there is one important difference when $n \geqq 2$ from the real number ordering. As is well known, for any two real numbers α and β, either (i) $\alpha \geqq \beta$ or (ii) $\alpha \leqq \beta$ must always hold. By contrast, it does not necessarily follow that either $x \geqq y$ or $x \leqq y$ hold for any two x and $y \in R^n$ $(n \geqq 2)$. For instance, if

$$x = \begin{bmatrix} 1 \\ -1 \end{bmatrix} \quad \text{and} \quad y = \begin{bmatrix} -1 \\ 2 \end{bmatrix} ,$$

* $x \geqq y$ may be expressed as $y \leqq x$ if necessary. The same applies to other inequalities.

neither $x \geqq y$ nor $x \leqq y$ holds. Real numbers can be ordered on a line. But any two elements cannot always be ordered according to the semi-ordering of vectors and matrices. A comparison is possible only for two elements standing in a very special relation to each other. Therefore, this sort of ordering should more exactly be called partial ordering or semi-ordering.

For $n = 2$, $x \leqq y$ may be graphically represented by fig. 15.1. In this case, y lies in the northeast of x and x lies in the southwest of y. But x and z cannot be ordered.

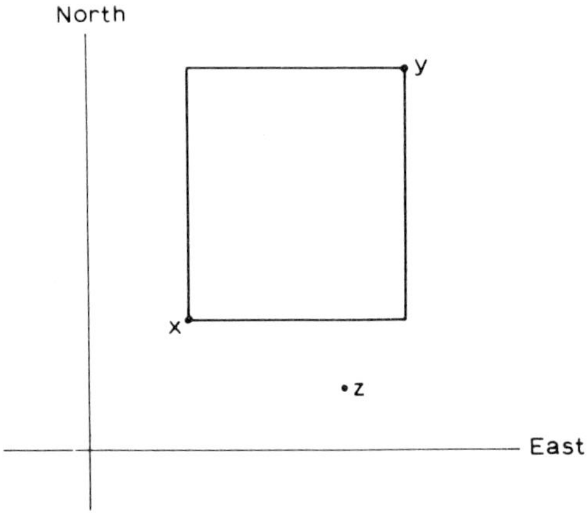

Fig. 15.1.

In short, when we understand correctly what is meant by the semi-ordering $\geqq$, we can easily prove the basic properties mentioned above as well as such as often employed rules like "$A \geqq 0, B \geqq C \Rightarrow AB \geqq AC$" that are not listed here.

Now we give a convenient criterion:

THEOREM 15.1. (i) *Let* $R^n \ni x, y$. $x \geqq y$ *if and only if* $(x, u) \geqq (y, u)$ *for any* $u \geqq 0$, $u \in R^n$.

(ii) *Let A and B be two nth order square matrices.* $A \geqq B$ *if and only if* $Au \geqq Bu$ *for any* $u \geqq 0$, $u \in R^n$.

Proof. Both (i) and (ii) can be easily and similarly proved. Here we present the proof of (ii) only. The necessity is obvious from the basic relations given above. To prove the sufficiency, take $u = e^j$ (a vector whose jth component is 1 and all others 0) for the criterion. Then, $Ae^j \geqq Be^j$ and $e^j \geqq 0$. Note that

Ae^j is the jth column vector a^j of A and Be^j the jth column vector b^j of B. $a^j \geqq b^j$ implies inequalities $a_{ij} \geqq b_{ij}$ $(i = 1, 2, ..., n)$. By changing j, we get $a_{ij} \geqq b_{ij}$ $(i, j = 1, 2, ..., n)$. $\therefore A \geqq B$.

Semi-ordering and topology. We saw many properties related to the concept of convergence in R^n. Now notice that an nth order square matrix is determined by n^2 elements and that the addition, subtraction, and scalar multiplication of matrices are defined as operations on matrix elements. They are equivalent to linear operations on vectors with n^2 components. Therefore, we are justified to treat the whole of nth order square matrices as an n^2-dimensional linear space R^{n^2}. The concept of convergence and topology can be carried over into it in a straightforward manner without any modifications. Almost all topological considerations in a linear space can be applied to matrices.

Let a_{ij} be the elements of a matrix A. Then, the norm of the matrix

$$\|A\| = \sqrt{\sum_{i,j=1}^{n} |a_{ij}|^2}, \quad \|A\|_1 = \sum_{i,j=1}^{n} |a_{ij}|, \quad \|A\|_2 = \max_{1 \leqq i,j \leqq n} |a_{ij}|$$

can be introduced just as in the case of a vector. Theorem 11.1 teaches us that the concept of convergence defined in terms of these norms is built up from that of convergence of each matrix element that is a real number. Whenever we encounter such a statement as "a sequence of matrices $\{A_\nu\}$ converges to a matrix A", we should take it to mean

$$(15.11) \qquad \lim_{\nu\to\infty} a_{ij\nu} = a_{ij} \quad \text{(for any } i \text{ and } j\text{)}$$

where $a_{ij\nu}$ and a_{ij} are the elements of A_ν and A respectively.

For sequences of matrices $\{A_\nu\}$ and $\{B_\nu\}$, a sequence of points $\{x^\nu\}$, and a sequence of numbers $\{\alpha_\nu\}$, we get the following relations on the assumption that $\lim_{\nu\to\infty} A_\nu = A$, $\lim_{\nu\to\infty} B_\nu = B$, $\lim_{\nu\to\infty} x^\nu = x$, and $\lim_{\nu\to\infty} \alpha_\nu = \alpha$;

$$(15.12) \qquad \lim_{\nu\to\infty} (A_\nu \pm B_\nu) = A \pm B,$$

$$(15.13) \qquad \lim_{\nu\to\infty} \alpha_\nu A_\nu = \alpha A,$$

$$(15.14) \qquad \lim_{\nu\to\infty} A_\nu B_\nu = AB.$$

$$(15.15) \qquad \lim_{\nu\to\infty} A_\nu x^\nu = Ax,$$

(15.16) if $A_\nu \geqq 0$ $(\nu = 1, 2, ...)$, then $A \geqq 0$; if $x^\nu \geqq 0$ $(\nu = 1, 2, ...)$, then $x \geqq 0$.

These relations can be easily proved in view of (15.11). The reader may try them.

Theorem 8.2 on bounded monotonic sequences can be extended to a sequence of points $\{x^{\nu}\}$ and a sequence of matrices $\{A_{\nu}\}$.

THEOREM 15.2. (i) *If* x^{ν} *is increasing, i.e.* $x^{\nu} \leqq x^{\nu+1}$ $(\nu = 1, 2, \ldots)$, *and bounded from above, i.e.* $x^{\nu} \leqq a$ $(\nu = 1, 2, \ldots)$, *then* $\{x^{\nu}\}$ *converges.*

(ii) *If* $\{A_{\nu}\}$ *is increasing, i.e.* $A_{\nu} \leqq A_{\nu+1}$ $(\nu = 1, 2, \ldots)$ *and bounded from above, i.e.* $A_{\nu} \leqq A$ $(\nu = 1, 2, \ldots)$, *then* $\{A_{\nu}\}$ *converges.*

a and A are upper bounds placed above these sequences in the semi-ordering sense. The same conclusions hold when "decreasing" is substituted for "increasing" and "bounded from below" for "bounded from above".

Proof. All sequences $\{x_i^{\nu}\}$ $(i = 1, 2, \ldots, n)$ whose terms are components of $\{x^{\nu}\}$ and all sequences $\{a_{ij\nu}\}$ $(i, j = 1, 2, \ldots, n)$ whose terms are elements of $\{A_{\nu}\}$ are bounded, increasing sequences by assumption. Hence, they converge. [Q.E.D.]

Non-negative inverse matrices. For its future applications, we may restate in a matrix notation what we learned about the equation system (3.1) in Section 3. Let B be the coefficient matrix of (3.1), c the vector of constant terms, and x the solution vector. The *off-diagonal elements* of B are 0 or negative $(b_{ij} \leqq 0, i \neq j)$. We have

$$(15.17) \qquad Bx = c.$$

We may restate the three (equivalent) conditions on this equation system (namely, (I), (II) and (H-S) in Section 3):

(I) weak solvability. For some $c > 0$, (15.17) has a non-negative solution $x \geqq 0$.

(II) strong solvability. For any $c \geqq 0$, (15.17) has a non-negative solution $x \geqq 0$.

(H-S) In

$$B = \begin{bmatrix} b_{11} & b_{12} & \cdots & b_{1n} \\ b_{21} & b_{22} & \cdots & b_{2n} \\ \cdots & \cdots & \cdots & \cdots \\ b_{n1} & b_{n2} & \cdots & b_{nn} \end{bmatrix},$$

its principal minors in the upper left-hand corner are positive, i.e.

$$\begin{vmatrix} b_{11} & b_{12} & \cdots & b_{1k} \\ b_{21} & b_{22} & \cdots & b_{2k} \\ \cdots & \cdots & \cdots & \cdots \\ b_{k1} & b_{k2} & \cdots & b_{kk} \end{vmatrix} > 0 \quad (k = 1, 2, \ldots, n) .$$

When (H-S) holds, we have $\det B \neq 0$ in particular so that there exists B^{-1} by virtue of Theorem 10.2. Letting c be an arbitrary non-negative vector, we see that there exists a non-negative solution $x \geqq 0$ because of (II). Indeed, $x = B^{-1}c$. Hence, for any $c \geqq 0$, we have $B^{-1}c \geqq 0$. Theorem 15.1 shows that $B^{-1} \geqq 0$. Conversely, assume that there exists B^{-1} and that $B^{-1} \geqq 0$. Then, as (II) holds, B satisfies (H-S). From this follows the theorem below.

THEOREM 15.3. *In order that a matrix B with 0 or negative off-diagonal elements may have a non-negative inverse matrix, it is necessary and sufficient that B satisfies (H-S).*

Applying this finding to the coefficient matrix of (15.1), we get

COROLLARY. *Let A be a non-negative nth order square matrix, I an nth order identity matrix, and ρ a real number. In order that $\rho I - A$ may have a non-negative inverse matrix $(\rho I - A)^{-1}$, it is necessary and sufficient that $\rho I - A$ satisfies (H-S).*

16. The non-negative eigenvalue problem

For a non-negative matrix A, let $B(\rho) = \rho I - A$ where I is an identity matrix and ρ a real-valued parameter. Consider M, the collection of all such real numbers ρ that $B(\rho)$ satisfies (H-S). M is a subset of the real number system. We can easily verify that M is not empty, as will be shown below. Take any positive vector $x > 0$. Then, by assigning a sufficiently large positive number to ρ, we can have $\rho x > Ax$ because the components of x are all positive. Hence, $B(\rho)x = \rho x - Ax > 0$. In other words, condition (I) holds for a sufficiently large value of ρ. Therefore, $B(\rho)$ satisfies condition (H-S) so that $\rho \in M$ in this case.

Next, we show that if some ρ belongs to M, all real numbers larger than ρ belong to M. Let $\eta \geqq \rho$. Then, $B(\eta) - B(\rho) = (\eta - \rho)I \geqq 0$. $\therefore B(\eta) \geqq B(\rho)$. As $\rho \in M$, we can get $B(\rho)x > 0$ by choosing some non-negative * $x \geqq 0$ accord-

* As is easily seen, we have in fact $x > 0$.

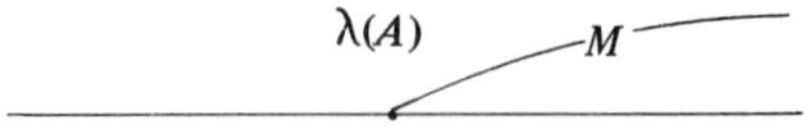

Fig. 16.1.

ing to condition (I). Then, for this x, we obtain $B(\eta)x \geqq B(\rho)x > 0$ so that $B(\eta)$ satisfies condition (I) and, hence, condition (H-S). Then, $\eta \in M$.

Then, what will happen if we try to make ρ as small as possible subject to condition (H-S). First of all, we can easily see that ρ cannot be made indefinitely small. That is, ρ is bounded from below. In fact, for $\rho \in M$, there exists $x \geqq 0$ such that $B(\rho)x > 0$ by virtue of (I). Then, $\rho x > Ax \geqq 0$ and hence $\rho > 0$, which indicates that M is bounded from below (0 is one of the lower bounds). With this in mind, let

(16.1) $\lambda(A) = \inf \rho$ (the infimum for all $\rho \in M$).

Then, obviously

$$\lambda(A) \geqq 0.$$

Now, if $\lambda(A) \in M$, $\lambda(A)$ would be the minimum of M. As a matter of fact, however, always $\lambda(A) \notin M$. We shall explain why. If $\lambda = \lambda(A) \in M$, there exists $x \geqq 0$ such that $B(\lambda)x = \lambda x - Ax > 0$ because of condition (I). Then, by choosing ρ that is less than but sufficiently close to λ, we still have $B(\rho)x = \rho x - Ax > 0$ for the same x so that $\rho \in M$. This contradicts the definition (16.1). $\therefore \lambda(A) \notin M$.

The preceding discussion has demonstrated that M is an open interval $(\lambda(A), +\infty)$. As $\lambda = \lambda(A) \notin M$, the equation

(16.2) $(\lambda I - A)x = c$

has no non-negative solution x for any $c > 0$ by the definition of M. Then, is it true that a homogeneous equation that puts $c = 0$ in (16.2), i.e.

(16.3) $(\lambda I - A)x = 0$,

has a non-negative solution x? $x = 0$ is, of course, a solution of (16.3). What we are now concerned with is a solution $x \geqq 0$ other than $x = 0$. To examine this problem is the main subject of the present section. Before proceeding further, however, let us first look at the problem from the point of view of the *eigenvalue problem* in general.

A given matrix * A induces a linear mapping $x \to Ax$: $R^n \to R^n$. If a vector $x \in R^n$ other than 0 is converted under this mapping into a vector which is λ times itself, namely

(16.4) $$\lambda x = Ax, \quad x \neq 0 ,$$

then λ is called an *eigenvalue* of A and x an *eigenvector* associated with λ. (16.4) can be rewritten as

(16.5) $$(\lambda I - A)x = 0 , \quad x \neq 0 .$$

Then, if λ is an eigenvalue, (16.5) has a solution $x \neq 0$ so that

(16.6) $$\varphi(\lambda) = \det(\lambda I - A) = 0 .$$

Conversely, if λ is a root of (16.6), (16.5) has a solution $x \neq 0$ and can be rewritten in the form of (16.4). Thus, the eigenvalues of A and the roots of (16.6) coincide with each other. (16.6) is called the *characteristic* or *latent equation* of A. For $A = [a_{ij}]$, we have

(16.7) $$\varphi(\lambda) = \begin{vmatrix} \lambda - a_{11} & -a_{12} & \cdots & -a_{1n} \\ -a_{21} & \lambda - a_{22} & \cdots & -a_{2n} \\ \cdots & \cdots & \cdots & \cdots \\ -a_{n1} & -a_{n2} & \cdots & \lambda - a_{nn} \end{vmatrix}$$

When expanded on λ according to the properties of determinants, $\varphi(\lambda)$ becomes an nth order polynomial:

(16.8) $$\varphi(\lambda) = \lambda^n + a_1 \lambda^{n-1} + \ldots + a_{n-1}\lambda + a_n .$$

The coefficients $a_1, a_2, \ldots, a_n$ are polynomials of the elements a_{ij}'s of A. Therefore, (16.8) is an nth order polynomial with real coefficients. The so-called fundamental theorem † in algebra demonstrates that (16.6) has n complex roots, which in general are not real numbers. For instance,

Example 16.1. $A = \begin{bmatrix} 0 & 1 \\ -1 & 0 \end{bmatrix}$ has a characteristic equation $\varphi(\lambda) = \begin{vmatrix} \lambda & -1 \\ 1 & \lambda \end{vmatrix} = \lambda^2 + 1 = 0$, whose roots $\lambda = \pm i$ (where i is the imaginary unit) are not real.

* A need not be subject to $A \geqq 0$ in the discussion of the eigenvalue problem in general.

† This fundamental theorem in algebra states that "an algebraic equation with complex coefficients always has some complex numbers as its roots". There are several proofs of the theorem, all of which require topological considerations, though elementary. The interested reader may consult, e.g. L.V.Ahlfors, *Complex Analysis* (McGraw-Hill, 1953), p. 99. As our discussions in this book are not based on this theorem, its proof is left to other books.

This indicates that we must introduce eigenvectors whose components are complex numbers in considering the eigenvalue problem in general even for a matrix A with real elements. As most of the basic theorems of determinants hold for complex numbers if complex vectors and matrices are introduced, it is certain that for each root of $\varphi(\lambda) = 0$ there is always a complex vector which is a solution of (16.5) and that λ is an eigenvalue.

We now proceed to examining the existence of a non-negative solution $x \geq 0$ of (16.3), while comparing it to the general discussion given above. The crux of the problem lies in a remarkable fact that, for a non-negative matrix A, $\lambda(A)$ as defined in (16.1) is not only a root of the characteristic equation but also has a non-negative vector among eigenvectors associated with itself.

THEOREM 16.1. *If $A \geqq 0$, equation (16.3) has a non-negative solution other than 0 for $\lambda = \lambda(A)$.*

Proof. Choose one $c > 0$ and keep it fixed. Then, consider equation

$$(16.9) \qquad (\rho I - A)x = c$$

for any $\rho \in M$, where M is the set that was defined earlier in this section.

Now, as the solution of (16.9) $x \geqq 0$ is uniquely determined for $\rho \in M$, we write it as $x(\rho)$. Then, an interesting relation

$$(16.10) \qquad x(\sigma) \geqq x(\tau) \qquad (\text{for } \sigma \leqq \tau;\ \sigma, \tau \in M)$$

holds. To prove this, subtract

$$(\sigma I - A)\, x(\sigma) = c \qquad \text{and} \qquad (\tau I - A) x(\tau) = c$$

from one another to get

$$(\sigma I - A)(x(\sigma) - x(\tau)) = (\tau - \sigma) x(\tau)\,;$$

as $\sigma \in M$, there exists $(\sigma I - A)^{-1} \geqq 0$ so that

$$x(\sigma) - x(\tau) = (\tau - \sigma)(\sigma I - A)^{-1} x(\tau) \geqq 0$$

by virtue of $\tau \geqq \sigma$ and $x(\tau) \geqq 0$. $\therefore x(\sigma) \geqq x(\tau)$.

Let $\{\rho_\nu\}$, $\rho_\nu \in M$ be a decreasing sequence for which $\lim_{\nu \to \infty} \rho_\nu = \lambda = \lambda(A)$. The existence of such a sequence is apparent from the definition (16.1) and the properties of the infimum. Then, (16.10) ensures that

$$(16.11) \qquad x(\rho_{\nu+1}) \geqq x(\rho_\nu) \qquad (\nu = 1, 2, \ldots)\,.$$

Putting

$$\eta_\nu = \sum_{j=1}^{n} x_j(\rho_\nu) \qquad \text{(the sum of components)} ,$$

we see from (16.11) that $\{\eta_\nu\}$ is an increasing sequence.

Consider first the case where $\{\eta_\nu\}$ is bounded from above. Then, the sequence of points $\{x(\rho_\nu)\}$ is also bounded from above in the sense of semi-ordered vectors *. With (16.11) taken into account, Theorem 15.2 shows that there exists $\lim\limits_{\nu\to\infty} x(\rho_\nu) = x \geqq 0$. Then, letting $\nu \to \infty$ ** in

$$(16.12) \qquad (\rho_\nu I - A)x(\rho_\nu) = c ,$$

we get

$$(\lambda I - A)x = c, \quad x \geqq 0$$

in the limit as $\nu \to \infty$. This implies $\lambda \in M$. This is a contradiction, as we have already demonstrated $\lambda \notin M$. Therefore, $\{\eta_\nu\}$ cannot be bounded from above. Hence, $\lim\limits_{\nu\to\infty} \eta_\nu = +\infty$ by Theorem 8.2.

Multiply $1/\eta_\nu$ on both sides of (16.12) and put $y^\nu = x(\rho_\nu)/\eta_\nu$ to get

$$(16.13) \qquad (\rho_\nu I - A)y^\nu = c/\eta_\nu \qquad (\nu = 1, 2, \ldots) .$$

Observe the set $S_n = \{x | x_j \text{ (component of } x) \geqq 0 \ (j = 1, 2, \ldots, n), \sum_{j=1}^{n} x_j = 1\}$. Obviously, $y^\nu \in S_n$ $(\nu = 1, 2, \ldots)$. As S_n is compact (see Example 14.4), $\{y^\nu\}$ contains a subsequence that converges within S_n. The corresponding subsequence of $\{\eta_\nu\}$ with indexes corresponding to it still diverges toward $+\infty$. Therefore, without loss of generality, we may assume that $\{y^\nu\}$ itself converges, namely $\lim\limits_{\nu\to\infty} y^\nu = x \in S^n$ †.

After these preliminaries, let $\nu \to \infty$ in (16.13). Its right-hand side converges to $\lim\limits_{\nu\to\infty} c/\eta_\nu = 0$. In the limit, therefore, we get

$$(\lambda I - A)x = 0, \qquad x \in S_n ,$$

* $x_j(\rho_\nu) \leqq \eta_\nu \leqq \sup\limits_\nu \eta_\nu < +\infty$.

** According to the properties given for semi-ordering and topology in Section 15.

† This procedure is a routine employed when we make use of the property of compactness. Its objective is to avoid the use of complicated suffixes in subsequences.

that is, $\lambda = \lambda(A)$ is an eigenvalue of A and x is a non-negative eigenvector associated with λ. [Q.E.D.]

Remark. As we have already noted, $\varphi(\lambda) = \det(\lambda I - A)$ is an nth order polynomial of λ. If it is considered a real-valued function of a real variable λ, we see from our findings above that, for a non-negative matrix A, $\varphi(\lambda) = 0$ when $\lambda = \lambda(A)$ and $\varphi(\lambda) > 0$ when $\lambda > \lambda(A)$ because of the (H-S) condition. This shows that $\lambda(A)$ is the largest real root of the equation $\varphi(\lambda) = 0$. We now move to a new section to present a number of important results including the relation of this largest root to other (in general, complex) roots.

17. The Frobenius root

Let A be a non-negative matrix and $\varphi(\lambda) = 0$ be the characteristic equation of A. Its largest root, whose existence was proved in the preceding section, is called the *Frobenius root.* This name is after G.Frobenius (1849–1917) who studied this type of problems. The theorem below summarizes a number of its important properties including those studied in the preceding section.

THEOREM 17.1 *(the Frobenius Theorem). Let A be a non-negative matrix.*

(i) *A has non-negative real eigenvalues. There exists a non-negative eigenvector $x \geq 0$ associated with the largest non-negative eigenvalue $\lambda(A)$.*

(ii) *The real number μ, for which $Ax \geqq \mu x$ holds for some $x \geq 0$, satisfies an inequality $\mu \leqq \lambda(A)$.*

In particular, let ω be any eigenvalue (in general, complex) of A. Then, $|\omega| \leqq \lambda(A)$ where $|\omega|$ is the absolute value of the complex number ω.

(iii) *$\lambda(A)$ is an increasing function of A; namely if $A_1 \geqq A_2 \geqq 0$, then $\lambda(A_1) \geqq \lambda(A_2)$.*

(iv) *Let ρ be a real number and I an nth order identity matrix. Then, $\rho I - A$ has a non-negative inverse matrix $(\rho I - A)^{-1}$ if and only if $\rho > \lambda(A)$.*

(v) $\lambda(A) = \lambda(A')$.

Proof. In Section 16, we learned that, for the set M of real numbers ρ for which $(\rho I - A)^{-1} \geqq 0$ exists,

(a) $M = (\lambda(A), +\infty)$ where $\lambda(A) = \inf \rho$ (the infimum of $\rho \in M$);

(b) A has a non-negative eigenvector $x \geq 0$ associated with $\lambda(A)$.

(i) and (iv) are both thereby proved. The remaining (ii), (iii), and (v) can be easily proved as follows:

(ii) Let $Ax \geqq \mu x$, $x \geq 0$. Then, we rewrite the first inequality as $(\mu I - A)x \leqq 0$. If $\mu > \lambda(A)$, there exists $(\mu I - A)^{-1} \geqq 0$ because of (iv). As the inequality is pre-multiplied by the latter, we get $x \leqq (\mu I - A)^{-1} 0 = 0$. $\therefore x \leqq 0$. This is in contradiction with $x \geq 0$. Hence, $\mu \leqq \lambda(A)$.

Next, denote by ω an eigenvalue in general. $z \neq 0$ is an eigenvector associated with it (in general, whose components are complex numbers). We have $Az = \omega z$, which is expressed as

$$\omega z_i = \sum_{j=1}^{n} a_{ij} z_j \quad (j = 1, 2, ..., n)$$

by component. Evaluating it in absolute values, we get

$$|\omega||z_i| = |\omega z_i| = |\sum_{j=1}^{n} a_{ij} z_j| \leqq \sum_{j=1}^{n} a_{ij} |z_j| \ .$$

Denote by $|z|$ the non-negative vector whose jth component is $|z_j|$. Then, this result is equivalent to

$$A|z| \geqq |\omega||z|, \quad |z| \geq 0 \ .$$

By virtue of the first half of (ii), we therefore obtain $|\omega| \leqq \lambda(A)$.

(iii) We defined M to be the set of ρ for which a non-negative inverse matrix $(\rho I - A)^{-1}$ exists. This set is changed as A is altered. Hence, we represent it as $M(A)$. Consider $M(A_1)$ and $M(A_2)$ for $A_1 \geqq A_2 \geqq 0$. We see $M(A_1) \subset M(A_2)$. In fact, if $\rho \in M(A_1)$, then $(\rho I - A_1)x > 0$ for some $x \geqq 0$. On the other hand, $\rho I - A_2 \geqq \rho I - A_1$ by assumption so that $(\rho I - A_2)x > 0$ for the same x. Hence, condition (I) (weak solvability) holds and $\rho \in M(A_2)$. This proves that $M(A_1) \subset M(A_2)$. As the range of real numbers for which an infimum is sought is broader in $M(A_2)$, we have

$$\lambda(A_2) = \inf_{\rho \in M(A_2)} \rho \leqq \inf_{\rho \in M(A_1)} \rho = \lambda(A_1).$$

(v) The characteristic equations of A and A' are $\det(\lambda I - A) = 0$ and $\det(\lambda I - A') = 0$ respectively. Their left-hand sides are transposes of each other so that their roots are identical. In particular, their largest non-negative roots, viz. the Frobenius roots, are equal. [Q.E.D.]

Remark 1. Let $L(A)$ be the set of real numbers μ which satisfy $Ax \geqq \mu x$ for some $x \geq 0$, as discussed in (ii) above. By virtue of (ii), $\mu \leqq \lambda(A)$ if

$\mu \in L(A)$. Also by virtue of (i), $Ax = \lambda(A)x$ for some $x \geqq 0$. This is a case where $Ax \geqq \mu x$ holds. Hence, $\lambda(A)$ itself belongs to $L(A)$. Further, for a real number μ such that $\mu \leqq \lambda(A)$, we have $Ax = \lambda(A)x \geqq \mu x$ for the eigenvector $x \geqq 0$ associated with $\lambda(A)$. Hence, $\mu \in L(A)$. $L(A)$ is therefore an interval which starts from a right-hand end point $\lambda(A)$ and runs toward infinity on the left, i.e. $L(A) = (-\infty, \lambda(A)]$. This divides the real number system R at $\lambda(A)$ into two intervals $L(A) = (-\infty, \lambda(A)]$ and $M(A) = (\lambda(A), +\infty)$.

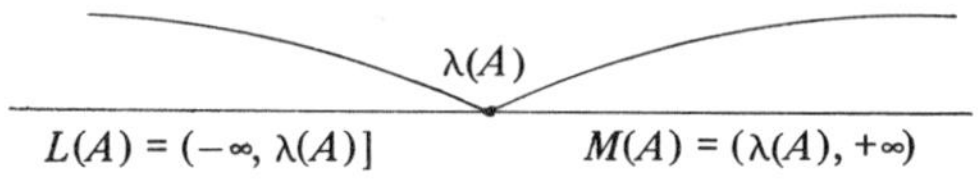

Fig. 17.1.

Remark 2. In this book, we have started from the (H-S) condition and arrived finally at the Frobenius root $\lambda(A)$ by gradually reducing the value of ρ within the set $M(A)$. We may recall that we have made effective use of the compactness of the set

$$S_n = \{x \mid x_i \geqq 0, \sum_{i=1}^{n} x_i = 1\}$$

in this approach. The existence of the Frobenius root can also be proved by Brouwer's fixed point theorem as we shall discuss later *. However, the fixed point theorem itself requires not only the compactness of S_n but also a deeper analysis of its topological properties for its proof. Therefore, it is very roundabout as the existence proof of the Frobenius root.

In what follows, we outline a more direct proof of the theorem than the one we have given above. This alternate proof provides a good exercise for making use of the basic knowledge we acquired in Chapter 2. The reader is urged to undertake the proof in full details along the lines to be indicated below.

In the foregoing proof we started from the set $M(A)$ and arrived at $\lambda(A)$. As a by-product, we clarified the structure of the set $L(A)$. In the alternate proof, we reverse the order and start from $L(A)$. The steps of the proof are outlined below.

Step 1. Indicate that $L(A) \neq \phi$ and that $L(A)$ is bounded from above.

Step 2. Let $\lambda = \sup \mu$ (the supremum of $\mu \in L(A)$). Consider a sequence of

* See Section 43.

numbers $\{\lambda_\nu\}$ and a sequence of points $\{x^\nu\}$ for which $\lim_{\nu\to\infty} \lambda_\nu = \lambda$, $Ax^\nu \geqq \lambda_\nu x^\nu$ and $x^\nu \in S_n$. Note that $\lambda \in L(A)$ by virtue of the compactness of S_n. This proves that λ is the largest number of $L(A)$. Put $\lambda = \lambda(A)$. Then, by definition, there exists some $x \geq 0$, for which

$$Ax \geqq \lambda(A)x \,. \tag{17.1}$$

Step 3. It can be easily shown that the equality sign holds in (17.1) for a positive matrix $A > 0$. (To see this, multiply both sides by A, assuming that the equality does not hold.) This shows that $\lambda(A)$ is the Frobenius root when A is a positive matrix.

Step 4. If $A_1 \geqq A_2 \geqq 0$, then $\lambda(A_1) \geqq \lambda(A_2)$. This proof immediately follows by definition from $L(A_1) \supset L(A_2)$, once the latter is proved. Then, to prove the existence of the Frobenius root for a non-negative $A = [a_{ij}] \geqq 0$ in general on the basis of the result obtained for a positive matrix, take a sequence of positive numbers $\{\epsilon_\nu\}$ converging monotonically toward 0 and consider a positive matrix $A_\nu = [a_{ij\nu}]$, $a_{ij\nu} = a_{ij} + \epsilon_\nu$ $(\nu = 1, 2, ...)$ that approaches A from above. Take an eigenvector $x^\nu \in S_n$ that is associated with $\lambda(A_\nu)$. Then,

$$A_\nu x^\nu = \lambda(A_\nu)x^\nu \quad (\nu = 1, 2, ...) \tag{17.2}$$

and

$$\lambda(A_1) \geqq \lambda(A_2) \geqq ... \geqq \lambda(A_\nu) \geqq \lambda(A_{\nu+1}) \geqq ... \geqq \lambda(A) \geqq 0 \,, \tag{17.3}$$

which shows that $\lambda(A_\nu)$ converges. However, as $\{x^\nu\}$ does not necessarily converge, take a suitable subsequence by virtue of the compactness of S_n to show that, in fact, $\lim_{\nu\to\infty} \lambda(A_\nu) = \lambda(A)$. This proves that there exists a non-negative eigenvector associated with $\lambda(A)$.

These steps provide an alternate proof of (i), (ii) and (iii) of Theorem 17.1. We next outline how to prove (iv). Step 4 has demonstrated that $\{\lambda(A_\nu)\}$ monotonically converges to $\lambda(A)$. Hence, if $\rho > \lambda(A)$, then $\rho > \lambda(A_\nu)$ at a certain appropriate number ν. Take $x^\nu \geq 0$, a non-negative eigenvector associated with $\lambda(A_\nu)$. Then, $A_\nu x^\nu = \lambda(A_\nu)x^\nu$. As $A^\nu > 0$, it follows that $A_\nu x^\nu > 0$. $\therefore$ $\lambda(A_\nu) > 0$, $x^\nu > 0$ so that $\lambda(A_\nu)x^\nu < \rho x^\nu$ and $A_\nu x^\nu < \rho x^\nu$. This together with $A \leqq A_\nu$ makes $Ax^\nu < \rho x^\nu$ hold, i.e. condition (I) (weak solvability) holds. Therefore, $(\rho I - A)^{-1}$ exists. The sufficiency of (iv) is thus proved. To prove its necessity, follow the original proof and take note that $\rho \in L(A)$ if $\lambda(A) \geqq \rho$, i.e. that $(\rho I - A)x \leqq 0$ for some $x \geq 0$. Pre-multiply it by $(\rho I - A)^{-1} \geqq 0$, the existence of which is assumed. Then, we obtain $x \leq 0$, which contradicts $x \geq 0$.

Remark 3. This reasoning can be applied directly to prove the following more general proposition *:

Consider the three assumptions below.

(a) Real-valued functions $\varphi_i(x)$ $(i = 1, 2, ..., n)$ are given and assumed to be continuous for $x \in R^n$, $x \geq 0$;

(b) They are increasing, namely $\varphi_i(x) \geqq \varphi_i(y)$ $(i = 1, 2, ..., n)$ for $x \geqq y$;

(c) They are subject to positive linear homogeneity, namely $\varphi_i(\lambda x) = \lambda \varphi_i(x)$ $(i = 1, 2, ..., n)$, $\lambda > 0$.

On these assumptions, there exists a maximum $\mu(\varphi)$ among μ such that $\varphi_i(x) \geqq \mu x_i$ $(i = 1, 2, ..., n)$ for some $x \geq 0$. Corresponding to this $\mu(\varphi)$,

$$\varphi_i(x) = \mu(\varphi) x_i \qquad (i = 1, 2, ..., n)$$

holds for an appropriate $x \geq 0$.

Its proof can be worked out in four steps similarly as outlined above. In this case, strictly increasing φ_i (i.e. $\varphi_i(x) > \varphi_i(y)$ $(i = 1, 2, ..., n)$ for $x \geq y$) play the role of the positive matrix. To approximate general φ_i (that satisfies (a), (b) and (c)) from above, take e.g.

$$\varphi_i(x) + \epsilon \sum_{j=1}^{n} x_j$$

and make the positive number ϵ less and less.

Looking back at our progress up to this point, we note that our start in Chapter 1 from the proof of equivalence of the three conditions (I), (II) and (H-S) with respect to the matrix $B = [b_{ij}]$ $(b_{ij} \leqq 0$ $(i \neq j))$ has brought us to the Frobenius root $\lambda(A)$ of a non-negative matrix A. Now as an application of our findings, let us examine the relation between the eigenvalues of the matrix B and the three conditions.

THEOREM 17.2. *Let the elements of the matrix B be $b_{ij} \leqq 0$ $(i \neq j)$. Its three (mutually equivalent) conditions (I), (II) and (H-S) are equivalent to the condition:*

(III) *The real part of any eigenvalue of B is positive.*

Proof. Denote the real part of a complex number α by Re (α). As off-diagonal elements of $-B$ are non-negative, we see that

$$(17.4) \qquad A = \rho I - B$$

* It was proved by R.M.Solow and P.A.Samuelson [50] by means of Brouwer's fixed point theorem.

is a non-negative matrix for a sufficiently large positive number ρ. Let $\lambda(A)$ be the Frobenius root of A. We prove that (H-S) $\Leftrightarrow$ (III).

(i) *Necessity.* Assume that B satisfies the (H-S) condition. Then, for any eigenvalue β (in general, complex number) of B, we have

$$0 = \det(\beta I - B) = \det(-\beta I + B) = \det((\rho - \beta) I - (\rho I - B))$$

$$= \det((\rho - \beta) I - A)\,.$$

Hence, $(\rho - \beta)$ is an eigenvalue of A so that $|\rho - \beta| \leqq \lambda(A)$ because of (ii) of Theorem 17.1.

$$\therefore \rho - \mathrm{Re}(\beta) = \mathrm{Re}(\rho - \beta) \leqq |\rho - \beta| \leqq \lambda(A)\,.$$

On the other hand, $\rho I - A = B$ from (17.4). As B satisfies the (H-S) condition, $(\rho I - A)$ satisfies it, too. Because of (iv) of Theorem 17.1, $\rho > \lambda(A)$. $\therefore \rho - \mathrm{Re}(\beta) \leqq \lambda(A) < \rho$, from which we get $\mathrm{Re}(\beta) > 0$.

(ii) *Sufficiency.* Let the real part of any eigenvalue of B be positive. Take an eigenvector $x \geq 0$ of A associated with $\lambda(A)$. Then,

$$Bx = (\rho I - A)x = \rho x - Ax = \rho x - \lambda(A)x = (\rho - \lambda(A))x\,.$$

Hence, $\rho - \lambda(A)$ is an eigenvalue of B and yet real.

$$\therefore \rho - \lambda(A) = \mathrm{Re}(\rho - \lambda(A)) > 0$$

(by assumption), viz. $\rho > \lambda(A)$.
Therefore, by (iv) of Theorem 17.1, $B = \rho I - A$ satisfies the (H-S) condition. [Q.E.D.]

COROLLARY. *Let the elements of a matrix B be $b_{ij} \geqq 0$ $(i \neq j)$. The real part of any eigenvalue of B is negative if and only if the principal minors of B in the upper left-hand corner alternate in sign between negative and positive:*

$$(-1)^k \begin{vmatrix} b_{11} & b_{12} & \cdots & b_{1k} \\ b_{21} & b_{22} & \cdots & b_{2k} \\ \cdots & \cdots & \cdots & \cdots \\ b_{k1} & b_{k2} & \cdots & b_{kk} \end{vmatrix} > 0 \quad (k = 1, 2, \ldots, n)\,.$$

Proof. The off-diagonal elements of the matrix $-B$ are 0 or negative. $-B$ satisfies the condition of Theorem 17.2. Now, an eigenvalue of B gives rise to that of $-B$ when the sign of the former is changed. Therefore, the condition that the real part of any eigenvalue of B is negative is equivalent to the condition that the real part of any eigenvalue of $-B$ is positive. This enables us to apply Theorem 17.2 to $-B$ to obtain the desired conclusion.

18. Economic significance of the Frobenius root

The Frobenius theorem was already established in 1908 by Frobenius as a mathematical theorem. But it was only in recent years that it had come to be applied in mathematical economics. Our exposition in Sections 16 and 17 might have made it sufficiently clear how important the Frobenius root is in economics. We shall refer to a few examples in this section to draw some economic implications from our mathematical findings.

Uniform average value-added ratio. Consider an economy and let $A = [a_{ij}] \geqq 0$ be its input coefficient matrix. A is a non-negative nth order square matrix. As we noted earlier, a_{ij} is the input of the ith commodity required for the production of one unit of the jth commodity during one production period.

Denoting the price vector by p, we get

$$(18.1) \qquad p - A'p = v$$

and

$$(18.2) \qquad v = (v_1, v_2, ..., v_n)' .$$

We already noted that v_j is value-added per unit of the (jth) good produced in the jth sector. In general, v_j is the sum of profits and wages. Denote by ω_j the ratio of v_j to its cost of production

$$\sum_{i=1}^{n} a_{ij} p_i ,$$

namely

$$(18.3) \qquad v_j = \omega_j \sum_{i=1}^{n} a_{ij} p_i \quad (j = 1, 2, ..., n) .$$

Denote by $\lambda(A')$ the Frobenius root of A'. (18.1) has a certain price vector $p \geq 0$ as its solution for any given average values added $v \geq 0$, when $1 > \lambda(A')$. But sectoral value-added ratios ω_j are not necessarily uniformly equal. They are generally different sector from sector. Is there then a price vector that equates all sectoral average value-added ratios? To answer this question, let us put $\omega_1 = \omega_2 = ... = \omega_n = \omega$. Substituting $v = \omega A'p$ for v on the right-hand side of (18.1) and rearranging terms, we get

$$(18.4) \qquad p = (1+\omega)A'p\,.$$

As $1+\omega \neq 0$, we divide (18.4) by it to obtain

$$(18.5) \qquad \mu p = A'p, \quad p \geq 0$$

where

$$(18.6) \qquad \mu = \frac{1}{1+\omega}\,.$$

Therefore, the existence of a price vector that equates the average value-added ratios among the sectors reduces to the solvability of the non-negative eigenvalue problem (18.5). It was proved that this eigenvalue problem can be solved for $\mu = \lambda(A')$. There might be another solution *. But such a solution of μ must always satisfy $\mu \leqq \lambda(A')$ because of (ii) of Theorem 17.1. Hence, if there exists a uniform average value-added ratio ω, it satisfies an inequality $\omega \geqq 1/\lambda(A') - 1$ because of (18.6) (provided that $\lambda(A') > 0$). If $\lambda(A') < 1$, then the uniform average value-added ratio is positive. In particular, there in fact exists a price vector that realizes the minimum uniform ratio

$$\omega = \frac{1}{\lambda(A')} - 1\,.$$

Uniform profit rate. We have treated value added as a whole without decomposing it to profits and wages. Now let us be more faithful to reality and look at the proportion of profits to total cost of production. Let l_j be the amount of labor required to produce one unit of the jth good and w the wage rate (unit price of labor). Then, the average value added of the jth sector is divided between profits π_j and wages $l_j w$ so that

$$(18.7) \qquad v_j = \pi_j + l_j w \quad (j = 1, 2, ..., n)\,.$$

The jth sector's profits, therefore, satisfy

$$(18.8) \qquad p_j = \sum_{i=1}^{n} a_{ij} p_i + l_j w + \pi_j \quad (j = 1, 2, ..., n)\,.$$

* There is no other solution if A is an indecomposable matrix as we shall see later.

Let π and l be vectors whose jth components are π_j and l_j respectively. Then, we have

$$(18.9) \qquad p = A'p + wl + \pi.$$

The sum of the first two terms on the right-hand side of (18.8) is the total unit cost of production including wages. Hence, let the sectoral profit rates be ω_j so that

$$(18.10) \qquad \pi_j = \omega_j \left(\sum_{i=1}^{n} a_{ij} p_i + l_j w\right) \quad (j = 1, 2, ..., n)\,.$$

If the uniformity condition $\omega_1 = \omega_2 = ... = \omega_n = \omega$ holds, we substitute $\pi = \omega(A'p + wl)$ in (18.9) and get

$$(18.11) \qquad (\rho I - A')p = wl\,,$$

where

$$(18.12) \qquad \rho = \frac{1}{1+\omega}.$$

If labor is an indispensable *factor of production* in all sectors, we have $l > 0$. Then, $\rho > \lambda(A')$ is the condition that (18.11) has a solution for a given wage rate $w > 0$. In this case, the solution is given by $p = w(\rho I - A')^{-1} l$. Rewritten as a relation in ω by using (18.12), we can conclude that if

$$(18.13) \qquad \frac{1}{1+\omega} > \lambda(A')\,,$$

there exists a price vector

$$(18.14) \qquad p = w(1+\omega)(I - (1+\omega)A')^{-1} l$$

that realizes the uniform profit rate ω.

Balanced growth rate. It is difficult to make a direct application of the basic equation system of the interindustry analysis $(I - A)x = c$, which is obtained by putting $\rho = 1$ in (15.1), for the purpose of analyzing the process of economic change. This equation system states that outputs x during a given period are completely consumed to cover final demands c and inputs Ax during the same period. However, in reality there is a certain difference in timing between production and consumption. In general, consumption is behind production. This delay in time is called a *time lag.* For simplicity, let this lag be a unit period of time. Consider a changing economy. Outputs and final demands of the tth period ($t = 1, 2, \ldots$) are given by $x(t) \geqq 0$ and $c(t) \geqq 0$. In this economy, $x(t)$ is produced in period t and consumed in period $t + 1$. In other words, $x(t)$ covers final demands $c(t + 1)$ and inputs $Ax(t + 1)$ in period $t + 1$. This relation is expressed by

(18.15) $$x(t) = Ax(t+1) + c(t+1)\,.$$

Let us examine whether balanced growth is possible in this economy. We mean by the balanced growth the state of expansion (or contraction) of outputs and final demands in all sectors at a uniform rate. In the state of balanced growth,

(18.16) $$\begin{aligned} x_j(t+1) &= \gamma x_j(t) \qquad (j = 1, 2, \ldots, n) \\ c_i(t+1) &= \gamma c_i(t) \qquad (i = 1, 2, \ldots, n)\,. \end{aligned}$$

We put $\gamma = 1 + \alpha$ and call α the *rate of growth.* Assuming (18.16), we write (18.15) as

(18.17) $$(\rho I - A)\,x(t) = c(t)\,,$$

where

(18.18) $$\rho = 1/\gamma\,.$$

(18.17) is a relation between $x(t)$ and $c(t)$ in the same period. Moreover, this relation is equivalent to

(18.19) $$(\rho I - A)x(0) = c(0)\,,$$

at $t = 0$ in view of (18.16). (18.19) has a non-negative solution $x(0)$ for $c(0) > 0$ if and only if $\rho > \lambda(A)$ as we have seen. Expressed in terms of $\gamma > 0$, this is stated as follows: If $\gamma - 1$ is the rate of growth implied in a balanced growth solution (18.16), we have

(18.20) $$1/\gamma > \lambda(A)\,.$$

Also, if γ satisfies (18.20), balanced growth (18.16) is feasible, starting from any $c(0) > 0$.

19. C.Neumann series

According to the basic system of equations of the interindustry analysis, gross outputs $x \geqq 0$ that yield net outputs exactly matching given final demands $c \geqq 0$ are obtained as $x = (I - A)^{-1}c$ by solving $(I - A)x = c$. In this section, we shall approach this correspondence between final demands and gross outputs from another direction.

To produce given final demands c, inputs Ac must be secured in the first instance. But Ac itself must be covered by outputs, for which $AAc = A^2c$ is required. Again the production of A^2c requires $AA^2c = A^3c$ and so on and so forth. We can keep on assessing the required inputs in this way. Therefore, we must produce

$$(19.1) \qquad c + Ac + A^2c + A^3c + \ldots + A^\nu c + \ldots$$

to realize net outputs c. It can be expected that this infinite series sums up exactly to actual gross outputs x. The purpose of this section is to examine this expectation of ours in mathematical terms.

In conjunction with (19.1) that is a series of vectors, we may consider a series of matrices

$$(19.2) \qquad \sum_{\nu=0}^{\infty} A^\nu = I + A + A^2 + \ldots + A^\nu + \ldots.$$

This is an extension of an infinite geometrical series

$$(19.3) \qquad \sum_{\nu=0}^{\infty} \alpha^\nu = 1 + \alpha + \alpha^2 + \ldots + \alpha^\nu + \ldots$$

to matrices. The sum of an infinite series like (19.1), (19.2), and (19.3) is defined as the limiting value of its partial sum up to its νth term. For instance, take the partial sum of (19.2)

$$T_\nu = I + A + A^2 + \ldots + A^\nu .$$

If there exists $\lim_{\nu \to \infty} T_\nu$ in the sense of a convergent sequence of matrices, the series (19.2) is said to be convergent and its sum is defined to be the limit of the sequence.

The problem of convergence of the vector series (19.1) is tantamount to that of convergence of (19.2) in view of our observations in Section 15, in particular the formula (15.15). Therefore, we shall examine a more general series

$$(19.4) \qquad \frac{1}{\rho}\sum_{\nu=0}^{\infty}\frac{A^\nu}{\rho^\nu} = \frac{1}{\rho}\,(I + \frac{1}{\rho}A + \frac{1}{\rho^2}A^2 + \ldots + \frac{1}{\rho^\nu}A^\nu + \ldots)$$

that covers (19.2) as a special case in order to clarify the relation of the convergence condition of this series to our earlier findings. C.Neumann (1832–1925) is a mathematician who studied infinite geometric series obtained as linear mappings in the linear space of infinite dimensions. This type of series is usually called C.Neumann series. The series (19.4) that we are going to study below is one of them.

THEOREM 19.1. *Let $\lambda(A)$ be the Frobenius root of a non-negative matrix A. Then,*

(i) *the series (19.4) converges if $\rho > \lambda(A)$, and its sum is $(\rho I - A)^{-1}$;*

(ii) *if the series (19.4) converges for some $\rho > 0$, then $\rho > \lambda(A)$ and its sum is $(\rho I - A)^{-1}$.*

Proof. In (i), $\rho > \lambda(A) \geqq 0$. Therefore, $\rho > 0$ both in (i) and (ii) so that each term in (19.4) is meaningful. The partial sum of (19.4) up to the νth term is given by

$$(19.5) \qquad T_\nu = \frac{1}{\rho}\left(I + \frac{1}{\rho}A + \frac{1}{\rho^2}A^2 + \dots + \frac{1}{\rho^\nu}A^\nu\right).$$

As $A \geqq 0$, we can easily see that $\{T_\nu\}$ is increasing, i.e.

$$(19.6) \qquad T_\nu \leqq T_{\nu+1} \quad (\nu = 0, 1, 2, \dots)$$

in the semi-ordering sense. We compute $(\rho I - A)T_\nu$ and obtain

$$\begin{aligned}(\rho I - A)\, T_\nu = T_\nu(\rho I - A) & \\ &= \left(I + \frac{1}{\rho}A + \frac{1}{\rho^2}A^2 + \dots + \frac{1}{\rho^\nu}A^\nu\right) \\ &\quad - \left(\frac{1}{\rho}A + \frac{1}{\rho^2}A^2 + \frac{1}{\rho^3}A^3 + \dots + \frac{1}{\rho^{\nu+1}}A^{\nu+1}\right) \\ &= I - \frac{1}{\rho^{\nu+1}}A^{\nu+1},\end{aligned}$$

so that

$$(19.7) \qquad (\rho I - A)T_\nu = T_\nu(\rho I - A) = I - \frac{1}{\rho^{\nu+1}}A^{\nu+1} \qquad (\nu = 0, 1, 2, \dots).$$

We now go on to prove (i) and (ii).

(i) As $A \geqq 0$ and $\rho > 0$, we have $-(1/\rho^{\nu+1})A^{\nu+1} \leqq 0$. Hence, from (19.7), we get

$$(19.8) \qquad (\rho I - A)T_\nu \leqq I \quad (\nu = 0, 1, 2, \ldots) .$$

By assumption, $\rho > \lambda(A)$ so that $\rho I - A$ has a non-negative inverse. Pre-multiplying both sides of (19.8) by $(\rho I - A)^{-1} \geqq 0$ does not change the inequality sign as we noted in Section 15.*. Hence,

$$T_\nu \leqq (\rho I - A)^{-1} \quad (\nu = 0, 1, 2, \ldots) .$$

Combined with (19.6), we see that $\{T_\nu\}$ is an increasing sequence bounded from above, i.e.

$$T_0 \leqq T_1 \leqq T_2 \ldots \leqq T_\nu \leqq T_{\nu+1} \leqq \ldots \leqq (\rho I - A)^{-1} .$$

$\{T_\nu\}$ converges because of (ii) of Theorem 15.2. Putting $\lim_{\nu\to\infty} T_\nu = T$, we get

$$(19.9) \qquad \lim_{\nu\to\infty} \frac{1}{\rho^\nu} A^\nu = \lim_{\nu\to\infty} \rho(T_{\nu+1} - T_\nu) = 0 .$$

Letting $\nu \to \infty$ in (19.7), we obtain

$$(\rho I - A)T = T(\rho I - A) = I .$$

$$\therefore T = (\rho I - A)^{-1}.$$

(ii) In view of $T_\nu \geqq 0$, we may observe that if (19.4) converges, and its limit is T, we have $T = \lim_{\nu\to\infty} T_\nu \geqq 0$, i.e. T is a non-negative matrix. As $\{T_\nu\}$ converges, the general term of (19.4) converges to 0 as in (19.9). Therefore, letting $\nu \to \infty$ in (19.7), we get $(\rho I - A)T = T(\rho I - A) = I$. Thus, $\rho I - A$ has a non-negative inverse matrix T so that $\rho > \lambda(A)$. [Q.E.D.]

As we have repeatedly pointed out, the solvability conditions (I), (II), and (H-S) of the equation system $(\rho I - A)x = c$ are all equivalent to the condition $\rho > \lambda(A)$. Therefore, Theorem 19.1 has clarified the relation between these conditions and that of convergence of (19.4). The corollary below deals with the special case of $\rho = 1$ in Theorem 19.1.

COROLLARY. *The condition* $1 > \lambda(A)$ *is necessary and sufficient for the convergence of the series (19.2).*

Iterative method. The series (19.4) provides an iterative method to obtain

* See (15.5).

the inverse matrix of $\rho I - A$. The partial sum T_ν gives an approximate solution to it. As a generalization of this, we get the following theorem:

THEOREM 19.2. *For $A \geqq 0$ and $\rho > \lambda(A)$, a sequence $\{T_\nu\}$ is formed as*

$$(19.10) \qquad T_{\nu+1} = \frac{1}{\rho}(AT_\nu + I) \quad (\nu = 0, 1, 2, \ldots)$$

starting from a square matrix T_0 with the same order as that of A. Then, it converges and $\lim_{\nu\to\infty} T_\nu = (\rho I - A)^{-1}$. In particular, starting from $T_0 = I/\rho$, $\{T_\nu\}$ is a sequence which has (19.5) as its general term.

Proof. As $\rho > \lambda(A)$, there exists $T = (\rho I - A)^{-1} \geqq 0$. Then, from $(\rho I - A)T = I$, we get

$$(19.11) \qquad T = \frac{1}{\rho}(AT + I) .$$

(19.10) and (19.11) lead to

$$(19.12) \qquad T_{\nu+1} - T = \frac{1}{\rho} A(T_\nu - T) .$$

Repeating (19.12) for $\nu = 1$ to ν, we have

$$(19.13) \qquad T_{\nu+1} = T + \frac{1}{\rho^\nu} A^\nu (T_1 - T) .$$

$\lim_{\nu\to\infty} (1/\rho^\nu)A^\nu = 0$ because $\rho > \lambda(A)$ as we showed above. Hence, letting $\nu \to \infty$ in (19.13), we get

$$\lim_{\nu\to\infty} T_{\nu+1} = T .$$

[Q.E.D.]

We may note from (19.7) that the convergence of the general term to 0 is not only necessary but also sufficient in order that the series (19.4) may converge. When $\rho = \lambda(A)$, Theorem 19.1 shows that (19.4) does not converge. In addition, this remark also reveals that the general term does not converge to 0 in this case.

20. Indecomposable matrices

Let n be the order of a non-negative matrix $A = [a_{ij}] \geqq 0$ and N the set consisting of numbers 1 to n, viz. $N = \{1, 2, ..., n\}$. When N is partitioned into two nonempty subsets I and J such that

$$(20.1) \qquad N = I \cup J, \ \ I \cap J = \phi, \ \ I \neq \phi, \ \ J \neq \phi$$

and

$$(20.2) \qquad a_{ij} = 0 \quad (\text{for } i \in I, \ \ j \in J),$$

A is said to be *decomposable.* If there is no such partition of N, A is said to be *indecomposable.*

We may illustrate this by the input coefficient matrix A in the interindustry analysis. When A is decomposable, it means that the jth sector ($j \in J$) does not purchase from the ith sector ($i \in I$). However, this does not necessarily preclude the possibility that the ith sector ($i \in I$) purchases from the jth sector ($j \in J$). If the ith sector ($i \in I$) does not purchase from the jth sector ($j \in J$) either,

$$a_{ji} = 0 \quad (\text{for } i \in I, \ \ j \in J)$$

holds in addition to (20.2). If the entire economy is completely separated into two mutually unrelated groups I and J, it may be said to be *completely decomposable.*

In what follows, we regard the non-negative matrix A in general as the input coefficient matrix for the sake of expository convenience.

If A is decomposable, there exists a partition of numbers into I and J. For instance, the matrix

$$\begin{bmatrix} 2 & 0 & 1 & 1 \\ 0 & 6 & 0 & 5 \\ 3 & 1 & 4 & 0 \\ 0 & 7 & 0 & 8 \end{bmatrix}$$

is decomposable; (20.1) and (20.2) hold for $I = \{2, 4\}$ and $J = \{1, 3\}$.

Assume that I consists of l numbers and J of k numbers. We renumber the rows and columns so that the first k numbers represent the sectors in J and the next l numbers the sectors in I. Correspondingly, goods are renumbered in the same manner. Then, A is rewritten as

$$(20.3) \qquad \begin{bmatrix} A_{11} & A_{12} \\ 0 & A_{22} \end{bmatrix}$$

where A_{11} and A_{22} are square matrices of orders k and l respectively. A_{12} is a (k, l) matrix and 0 in the southwest corner is an (l, k) zero matrix. In the numerical example above, $J = \{1, 3\}$ is renumbered as $\{1, 2\}$ and $I = \{2, 4\}$ as $\{3, 4\}$. This can be done by applying a permutation

$$\begin{pmatrix} 1 & 2 & 3 & 4 \\ 1 & 3 & 2 & 4 \end{pmatrix}$$

on the row and column numbers simultaneously. It is nothing but interchanging 2 and 3. By interchanging rows 2 and 3 and columns 2 and 3, the matrix in the example becomes

$$\begin{bmatrix} 2 & 1 & 0 & 1 \\ 3 & 4 & 1 & 0 \\ 0 & 0 & 6 & 5 \\ 0 & 0 & 7 & 8 \end{bmatrix}.$$

Similarly, by performing appropriate but identical permutations on the rows and columns of the decomposable matrix A, we get a new matrix in the form of (20.3). Further, if it is completely decomposable, we can have $A_{12} = 0$.

Let P be the matrix obtained after applying the above-mentioned permutation on the columns of the identity matrix I. Its transpose P' is the matrix derived by applying the same permutation on the rows of the identity matrix. By post-multiplying A by P, we get AP. AP is the matrix obtained by applying this permutation on the columns of A. By pre-multiplying AP by P', we get $P'AP$. $P'AP$ is the matrix obtained by performing this permutation on the rows of AP. As $P' = P^{-1}$, $P^{-1}AP$ is the matrix resulting from the identical permutation applied on both the columns and rows of A. Therefore, a decomposable matrix can be transformed into

$$(20.4) \qquad P^{-1}AP = \begin{bmatrix} A_{11} & A_{12} \\ 0 & A_{22} \end{bmatrix}$$

via the use of an appropriate permutation matrix P. In our numerical example, we have

$$P = \begin{bmatrix} 1 & 0 & 0 & 0 \\ 0 & 0 & 1 & 0 \\ 0 & 1 & 0 & 0 \\ 0 & 0 & 0 & 1 \end{bmatrix}.$$

Remark. If A of order higher than 1 * is indecomposable, it follows from the definition that

* A first order square matrix is always indecomposable due to the nonexistence of any partition satisfying (20.1). Propositions (a) and (b) do not hold for such a matrix.

(a) for any j, there exists i such that $a_{ij} > 0$, $i \neq j$, and that (b) for any i, there exists j such that $a_{ij} > 0$, $j \neq i$. Its proof is left to the reader as an exercise.

Let us now characterize indecomposable matrices. For this, it suffices to prove the following lemma that characterizes decomposable matrices.

LEMMA. *$A \geqq 0$ is decomposable if and only if $Ax \leqq \mu x$ holds for a real number μ and an appropriate vector $x \geq 0, \ngtr 0$.*

Proof. (i) *Necessity.* If A is decomposable, there exists an appropriate permutation matrix P that transforms A into the form of (20.4). Denote the Frobenius root of A_{11} by $\lambda(A_{11}) = \mu$. Then, there exists an eigenvector $y \geq 0$ associated with it, for which $A_{11}y = \mu y$. Now let

$$z = \begin{bmatrix} y \\ 0 \\ 0 \\ \vdots \\ 0 \end{bmatrix} \left.\begin{matrix} \\ \\ \\ \\ \end{matrix}\right\} l$$

where l is the order of A_{22}. Then, $z \geq 0$, $z \ngtr 0$ and

$$\begin{bmatrix} A_{11} & A_{12} \\ 0 & A_{22} \end{bmatrix} z = \mu z \, .$$

In other words, $P^{-1}APz = \mu z$. Pre-multiplying it by the permutation matrix, we get $APz = \mu Pz$. Putting $Pz = x$, we find that $x \geq 0, x \ngtr 0$ because x is a rearrangement of z and that $Ax = \mu x$. The latter is a special case of $Ax \leqq \mu x$ where we have the equality sign.

(ii) *Sufficiency.* If there exist such x and μ as described above, we may write out $Ax \leqq \mu x$ by component:

$$(20.5) \qquad \mu x_i \geqq \sum_{j=1}^{n} a_{ij}x_j \geqq 0 \quad (i = 1, 2, ..., n) \, .$$

Let $J = \{j \,|\, x_j > 0\}$. Then, because of the assumption $x \geq 0$, $x \ngtr 0$, we have $\phi \subsetneqq J \subsetneqq N = \{1, 2, ..., n\}$. Denote the complement of J in N by I. Then, I and J satisfy (20.1). If $i \in I$, then $x_i = 0$ and we get from (20.5)

$$0 \geqq \sum_{j=1}^{n} a_{ij}x_j \geqq 0 \quad (\text{for } i \in I) \, ,$$

in which individual terms between the two zeros are all non-negative, i.e. $a_{ij}x_j \geqq 0$, while they sum up to 0. Hence, we have

$$(20.6) \qquad a_{ij}x_j = 0 \quad (i \in I;\ j = 1, 2, ..., n)\,.$$

In (20.6), $x_j > 0$ for $j \in J$ so that $a_{ij} = 0$ $(i \in I,\ j \in J)$. Hence, A is decomposable.

If A is indecomposable, Theorem 17.1 is made more precise as follows:

THEOREM 20.1. *If A is an indecomposable matrix of order higher than 1,*

(i) *the Frobenius root of A is $\lambda(A) > 0$; there exists a positive eigenvector $x > 0$ associated with it; any real eigenvector is uniquely determined up to multiplication by scalars;*

(ii) *the non-negative eigenvalue problem $Ay = \mu y$, $\mu \geqq 0$, $y \geq 0$ has no solution other than $\mu = \lambda(A)$;*

(iii) $\lambda(A_1) > \lambda(A_2)$, *provided that $A_1 \geq A_2 \geqq 0$ and at least either of A_1 and A_2 is indecomposable;*

(iv) $\lambda(A)$ *is a simple root of the characteristic equation.*

Proof. (i) Let $\lambda(A) = \lambda$. $x \geq 0$ represents an eigenvector associated with it. Then, $\lambda x = Ax$. If $x \not> 0$, then A is decomposable by the lemma above. This contradicts the assumption. Hence, $x > 0$. As A contains some positive elements in each row (see the remark above), we get $Ax > 0$ in view of $x > 0$. Hence, $\lambda x = Ax > 0$ yields $\lambda > 0$.

Denote by $y \neq 0$ any real eigenvector associated with λ. Compare its components with those of the positive eigenvector x and put

$$(20.7) \qquad \min_{1 \leqq i \leqq n} y_i/x_i = \theta\,.$$

Then, $z = y - \theta x \geqq 0$ and $z \not> 0$. Moreover,

$$Az = A(y - \theta x) = Ay - \theta Ax = \lambda y - \theta \lambda x = \lambda z$$

so that $Az = \lambda z$, $z \geqq 0$, $z \not> 0$. As A is indecomposable, we must have $z = 0$ because of the lemma. Hence, $y = \theta x$ and y is a scalar multiple of x.

(ii) The indecomposability of A is equivalent by definition to that of A'. As $\lambda(A) = \lambda(A') = \lambda$, there exists a positive eigenvector $x > 0$ of A' associated with λ so that $A'x = \lambda x$. Putting

$$Ay = \mu y, \quad y \geq 0$$

and forming an inner product, we get

$$\mu(x, y) = (x, \mu y) = (x, Ay) = (A'x, y) = (\lambda x, y) = \lambda(x, y) .$$

$$\therefore (\lambda - \mu)(x, y) = 0.$$

Because $x > 0$ and $y \geq 0$, we get $(x, y) > 0$. $\therefore \lambda = \mu$.

(iii) As $A_1 \geq A_2 \geqq 0$, A_2 is decomposable if A_1 is decomposable. This contradicts the assumption. Hence, A_1 is indecomposable. $C = (½)(A_1 + A_2)$ is also indecomposable as can easily be verified from the definition of indecomposability. (The proof is left to the reader).

Take a positive eigenvector $z > 0$ associated with $\lambda(C)$ (see (i) for its existence). As $A_1 \geq C$, we have $\lambda(C)z = Cz \leq A_1 z$. Take a positive eigenvector $y > 0$ associated with $\lambda(A_1')$ and form an inner product

$$\lambda(C)(y, z) = (y, \lambda(C)z) = (y, Cz) < (y, A_1 z)$$

$$= (A_1' y, z) = (\lambda(A_1')y, z) = \lambda(A_1')(y, z) \ ,$$

$$\therefore (\lambda(A_1') - \lambda(C))(y, z) > 0 .$$

$(y, z) > 0$ because $y > 0$ and $z > 0$ so that $\lambda(C) < \lambda(A_1') = \lambda(A_1)$.

On the other hand, $\lambda(A_2) \leqq \lambda(C)$ because of $A_2 \leqq C$ by virtue of (ii) of Theorem 17.1. Combining these results, we get $\lambda(A_2) < \lambda(A_1)$.

(iv) Denote any principal submatrix of A by $C = [a_{ij}]$ $(i, j \in J)$ where J is a proper subset of $\{1, 2, ..., n\}$. Now forming an nth order square matrix $B = [b_{ij}] \geqq 0$ according to

$$b_{ij} = \begin{cases} a_{ij} & (i, j \in J) \\ 0 & \text{(otherwise)} \end{cases} \tag{20.8}$$

we obviously have $A \geqq B$. Clearly, B is decomposable, whereas A is indecomposable by assumption so that $A \neq B$. Hence, $A \geq B$ and it follows from (iii) that $\lambda(A) > \lambda(B)$. On the other hand, obviously * $\lambda(B) \geqq \lambda(C)$. Thus, we get $\lambda(A) > \lambda(C)$ from these inequalities.

Now let the order of C be k and the kth order identity matrix be I_k. Then, as $\lambda(A) > \lambda(C)$, we have $\det(\lambda I_k - C) > 0$, $\lambda = \lambda(A)$ because of the (H-S) condition on $\rho I_k - C$. Therefore, principal minors of orders lower than n of

* In fact, $\lambda(B) = \lambda(C)$.

det $(\lambda I - A)$ are positive. Now from

$$\varphi(\rho) = \det(\rho I - A) = \begin{vmatrix} \rho - a_{11} & -a_{12} & \cdots & -a_{1n} \\ -a_{21} & \rho - a_{22} & \cdots & -a_{2n} \\ \cdots & \cdots & \cdots & \cdots \\ -a_{n1} & -a_{n2} & \cdots & \rho - a_{nn} \end{vmatrix},$$

we see that the derivative of $\varphi(\rho)$ is given by

$$\varphi'(\rho) = \text{the sum of all principal minors of the } (n-1)\text{st order}$$

so that $\varphi'(\lambda) > 0$. Then, $\rho = \lambda$ is a simple root of $\varphi(\rho) = 0$. [Q.E.D.]

We have shown the equivalence of the four conditions on a non-negative matrix $A \geqq 0$, i.e. the weak solvability (I), the strong solvability (II), the (H-S) condition, and the condition that $\rho > \lambda(A)$ with respect to the equation system $(\rho I - A)x = c$. We may now add the following condition:

(0) $(\rho I - A)x = c$ has a solution $x \geqq 0$ for some $c \geq 0$.

Then, we have

THEOREM 20.2. *If* $A \geqq 0$ *is indecomposable,*

(i) *condition* (0) *is equivalent to* (I), (II), (H-S), *and* $\rho > \lambda(A)$;

(ii) *provided that* $\rho I - A$ *has a non-negative inverse matrix, this inverse is always a positive matrix, i.e.* $(\rho I - A)^{-1} > 0$.

Proof. (i) We assume (0). If $(\rho I - A)x = c$ has a solution $x \geqq 0$ for some $c \geq 0$, then $x \geq 0$. Let $y > 0$ represent a positive eigenvector of A' associated with $\lambda = \lambda(A')$. Then, $A'y = \lambda y$. The inner product of y and $\rho x = Ax + c \geq Ax$ satisfies

$$\rho(y, x) > (y, Ax) = (A'y, x) = \lambda(y, x).$$

As $(y, x) > 0$, we get $\rho > \lambda = \lambda(A')$. We have $\rho > \lambda(A)$ because $\lambda(A') = \lambda(A)$. Hence, (0) $\Rightarrow \rho > \lambda(A)$. On the other hand, it is obvious that (I) $\Rightarrow$ (0).

(ii) If $(\rho I - A)^{-1} \geqq 0$ exists, the solution of $(\rho I - A)x = c$ for any $c \geq 0$ is naturally non-negative. Then, it suffices to show that $x > 0$. Indeed, as

$$\rho x = Ax + c \geq Ax, \quad x \geq 0,$$

we must have $x > 0$ according to the lemma. To see that $(\rho I - A)^{-1} > 0$, take the jth unit vector e^j for c ($e^j \geq 0$) and note that $(\rho I - A)^{-1}e^j > 0$ because of what we have proved. $(\rho I - A)^{-1}e^j$ is exactly the jth column of $(\rho I - A)^{-1}$. Repeating this procedure, we see that each column is a positive vector. Hence, it follows that $(\rho I - A)^{-1} > 0$.

Row sums, column sums, and the Frobenius root. We described row sums of a non-negative matrix in Section 3. We gave an interesting corollary that shows how they are related to the (H-S) condition. This corollary states that $\rho I - A$ satisfies the (H-S) condition if (i) $\rho > r_i$ ($i = 1, 2, ..., n$) or (ii) $\rho > s_j$ ($j = 1, 2, ..., n$) where r_i is a row sum and s_j a column sum of $A \geqq 0$.

We give some additional findings on the row sums and column sums.

THEOREM 20.3.

(i) $\min_{1 \leqq j \leqq n} s_j \leqq \lambda(A) \leqq \max_{1 \leqq j \leqq n} s_j$;

(ii) $\min_{1 \leqq i \leqq n} r_i \leqq \lambda(A) \leqq \max_{1 \leqq i \leqq n} r_i$;

(iii) *Let A be indecomposable. Then, the following three conditions are equivalent:* (a) $\lambda(A) = \max_{1 \leqq j \leqq n} s_j$; (b) $\lambda(A) = \min_{1 \leqq j \leqq n} s_j$; (c) *$n$ column sums s_j are all equal.*

(iv) *Let A be indecomposable. Then, the following three conditions are equivalent:* (a) $\lambda(A) = \max_{1 \leqq i \leqq n} r_i$; (b) $\lambda(A) = \min_{1 \leqq i \leqq n} r_i$; (c) *$n$ row sums r_i are all equal.*

Proof. (i) Let $x \geq 0$ represent a non-negative eigenvector associated with $\lambda(A)$. As $\lambda(A)x = Ax$ is homogeneous in x, we may assume that

$$\sum_{j=1}^{n} x_j = 1.$$

Writing out $\lambda(A)x = Ax$ by component, we have

$$\lambda(A)x_i = \sum_{j=1}^{n} a_{ij}x_j \quad (i = 1, 2, ..., n). \tag{20.9}$$

Summing them up over i, we get

$$\lambda(A) = \lambda(A)\sum_{i=1}^{n} x_i = \sum_{i,j=1}^{n} a_{ij}x_j = \sum_{j=1}^{n}\Big(\sum_{i=1}^{n} a_{ij}\Big)x_j = \sum_{j=1}^{n} s_j x_j .$$

Considering $x_j \geqq 0$ and

$$\sum_{j=1}^{n} x_j = 1,$$

we have

$$\min_{1 \leqq j \leqq n} s_j \leqq \lambda(A) \leqq \max_{1 \leqq i \leqq n} s_j .$$

(ii) It can be proved just like (i). Note that $\lambda(A) = \lambda(A')$ in the proof.

(iii) From $\lambda(A) = \sum_{j=1}^{n} s_j x_j$, we have

$$(20.10) \qquad \sum_{j=1}^{n} (\lambda(A) - s_j) x_j = 0 .$$

If $\lambda(A) = \max s_j$, then

$$(20.11) \qquad \sum_{j=1}^{n} (\max_{1 \leqq j \leqq n} s_j - s_j)\, x_j = 0 .$$

As A is indecomposable, we have $x_j > 0$ $(i = 1, 2, ..., n)$ and $\max_{1 \leqq j \leqq n} s_j \geqq s_j$ $(j = 1, 2, ..., n)$. Hence, it follows from (20.11) that $s_j = \max_{1 \leqq j \leqq n} s_j$ $(j = 1, 2, ..., n)$. This proves (a) ⇒ (c). (b) ⇒ (c) can be proved in a similar manner. On the other hand, (c) ⇒ (a) and (c) ⇒ (b) are evident. Thus, (a), (b) and (c) are equivalent.

(iv) As $\lambda(A) = \lambda(A')$, we simply rewrite (iii) for A' to get (iv).

21. Indecomposable matrices (continued)

This section is not related to the rest of the book. The reader may skip it.

Imprimitive matrices. Let A be an indecomposable non-negative matrix. The order of A is n as before. For the sake of expository convenience, consider A as the input coefficient matrix. As A is indecomposable, we see that for any nonempty proper subset $J \subsetneqq \{1, 2, ..., n\}$, there always is a sector j in J that uses output of a sector outside the group J as input. This sector j in general purchases inputs also from sectors within the group J. However, it is possible for a special set J that sectors in J purchase inputs from sectors outside J but not from sectors within J. Such occurs if a special structure is given the technical interdependence among sectors that is represented by A. In this case, input coefficients satisfy

$$a_{ij} = 0 \quad (\text{for } i, j \in J)$$

$$\sum_{i \notin J} a_{ij} > 0 \quad (\text{for } j \in J)\,.$$

Now assume that the entire economy is divided into s mutually non-intersecting groups $J_1, J_2, \dots, J_s$ and that inputs into sectors in the group J_ν are outputs of sectors in the group $J_{\nu-1}$ only. We set $J_0 = J_s$. If such a partition $\{J_1, J_2, \dots, J_s\}$ $(s \geqq 2)$ is possible, A is said to be *imprimitive.* In this case, the coefficients satisfy

$$a_{ij} = 0 \quad (i \notin J_{\nu-1},\ j \in J_\nu) \quad (\nu = 1, 2, \dots, s) \tag{21.1}$$

$$\sum_{i \in J_{\nu-1}} a_{ij} > 0 \quad (j \in J_\nu) \qquad (\nu = 1, 2, \dots, s)\ . \tag{21.2}$$

When such a partition is impossible, A is said to be *primitive*. Let A be imprimitive and decomposable into $J_1, J_2, \dots, J_s$ $(s \geqq 2)$. The number of sectors in J_ν is denoted by $n(J_\nu)$. Renumber sectors and commodities so that the group J_1 is placed in the first $n(J_1)$ sectors, the group J_2 in the next $n(J_2)$ sectors and so on until the group J_s is placed as the last $n(J_s)$ sectors. This renumbering is done by applying an identical permutation simultaneously on the rows and columns of A. Denote this permutation matrix by P. Then, A is transformed into

$$P^{-1}AP = \begin{bmatrix} 0 & A_{12} & 0 & \cdots & 0 \\ 0 & 0 & A_{23} & \cdots & 0 \\ \vdots & & 0 & \ddots & \vdots \\ \vdots & & & \ddots & 0 \\ \vdots & & & & A_{s-1\,s} \\ A_{s1} & 0 & & \cdots & 0 \end{bmatrix} \tag{21.3}$$

where $A_{\nu-1\,\nu}$ is an $(n(J_{\nu-1}), n(J_\nu))$ non-negative rectangular matrix. We have $n(J_\nu)$th order square 0 matrices along the principal diagonal. All the other elements are zero.

Example 21.1.

$$A = \begin{bmatrix} 0 & 0 & 0 & 0 & 0 & 1 \\ 0 & 0 & 0 & 0 & 5 & 0 \\ 0 & 0 & 0 & 3 & 0 & 0 \\ 0 & 4 & 0 & 0 & 0 & 0 \\ 6 & 0 & 0 & 0 & 0 & 0 \\ 0 & 0 & 2 & 0 & 0 & 0 \end{bmatrix}$$

has a partition $J_1 = \{1, 4\}$, $J_2 = \{2, 6\}$, and $J_3 = \{3, 5\}$. Hence, applying the permutation *

$$\begin{pmatrix} 1 & 2 & 3 & 4 & 5 & 6 \\ 1 & 4 & 2 & 6 & 3 & 5 \end{pmatrix},$$

we get

$$P^{-1}AP = \begin{bmatrix} 0 & 0 & 0 & 1 & 0 & 0 \\ 0 & 0 & 4 & 0 & 0 & 0 \\ 0 & 0 & 0 & 0 & 0 & 5 \\ 0 & 0 & 0 & 0 & 2 & 0 \\ 0 & 3 & 0 & 0 & 0 & 0 \\ 6 & 0 & 0 & 0 & 0 & 0 \end{bmatrix}.$$

A has another partition $J_1 = \{1\}$, $J_2 = \{6\}$, $J_3 = \{3\}$, $J_4 = \{4\}$, $J_5 = \{2\}$, and $J_6 = \{5\}$. Hence, applying the permutation

$$\begin{pmatrix} 1 & 2 & 3 & 4 & 5 & 6 \\ 1 & 6 & 3 & 4 & 2 & 5 \end{pmatrix},$$

we get

$$Q^{-1}AQ = \begin{bmatrix} 0 & 1 & 0 & 0 & 0 & 0 \\ 0 & 0 & 2 & 0 & 0 & 0 \\ 0 & 0 & 0 & 3 & 0 & 0 \\ 0 & 0 & 0 & 0 & 4 & 0 \\ 0 & 0 & 0 & 0 & 0 & 5 \\ 6 & 0 & 0 & 0 & 0 & 0 \end{bmatrix}.$$

The reader may obtain the permutation matrices P and Q in these two cases and verify the above results by matrix multiplications.

* $\begin{pmatrix} 1 & 2 & 3 & 4 & 5 & 6 \\ 1 & 4 & 2 & 6 & 3 & 5 \end{pmatrix}$ represents a permutation: $1 \to 1$, $2 \to 4$, $3 \to 2$, $4 \to 6$, $5 \to 3$ and $6 \to 5$. The rows (columns) 1, 2, 3, 4, 5, and 6 of the matrix after this permutation are the rows (columns) 1, 4, 2, 6, 3, and 5 of the original matrix.

This example has revealed that the partition $J_1, J_2, ..., J_s$ in the imprimitive case is in general not unique. Thus, we pay special attention to the partition that maximizes the group number s.

A relation with eigenvalues. How can we determine whether A is primitive or imprimitive? If it is imprimitive, what characterizes the maximum k that is to be taken by the group number s in the partition discussed above? These questions are answered by a theorem below that reveals a complete correspondence between the number of certain eigenvalues and the maximum of s.

As we already noted, an indecomposable non-negative matrix (of order higher than 1) has a positive Frobenius root $\lambda(A) = \lambda$ that is a simple root. Further, we have the following theorem.

THEOREM 21.1. *Let $\rho_1, \rho_2, ..., \rho_k$ be different roots of* $\det(\rho I - A) = 0$, *the characteristic equation of an indecomposable non-negative matrix A of order higher than 1, that are equal to λ in absolute values. Then, the maximum of the group number s in the partition is k* *.

Proof. The proof will be worked out in two steps (i) and (ii), of which the latter will be divided further to four steps (ii.a) ~ (ii.d).

(i) Let the number of groups in any partition be s. Then, we show $s \leqq k$. A can be transformed into the form of (21.3) by an appropriate permutation. We may first verify that the eigenvalues of A are completely identical with those of $P^{-1}AP$. Denote an eigenvalue of A by ρ and the eigenvector associated with it by z. Then, $Az = \rho z$. $\therefore P^{-1}APP^{-1}z = P^{-1}z$. Namely, ρ is an eigenvalue of $P^{-1}AP$, whose eigenvector is $P^{-1}z$. By the same token, an eigenvalue of $P^{-1}AP$ is shown to be that of A.

Let $P^{-1}AP = B$ in (21.3). Needless to say, B is indecomposable and $\lambda(B) = \lambda(A) = \lambda > 0$. Take a positive eigenvector of B, $x > 0$, associated with λ. Let x^1 be the positive vector consisting of the first $n(J_1)$ components of x, x^2 the positive vector consisting of the next $n(J_2)$ components of x, and so on. x^t, therefore, represents the positive vector consisting of components numbered

$$\sum_{\nu=1}^{t-1} n(J_\nu) + 1 \quad \text{to} \quad \sum_{\nu=1}^{t} n(J_\nu) .$$

* When $k = 1$, i.e. when there are no other roots than λ that are equal to λ in absolute value, the maximum of s is equal to one, that is, the matrix is primitive.

Thus, we have

$$(21.4) \qquad x = \begin{bmatrix} x^1 \\ x^2 \\ \vdots \\ x^s \end{bmatrix} .$$

By using $Bx = \lambda x$, we write this out individually for $x^1, x^2, \ldots, x^s$ as

$$(21.5) \qquad \begin{cases} \lambda x^1 = A_{12} x^2 \\ \lambda x^2 = A_{23} x^3 \\ \cdots\cdots\cdots \\ \lambda x^\nu = A_{\nu\nu+1} x^{\nu+1} \\ \cdots\cdots\cdots \\ \lambda x^s = A_{s1} x^1 . \end{cases}$$

Let $\omega = \exp(2\pi m/s)i \quad (m=0,1,\ldots, s-1)$ be the sth roots of unity. Take one of them and multiply both sides of the νth equation of (21.5) by ω^ν to get

$$(21.6) \qquad \begin{cases} \lambda\omega x^1 = A_{12}\omega x^2 \\ \lambda\omega\omega x^2 = A_{23}\omega^2 x^3 \\ \cdots\cdots\cdots\cdots \\ \lambda\omega\omega^{\nu-1} x^\nu = A_{\nu\nu+1}\omega^\nu x^{\nu+1} \\ \cdots\cdots\cdots\cdots \\ \lambda\omega\omega^{s-1} x^s = A_{s1}\omega^s x^1 \end{cases}$$

and

$$(21.7) \qquad \omega^s - 1 .$$

Now define a complex vector $z \neq 0$ as

$$z = \begin{bmatrix} x^1 \\ \omega x^2 \\ \omega^2 x^3 \\ \vdots \\ \omega^{s-1} x^s \end{bmatrix} .$$

Taking (21.7) into consideration, we see that (21.6) reduces to $Bz = \rho z$, $\rho = \lambda\omega$, which shows that ρ is an eigenvalue of B. Hence, B has at least s different eigenvalues $\rho = \lambda \exp(2\pi m/s)i \quad (m=0,1,\ldots, s-1)$, equal to λ in absolute values. $\therefore s \leqq k$.

(ii) In fact, it can be shown that the economy can be partitioned into k groups of sectors. Let $\lambda(A) = \lambda$. An eigenvalue of $(1/\lambda)A$ is $1/\lambda$ times the corresponding eigenvalue of A. In particular, the Frobenius root of $(1/\lambda)A$ is unity. Any permutation matrix P transforms A and $(1/\lambda)A$ into the same matrix form. Positive elements are identically arrayed in $P^{-1}AP$ and $P^{-1}(1/\lambda)AP$. Then, without loss of generality, we may assume that $\lambda(A) = 1$.

Suppose that there are k different eigenvalues of A that are equal to unity in absolute value. The set consisting of them is denoted by Ω.

The proof is given in four steps below.

(ii.a) Let $\sigma \in \Omega$ and $z \neq 0$ be a (complex) eigenvector associated with σ, namely

$$\sigma z = Az \,. \tag{21.8}$$

In terms of components, we have

$$\sigma z_i = \sum_{j=1}^{n} a_{ij} z_j \quad (i = 1, 2, \ldots, n) \,.$$

Take the absolute value and consider $|\sigma| = 1$ to get

$$|z_i| = |\sigma|\,|z_i| = |\sum_{j=1}^{n} a_{ij} z_j| \leqq \sum_{j=1}^{n} a_{ij} |z_j| \,. \tag{21.9}$$

Define a non-negative vector

$$z = \begin{bmatrix} |z_1| \\ |z_2| \\ \vdots \\ |z_n| \end{bmatrix} .$$

Then, (21.9) is rewritten as

$$|z| \leqq A|z| \,. \tag{21.10}$$

It can be shown that the equality sign holds in (21.10). As $\lambda(A') = \lambda(A) = 1$, we get the inner product between $y > 0$, that is a positive eigenvector of A' associated with unity, and $|z| \leq A|z|$:

$$(y, |z|) < (y, A|z|) = (A'y, |z|) = (y, |z|) \,.$$

This is a contradiction. Hence, both sides of (21.10) must be equal to each other so that

$$|z| = A|z| \,. \tag{21.11}$$

Now let $x > 0$ be a positive eigenvector of A associated with the eigenvalue 1. Then, by virtue of (i) of Theorem 20.1, we see that $|z|$ is a positive multiple of x. Thus, we may be permitted to assume $|z| = x$ by multiplying x by an appropriate positive number. In this case, the individual components of z can be written as

$$(21.12) \qquad z_i = x_i \delta_i \quad (i = 1, 2, ..., n)$$

where δ_i is a complex number and $|\delta_i| = 1$. Let a complex diagonal matrix D be given by

$$(21.13) \qquad D = \begin{bmatrix} \delta_1 & & & \\ & \delta_2 & & 0 \\ & 0 & \ddots & \\ & & & \delta_n \end{bmatrix} .$$

It is easily verified that

$$D^{-1} = \begin{bmatrix} 1/\delta_1 & & & \\ & 1/\delta_2 & & 0 \\ & 0 & \ddots & \\ & & & 1/\delta_n \end{bmatrix} .$$

Hence, we get

$$(21.14) \qquad z = Dx .$$

(21.8) reduces to $\sigma Dx = ADx$, which, when pre-multiplied by $\sigma^{-1}D^{-1}$, becomes $x = \sigma^{-1}D^{-1}ADx$. Its left-hand side is equal to Ax because of the manner in which x is defined. Thus,

$$(21.15) \qquad Ax = \sigma^{-1}D^{-1}ADx .$$

Put $C = \sigma^{-1}D^{-1}AD = [c_{ij}]$. c_{ij} is a complex number. Matrix multiplications reveal that $c_{ij} = \sigma^{-1}\delta_i^{-1}a_{ij}\delta_j$. Taking $|\sigma| = |\delta_i| = 1$ into consideration, we get

$$(21.16) \qquad |c_{ij}| = |\sigma|^{-1}|\delta_i|^{-1}a_{ij}|\delta_j| = a_{ij} .$$

It follows from this that the real part of c_{ij} is subject to

$$\text{Re}(c_{ij}) \leqq a_{ij} \quad (i, j = 1, 2, ..., n).$$

Rewriting (21.15) and writing out its real part by component, we find

$$\sum_{j=1}^{n} (a_{ij} - \mathrm{Re}(c_{ij}))x_j = 0 \quad (i = 1, 2, ..., n) .$$

As x_j's are all positive and $a_{ij} \geqq \mathrm{Re}\,(c_{ij})$, we see that $a_{ij} = \mathrm{Re}\,(c_{ij})$. Considering (21.16), we get the imaginary part of c_{ij}: $\mathrm{Im}\,(c_{ij}) = 0$.

We have shown that $c_{ij} = a_{ij}$ $(i, j = 1, 2, ..., n)$. This is expressed in a matrix form as

$$\sigma^{-1}D^{-1}AD = A .$$

When it is pre-multiplied by σD and post-multiplied by D^{-1}, we get

$$A = \sigma DAD^{-1} . \tag{21.17}$$

This holds for any $\sigma \in \Omega$. Denote the D matrices (21.13) corresponding to any $\sigma, \tau \in \Omega$ by D_σ and D_τ. Then, we have

$$\sigma D_\sigma x = AD_\sigma x \quad \text{and} \quad \tau D_\tau x = AD_\tau x .$$

Noting that $\sigma D_\sigma A = AD_\sigma$ because of the general formula (21.17) of the D matrix, we get

$$\sigma\tau D_\sigma D_\tau x = \sigma D_\sigma \tau D_\tau x = \sigma D_\sigma AD_\tau x = AD_\sigma D_\tau x \ .$$

As $D_\sigma D_\tau x \neq 0$, this equation indicates that $\sigma\tau$ is an eigenvalue of A. Moreover, $|\sigma\tau| = |\sigma||\tau| = 1$. Hence, we have proved that

$$\sigma\tau \in \Omega \quad \text{if} \quad \sigma, \tau \in \Omega .$$

(ii.b) The finding above shows that $\sigma^\nu \in \Omega$ $(\nu = 1, 2, 3, ...)$ if $\sigma \in \Omega$. As Ω is a finite set, σ^ν's cannot all be different complex numbers. By taking appropriate natural numbers μ and ν $(\mu > \nu)$, we can make $\sigma^\mu = \sigma^\nu$. Hence, $\sigma^{\mu-\nu} = 1$. In other words, we get unity after σ is raised to an appropriate power if $\sigma \in \Omega$. We assumed that Ω consists of k elements. We now show that $\sigma^k = 1$ for any $\sigma \in \Omega$. Let p be the minimum exponent at which σ^p is equal to unity, i.e. $\sigma^p = 1$, $\sigma^\nu \neq 1$ $(\nu = 1, 2, ..., p-1)$. Then, we can demonstrate that $\sigma^k = 1$ if we show that k is divisible by p.

Put

$$\Omega_0 = \{1, \sigma, \sigma^2, ..., \sigma^{p-1}\} ,$$

which is a set consisting of p elements and $\Omega_0 \subset \Omega$ by (ii.a). Let ν be an arbitrarily given integer ($\nu = 0, \pm 1, \pm 2, \ldots$). Then, it can be expressed as $\nu = pq + r$, $0 \leqq r < p$ so that $\sigma^\nu = (\sigma^p)^q \sigma^r = \sigma^r \in \Omega_0$. Suppose that $\Omega_0 \neq \Omega$. Then, choose an element τ_1 such that $\tau_1 \in \Omega, \notin \Omega_0$ and form a set

$$\Omega_1 = \{\tau_1, \sigma\tau_1, \sigma^2\tau_1, \ldots, \sigma^{p-1}\tau_1\} \subset \Omega .$$

Now $\Omega_0 \cap \Omega_1 \neq \phi$. To see this, assume that the two sets have a common element. Then, $\sigma^\nu\tau_1 = \sigma^\mu$ (for some μ, ν; $0 \leqq \mu, \nu < p$) and $\tau_1 = \sigma^{\mu-\nu} \in \Omega_0$, which is a contradiction. Further, if $\Omega_0 \cup \Omega_1 \neq \Omega$, we take $\tau_2 \in \Omega, \notin \Omega_0 \cup \Omega_1$ and form

$$\Omega_2 = \{\tau_2, \sigma\tau_2, \sigma^2\tau_2, \ldots, \sigma^{p-1}\tau_2\} \subset \Omega .$$

Just as in the case of Ω_1, it can be shown that Ω_2 has no element in common with either of Ω_0 and Ω_1. Repeating this process, we form $\Omega_3, \Omega_4, \ldots$ in the same fashion. As Ω is a finite set, the elements of Ω are exhausted after finite times. We have

$$\Omega = \bigcup_{\nu=0}^{m} \Omega_\nu$$

$$\Omega_\nu = \{\tau_\nu, \sigma\tau_\nu, \sigma^2\tau_\nu, \ldots, \sigma^{p-1}\tau_\nu\}$$

$$\Omega_\mu \cap \Omega_\nu = \phi \qquad (\mu \neq \nu) .$$

Obviously, all the elements of each Ω_ν are different (why?) so that each Ω_ν consists of p complex numbers. Thus, $k = p(m+1)$ and p is a divisor of k.

(ii.c) We have demonstrated that $\sigma^k = 1$ if $\sigma \in \Omega$. Hence, the elements of Ω are roots of the equation $\omega^k - 1 = 0$, whose roots are a total of k numbers $\omega = \exp(2\pi t/k)i$ ($t = 0, 1, 2, \ldots, k-1$) as is well known. As Ω consists of k elements, we see that $\Omega = \{\exp(2\pi t/k)i \mid t = 0, 1, 2, \ldots, k-1\}$.

(ii.d) We continue this proof by choosing and fixing an element $\sigma \in \Omega$ that becomes equal to unity for the first time when it is raised to the kth power. This is, e.g., $\sigma = \exp(2\pi i/k)$. Then, we can write $\Omega = \{1, \sigma, \sigma^2, \ldots, \sigma^{k-1}\}$. Let the D matrix corresponding to this σ be D. In terms of elements, (21.17) is expressed as

$$a_{ij} = \sigma\delta_i a_{ij} \delta_j^{-1} \qquad (i, j = 1, 2, \ldots, n) . \tag{21.18}$$

Define k subsets of $N = \{1, 2, \ldots, n\}$:

$$J_\nu = \{i \mid \delta_i = \delta_1 \sigma^{\nu-1}\} \quad (\nu = 1, 2, \ldots, k) , \tag{21.19}$$

which obviously satisfy

(21.20) $J_\mu \cap J_\nu = \phi \quad (\mu \neq \nu)$.

Let us now prove that

(21.21) $J_\nu \neq \phi \quad (\nu = 1, 2, \ldots, k)$.

Suppose that there exists ν such that $J_\nu = \phi$. Let the smallest of such ν be $\mu + 1$. As $J_1 \ni 1$, certainly $J_1 \neq \phi$ and $\mu \geqq 1$. We have $J_\mu \neq \phi, J_{\mu+1} = \phi$ by the definition of μ. Then, if $i \in J_\mu$, we have $\sigma\delta_i = \delta_1\sigma^\mu$. Also $\delta_j \neq \delta_1\sigma^\mu$ ($j = 1, 2, \ldots, n$). The latter is due to $J_{\mu+1} = \phi$ because $\delta_j \neq \delta_1\sigma^{(\mu+1)-1}$ as none of j ($= 1, 2, \ldots, n$) is an element of $J_{\mu+1}$. Hence, $\sigma\delta_i\delta_j^{-1} \neq 1$ ($i \in J_\mu, j = 1, 2, \ldots, n$). Therefore, from (21.18), we get $a_{ij} = 0$ ($i \in J_\mu, j = 1, 2, \ldots, n$). This contradicts the indecomposability of A. Thus, (21.21) has been proved. Next, we prove that

(21.22) $N = \bigcup_{\nu=1}^{k} J_\nu$.

If (21.22) is denied, the set on the right-hand side is a proper subset of N. Let

$$I = \bigcup_{\nu=1}^{k} J_\nu \ .$$

and $I^c = J$ (complement of I). Then, $\sigma\delta_i\delta_j^{-1} \neq 1$ ($i \in I, j \in J$). By (21.18), we get $a_{ij} = 0$ ($i \in I, j \in J$), which again contradicts the indecomposability of A. Hence, (21.22) must hold. N is thus partitioned into k nonempty subsets $J_1, J_2, \ldots, J_k$. The proof will be completed when this partition is shown to satisfy (21.1) and (21.2). In fact, for $i \notin J_{\nu-1}, j \in J_\nu$, we have $\sigma\delta_i\delta_j^{-1} \neq 1$, so that in the same way as above, (21.1) follows from (21.18). If (21.1) holds, then (21.2) holds because of the indecomposability of A. [Q.E.D.]

COROLLARY. *An indecomposable matrix $A \geqq 0$ of order higher than 1 is primitive if and only if there is no eigenvalue other than $\lambda = \lambda(A)$ that is equal to $\lambda(A)$ in absolute value. A positive matrix is a special case of it.*

Remark. We showed above in the proof of (i) that there exists an eigenvalue ρ such that unity is obtained for the first time after ρ/λ is raised to the sth power if there is a partition of the sectors into s groups. (ii.b) of the proof revealed that k is always divisible by such s. Thus, the group number s of a partition under study must be a divisor of k. Conversely, if s is a divisor of k, there exists such a partition of the sectors into s groups. This can be shown by putting $\sigma = \exp(2\pi i/s)$ in (ii.d) of the proof and repeating the argument given there. Unity is obtained for the first time by raising this σ to the sth power. As $k = sd$, we get $\sigma = \exp(2\pi d/k)i$ so that certainly $\sigma \in \Omega$.

22. Relative stability of the balanced growth path

Let an nth order square matrix $A > 0$ be given and let $\lambda(A) = \lambda$, $\lambda x = Ax$, $x > 0$.

$$x(t) = \lambda^t x \quad (t = 0, 1, 2, ...) \tag{22.1}$$

is a special solution of a difference equation

$$y(t+1) = Ay(t) \quad (t = 0, 1, 2, ...)\,. \tag{22.2}$$

It is called a *balanced growth solution* in correspondence to the exposition in Section 18. In this section, we prove the following theorem:

THEOREM 22.1. * *For the solution $y(t)$ of (22.2) that starts from an arbitrary $y(0) \geq 0$ and the balanced growth solution $x(t)$, there exist $\lim_{t\to\infty} y_i(t)/x_i(t)$ $(i = 1, 2, ..., n)$. These n limits are positive and equal to each other.*

Before proceeding to its proof, let us explain what is meant by this theorem. Each component of $x(t)$ strictly increases toward infinity if $\lambda > 1$ and strictly decreases toward 0 if $\lambda < 1$. If $\lambda = 1$, $x(t)$ is constant. The conclusion of the theorem refers not to the behaviors of $x(t)$ and $y(t)$ themselves but to how the ratios of components would change as time passes. As $x(t)$ always lies on a ray generated by the vector $x > 0$, the direction of $x(t)$ as seen from the origin is always the same. In contrast, the path of $y(t)$ is, in general, not on a straight line. Its direction as seen from the origin is always changing. However, at the passage of time, the direction of $y(t)$ approaches that of x. This is what the theorem states. (Cf. fig. 22.1.)

Proof. Put

$$y_i(t)/x_i(t) = c_i(t) \quad (i = 1, 2, ..., n) \tag{22.3}$$

* This theorem was proved for a more general type of functions by R.M.Solow and P.A.Samuelson. See ref. [50] for details.

and define n sequences of numbers $\{c_i(t)\}$. Each term of these sequences is obviously $c_i(t) \geqq 0$ $(t = 0, 1, 2, \ldots)$. Now put

(22.4) $$\alpha(t) = \min_{1 \leqq i \leqq n} c_i(t) \quad \text{and} \quad \beta(t) = \max_{1 \leqq i \leqq n} c_i(t) \; .$$

We shall prove

(22.5) $$\lim_{t\to\infty} \alpha(t) = \lim_{t\to\infty} \beta(t) \, .$$

As $\alpha(t) \leqq c_i(t) \leqq \beta(t)$, it follows that $c_i(t)$ converges to the same limit.

For any time point t, choose an index k such that $\alpha(t) = c_k(t)$ *. Then, for any i,

$$y_i(t+1) = \sum_{j=1}^{n} a_{ij} y_j(t) = \sum_{j=1}^{n} a_{ij} c_j(t) x_j(t)$$

$$= \alpha(t) a_{ik} x_k(t) + \sum_{j \neq k} a_{ij} c_j(t) x_j(t)$$

$$= \alpha(t) a_{ik} x_k(t) - \beta(t) a_{ik} x_k(t) + \beta(t) a_{ik} x_k(t)$$

$$+ \sum_{j \neq k} a_{ij} c_j(t) x_j(t)$$

$$\leqq (\alpha(t) - \beta(t)) a_{ik} x_k(t) + \beta(t) \sum_{j=1}^{n} a_{ij} x_j(t)$$

$$= (\alpha(t) - \beta(t)) a_{ik} x_k(t) + \beta(t) x_i(t+1) \, .$$

Dividing this inequality through by $x_i(t+1)$, we get

$$y_i(t+1)/x_i(t+1) \leqq (\alpha(t) - \beta(t)) a_{ik} x_k(t)/x_i(t+1) + \beta(t) \, .$$

Noting that $x_k(t)/x_i(t+1) = x_k/\lambda x_i$ and $\alpha(t) - \beta(t) \leqq 0$ and putting

(22.6) $$\min_{i,\, j} a_{ij} = \delta > 0 \quad \text{and} \quad \min_{i,\, j} x_j/x_i = \epsilon > 0 \, ,$$

we can transform this inequality into

(22.7) $$y_i(t+1)/x_i(t+1) \leqq (\alpha(t) - \beta(t)) \frac{\epsilon\delta}{\lambda} + \beta(t) \qquad (i = 1, 2, \ldots, n) \, .$$

* The value of k varies as t varies.

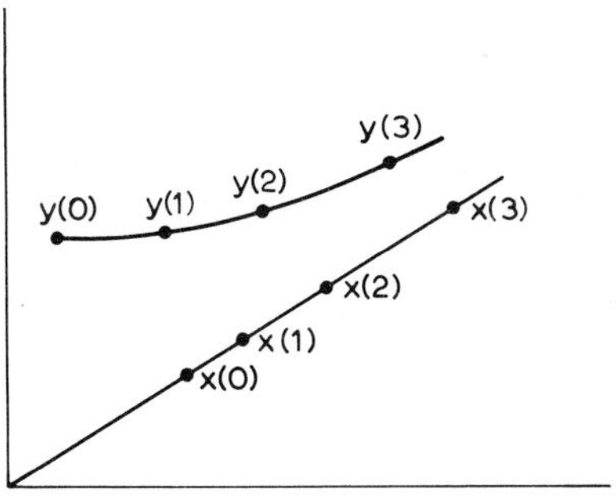

Fig. 22.1.

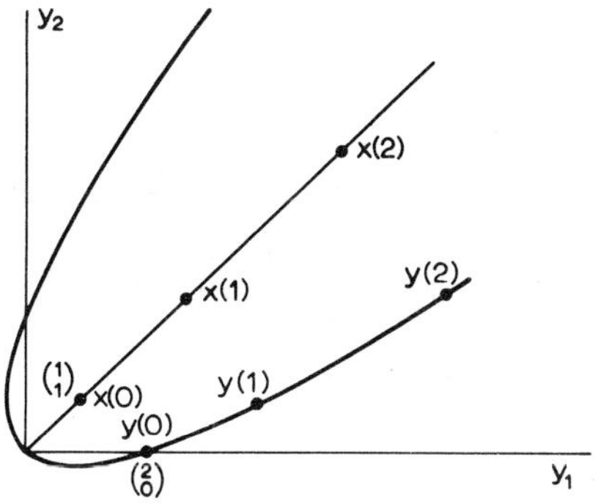

Fig. 22.2.

Hence, taking the maximum of the left-hand side of (22.7), we get

$$\beta(t+1) \leqq (\alpha(t) - \beta(t)) \frac{\epsilon\delta}{\lambda} + \beta(t)\,,$$

which is transformed into

$$0 \leqq \beta(t) - \alpha(t) \leqq \frac{\lambda}{\epsilon\delta} (\beta(t) - \beta(t+1)) \quad (t = 0, 1, 2, \ldots)\,. \tag{22.8}$$

By the same token, we obtain

$$0 \leqq \beta(t) - \alpha(t) \leqq \frac{\lambda}{\epsilon\delta} (\alpha(t+1) - \alpha(t)) \quad (t = 0, 1, 2, \ldots)\,. \tag{22.9}$$

These inequalities establish

$$0 \leqq \alpha(0) \leqq \alpha(1) \leqq \ldots \leqq \alpha(t) \leqq \alpha(t+1) \leqq \ldots$$

$$\leqq \beta(t+1) \leqq \beta(t) \leqq \ldots \leqq \beta(1) \leqq \beta(0)$$

with

$\{\alpha(t)\}$ increasing and bounded from above

and

$\{\beta(t)\}$ decreasing and bounded from below.

Therefore, there exist $\lim_{t\to\infty} \alpha(t) = \alpha$ and $\lim_{t\to\infty} \beta(t) = \beta$. As $t \to \infty$ in (22.8) and (22.9), the right-hand sides converge to 0 so that the left-hand sides also converge to 0. Thus, $\alpha = \beta$. As the initial vector $y(0) \geq 0$ and $A > 0$, we have $y(1) = Ay(0) > 0$, i.e. $c_i(1) = y_i(1)/\lambda x_i > 0$ $(i = 1, 2, \ldots, n)$, from which $\alpha(1) = \min_{1 \leqq i \leqq n} c_i(1) > 0$. As $\{\alpha(t)\}$ is increasingly convergent, $\alpha \geqq \alpha(t) > 0$. This proves that the limit is positive.

COROLLARY. *For two solutions of (22.2) that start from arbitrarily given* $y(0) \geq 0$ *and* $z(0) \geq 0$, *there exists* $\lim_{t\to\infty} z_i(t)/y_i(t)$ *and the limit is a positive number independent of i.*

Proof. From $y(0) \geq 0$ and $z(0) \geq 0$, we get $y(1) = Ay(0) > 0$ and $z(1) = Az(0) > 0$, so that $y_i(t)$ and $z_i(t)$ are always positive at time points after $t=1$. Then, sequences of numbers $\{z_i(t)/y_i(t)\}$ are meaningful at $t \geqq 1$. Let $x(t)$ be the balanced growth solution of (22.2). Then, Theorem 22.1 states that $y_i(t)/x_i(t)$ and $z_i(t)/x_i(t)$ converge to positive numbers independent of i. Therefore,

$$d_i(t) = z_i(t)/y_i(t) = \frac{z_i(t)}{x_i(t)} \Big/ \frac{y_i(t)}{x_i(t)}$$

also converges to a positive number independent of i.

Remark. In this case, for

$$\sigma(t) = \min_{1 \leqq i \leqq n} d_i(t) \quad \text{and} \quad \tau(t) = \max_{1 \leqq i \leqq n} d_i(t) , \tag{22.10}$$

we find $\{\sigma(t)\}$ increasing and $\{\tau(t)\}$ decreasing. This can be obtained from a more simplified form of evaluating inequalities than that used in the proof of Theorem 22.1. To see this, write $z_i(t) = d_i(t)y_i(t)$. Then, for any i,

$$z_i(t+1) = \sum_{j=1}^{n} a_{ij} z_j(t) = \sum_{j=1}^{n} a_{ij} d_j(t) y_j(t)$$

$$\leqq \tau(t) \sum_{j=1}^{n} a_{ij} y_j(t) = \tau(t) y_i(t+1) ,$$

so that

$$d_i(t+1) \leqq \tau(t) \quad (i = 1, 2, ..., n),$$

whence,

$$\tau(t+1) \leqq \tau(t) .$$

By the same token, we have

$$\sigma(t+1) \geqq \sigma(t) .$$

Successive approximations of the Frobenius root of a positive matrix. Consider a solution $y(t)$ of (22.2) that starts from an arbitrary $y(0) \geq 0$. Let $y(t)$

be a vector representing the economic state at time t. Then,

$$\lambda_i(t) = y_i(t+1)/y_i(t)$$

is the sectoral growth factor, i.e. 1 + the growth rate of the ith sector. In general, the value of $\lambda_i(t)$ is dependent on i and t, but it approaches to $\lambda(A)$, the Frobenius root of A or 1 + the balanced growth rate, as time passes and in the limit

$$(22.11) \qquad \lim_{t\to\infty} \lambda_i(t) = \lambda(A) \qquad (i = 1, 2, ..., n)\,.$$

It can be explained very simply. Put $z(t) = y(t+1)$. Then, $z(t)$ is a solution of (22.2) that starts from $z(0) \geq 0$. Hence, the corollary and the remark given above show that $\{\min \lambda_i(t)\}$ converges increasingly and $\{\max \lambda_i(t)\}$ decreasingly to the same limit. Moreover,

$$\lambda_i(t) = \lambda\left(\frac{y_i(t+1)}{\lambda^{t+1} x_i} \bigg/ \frac{y_i(t)}{\lambda^t x_i}\right)$$

and

$$\lim_{t\to\infty} \frac{y_i(t+1)}{\lambda^{t+1} x_i} = \lim_{t\to\infty} \frac{y_i(t)}{\lambda^t x_i} = \alpha = \beta > 0\,,$$

from which (22.11) follows.

$\lambda(A)$ is bounded from above and below by $\{\min \lambda_i(t)\}$ and $\{\max \lambda_i(t)\}$ that monotonically converge to it. Therefore, they provide convenient means to get approximations of $\lambda(A)$.

On the other hand, the eigenvector of A associated with $\lambda(A)$ is approximated as follows: For the solution $y(t)$ given above, put

$$(22.12) \qquad w_i(t) = y_i(t) \bigg/ \sum_{j=1}^{n} y_j(t)$$

and

$$w(t) = \begin{bmatrix} w_1(t) \\ w_2(t) \\ \vdots \\ w_n(t) \end{bmatrix}.$$

Then, $\{w(t)\}$ converges to $\lim_{t\to\infty} w(t)$, which is one of the eigenvectors of A associated with $\lambda(A)$. In fact, as $y_i(t) = c_i(t)\lambda^t x_i$ from (22.3), we have

$$w_i(t) = \frac{c_i(t)\lambda^t x_i}{\sum_{j=1}^{n} c_j(t)\lambda^t x_j} = \frac{c_i(t)x_i}{\sum_{j=1}^{n} c_j(t)x_j} \to \frac{x_i}{\sum_{j=1}^{n} x_j} \quad (t \to \infty)$$

because of $\lim_{\nu\to\infty} c_i(t) = \alpha > 0$.

Note. The term, ***relative stability***, stems from the fact that the theorem has to do with the convergence of (relative) ratios of components $y_1(t)$, $y_2(t), \ldots, y_n(t)$ rather than the behavior of the solution $y(t)$ itself. The conclusion of the theorem refers to the convergence of ratios $y_1(t) : y_2(t) : \ldots : y_n(t)$ to constant ratios $x_1 : x_2 : \ldots : x_n$.

Now if $\lambda(A) > 1$, then each component of $y(t)$ expands at a rate commensurate to $\lambda(A)^t$. Geometrically speaking, $y(t)$ departs from the origin along a curve. But $y(t)$ does not always approach the $x(t)$ line. Fig. 22.1 is an illustration contained in many textbooks of economics and represents the case where $y(t)$ approaches the $x(t)$ line. However, the relative stability does not necessarily ensure that the $x(t)$ line is an asymptote of the trajectory of $y(t)$. To keep the relative stability from being misunderstood in this way, let us present a case in which $y(t)$ diverges from the x line as time passes.

Example 22.1. The eigenvalues of $A = \begin{bmatrix} 3 & 1 \\ 1 & 3 \end{bmatrix}$ are 4 and 2; the associated eigenvectors are $\begin{bmatrix} 1 \\ 1 \end{bmatrix}$ and $\begin{bmatrix} 1 \\ -1 \end{bmatrix}$. Hence, the Frobenius root is $\lambda(A) = 4$. Now

$$y_1(t) = 4^t + 2^t$$
$$y_2(t) = 4^t - 2^t$$

is a solution of (22.2) that starts from $y_1(0) = 2$ and $y_2(0) = 0$. To see what sort of a trajectory this solution has, we eliminate t from the solution. We see that the solution $y(t)$ lies on a curve $2(y_1 + y_2) = (y_1 - y_2)^2$. This curve is a parabola, as shown in fig. 22.2, with a straight line $y_1 - y_2 = 0$ as its principal axis and

$$\begin{bmatrix} 1/4 \\ 1/4 \end{bmatrix}$$

as its focus. It is easily computed that the distance between $y(t)$ and the balanced growth line is $\sqrt{2} \cdot 2^t$ at time t. This distance diverges to infinity as time passes.

Chapter 4

OPTIMIZATION PROBLEMS

23. The microeconomic approach

The interindustry analysis that we have studied assumes that there exists a fixed process of production in each sector so that there is an invariant technological interdependence among sectors. The technological structure is thus fixed in the national economy. The interindustry analysis primarily aims at examining the relation of correspondence between final demands c and total outputs x through this fixed technological structure of the economy.

The thesis traditionally expounded in economics since Adam Smith (1723–1790) is the maximization principle of economic behavior, i.e. the greatest gain with the least cost. The basic idea was systematically incorporated into economic theory by the marginalists represented by Walras, C. Menger *, and S.Jevons **. In particular, Walras developed his mathematical analysis of economic phenomena on this ideological foundation and paved the way for later developments.

Constituents of a national economy, e.g. firms and households, are engaged in economic activities like production and consumption subject to the restrictions placed by natural resource availability and technology on the one hand and to the existing social system and institutions on the other. Constituents' interests are intricately intertwined *via* these constraints. However, they are not necessarily completely deprived of freedom of action even though they are placed in a complex environment. There is a certain degree of freedom that enables them to choose the most desirable one from among a number of feasible actions. For instance, a firm selects a technical process that is

* Austrian economist (1840–1921).
** British economist (1815–1882).

the most advantageous in the light of a certain criterion, say that of profit maximization, from among several technical processes available for the production of a given commodity. However, the interindustry analysis assumes that technology is completely fixed in each industry so that there is no room for choice in this respect. Even if there are a number of technical processes available in each industry, the choice of the optimum process is assumed to have been completed. The analysis begins at this point. No further analysis is made of the choice of techniques. Thus, the interindustry analysis is simple-minded and incomplete as regards the analysis of economic motivations. Inspite of this serious handicap, the interindustry analysis has practical relevance, unlike the elaborate general Walrasian theory, that is sufficient for studying the actual workings of a national economy. It has witnessed popular applications in many countries including Western nations and Japan.

In the orthodox Walrasian approach, an economy is theoretically analyzed with respect to (a) the economic behaviors of individual economic units and (b) their coordination in the presence of a multitude of individual economic units. Let us give a brief account of these two steps. It is firms and households that play important roles as constituents of an economy. A firm purchases inputs (labor, raw materials and semi-finished goods), produces finished goods by combining these inputs, and sells them to make profits. As techniques vary that the firm adopts, inputs are combined in different proportions and input-output ratios change. Therefore, there are in general a number of production programmes that the firm can employ. One specific programme is chosen for the actual adoption from among them. What objectives has the firm in view when it makes this selection? In reality, business objectives are complex. But of primary importance to a modern firm is, in many instances, the volume or rate of profits. Thus, we shall highlight this point and accept the approach that analyzes business behaviors on the basis of the *profit maximization principle,* i.e. the axiom that a firm adopts the production programme that would maximize profits (or similar targets). This is certainly a bold simplification. Bodily motions on earth are always accompanied by friction due to air resistance and other factors. There are no motions without friction. However, it is well known that the essence of dynamic laws of motion was brought to light by examining laws of motion without friction as accomplished by Galilei and Newton. This enables us to study laws of motion in general situations. Economic theory may follow an approach that is formally analogous to it.

Households (of workers, entrepreneurs and capitalists), on the other hand, spend their income (wages, profits, interest and so on) to purchase a number of commodities. The theory of consumer behavior examines in what proportions households would apportion their income on various goods that are to be purchased. In its traditional approach, this theory is based on the *utility maximization principle,* i.e. the principle that a consumer determines the amounts of the purchases of various commodities to maximize his *utility,* namely the degree of convenience and satisfaction that these commodities accord him.

As is clear from this description, the Walrasian analysis formalizes theories of economic behavior as problems of maximization or minimization in many instances.

Let us explain the prefix "micro" in the heading of this section. In natural sciences, this word means microscopic or very minute. Microwave, microbes, and nuclei are representatives of the micro world. In economics, there appear no such microscopic entities. But individual economic units (households, firms, etc.) are engaged in economic activities whose scales are minute in comparison to that of the economy as a whole. The economy is something like a giant body consisting of a multitude of "atoms" that are individual economic units. In the kinetic theory of gases in physics, a study of the average behavior of many gaseous molecules is called a macroscopic study. On the other hand, we find ourselves working in a field of microscopic study, once we are concerned with the behaviors of individual molecules. Analogously, in economics, a microscopic study analyzes behavioral motivations of individual elements in an economy. "Micro" refers to the analysis of motivations of individual economic units rather than to the size of these units under study. The Walrasian analysis is typical of microeconomics. It first pursues behaviors of economic units on the basis of the profit and utility maximization principles and then comes to explaining the working of the national economy as a whole on the basis of these micro behaviors. The former, i.e. the analysis of behaviors of economic units on the basis of the maximization principles, is the study (a) referred to above. The latter, i.e. the coordination of individual economic behaviors over the economy as a whole, is the step (b). As we have explained, outputs, inputs (including employment), and consumption by individual economic units are determined by the profit and utility maximization principles. Aggregate demand and supply are then determined by aggregating these amounts over the society as a whole. If aggregate demand and supply are not identical, production is not equal to sales and demand not equal to purchases. With such a disequilibrium between demand and supply, individual pursuits of maximum profits and utility are possible merely as expected values. They are infeasible in practice because of the constraints imposed by circular flows in the national economy. Thus, the balance between demand and supply is presupposed in order to make individual programmes (based on the maximization principles) feasible. The coordination or harmonization of individual actions of these economic units is succinctly represented by the equilibrium between demand and supply. Therefore, the step (b) is a theoretical examination of the feasibility of the demand-and-supply equilibrium.

This is the programme of the Walrasian approach in mathematical economics. It was methodologically established for the first time by Walras and has been inherited by contemporary economics. Needless to say, here lies the greatness of Walras as an economist. Though Walras (and many subsequent mathematical economists) used to apply calculus mechanically to prove the programme established by himself, this is not sufficient for our purpose. We need more penetrating mathematical analysis. In particular, with respect to the step (b) above, Walras presented only a conjecture for the existence of the demand-and-supply equilibrium. It is only in recent years that his conjecture was examined in truly mathematical terms and was given an affirmative proof. This is the existence problem of the equilibrium solution. The latter part of the present book will be devoted to explaining this problem.

The present chapter will discuss the maximization and minimization problems that are contained in the step (a) in view of their own interest as well as for the purpose of preparing ourselves for the step (b).

Classical mathematical economics dealt with optimization problems through the mechanical application of differential and integral calculus. This approach, however, is very much imperfect as a means of mathematical analysis not because calculus was in error but because it was applied in an inexact manner. However, as we stated at the very beginning of this book, the development of the new approach as exemplified by the theory of games helped to rectify this situation. A correct orientation is now under way. We are going to study the modern analysis of the maximization and minimization problems. Under the heading of optimization problems, we shall cover these problems including the analysis of production through linear programming and activity analysis in view of their affinity and similarity in treatment.

24. Interior optima and corner optima

This section will introduce the reader to the modern approach by critically examining the classical analysis in the theory of production planning. Let us begin with discussing the concept of the production function that underlies the theory of firms.

In general, there are a number of techniques available to a firm. We concentrate our attention not so much on the engineering aspect of techniques but on the production planning that would be made feasible by applying these techniques, i.e. the quantitative relations between inputs and outputs. For instance, electric power is produced by techniques of hydraulic, thermal, and nuclear power generation. To be more specific, hydraulic power generation includes a large number of techniques with varying capacities of water flows and turbines to be installed in a power plant. However, what is economically important is simply how much power is to be produced from given amounts of inputs (labor, raw materials, etc.).

Denote outputs by $x_1, x_2, ..., x_m$ and inputs by $y_1, y_2, ..., y_n$ in a given production plan. Outputs and inputs are numbered here because there are in general many outputs and inputs. $m \geqq 2$ represents the case where there are by-products or the case of joint production. For instance, the production of coal gas is always accompanied by that of cokes. Such specific cases are numerous. Moreover, there can be a good that appears both as output and input in the present formulation.

Now for a firm, a technically feasible combination of outputs and inputs $(x_1, x_2, ..., x_m, y_1, y_2, ..., y_n)$ is constrained by an implicit function

$$(24.1) \qquad F(x_1, x_2, ..., x_m, y_1, y_2, ..., y_n) = 0 .$$

This formulation is due to J.R.Hicks (1904–), who is regarded as a foremost authority of classical mathematical economics. (24.1) is a *production function.* This itself is a fairly general formulation, but the modern approach goes a few steps further. It regards the whole of feasible combinations $(x_1, x_2, ..., x_m, y_1, y_2, ..., y_n)$ as a set Δ in R^{m+n} and analyzes the structure of Δ.

In the interindustry analysis, we disregard the fact that an industry consists of a number of firms and examine the production function of the industry. As we stated earlier, let output of the jth industry be x_j and its inputs x_{ij}. They are related to each other by the proportionality relations $x_{ij} = a_{ij}x_j$ $(i = 1, 2, ..., n)$ where a_{ij} is an input coefficient. In order to simplify the problem in this section, we omit subscript j and put $x = x_j$, $y_i = x_{ij}$, and $a_i = a_{ij}$. Then, the technological structure of this industry is represented by

$$(24.2) \qquad y_i = a_i x \quad (i = 1, 2, ..., n) .$$

Note that technically feasible input ratios are fixed as $a_1 : a_2 : ... : a_n$. Hence, for arbitrarily given $y_1, y_2, ..., y_n$, the (maximum) amount of x that can be produced from the combination of inputs at the fixed ratios is given by $x = \min y_i/a_i$ (the minimum for i where $a_i > 0$). For each input, $y_i - a_i x$ $(\geqq 0)$ is left idle. This can be expressed as

$$(24.3) \qquad x - \min_{i \in I} y_i/a_i = 0 ,$$

corresponding to (24.1) à la Hicks, where $I = \{i \mid a_i > 0\}$ is a set of subscripts.

The Hicksian approach proceeds on the assumption of differentiability of the function F on the left-hand side of (24.1). It excludes non-differentiable functions like (24.3). This is the first difficulty of the classical approach, to which we shall return later. We shall discuss the second difficulty first.

As a typical optimization problem in the theory of firms, we may cite the least-cost problem for a firm under free competition. It is assumed that this firm behaves as follows: The firm can exert no appreciable influence on the market through artificial means like price administration because its scale is miniscule in comparison to that of the economy as a whole. Therefore, this firm would consider commodity prices as *data* that cannot be altered by itself, i.e. as given constraints in establishing its production plan. In reality, as the firm gets larger in size, its influence on the market becomes more and more significant. However, for the sake of analytical convenience, an economic unit which takes prices as given is called *competitive* in its behavioral pattern irrespective of its size. Given output prices $p_1, p_2, ..., p_m$ and input prices $q_1, q_2, ..., q_n$, a competitive firm that produces given outputs $x_1, x_2, ..., x_m$ subject to the production function (24.1) would determine inputs $y_1, y_2, ..., y_n$ so as to maximize its profit $\sum p_j x_j - \sum q_i y_i$ or to minimize the cost of production

$$(24.4) \qquad C = C(y_1, y_2, ..., y_n) = \sum_{i=1}^{n} q_i y_i$$

subject to (24.1) *. In other words, the problem is formulated as a minimization problem

$$\min C(y_1, y_2, ..., y_n) \text{ subject to}$$

$$F(x_1, x_2, ..., x_m, y_1, y_2, ..., y_n) = 0\,.$$

In the classical approach, this problem is answered as follows: It has a solution $\hat{y}_1, \hat{y}_2, ..., \hat{y}_n$. Provided that F is differentiable, a theorem in differential calculus gives a necessary condition that there should be a proportionality relation

$$(24.5) \qquad \frac{\partial C}{\partial y_1} : \frac{\partial C}{\partial y_2} : ... : \frac{\partial C}{\partial y_n} = \frac{\partial F}{\partial y_1} : \frac{\partial F}{\partial y_2} : ... : \frac{\partial F}{\partial y_n}$$

at $\hat{y}_1, \hat{y}_2, ..., \hat{y}_n$. Let us examine whether this condition is correct.

* In the present problem, $x_1, x_2, ..., x_m$ are given constants.

Example 24.1. Assume that $m = 1$ and $n = 2$. Suppose that the firm combines inputs y_1 and y_2 and produces output $x = f(y_1, y_2) = a_1 y_1 + a_2 y_2$ (where a_1 and a_2 are positive constants). In this case, the two inputs are perfect substitutes. This is an economically significant case. This problem is reduced to a minimization problem, i.e.

$$\min (q_1 y_1 + q_2 y_2) \text{ subject to } a_1 y_1 + a_2 y_2 - x = 0 .$$

If we interpret the constraint $a_1 y_1 + a_2 y_2 = x$ literally with no additional restraints, then the variables are allowed to range along the straight line $a_1 y_1 + a_2 y_2 = x$. If $q_1 : q_2 \neq a_1 : a_2$, the cost of production $C(y_1, y_2)$ is made as small as one likes so that it is minimized at no point. To exclude this unreasonable consequence, it is natural to add the non-negativity constraints $y_1 \geqq 0$ and $y_2 \geqq 0$. It is obvious that C is minimized at $\hat{y}$ in fig. 24.1. However, (24.5) does not hold at $\hat{y}$ if $q_1 : q_2 \neq a_1 : a_2$, for clearly $\partial C / \partial y_1 = q_1$, $\partial C / \partial y_2 = q_2$, $\partial F / \partial y_1 = a_1$, and $\partial F / \partial y_2 = a_2$.

This example suggests the following important fact: In the classical approach, (24.1) was formulated seldom with proper considerations of the domain of the function F. Thus, little attention was paid to the domain (i.e. a set) in which the variables are allowed to range in the minimization problem and to the non-negativity constraints that are economically significant. It was quite often the case that theorems in calculus were mechanically applied with the complete neglect of premises of the problem under study. It is close to mathematical nonsense to examine an optimization problem without clear awareness of the domain of the variables.

Example 24.2. Let us examine the same minimization problem for the production function $x = f(y_1, y_2) = \sqrt{y_1 y_2}$, $y_1 \geqq 0$ and $y_2 \geqq 0$. $F(x, y_1, y_2) = \sqrt{y_1 y_2} - x$ is a differentiable function * for $x \geqq 0$, $y_1 \geqq 0$, $y_2 \geqq 0$, and $\sqrt{y_1 y_2} = x$ is the hyperbola $y_1 y_2 = x^2$ in the first quadrant. C is minimized at a point like $\hat{y}$ in fig. 24.2.

The condition (24.5) holds at this point, as can be easily verified. (The calculation is left to the reader.)

Thus, the condition (24.5) holds in one case but not in another even though the minimization problem is formally the same in the two cases. More rigorously stated, (24.5) is to be replaced by a necessary condition expressed correctly as inequalities subject to properly stated premises on the domain in which the variables are allowed to range. (24.5) is a special case where condi-

* More exactly, differentiable for $x \geqq 0$, $y_1 > 0$, $y_2 > 0$.

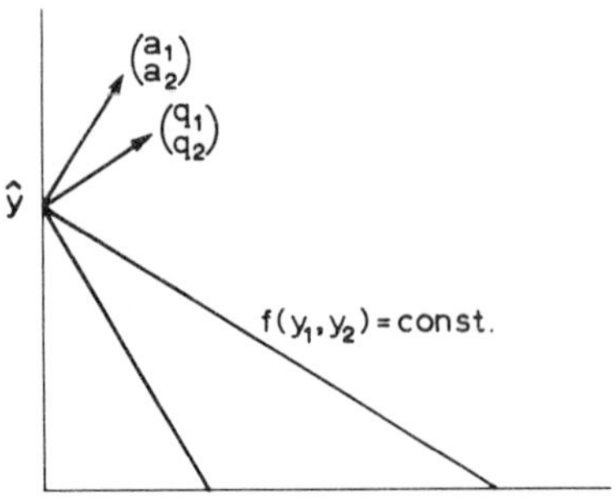

Fig. 24.1.

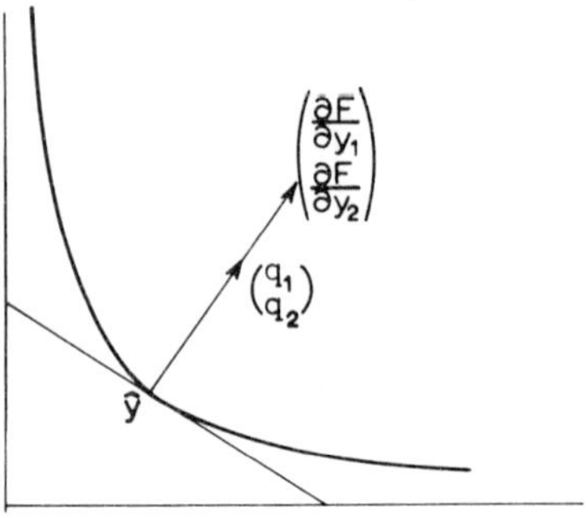

Fig. 24.2.

tions are more stringent. A comparison of figs. 24.1 and 24.2 reveals a big difference between the two cases. In the former the minimum point is reached at an end point of the domain, while in the latter case it is attained at a point inside the domain. The location of the minimum point in the domain is really important in determining the minimization condition when proper considerations are accorded to the structure and properties of the domain as a set. In the terminology to be introduced (Section 28), the minimum point is a boundary point of the domain in fig. 24.1 and an interior point in fig. 24.2. They are called a *corner minimum point* and an *interior minimum point* respectively. (24.5) holds at an interior minimum point but not necessarily at a corner minimum point. To make this situation clear, let us consider the minimization problem for a function of a single variable $f(t)$, $a \leqq t \leqq b$. Provided that $f(t)$ is continuous in the closed interval $[a, b]$, $f(t)$ assumes a minimum value at some point $\hat{t}$ of the interval because the interval is compact.

Let $f(t)$ be differentiable. Then, as is well known,

(i) $$f'(\hat{t}) = 0 \quad \text{if} \quad a < \hat{t} < b ,$$

but

(ii) $$f'(\hat{t}) \geqq 0 \quad \text{if} \quad \hat{t} = a ,$$

and

(iii) $$f'(\hat{t}) \leqq 0 \quad \text{if} \quad \hat{t} = b ,$$

where the equality sign does not necessarily hold. This point is made clear by a visual inspection of figs. 24.3 and 24.4. It is also easy to give a rigorous proof. This shows how important it is to distinguish corner and interior optimum points.

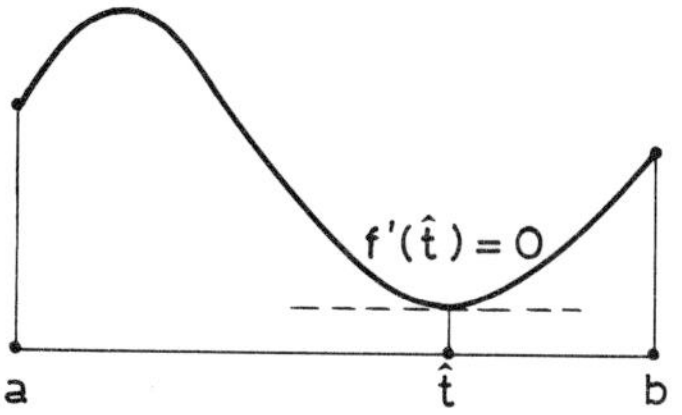

Fig. 24.3.

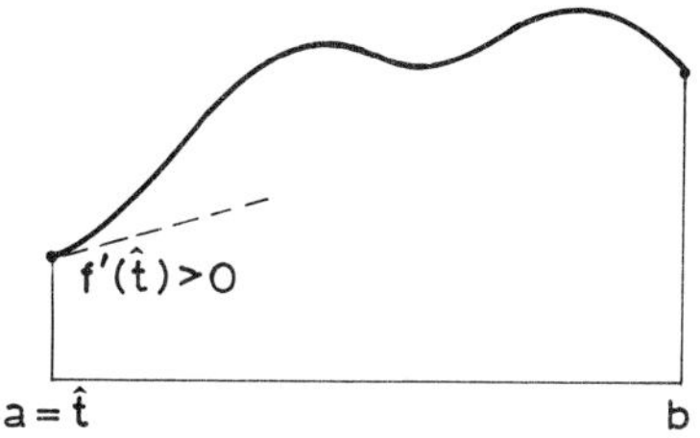

Fig. 24.4.

25. Linear programming problems

In the preceding section we pointed out the neglect of non-negativity constraints and the lack of distinction between corner optima and interior optima in the classical theory of firms. Proper considerations of the non-negativity conditions invalidate the optimum conditions (24.5) as equalities. Thus, theorems in the classical theories of firms and consumer behavior that are derived from equality conditions like (24.5) are assured of their validity only on very strong restrictions.

Then, what about the assumption of differentiability that is one of the building blocks of classical theory? This assumption does not seem to have much to do with an economic appropriateness of the theory of consumer behavior. The situation, however, is quite different in the theories of firms and production. It is certainly not impossible to formulate the techniques of fixed proportions in the input-output analysis in terms of the classical production function (24.3) with variable proportions. But as already noted, the production function (24.3) becomes nondifferentiable in our case so that it is beyond the reach of the classical analysis. In view of the realistic importance of the case of fixed proportions, its omission is a significant defect of the classical approach. The modern approach would analyze not the production function itself but the production possibility set Δ, i.e. the set of technically feasible combinations of inputs and outputs. This general analysis covers both the classical case and the fixed-proportions case as special cases.

Thus, the modern approach in mathematical economics not only concentrates on the structure of Δ as a set in its general theory of production, but also has constructed a highly specific operational theory for the case of fixed proportions. One example of it is the interindustry analysis, whose theoretical basis was already presented. Another example is the theory of *linear programming* (abbreviated as LP) that may be regarded as an extension and generalization of the former.

The canonical form of a linear programming problem. Linear programming is mathematically formalized as a maximization problem, namely that of maximizing a linear function

$$(25.1) \qquad c_1y_1 + c_2y_2 + \dots + c_ny_n$$

subject to linear inequalities

$$(25.2) \qquad \begin{array}{l} a_{11}y_1 + a_{12}y_2 + \dots + a_{1n}y_n \leqq b_1 \\ a_{21}y_1 + a_{22}y_2 + \dots + a_{2n}y_n \leqq b_2 \\ \dots\dots\dots\dots\dots\dots\dots\dots\dots\dots \\ a_{m1}y_1 + a_{m2}a_2 + \dots + a_{mn}y_n \leqq b_m \end{array}$$

and to

$$(25.3) \qquad y_1 \geqq 0, \ y_2 \geqq 0, \ \dots, \ y_n \geqq 0 .$$

This is the canonical form of a linear programming problem. a_{ij}, b_i and c_j are given constants which may be positive, negative or zero.

A great many problems may be formulated as problems of linear programming. Space does not permit us to introduce its applications in the present book that is primarily concerned with its theoretical features. The interested reader should consult reference books cited in Bibliography of this book. We shall present here two important examples in the production planning of a firm and the production and distribution problem in a national economy.

Example 25.1. Production planning of a firm.

Consider a production process that produces k outputs from m inputs. In this process, the proportions among inputs and outputs are fixed. Moreover, outputs would be λ times as large if all inputs are increased (or decreased) by λ times ($\lambda > 0$) in the given fixed proportions. Namely, there prevail ***constant returns to scale***. The processes that are postulated in the interindustry analysis are an example – a special case of $k = 1$.

Suppose that there are n such processes. The jth process produces $h_{1j}, h_{2j}, \dots, h_{kj}$ units of outputs from $a_{1j}, a_{2j}, \dots, a_{mj}$ units of inputs. Then, because of the assumption of constant returns to scale, $h_{1j}y_j, h_{2j}y_j, \dots, h_{kj}y_j$ units of outputs are produced out of $a_{1j}y_j, a_{2j}y_j, \dots, a_{mj}y_j$ units of inputs. Expressed in vector notation, the jth process is given by

$$(25.4) \qquad \text{inputs } y_j \begin{bmatrix} a_{1j} \\ a_{2j} \\ \vdots \\ a_{mj} \end{bmatrix} \to \text{outputs } y_j \begin{bmatrix} h_{1j} \\ h_{2j} \\ \vdots \\ h_{kj} \end{bmatrix} .$$

Because of the fixity of proportions among inputs and outputs and of constant returns to scale, the operation of the jth process is determined by the scalar $y_j \geqq 0$, which is called the *activity level* of the jth process.

Now what would follow if the n processes are simultaneously operated, each at the level of y_j respectively? As these processes are technically independent of each other in their operations, the inputs and outputs of one process would not be affected by the activity levels in other processes. Hence, when the processes are simultaneously operated, outputs and inputs are the sum total of outputs and inputs of the individual processes and given by

$$(25.5) \quad \text{inputs} \sum_{j=1}^{n} y_j \begin{bmatrix} a_{1j} \\ a_{2j} \\ \vdots \\ a_{mj} \end{bmatrix} \rightarrow \text{outputs} \sum_{j=1}^{n} y_j \begin{bmatrix} h_{1j} \\ h_{2j} \\ \vdots \\ h_{kj} \end{bmatrix} .$$

Denote output prices by p_i ($i = 1, 2, \ldots, k$) and input prices by q_i ($i = 1, 2, \ldots, m$). Then, the unit profit of the jth process is

$$(25.6) \quad c_j = \sum_{i=1}^{k} p_i h_{ij} - \sum_{i=1}^{m} q_i a_{ij} .$$

As can easily be derived from (25.5) and (25.6), the total profit arising from the simultaneous operations of all processes is expressed exactly as (25.1). For a competitive firm, p_i's and q_i's are data so that c_j is also a given constant. Thus, the strategic variables that the firm can select and adjust are only the activity levels $y_1, y_2, \ldots, y_n$. If the available amounts of inputs $b_1, b_2, \ldots, b_m$ are given as constants, the amounts of inputs required for the operation of the processes must satisfy (25.2). Hence, the firm decides on $y_1, y_2, \ldots, y_n$ so as to maximize (25.1) subject to (25.2) and (25.3). This is the production planning problem of a firm.

Example 25.2. Production assignment and income distribution in a national economy.

Suppose that there are n processes (25.4) in an economy. Unit value added of the jth process is given by c_j (constant). Factors of production that are used as inputs include land services, labor, and capital services (of machinery, equipment, structures, etc.). Suppose that there are m factors of production, whose existing amounts are $b_1, b_2, \ldots, b_m$. (25.2) and (25.3) represent activities that are feasible in this economy, while (25.1) is the corresponding aggregate value added. Thus, the maximization problem (25.1) ~ (25.3) is interpreted as the problem of optimal economy-wide production planning.

Factors of production contribute to production as inputs on the one hand and share value added as returns on their services on the other. Distribution of value added is effected through the market pricing mechanism. Let the price of the ith factor of production be $x_i \geqq 0$. The value added of the jth process is entirely distributed to the factors of production used as inputs in this process.

$$(25.7) \qquad b_1x_1 + b_2x_2 + \ldots + b_mx_m$$

is the sum total of value added that is to be distributed to the factors of production. It is subject to the following inequalities:

$$(25.8) \qquad \begin{aligned} a_{11}x_1 + a_{21}x_2 + \ldots + a_{m1}x_m &\geqq c_1 \\ a_{12}x_1 + a_{22}x_2 + \ldots + a_{m2}x_m &\geqq c_2 \\ \cdots\cdots\cdots\cdots\cdots\cdots\cdots\cdots& \\ a_{1n}x_1 + a_{2n}x_2 + \ldots + a_{mn}x_m &\geqq c_n \end{aligned}$$

and

$$(25.9) \qquad x_1 \geqq 0,\ x_2 \geqq 0,\ \ldots,\ x_m \geqq 0\,.$$

We thus have the minimization problem of the total distributed income (25.7) subject to (25.8) and (25.9). This is another canonical form of linear programming problems. In economics, this is the valuation problem of factors of production.

The problem may be given a more economic interpretation. (25.1) represents the sum total of value added produced and should be regarded as national income produced *. On the other hand, (25.7) is the sum total of net values that are to be distributed to the factors of production, i.e. national income distributed or earned.

Then, for the activity levels $y_1, y_2, \ldots, y_n$ that satisfy (25.2) and (25.3) and the prices $x_1, x_2, \ldots, x_m$ that satisfy (25.8) and (25.9), there holds in general an inequality

$$(25.10) \qquad b_1x_1 + b_2x_2 + \ldots + b_mx_m \geqq c_1y_1 + c_2y_2 + \ldots + c_ny_n\,.$$

This fact can be easily proved as follows: multiply the ith inequality of (25.2)

* See Section 4.

by $x_i \geqq 0$ and sum up over i to get

$$(25.11) \qquad \sum_{i,j=1}^{m,n} a_{ij} x_i y_j \leqq \sum_{i=1}^{m} b_i x_i .$$

Similarly, multiply the jth inequality of (25.8) by y_j and sum up over j to get

$$(25.12) \qquad \sum_{i,j=1}^{m,n} a_{ij} x_i y_j \geqq \sum_{j=1}^{n} c_j y_j .$$

As the left-hand side is identical in (25.11) and (25.12), we obtain (25.10).

(25.10) assures that national income distributed $\geqq$ national income produced at all times. However, for activity levels and prices that are arbitrarily fixed, there follows in general a strict inequality: national income distributed $>$national income produced. In this case, the circular flow of value within the economy would be obstructed. For it is impossible to distribute more income than produced. Then, are there particular sets of the activity levels and prices that would equate both sides of the national income inequality? This is the existence problem of equilibrium activity levels and prices – a simple case of the problem (b) proposed in Section 23. This problem will be solved in the affirmative. The solution demonstrates the property of *duality* *, which provides the fundamental theorems in linear programming.

The theorems show that there exist the maximum of (25.1) subject to (25.2) and (25.3) and the minimum of (25.7) subject to (25.8) and (25.9) and that the two extremum values coincide with each other. Thus, the equilibrium sets of the activity levels and prices are obtained as solutions of the maximization and minimization problems.

It was implicitly assumed in these economic interpretations that the constants a_{ij}, b_i and c_j are non-negative real numbers. However, it is clear that the signs of the coefficients are immaterial to the mathematical content of these interpretations. The re-examination of Example 25.2 above, with this point in mind, leads us to the fact that there is a close connection between the maximization problem (25.1) ~ (25.3) and the minimization problem (25.7) ~ (25.9). We list special relations between the two optimization problems:

(a) The arrays of coefficients a_{ij} in the two problems are transposes to each other.

(b) Coefficients $b_1, b_2, \ldots, b_m$ in the function (25.7) that is to be mini-

* See Section 4, especially Theorem 4.1.

mized in the minimization problem, i.e. the *objective functional*, are identical to the constants on the right-hand side of (25.2), the constraints in the maximization problem.

(c) Coefficients $c_1, c_2, ..., c_n$ in the objective functional (25.1) in the maximization problem are identical to the constants on the right-hand side of (25.8), the constraints in the minimization problem.

(d) The inequality sign of (25.2) is reversed in (25.8).

The two linear programming problems that stand in such relations as these are called *dual* to each other. One is considered the primal problem and the other its dual problem.

Before going into a more detailed study, it should be noted that there is an important reason for having used the adjective, "operational", in describing linear programming problems. There are not only qualitative findings for linear programming that are to be explained below, but also establihsed practical computational solutions *. Thus, it is possible to apply linear programming to actual problems as it witnessed in many practical applications. In this sense, computational methods are important and a theoretical examination of these methods is an interesting task, but space does not permit us to introduce them in this book. The reader should consult other reference books on linear programming for this.

In a matrix and vector form, we put

$$A = \begin{bmatrix} a_{11} & a_{12} & \cdots & a_{1n} \\ a_{21} & a_{22} & \cdots & a_{2n} \\ & & & \\ a_{m1} & a_{m2} & \cdots & a_{mn} \end{bmatrix}, \quad b = \begin{bmatrix} b_1 \\ b_2 \\ \vdots \\ b_m \end{bmatrix}, \quad c = \begin{bmatrix} c_1 \\ c_2 \\ \vdots \\ c_n \end{bmatrix}, \quad x = \begin{bmatrix} x_1 \\ x_2 \\ \vdots \\ x_m \end{bmatrix}, \text{ and } y = \begin{bmatrix} y_1 \\ y_2 \\ \vdots \\ y_n \end{bmatrix}.$$

Then, our linear programming problems are summarized as follows:

(M) maximization problem: max (c, y) subject to $Ay \leqq b$, $y \geqq 0$;
(m) minimization problem: min (b, x) subject to $A'x \geqq c, x \geqq 0$;

The two problems are dual to each other **.

Remark 1. A minimization problem

$$\min (5x_1 - 2x_2 + 6x_3)$$

* The simplex method is the most standard one. Many textbooks on linear programming are devoted to introducing applications and computational methods, in particular the simplex method.

** (b, x) and (c, y) are inner products.

subject to

$$\begin{cases} -x_1 + 2x_2 + 4x_3 \leqq -1 \\ -3x_1 + x_2 + x_3 \geqq 2 \\ x_1 \geqq 0,\ x_2 \geqq 0,\ x_3 \geqq 0 \end{cases}$$

is transformed into a minimization problem of type (m) by rearranging the first inequality. Then, we have

$$\min\,(5x_1 - 2x_2 + 6x_3)$$

subject to

$$\begin{cases} x_1 - 2x_2 - 4x_3 \geqq 1 \\ -3x_1 + x_2 + x_3 \geqq 2 \\ x_1 \geqq 0,\ x_2 \geqq 0,\ x_3 \geqq 0\,. \end{cases}$$

Any optimization problem of a linear function subject to linear inequalities and non-negativity constraints of variables can be standardized into a linear programming problem of type (M) or (m) by rearranging the inequalities and, if necessary, by changing the signs of constants in the objective functional.

Remark 2. There may not necessarily exist a vector that satisfies the constraints in an arbitrarily posed linear programming problem. For instance, there is no solution for the inequalities in the example of Remark 1. By adding up its two inequalities, we obtain $-2x_1 - x_2 - 3x_3 \geqq 3$. Its left-hand side cannot be positive because of the non-negativity conditions $x_1 \geqq 0$, $x_2 \geqq 0$, and $x_3 \geqq 0$. It is therefore less than 3 and contradicts the assumed existence of the solution. Hence, there is no solution of this problem.

Remark 3. Examine the following problem:
Maximize $(y_1 + y_2)$ subject to

$$\begin{cases} y_1 - y_2 \leqq 2 \\ y_1 - 2y_2 \leqq 1 \\ y_1 \geqq 0,\ y_2 \geqq 0\,. \end{cases}$$

Let $\lambda > 0$ be any positive number. Then, $y_1 = y_2 = \lambda$ satisfy the inequalities. The objective functional assumes the value $y_1 + y_2 = 2\lambda$, which can be made as large as one likes. Therefore, there are vectors that satisfy the constraints, while there is no maximum *. The reader should construct its dual problem and verify that there is no vector that satisfies its constraints.

These remarks demonstrate that linear programming problems may and may not have solutions. It is the duality theorems that in a systematic way clarify an important property that underlies these phenomena.

Let X be the set of vectors x that satisfy the constraints of the problem (m), i.e.

$$X = \{x \mid x \geqq 0, A'x \geqq c\} \tag{25.13}$$

and let Y be the set of vectors y that satisfy the constraints of the problem (M), i.e.

$$Y = \{y \mid y \geqq 0, Ay \leqq b\}\,. \tag{25.14}$$

Elements of X and Y are called *feasible*. If $X \neq \phi$, then it is also said that "the problem (m) is feasible". The same mode of expression applies to (M).

DUALITY THEOREM 25.1. *If $X \neq \phi$ and $Y \neq \phi$, then*

(i) $(b, x) \geqq (c, y)$ *(for any $x \in X$ and any $y \in Y$)*

and

(ii) $(b, \hat{x}) = (c, \hat{y})$ *(for some $\hat{x} \in X$ and some $\hat{y} \in Y$)*.

DUALITY THEOREM 25.2. *For $X \neq \phi$,*

(i) *If $Y \neq \phi$, then the problem (m) has* $\min_{x \in X} (b, x)$.

(ii) *If $Y = \phi$, then the objective functional (b, x) of the problem (m) can be made as small as one likes, i.e.* $\inf_{x \in X} (b, x) = -\infty$.

(iii) *If the problem (m) has* $\min_{x \in X} (b, x)$, *then $Y \neq \phi$ and the problem (M) has* $\max_{y \in Y} (c, y)$. *The two extremum values are equal.*

DUALITY THEOREM 25.2d. *For $Y \neq \phi$,*

(i) *If $X \neq \phi$, then the problem (M) has* $\max_{y \in Y} (c, y)$.

* One may symbolically write this as $\max (y_1 + y_2) = +\infty$.

(ii) *If* $X = \phi$, *then the objective functional* (c, y) *of the problem (M) can be made as large as one likes, i.e.* $\sup_{y \in Y} (c, y) = +\infty$.

(iii) *If the problem (M) has* $\max_{y \in Y} (c, y)$, then $X \neq \phi$ *and the problem (m) has* $\min_{x \in X} (b, x)$. *The two extremum values are equal.*

Now how can we prove these theorems? In linear programming, corner optima play an essential role so that it is not possible to make a mechanical application of differential calculus in solving its problems. This has led us to a positive use of various properties of convex sets, in particular the separation theorems, as a standard and efficient way of dealing with the duality theorems and many other similar problems. The separation theorems on convex sets have been powerful in the analysis of mathematically analogous problems in linear programming, game theory, and linear economic models. To cite an example, the proof of the fundamental theorem in game theory was initially based on the fixed point theorem that is a relatively sophisticated theorem in the convex set theory. But J. von Neumann, the initiator of game theory himself, later gave an elementary proof by applying a separation theorem. Since then, the separation theorems seem to have become a standard routine in mathematical economics. This book will devote a few subsequent chapters on the separation theorems and their applications, where a standard proof will be given to the duality theorems.

However, this does not mean that it is impossible to treat the duality theorems by means of differential calculus. Rather, such an undertaking is possible, though some special devices must be adopted. We shall describe this treatment in the next section as a prelude to the modern approach. It would, in my belief, pave our way from differential calculus to the separation theorems.

To conclude this section, we add several remarks on the duality theorems.

Remark 4. Duality theorems 25.2 and 25.2d are dual to each other. Further, the problem (m) can be rearranged to a problem of type (M): $\max (-b, x)$ subject to $-A'x \leqq -c$, $x \geqq 0$. Similarly, the problem (M) can be transformed into a problem (m). Hence, the two theorems are identical in substance.

Remark 5. By virtue of (i) and (ii) of Duality theorem 25.1, we get

(a) $(b, \hat{x}) \leqq (b, x)$ for any $x \in X$, i.e. $(b, \hat{x}) = \min_{x \in X} (b, x)$, and

(b) $(c, \hat{y}) \geqq (c, y)$ for any $y \in Y$, i.e. $(c, \hat{y}) = \max_{y \in Y} (c, y)$, from which (i) of Duality Theorems 25.2 and 25.2d can be derived.

Remark 6. (iii) of Duality Theorems 25.2 and 25.2d can be easily derived from the other parts of the theorems. In fact, the optimum of the primal problem, if it exists, is neither positively nor negatively infinite so that the dual problem is feasible because of (ii) of Duality Theorems 25.2 and 25.2d. For subsequent steps of the proof, we may consult Remark 5.

From Remarks 5 ~ 6 it is now clear that only Duality Theorem 25.1 and (ii) of Duality Theorems 25.2 and 25.2d remain to be proved. Their proofs can be worked out by means of a method such as explained in the following section as well as the separation theorems.

Remark 7. Example 25.2 already demonstrated how to derive (i) of Duality Theorem 25.1 *. Now let $\hat{x} \in X$ and $\hat{y} \in Y$ be solutions that satisfy (ii) of Duality Theorem 25.1 (called the *optimal solutions*). Substituting them into (25.11) and (25.12), we see that their right-hand sides are identical. Thus, (25.11) and (25.12) hold with equality signs. By rearranging terms, we get

$$(25.15) \qquad \sum_{i=1}^{m} (b_i - \sum_{j=1}^{n} a_{ij}\hat{y}_j)\,\hat{x}_i = 0$$

and

$$(25.16) \qquad \sum_{j=1}^{n} (\sum_{i=1}^{m} a_{ij}\hat{x}_i - c_j)\,\hat{y}_j = 0\,.$$

As $\hat{x} \in X$ and $\hat{y} \in Y$, we have $\hat{x}_i \geqq 0$ and $\hat{y}_j \geqq 0$. It is also seen that the expressions in the parentheses, i.e. the coefficients of the variables in (25.15) and (25.16) are non-negative. We can easily see from these results that

$$(\alpha) \text{ if } \qquad \sum_{j=1}^{n} a_{ij}\hat{y}_j < b_i\,, \quad \text{then } \hat{x}_i = 0 \text{ for this } i$$

and

$$(\beta) \text{ if } \qquad \sum_{i=1}^{m} a_{ij}\hat{x}_i > c_j\,, \quad \text{then } \hat{y}_j = 0 \text{ for this } j\,.$$

* See eq. (25.10).

This fact can be economically interpreted as follows in reference to Example 25.2: In equilibrium, (α) the factor of production i would become a free good with a zero price if it exists in excess of what is required for the actual use and (β) a process would not be operated if the factors of production require returns in excess of value added produced in this process; in other words, a process with operating deficits would not be employed.

26. The differential-calculus approach to linear programming *

In this section, we apply differential calculus to prove (ii) of Duality Theorem 25.1.

For this proof, it is sufficient to demonstrate that an inequality $(b, \hat{x}) \leqq (c, \hat{y})$ holds for appropriate $\hat{x} \in X$ and $\hat{y} \in Y$ **. For it is known that $(b, \hat{x}) \geqq (c, \hat{y})$ in (i) of this theorem. Hence, immediately we get $(b, \hat{x}) = (c, \hat{y})$. Thus, we are required to prove the next theorem.

THEOREM 26.1. *If $X \neq \phi$ and $Y \neq \phi$, then the system of inequalities (25.2), (25.3), (25.8), (25.9) and*

$$\sum_{i=1}^{m} b_i x_i - \sum_{j=1}^{n} c_j y_j \leqq 0$$

has a solution. The last inequality makes conditions more stringent.

For the proof of the theorem, we begin with two preliminary observations.

Observation 1. Let us begin with introducing a function of a special form that will be employed in the proof. A function of a real variable t

(26.1) $\qquad \theta(t) = \max(t, 0)$

is a continuous function represented by

$$\theta(t) = \begin{cases} t & \text{for } t \geqq 0 \\ 0 & \text{for } t < 0 . \end{cases}$$

Its graph is shown in fig. 26.1. At $t = 0$, the function is not differentiable as

* This section is based on Nikaido [48, 49].

** X and Y are as defined in (25.13) and (25.14).

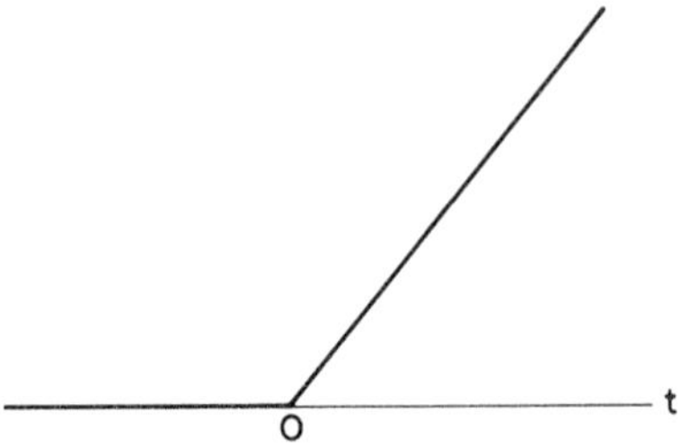

Fig. 26.1.

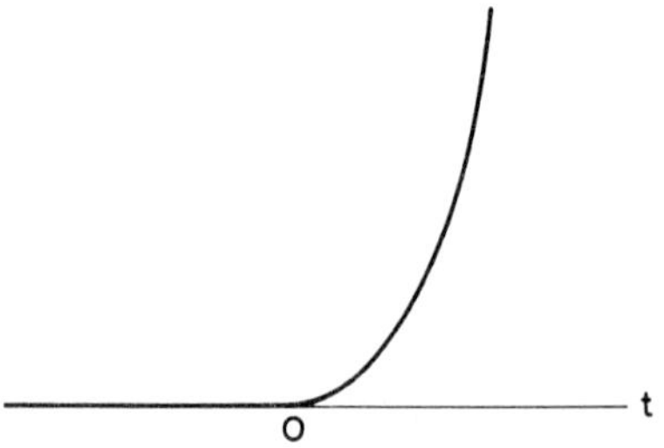

Fig. 26.2.

its right-hand derivative is 1 and its left-hand derivative is 0 at this point. However, the square of this function

(26.2) $\quad f(t) = \theta(t)^2$

is everywhere differentiable. In fact, $f(t)$ is represented intervalwise by

$$f(t) = \begin{cases} t^2 & \text{for } t \geqq 0 \\ 0 & \text{for } t < 0\,, \end{cases}$$

which is 0 always for $t < 0$ and a quadratic function t^2 for $t > 0$. It is differentiable in these intervals. On the other hand, at $t = 0$, its right-hand and left-hand derivatives are both 0. Hence, $f(t)$ has a derivative

$$f'(t) = \begin{cases} 2t & \text{for } t \geqq 0 \\ 0 & \text{for } t < 0\,, \end{cases}$$

which is

(26.3) $\quad f'(t) = 2\theta(t)$

in view of (26.1). Thus, this derivative is continuous. Fig. 26.2 is the graph of $f(t)$.

Let $g(x_1, x_2, ..., x_k)$ be a partially differentiable function in k variables. Then, the function

$$F(x_1, x_2, ..., x_k) = f(g(x_1, x_2, ..., x_k))$$

is partially differentiable. Its partial derivatives are given by

(26.4) $\quad \partial F/\partial x_i = 2\theta(g(x_1, x_2, ..., x_k))\dfrac{\partial g}{\partial x_i} \qquad (i = 1, 2, ..., k)\,,$

because of the rule on composed functions in differential calculus and (26.3).

Observation 2. The lemma given below provides a necessary condition that is satisfied in general by minima including corner minima. It will be employed in our proof.

LEMMA. *Let $F(x)$, a function of k numerical variables * be defined for non-negative vectors $x \geqq 0$ in R^k and have continuous partial derivatives. If $F(x)$ attains a minimum at $x = \hat{x} \geqq 0$, the following two conclusions hold **:*

(i) $$\left[\frac{\partial F}{\partial x_i}\right]_{x=\hat{x}} \geqq 0 \quad (i = 1, 2, ..., k)$$

and

(ii) $$\sum_{i=1}^{k} \hat{x}_i \left[\frac{\partial F}{\partial x_i}\right]_{x=\hat{x}} = 0$$

so that $[\partial F/\partial x_i]_{x=\hat{x}} = 0$ *for* $\hat{x}_i > 0$ *because of* (i) *and* (ii) *in view of* $\hat{x}_i \geqq 0$.

Proof. For any $y \geqq 0$, form a segment connecting $\hat{x}$ and y

(26.5) $$x(t) = (1-t)\hat{x} + ty \quad (0 \leqq t \leqq 1)\,.$$

As the components of $x(t)$ are all non-negative, we have $x(t) \geqq 0$. Now $F(x)$ reaches a minimum at $x = \hat{x}$ by assumption so that

$$F(\hat{x}) \leqq F(x(t)) \quad (0 \leqq t \leqq 1)\,,$$

from which we get

(26.6) $$0 \leqq \frac{1}{t}\,(F(x(t)) - F(x(0))) \quad (0 < t \leqq 1)$$

as $x(0) = \hat{x}$. As $F(x(t))$ is differentiable from the assumptions, we obtain

(26.7) $$0 \leqq \left[\frac{\mathrm{d}}{\mathrm{d}t} F(x(t))\right]_{t=0}$$

by letting $t \to 0$ in (26.6). On the other hand, the rule on composed functions

* x is a vector with components $x_1, x_2, ..., x_k$.

** $[\partial F/\partial x_i]_{x=\hat{x}}$ that appears below represents the value of the partial derivative $\partial F/\partial x_i$ at $x = \hat{x}$.

gives us

$$(26.8)\qquad \left[\frac{\mathrm{d}}{\mathrm{d}t}F(x(t))\right]_{t=0} = \sum_{i=1}^{k}(y_i - \hat{x}_i)\left[\frac{\partial F}{\partial x_i}\right]_{x=\hat{x}} .$$

(26.7) and (26.8) lead to

$$(26.9)\qquad \sum_{i=1}^{k} \hat{x}_i \left[\frac{\partial F}{\partial x_i}\right]_{x=\hat{x}} \leqq \sum_{i=1}^{k} y_i \left[\frac{\partial F}{\partial x_i}\right]_{x=\hat{x}} ,$$

which holds for any $y \geqq 0$. Set $y_i = \lambda > 0$ and all the other components of y zero. Also put the left-hand side of (26.9) equal to μ (= constant!). Then, we get

$$\frac{\mu}{\lambda} \leqq \left[\frac{\partial F}{\partial x_i}\right]_{x=\hat{x}} .$$

By letting $\lambda \to +\infty$ in this relation, we see that its left-hand side converges toward 0. Thus, we get (i). Then, $\hat{x} \geqq 0$ and (i) imply that the left-hand side of (26.9) is non-negative. Moreover, setting $y = 0$ in (26.9) yields its left-hand side $\leqq 0$. Combining these results together, we get (ii).

Proof of Theorem 26.1. Define a function of $m + n$ variables, $x_1, x_2, \ldots, x_m, y_1, y_2, \ldots, y_n$:

$$(26.10)\qquad F(x, y) = \sum_{i=1}^{m} \sigma_i(y)^2 + \sum_{j=1}^{n} \tau_j(x)^2 + \rho(x, y)^2$$

where x is a vector with components $x_1, x_2, \ldots, x_m$ and y is a vector with components $y_1, y_2, \ldots, y_n$. $\sigma_i(y)$, $\tau_j(x)$ and $\rho(x, y)$ are defined as follows:

$$(26.11)\qquad \sigma_i(y) = \max\left(\sum_{j=1}^{n} a_{ij}y_j - b_i, 0\right) \quad (i = 1, 2, \ldots, m)$$

$$(26.12)\qquad \tau_j(x) = \max\left(c_j - \sum_{i=1}^{m} a_{ij}x_i, 0\right) \quad (j = 1, 2, \ldots, n)$$

$$(26.13)\qquad \rho(x, y) = \max\left(\sum_{i=1}^{m} b_i x_i - \sum_{j=1}^{n} c_j y_j, 0\right) .$$

As is clear from the form of (26.10), each of the terms on the right-hand side is non-negative so that we always have $F(x, y) \geqq 0$. If $F(x, y) = 0$ for appropriate $x \geqq 0$ and $y \geqq 0$, the terms on the right-hand side are all 0, i.e. $\sigma_i(y) = \tau_j(x) = \rho(x, y) = 0$ (for all i and j). Then, the definitional equations (26.11), (26.12), and (26.13) reveal that

$$\sum_{j=1}^{n} a_{ij}y_j - b_i \leqq \sigma_i(y) = 0 \quad (i = 1, 2, ..., m) ,$$

$$c_j - \sum_{i=1}^{m} a_{ij}x_i \leqq \tau_j(x) = 0 \quad (j = 1, 2, ..., n) ,$$

and

$$\sum_{i=1}^{m} b_i x_i - \sum_{j=1}^{n} c_j y_j \leqq \rho(x, y) = 0 ,$$

which prove the theorem.

Thus, it suffices to give the proof in two stages:
(a) $F(x, y)$ attains a minimum in the domain $x \geqq 0$ and $y \geqq 0$;
(b) if $X \neq \phi$ and $Y \neq \phi$, then $\min_{x \geqq 0, y \geqq 0} F(x, y) = 0$.

The proof of (a) will be given in the next chapter *. Here we give a proof of (b), on the assumption that (a) holds.

Assume that $F(x, y)$ reaches a minimum in the domain at $x = \hat{x}$ and $y = \hat{y}$. Then, the lemma shows that the conditions described in (i) and (ii) hold there. Applying (26.4) to σ_i^2, τ_j^2, and ρ^2, we see that (i) and (ii) of the lemma are given by

$$(26.14) \qquad \frac{1}{2}\left[\frac{\partial F}{\partial x_i}\right]_{\substack{x=\hat{x}\\ y=\hat{y}}} = -\sum_{j=1}^{n} a_{ij}\tau_j(\hat{x}) + \rho(\hat{x}, \hat{y})\, b_i \geqq 0 \quad (i = 1, 2, ..., m),$$

$$(26.15) \qquad \frac{1}{2}\left[\frac{\partial F}{\partial y_j}\right]_{\substack{x=\hat{x}\\ y=\hat{y}}} = \sum_{i=1}^{m} a_{ij}\sigma_i(\hat{y}) - \rho(\hat{x}, \hat{y})\, c_j \geqq 0 \quad (j = 1, 2, ..., n) ,$$

* See applications in Section 27. It is obvious that $\inf_{x \geqq 0,\, y \geqq 0} F(x, y) \geqq 0$ because $F(x, y) \geqq 0$ everywhere.

and

$$(26.16)\qquad \frac{1}{2}\sum_{i=1}^{m}\hat{x}_i\left[\frac{\partial F}{\partial x_i}\right]_{\substack{x=\hat{x}\\ y=\hat{y}}}+\frac{1}{2}\sum_{j=1}^{n}\hat{y}_j\left[\frac{\partial F}{\partial y_j}\right]_{\substack{x=\hat{x}\\ y=\hat{y}}}$$

$$=-\sum_{j=1}^{n}\tau_j(\hat{x})\sum_{i=1}^{m}a_{ij}\hat{x}_i+\sum_{i=1}^{m}\sigma_i(\hat{y})\sum_{j=1}^{n}a_{ij}\hat{y}_j$$

$$+\rho(\hat{x},\hat{y})\,(\sum_{i=1}^{m}b_i\hat{x}_i-\sum_{j=1}^{n}c_j\hat{y}_j)=0\,.$$

The function $\theta(t)$ of (26.1) is such that $\theta(t)^2 = t\theta(t) = 0$ for $\theta(t) = 0$, and $\theta(t)^2 = t\theta(t)$ for $\theta(t) > 0$. Thus, it always follows that

$$(26.17)\qquad \theta(t)^2 = t\theta(t)\,.$$

We may rewrite (26.16) in a simpler form by means of (26.17). Applying (26.17) and referring to the definitions (26.11), (26.12) and (26.13), we obtain

$$\sigma_i(\hat{y})^2=\sigma_i(\hat{y})\,(\sum_{j=1}^{n}a_{ij}\hat{y}_j-b_i)\qquad(i=1,2,\ldots,m),$$

$$\tau_j(\hat{x})^2=\tau_j(\hat{x})\,(c_j-\sum_{i=1}^{m}a_{ij}\hat{x}_i)\qquad(j=1,2,\ldots,n)\,,$$

and

$$\rho(\hat{x},\hat{y})^2=\rho(\hat{x},\hat{y})\,(\sum_{i=1}^{m}b_i\hat{x}_i-\sum_{j=1}^{n}c_j\hat{y}_j)\,.$$

They sum up to $F(\hat{x}, \hat{y})$ on the left-hand side because of the definition (26.10). On the right-hand side, all the terms except

$$\sum_{j=1}^{n}c_j\tau_j(\hat{x})-\sum_{i=1}^{m}b_i\sigma_i(\hat{y})$$

add up to 0 because of (26.16). Hence,

$$(26.18)\qquad F(\hat{x},\hat{y})=\sum_{j=1}^{n}c_j\tau_j(\hat{x})-\sum_{i=1}^{m}b_i\sigma_i(\hat{y})\,.$$

We should note that the assumption that $X\neq\phi$ and $Y\neq\phi$ has not been employed at all so far in our proof. Thus, (26.14), (26.15) and (26.18) hold regardless of this assumption.

Next, let us show that $F(\hat{x},\hat{y})=0$ when $X\neq\phi$ and $Y\neq\phi$. For this purpose, let

$$(26.19)\qquad \gamma=\inf\,[(b,x)-(c,y)]\quad(\text{for all } x\in X \text{ and } y\in X)\,.$$

(i) of Duality Theorem 25.1 shows that $\gamma\geqq 0$. By the definition of the infimum, for any $\epsilon>0$ there should exist $x\in X$ and $y\in Y$ such that

$$(26.20)\qquad \gamma+\epsilon>(b,x)-(c,y)\,.$$

Define non-negative vectors $\sigma(\hat{y})$ and $\tau(\hat{x})$ to be

$$\sigma(\hat{y})=\begin{bmatrix}\sigma_1(\hat{y})\\ \sigma_2(\hat{y})\\ \vdots\\ \sigma_m(\hat{y})\end{bmatrix}\quad\text{and}\quad\tau(\hat{x})=\begin{bmatrix}\tau_1(\hat{x})\\ \tau_2(\hat{x})\\ \vdots\\ \tau_n(\hat{x})\end{bmatrix}\,.$$

Then, (26.14) and (26.15) are expressed in matrix notation as

$$(26.21)\qquad A\tau(\hat{x})\leqq\rho(\hat{x},\hat{y})b$$

and

$$(26.22)\qquad A'\sigma(\hat{y})\geqq\rho(\hat{x},\hat{y})c\,.$$

On the other hand, $x\in X$ and $y\in Y$ that satisfy (26.20) also fulfil

$$(26.23)\qquad Ay\leqq b$$

and

$$(26.24)\qquad A'x\geqq c\,.$$

Adding (26.23) to (26.21) and (26.24) to (26.22) and dividing them by

$1+\rho(\hat{x},\hat{y})>0$, we get

$$A\frac{y+\tau(\hat{x})}{1+\rho(\hat{x},\hat{y})}\leqq b \quad\text{and}\quad A'\frac{x+\sigma(\hat{y})}{1+\rho(\hat{x},\hat{y})}\geqq c\,,$$

so that

$$\frac{x+\sigma(\hat{y})}{1+\rho(\hat{x},\hat{y})}\in X \quad\text{and}\quad \frac{y+\tau(\hat{x})}{1+\rho(\hat{x},\hat{y})}\in Y.$$

Hence, because of (26.19),

$$(b,\frac{x+\sigma(\hat{y})}{1+\rho(\hat{x},\hat{y})})-(c,\frac{y+\tau(\hat{x})}{1+\rho(\hat{x},\hat{y})})\geqq\gamma\,,$$

which is rearranged into

$$(b,\sigma(\hat{y}))-(c,\tau(\hat{x}))\geqq\gamma\rho(\hat{x},\hat{y})+\gamma-[(b,x)-(c,y)]\,.$$

Now since $\gamma\rho(\hat{x},\hat{y})\geqq 0$ and $\gamma-[(b,x)-(c,y)]>-\epsilon$ by (26.20), we get

(26.25) $$(b,\sigma(\hat{y}))-(c,\tau(\hat{x}))>-\epsilon\,.$$

The left-hand side of (26.25) is a constant, while ϵ on the right-hand side is arbitrary. Then,

$$(b,\sigma(\hat{y}))-(c,\tau(\hat{x}))\geqq 0\,,$$

i.e.

$$\sum_{j=1}^{n}c_j\tau_j(\hat{x})-\sum_{i=1}^{m}b_i\sigma_i(\hat{y})\leqq 0\,,$$

which shows that the left-hand side of (26.18) is not positive so that $F(\hat{x},\hat{y})\leqq 0$. It follows from $0\leqq F(\hat{x},\hat{y})\leqq 0$ that $F(\hat{x},\hat{y})=0$. [Q.E.D.]

(ii) of Duality Theorems 25.2 and 25.2d can be proved by following the same procedure.

Chapter 5

INTRODUCTION TO MATHEMATICS (II) PROPERTIES OF CONVEX SETS

27. Convex sets

This chapter supplements point set theory outlined in Chapter 2. It concentrates on properties of convex sets – primarily on the separation theorems – as we announced earlier. Unless otherwise noted, all points and sets appearing below refer to those of R^n.

As noted in the preceding section *, a segment connecting two end points x and y in R^n is a point set represented by the expression

(27.1) $\alpha x + \beta y; \quad \alpha, \beta \geqq 0, \quad \alpha + \beta = 1.$

This set is denoted notationally by $[x, y]$, just like a closed interval of real numbers. Individual points of the segment $[x, y]$ are called *convex linear combinations* of x and y. A subset X of R^n is called a *convex set* if a segment $[x, y]$ with any two end points x and y in X is always included in X. In fig. 27.1, the set in the right-hand figure is convex, but the one on the left is not.

For the sake of convenience, we count an empty set as a convex set. Hence, in order to prove that a set X is convex, it suffices to show that $X \ni x, y \Rightarrow \alpha x + \beta y \in X$ (for any $\alpha \geqq 0, \beta \geqq 0$, and $\alpha + \beta = 1$).

There are many examples of convex sets.

Example 27.1. A set represented by a system of linear inequalities, like the constraints (25.2) in a linear programming problem, is convex. In general, a set formed by solutions to a system of some ** linear inequalities or that of

* See equation (26.5).
** A finite or infinite number.

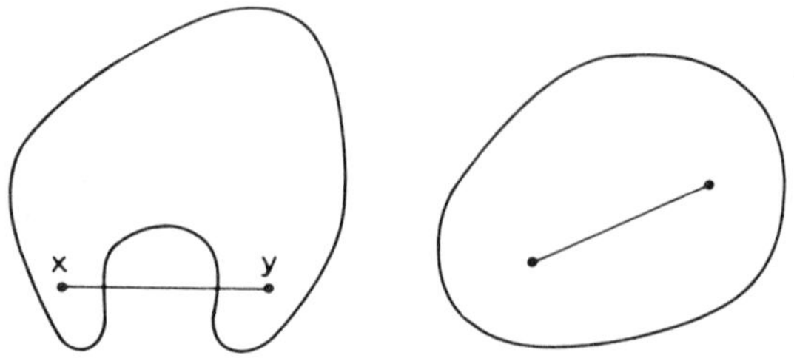

Fig. 27.1.

linear equations or their mixed system is convex. In other words, given non-homogeneous linear functions

$$f_\lambda(x) = \sum_{j=1}^{n} a_{\lambda j} x_j + b_\lambda \quad (\lambda \in \Lambda)\,,$$

the set of solutions to a system of inequalities $f_\lambda(x) \geqq 0$,

$$(27.2) \qquad X = \{x \mid f_\lambda(x) \geqq 0,\ \lambda \in \Lambda\}$$

is a convex set where Λ is the set of suffixes. In this case, for all or some of λ, the inequality $\geqq$ may be changed to a strict inequality $>$ or equality $=$, or reversed without affecting the conclusion.

Proof. This is easily proved, but we shall give the proof for the reader's benefit. For $x, y \in X$, we have $f_\lambda(x) \geqq 0$ and $f_\lambda(y) \geqq 0$. As $f_\lambda(x) - b_\lambda$ is a homogeneous linear function, $f_\lambda(\alpha x + \beta y) - b_\lambda = \alpha(f_\lambda(x) - b_\lambda) + \beta(f_\lambda(y) - b_\lambda) \geqq \alpha(-b_\lambda) + \beta(-b_\lambda) = -(\alpha+\beta)b_\lambda = -b_\lambda$ for any $\alpha \geqq 0, \beta \geqq 0$ and $\alpha + \beta = 1$. $\therefore f_\lambda(\alpha x + \beta y) \geqq 0$. As this holds for any $\lambda \in \Lambda$, we get $\alpha x + \beta y \in X$. The same holds true for the other cases.

As special cases of this finding, we may establish the following properties:

(i) The set of all non-negative vectors in R^n, i.e. the *positive orthant*

$$R_+^n = \{x \mid x \in R^n,\ x \geqq 0\}$$

is a convex set. (Cf. fig. 27.2).

(ii) In the linear programming problem of type (M), the domain Y in which the variables are allowed to range and the collection Y_0 of all optimal solutions are convex subsets in R_+^n. Of course, $Y_0 \subset Y$. Similarly, in the problem of type (m), the domain X in which the variables are allowed to range and the

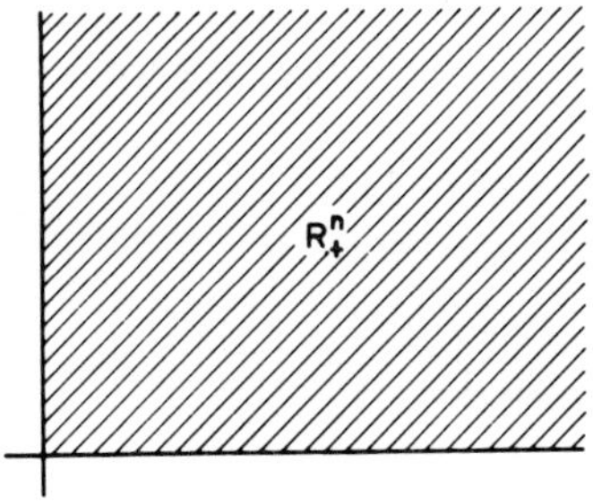

Fig. 27.2.

collection X_0 of all optimal solutions are convex subsets in R^m_+.

Example 27.2. A subset L of R^n is called a *linear subspace* when $\alpha x + \beta y \in L$ (for any real numbers α and β), if $L \ni x, y$. L is called an *affine subspace* when $\alpha x + \beta y \in L$ (for any real numbers α, β, and $\alpha + \beta = 1$) if $L \ni x, y$. It is readily noted from the definitions that they are convex sets. A linear subspace is such a special affine subspace as passes through the origin.

Example 27.3. A set $L = \{x \mid f(x) = 0\}$, defined for a linear function

$$f(x) = \sum_{j=1}^{n} a_j x_j + b:$$

$R^n \to R$ (provided that some of the coefficients a_j are not 0), is called a *hyperplane.* This is an affine subspace. A straight line in R^2 and a plane in R^3 are its examples.

A hyperplane separates R^n into two convex sets, $X_+ = \{x \mid f(x) \geqq 0\}$ and $X_- = \{x \mid f(x) \leqq 0\}$, which are called *half-spaces.* The intersection of X_+ and X_- is the original hyperplane so that $L = X_+ \cap X_-$. Hence, the set of solutions to the inequalities (27.2) can be regarded as the intersection of a finite or infinite number of half-spaces except for a special case where it coincides with R^n itself.

Example 27.4. Let X be a convex set in R^n. A function φ: $X \to R$ is called a *convex function* if it satisfies

$$(27.3) \qquad \varphi(\alpha x + \beta y) \leqq \alpha\varphi(x) + \beta\varphi(y)$$

(for any $x, y \in X$, $\alpha \geqq 0$, $\beta \geqq 0$, and $\alpha + \beta = 1$).

$\varphi(x)$ is called a *concave function* if $-\varphi(x)$ is a convex function.

Suppose that there are a finite or infinite number of convex functions $\varphi_\lambda (\lambda \in \Lambda)$, all defined on the same domain. Then, a set

$$(27.4) \qquad \{x \mid \varphi_\lambda(x) \leqq \alpha_\lambda, \lambda \in \Lambda\},$$

where α_λ is a given constant, is a convex subset of X. This can be easily proved by (27.3). This result holds for strict inequalities $<$ as well as $\leqq$. It may be noted that the norms $\|x\|$, $\|x\|_1$, and $\|x\|_2$, introduced in section 11, are all good examples of convex functions (defined on the whole of R^n). The reader should verify this fact. This finding can be used to show that, for any norm, the spherical ϵ-neighborhood * $U(a, \epsilon)$ and the closed spherical ϵ-neighborhood ** $\bar{U}(a, \epsilon)$ are convex sets. In fact, $\varphi(x) = \|x - a\|$ is a convex function; we may write $U(a, \epsilon) = \{x \mid \varphi(x) < \epsilon\}$, a special case of the present example. The same also holds for $\bar{U}(a, \epsilon)$.

Convex linear combinations of multiple points. A linear combination

$$\sum_{i=1}^{s} \alpha_i x^i$$

that is formed by assigning weights

$$\alpha_i \geqq 0, \quad \sum_{i=1}^{s} \alpha_i = 1$$

to a finite number of points $x^1, x^2, \ldots, x^s$ in R^n is called a convex linear combination of these points.

A convex set X was defined to be a set that contains a convex linear combination of any two points in it. In general, the following theorem holds:

THEOREM 27.1. *Let X be a convex subset. If $x^i \in X$ $(i = 1, 2, \ldots, s)$, then a convex linear combination of $x^1, x^2, \ldots, x^s$ is contained in X.*

Proof. If $s = 2$, the assertion is nothing but the definition of a convex set. Suppose that the theorem holds for $s = m$. We prove the theorem for $s = m + 1$ by induction. If one of the $m + 1$ weights α_i $(i = 1, 2, \ldots, m + 1)$ is 0, the convex linear combination can be regarded as a convex linear combination of m points and is contained in X because of the inductive hypothesis. If $\alpha_i > 0$ $(i = 1, 2, \ldots, m + 1)$, rewrite it as

* Eq. (12.5).
** Example 14.5.

$$(27.5) \qquad \sum_{i=1}^{s} \alpha_i x^i = \alpha_1 x^1 + (1-\alpha_1) \sum_{i=2}^{m+1} \frac{\alpha_i}{1-\alpha_1} x^i ,$$

which is contained in X as a convex linear combination of two points x^1 and

$$\sum_{i=2}^{m+1} \frac{\alpha_i}{1-\alpha_1} x^i$$

in X. For the former is contained in X by assumption and the latter by the inductive hypothesis.

Intersection of multiple convex sets.

THEOREM 27.2. *Given a finite or infinite number of convex sets $X_\lambda (\lambda \in \Lambda)$, their intersection $\bigcap_{\lambda \in \Lambda} X_\lambda$ is also a convex set.*

Proof. If $x, y \in \bigcap_{\lambda \in \Lambda} X_\lambda$, then $x, y \in X_\lambda$ $(\lambda \in \Lambda)$. As each of X_λ is convex, $[x, y] \subset X_\lambda$ $(\lambda \in \Lambda)$. As this holds for any $\lambda \in \Lambda$, it follows that $[x, y] \subset \bigcap_{\lambda \in \Lambda} X_\lambda$. Hence, the intersection (though it might be empty) is a convex set. [Q.E.D.]

If a set X in R^n is not convex, we can think of augmenting it into a convex set by adding the fewest possible points to it. This procedure compares to forming the closure of a set that was considered in Section 12 in connection with the concept of closed sets. Let all convex sets that include X be X_λ $(\lambda \in \Lambda)$. Then, $C(X) = \bigcap_{\lambda \in \Lambda} X_\lambda$ is the smallest convex set that includes X. It is called the *convex hull* of X. As R^n is counted as one of X_λ, we know that $C(X)$ is obtained as a nonempty convex set that includes X if $X \neq \phi$. Theorem 27.2 asserts that it is convex. Needless to say, $C(X) = X$ if X itself is a convex set. If we look at $C(X)$ from another angle, we have the next theorem.

THEOREM 27.3. *$C(X)$ is the set of all convex linear combinations of any finite number of points in X, i.e.*

$$(27.6) \qquad C(X) = \{ \sum_{i=1}^{s} \alpha_i x^i \,|\, x^i \in X,\ \alpha_i \geqq 0,\ \sum_{i=1}^{s} \alpha_i = 1 \} ,$$

where the number and choice of x^i, the choice of α_i, etc. are completely arbitrary.

Proof. Denote the right-hand side of (27.6) by Y. Then, obviously, $Y \supset X$. Next, for $\lambda, \mu \geqq 0$, $\lambda + \mu = 1$,

$$\lambda \sum_{i=1}^{s} \alpha_i x^i + \mu \sum_{j=1}^{t} \beta_j y^j = \sum_{i=1}^{s} \lambda\alpha_i x^i + \sum_{j=1}^{t} \mu\beta_j y^j .$$

As $\lambda\alpha_i \geqq 0$, $\mu\beta_j \geqq 0$ and they sum up to 1, a convex linear combination of any two points in Y is contained in Y. Thus, Y itself is a convex set. Further, any convex set that includes X must contain convex linear combinations of points in X and, hence, points in Y. Thus, Y is the smallest convex set that includes X so that $Y = C(X)$. [Q.E.D.]

Non-negative or positive linear combinations are concepts analogous to convex linear combinations. They are obtained by removing the condition that the sum of coefficients is unity and only retaining the non-negativity condition. In other words, a linear combination

$$(27.7) \qquad \sum_{i=1}^{s} \alpha_i x^i$$

of $x^i \in R^n$ $(i = 1, 2, \ldots, s)$ is called a *non-negative linear combination* if the coefficients α_i are non-negative and a *positive linear combination* if they are positive.

THEOREM 27.4. *If a point x in R^n is represented by a non-negative linear combination* (27.7) *of a finite number of x^i $(i = 1, 2, \ldots, s)$, it is possible to limit the number of its positive coefficients at most to n (which is the dimension of R^n) by appropriately selecting the values of the coefficients α_i.*

In the expression (27.7) *in which the number of positive coefficients is the smallest among all non-negative linear combinations of given x^i $(i = 1, 2, \ldots, s)$, all of the x^i with positive coefficients form a set of linearly independent vectors.*

Proof. The first half of the theorem immediately follows from the second half because a set of linearly independent vectors in R^n always consists of not more than n elements by virtue of Theorem 9.1 so that the minimal number of positive coefficients in all linear combinations (27.7) that express x is at most n.

To prove the second half of the theorem, it suffices to show the following property: Corresponding to the expression

(27.8) $$x = \sum_{i=1}^{s} \alpha_i x^i, \quad \alpha_i \geqq 0\,,$$

determine a set of indexes $I \subset \{1, 2, ..., s\}$ by

(27.9) $$I = \{i \mid \alpha_i > 0\}\,.$$

If $I \neq \phi$ and if a set of vectors $\{x^i \mid i \in I\}$ is linearly dependent, it satisfies a linear relation

(27.10) $$\sum_{i \in I} \beta_i x^i = 0\,,$$

some of whose coefficients are non-zero. As we can assume that there is a positive coefficient among the non-zero coefficients of (27.10) *, we get

$$\min_{\beta_i > 0} \frac{\alpha_i}{\beta_i} = \theta$$

where $\theta > 0$. Multiply (27.10) by θ and subtract it from (27.8) to get

(27.11) $$x = \sum_{i \in I} (\alpha_i - \theta\beta_i) x^i\,,$$

in which $\alpha_i - \theta\beta_i \geqq 0$ $(i \in I)$ by the definition of θ and at least one of them is zero. Thus, the number of positive coefficients in (27.11) is at least less by one than the number of elements of I. Hence, $\{x^i \mid i \in I\}$ is linearly independent, provided that (27.8) already has the smallest number of positive coefficients. It may be noted that $I = \phi$ in a certain case (i.e. where $x = 0$). [Q.E.D.]

COROLLARY. *The number of x^i in the expression of $C(X)$ in Theorem 27.3 may be at most $n + 1$. To paraphrase, the entire collection of convex linear combinations formed by $n + 1$ points that are arbitrarily taken from X is $C(X)$.*

Proof. Add 1 as the $(n+1)$st component to a point x in R^n to obtain a point $\underline{x} = \begin{bmatrix} x \\ 1 \end{bmatrix}$ in R^{n+1}. Then, the fact that $\underline{x}$ is a non-negative linear combination of

* If not, multiply both sides by -1.

$\underline{x}^i$ ($i = 1, 2, ..., s$) in R^{n+1} is equivalent to that of x being a convex linear combination of x^i in R^n. In the light of Theorem 27.4, the minimal number of positive coefficients in representing $\underline{x}$ by a non-negative linear combination of $\underline{x}^i$ in R^{n+1} is at most $n + 1$.

Convex cones. A convex cone is a special type of a convex set. Let a subset of $R^n, K \neq \phi$, satisfy conditions

(a) $$x + y \in K \quad \text{if} \quad x, y \in K$$

and

(b) $$\alpha x \in K \quad \text{if} \quad \alpha \geqq 0, \quad x \in K .$$

Then, K is called a *convex cone.* It is easy to show from (a) and (b) that a convex cone is a convex set. It follows from (b) that $0 \in K$. In parallel to those of convex sets, the following properties hold for convex cones (their proof is left to the reader):

(a) If K_λ $(\lambda \in \Lambda)$ are convex cones, then $\bigcap_{\lambda \in \Lambda} K_\lambda$ is also a convex cone;

(b) There exists the smallest convex cone $K(X)$ that includes a subset of R^n, $X \neq \phi$. This is called the *convex cone spanned by X.* We have

$$(27.12) \qquad K(X) = \{\sum_{i=1}^{s} \alpha_i x^i \,|\, x^i \in X, \ \alpha_i \geqq 0\} ,$$

which is equivalent to (27.6) with the condition $\sum \alpha_i = 1$ removed. (Cf. fig. 27.3).

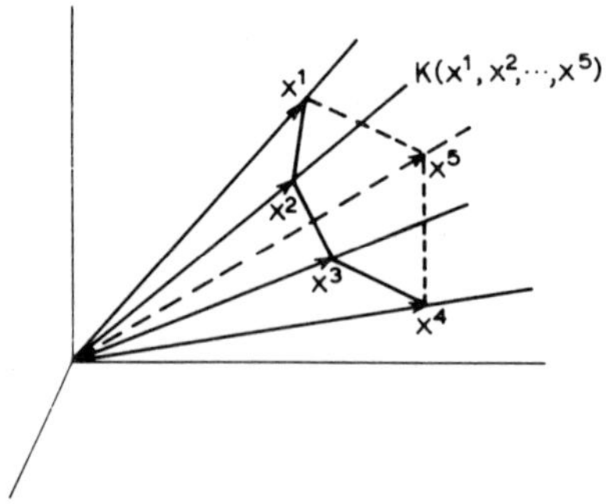

Fig. 27.3.

In particular, when X is a finite set $X = \{x^1, x^2, ..., x^s\}$, $K(X)$ is called a *convex polyhedral cone* and denoted, if necessary, by $K(x^1, x^2, ..., x^s)$. For instance, R^n_+ is a convex polyhedral cone $K(e^1, e^2, ..., e^n)$ *.

The following theorem holds for a convex polyhedral cone:

THEOREM 27.5. *A convex polyhedral cone $K(x^1, x^2, ..., x^s)$ is a closed set in R^n.*

Proof. The reader should recall how a closed set was defined in Section 12. In order to show that $K(x^1, x^2, ..., x^s)$ is a closed set, it is sufficient to demonstrate that, if $y^\nu \in K(x^1, x^2, ..., x^s)$ $(\nu = 1, 2, 3, ...)$ and $\lim_{\nu\to\infty} y^\nu = y$, then $y \in K(x^1, x^2, ..., x^s)$. As each term of the sequence $\{y^\nu\}$ is contained in the convex polyhedral cone, it is a non-negative linear combination of $x^1, x^2, ..., x^s$. Hence by Theorem 27.4, a set of indexes $I_\nu \subset \{1, 2, ..., s\}$ is determined for each ν such that

$$(27.13) \qquad y^\nu = \sum_{i=1}^{s} \alpha_{i\nu} x^i, \quad \alpha_{i\nu} > 0 \ (i \in I_\nu), \quad \alpha_{i\nu} = 0 \ (i \notin I_\nu),$$

and

$$(27.14) \qquad \{x^i \mid i \in I_\nu\} \quad \text{is linearly independent} \quad (\nu = 1, 2, ...).$$

I_ν is a subset of a finite set $\{1, 2, ..., s\}$. As ν is changed, I_ν would coincide with a certain subset $I \subset \{1, 2, ..., s\}$ for infinite times so that we may assume $I_\nu = I$ $(\nu = 1, 2, ...)$ without loss of generality **. Our subsequent discussion is divided into two cases.

(i) If $I = \phi$, then $y^\nu = 0$ $(\nu = 1, 2, ...)$. As $y = \lim_{\nu\to\infty} y^\nu = 0$, we get $y = 0 \in K(x^1, x^2, ..., x^s)$.

(ii) If $I \neq \phi$, then $\{x^i \mid i \in I\}$ can be extended to a basis of R^n $\{x^i (i \in I), w^j (j \in J)\}$ according to Theorem 9.2. Any point x in R^n is uniquely representable as a linear combination of x^i and w^j, with their coefficients $\alpha_i(x)$ and $\omega_j(x)$ as continuous functions of x (as shown in the latter half of (2) in Section 13). Thus,

$$(27.15) \qquad \lim_{\nu\to\infty} \alpha_i(y^\nu) = \alpha_i(y) \quad (i \in I).$$

* e^i is a unit vector.

** Take a subsequence as usual.

On the other hand, (27.13) is nothing but

$$y^\nu = \sum_{i \in I} \alpha_i(y^\nu)\, x^i \quad (\nu = 1, 2, \ldots) ;$$

in the limit with $\nu \to \infty$, we have

$$(27.16) \qquad y = \sum_{i \in I} \alpha_i(y)\, x^i .$$

As $\alpha_i(y^\nu) > 0$ in (27.15), we have $\alpha_i(y) \geqq 0$ in the limit. This proves that $y \in K(x^1, x^2, \ldots, x^s)$.

COROLLARY. *Let A be an (m, n) matrix, b^ν, $b \in R^m$, and* $\lim_{\nu \to \infty} b^\nu = b$. *If linear inequalities*

$$(27.17) \qquad Ay \leqq b^\nu, \quad y \geqq 0$$

have a solution with respect to each ν, then linear inequalities

$$(27.18) \qquad Ay \leqq b\,, \quad y \geqq 0$$

have a solution.

Proof. Let $b - Ay = v \geqq 0$ in order to rewrite the inequalities (27.18) as equations with non-negative unknowns. Then, $v \in R^m_+$. (27.18) has a solution y if and only if

$$(27.19) \qquad Ay + v = b, \quad y \geqq 0, \quad v \geqq 0$$

has a solution y and v. The components of v are called *slack variables.* Now let the n column vectors of A be a^j, the m column vectors of a unit matrix of the mth order be e^i, and the components of y and v be y_j and v_i. Then, (27.19) is rewritten as

$$(27.20) \qquad \sum_{j=1}^{n} y_j a^j + \sum_{i=1}^{m} v_i e^i = b\,, \quad y_j \geqq 0\,, \quad v_i \geqq 0\,.$$

(27.20) shows that b is contained in the convex polyhedral cone $K(a^1, a^2, \ldots, a^n, e^1, e^2, \ldots, e^m)$ spanned by $a^1, a^2, \ldots, a^n, e^1, e^2, \ldots, e^m$. Then, this corollary immediately follows from Theorem 27.5. Its assumption is expressed as

$$K(a^1, a^2, ..., a^n, e^1, e^2, ..., e^m) \ni b^\nu \quad (\nu = 1, 2, ...)$$

$$\lim_{\nu\to\infty} b^\nu = b ,$$

in terms of the convex polyhedral cone, introduced above, which is a closed set by Theorem 27.5 so that $b \in K(a^1, a^2, ..., a^n, e^1, e^2, ..., e^m)$. This is the conclusion of the corollary.

Applications. We give the proof of (a) in Section 26, a pending stage in the differential-calculus approach to duality in linear programming. For this purpose, it suffices to prove the following more general proposition: A function of u defined for l linear functions

$$\sum_{j=1}^{k} h_{ij}u_j + d_i \quad (i = 1, 2, ..., l) ,$$

$$F(u) = \sum_{i=1}^{l} \omega_i(u)^2 , \tag{27.21}$$

where

$$\omega_i(u) = \max \left(\sum_{j=1}^{k} h_{ij}u_j + d_i, 0\right) \quad (i = 1, 2, ..., l) , \tag{27.22}$$

has a minimum in R^k_+.

Let H be an (l, k) matrix $[h_{ij}]$ and d a vector of l elements whose ith component is d_i. Then, the components of $Hu + d$ are the linear functions given above. (a) in Section 26 is a special case of it specified by

$$H = \begin{bmatrix} 0 & A \\ -A' & 0 \\ b' & -c' \end{bmatrix} , \quad c = \begin{bmatrix} -b \\ c \\ 0 \end{bmatrix} , \quad u = \begin{bmatrix} x \\ y \end{bmatrix} , \quad \begin{matrix} l = m + n + 1 , \\ k = m + n . \end{matrix}$$

We give below the proof of this general proposition. Obviously, $\delta \geqq 0$ where $\inf_{u \geqq 0} F(u) = \delta$. Choose a sequence $\{u^\nu\}$ from R^k_+ that satisfies $\lim_{\nu\to\infty} F(u^\nu) = \delta$. This makes a point sequence $\{\omega(u^\nu)\}$ in R^l (whose ith component is $\omega_i(u^\nu)$) bounded. Then, because of the compactness *, this sequence

* Compare Section 14.

of points can be made convergent by extracting a subsequence from it. Hence, without loss of generality, we may assume that $\{\omega(u^\nu)\}$ itself converges. Thus, setting

$$(27.23) \qquad \lim_{\nu\to\infty} \omega_i(u^\nu) = \delta_i \quad (i = 1, 2, \ldots, l)\,,$$

we see that $\delta_i \geqq 0$ and

$$(27.24) \qquad \sum_{i=1}^{l} \delta_i^2 = \delta\,,$$

because of continuity. On the other hand, the definition (27.22) shows that

$$\sum_{j=1}^{k} h_{ij} u_j^\nu + d_i \leqq \omega_i(u^\nu) \quad (i = 1, 2, \ldots, l)\,.$$

In other words, the inequalities

$$(27.25) \qquad \sum_{j=1}^{k} h_{ij} u_j \leqq \omega_i(u^\nu) - d_i \quad (i = 1, 2, \ldots, l)\,,$$

$$u_j \geqq 0 \quad (j = 1, 2, \ldots, k)$$

have a solution $u = u^\nu$ for each ν and the constant terms on the right-hand side converge to $\delta_i - d_i$. Then, by the corollary given above, a system with $\omega_i(u^\nu) - d_i$ replaced by $\delta_i - d_i$ has a solution. Hence,

$$(27.26) \qquad \sum_{j=1}^{k} h_{ij} u_j + d_i \leqq \delta_i \quad (i = 1, 2, \ldots, l)\,,$$

$$u_j \geqq 0 \quad (j = 1, 2, \ldots, k)$$

have solutions, one of which is selected as u. Then, again by (27.22), this u satisfies

$$\omega_i(u) \leqq \delta_i \quad (i = 1, 2, \ldots, l)$$

and $F(u) \leqq \sum_{i=1}^{l} \delta_i^2 = \delta$. Therefore, by the definition of δ, we get $F(u) = \delta$.

[Q.E.D.]

28. Basic properties of convex sets

In this section, we shall introduce topological concepts that we were unable to explain in Chapter 2, and investigate the structure of convex sets with the help of these concepts.

When a point a in R^n together with its appropriate neighborhood $U(a, \epsilon)$ is contained in a set X, a is called an *interior point* of X. The set of all interior points of X is called the *interior* of X and denoted by X^o.

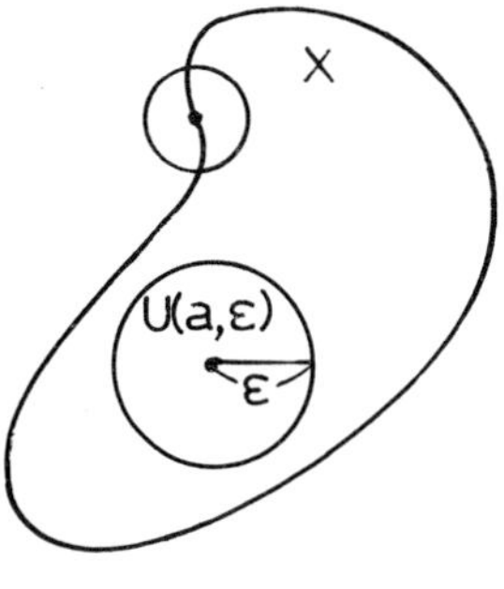

Fig. 28.1.

Example 28.1. It is easy to check that the interior of a disc in R^2, $X = \{x | x_1^2 + x_2^2 \leqq 1\}$, is $X^o = \{x | x_1^2 + x_2^2 < 1\}$. On the other hand, the interior of a disc in R^3, $X = \{x | x_3 = 0, x_1^2 + x_2^2 \leqq 1\}$, is $X^o = \phi$. This is because no point a in R^3 can be an interior point of X. For any ϵ-neighborhood $U(a, \epsilon)$ of any point a in R^3 contains always a point x whose third component is $x_3 \neq 0$ so that it is impossible that a neighborhood of a is completely included in X.

As this example indicates, X^o may be empty or non-empty. However, the definition makes it clear that we always have $X^o \subset X$. We also note that the closure $\bar{X}$ of X always satisfies * $X \subset \bar{X}$ so that we have $X^o \subset \bar{X}$. A point a of $\bar{X}$ such that $a \notin X^o$ is called a *boundary point* of X. The set of all boundary points of X is called the *boundary* of X and denoted by X^b, i.e. $X^b = \{a | a \in \bar{X}, \notin X^o\}$. A point of X^b can also be characterized as follows: $a \in \bar{X}$ if and only if the distance $d(a, X)$ is 0 **. This means that any ϵ-neighborhood of a satisfies $U(a, \epsilon) \cap X \neq \phi$. At the same time, $a \notin X^o$ is equivalent to the fact that no neighborhood of a satisfies $U(a, \epsilon) \subset X$ and, hence, to $U(a, \epsilon) \cap X^c \neq \phi$. We combine these two properties and characterize a boundary point

* See the definition of a closure in Section 12.

** See Section 12.

a as follows: "A boundary point is a point such that its ϵ-neighborhood contains both points belonging to X and points not belonging to X". We may note that this characterization has proved the following property:

$$X^{\mathrm{b}} = \overline{X} \cap \overline{X^{\mathrm{c}}} . \tag{28.1}$$

As $\overline{X}$ and $\overline{X^{\mathrm{c}}}$ are both closed sets, their intersection X^{b} is also a closed set. As the right-hand side of (28.1) is symmetric with respect to X and X^{c}, it also follows that the boundaries of X and X^{c} are the same set. Let us now examine properties of the closure, interior, and boundary of a convex set X.

THEOREM 28.1. (i) *If X is a convex set, its closure $\overline{X}$ is also a convex set.* (ii) *Let a be an interior point of a convex set X and $b \in \overline{X}$. Then, all points on the segment $[a, b]$ except b are interior points of X* *.

Proof. (i) Let $x, y \in \overline{X}$. Then, there exist sequences of points $\{x^\nu\}$, $\{y^\nu\}$ such that

$$\lim_{\nu\to\infty} x^\nu = x, \quad \lim_{\nu\to\infty} y^\nu = y, \quad x^\nu, y^\nu \in X \quad (\nu = 1, 2, \ldots) .$$

We have first of all $\lim_{\nu\to\infty} (\alpha x^\nu + \beta y^\nu) = \alpha x + \beta y$ for any $\alpha \geqq 0, \beta \geqq 0, \alpha + \beta = 1$. As X is convex, $\alpha x^\nu + \beta y^\nu \in X$ $(\nu = 1, 2, \ldots)$ so that $\alpha x + \beta y$ is the limit of a sequence of points $\{\alpha x^\nu + \beta y^\nu\}$ and is contained in $\overline{X}$, i.e. $\alpha x + \beta y \in \overline{X}$ by the definition of closures.

(ii) As a is an interior point, we have $U(a, \epsilon) \subset X$ for an appropriate $\epsilon > 0$. Now a point on $[a, b]$ except b is expressed by $c_t = (1 - t)a + tb, 0 \leqq t < 1$. The objective of the proof is to show $c_t \in X^{\mathrm{o}}$ and it suffices to show that $U(c_t, (1 - t)\epsilon) \subset X$. Let $x \in U(c_t, (1 - t)\epsilon)$. Then, $\|x - c_t\| < (1 - t)\epsilon$. As $b \in \overline{X}$, there should exist a point d in X close enough to b to make $t\|b - d\| < (1 - t)\epsilon - \|x - c_t\|$ hold. Hence,

$$\|x - (1 - t)a - td\| \leqq \|x - (1 - t)a - tb\| + t\|b - d\| < (1 - t)\epsilon.$$

Dividing both sides by $(1 - t)$ and rearranging terms, we get

$$\left\| \frac{1}{1 - t}(x - td) - a \right\| < \epsilon$$

* b itself may or may not be an interior point.

so that

$$e = \frac{1}{1-t}(x - td) \in U(a, \epsilon) \subset X \ .$$

Thus,

$$x = (1-t)e + td \in [e, d] \subset X \ .$$

This proves $U(c_t, (1-t)\epsilon) \subset X$. [Q.E.D.]

A number of important corollaries follow from this theorem.

COROLLARY 1. *There exists at most only one boundary point of a convex set X on a ray that emanates from an interior point a of X.*

Proof. Suppose that there are two or more boundary points on this ray. Let two of these boundary points be b and c. b is situated farther away from a than c is. Then, $c \in [a, b]$ and $c \neq b$. As $a \in X^{\text{o}}$ and $b \in \bar{X} \cap \overline{X^{\text{c}}} \subset \bar{X}$, c is an interior point of X because of (i) of Theorem 28.1. This contradicts the assumption that c is a boundary point.

COROLLARY 2. *If X is a convex set, then X^{o}, the interior of X, is a convex set.*

Proof. Let $a, b \in X^{\text{o}}$. As $X^{\text{o}} \subset \bar{X}$, we have $b \in \bar{X}$. The application of (ii) of Theorem 28.1 indicates that points on $[a, b]$ except b are interior points of X. b itself is an interior point by assumption. Hence, $[a, b] \subset X^{\text{o}}$, i.e. X^{o} is convex.

COROLLARY 3. *If X is a convex set and $X^{\text{o}} \neq \phi$, then $\bar{X} = \overline{X^{\text{o}}}$.*

Proof. As $X \supset X^{\text{o}}$, it immediately follows that $\bar{X} \supset \overline{X^{\text{o}}}$ *. Conversely, select an interior point a. Then, for any $b \in \bar{X}$, points on $[a, b]$ except b are contained in X^{o} so that one can find a point of X^{o} as close to b as one likes. Thus, $b \in \overline{X^{\text{o}}}$, i.e. $\bar{X} \subset \overline{X^{\text{o}}}$. [Q.E.D.]

We defined affine subspaces earlier. We now define an affine mapping f: $R^n \to R^m$. This is a mapping satisfying

(28.2) $$f(\alpha x + \beta y) = \alpha f(x) + \beta f(y) \qquad (\text{for any } x, y \in R^n, \ \alpha + \beta = 1) \ .$$

* See Section 12.

The condition (28.2) is less restrictive than that of a linear mapping *. Obvioulsy, linear mappings are affine mappings of a special type. If f is an affine mapping, then $g(x) = f(x) - f(0)$ is a linear mapping. Its converse also holds. Because of this fact, an affine mapping is given a specific expression $f(x) = Ax + b$ where A is an (m, n) matrix and b a constant vector. In other words, an affine mapping is a mapping composed of a linear mapping and a parallel translation. The reader should prove these properties.

THEOREM 28.2. *Let f: $R^n \to R^m$ be an affine mapping and X a convex set in R^n. Then, the image $f(X)$ is a convex set in R^m.*

Proof. If $y^1, y^2 \in f(X)$, then one may write $y^1 = f(x^1)$ and $y^2 = f(x^2)$ (for some $x^1, x^2 \in X$). We have $\alpha_1 y^1 + \alpha_2 y^2 = \alpha_1 f(x^1) + \alpha_2 f(x^2) = f(\alpha_1 x^1 + \alpha_2 x^2) \in f(X)$ for any $\alpha_1 \geqq 0$, $\alpha_2 \geqq 0$, $\alpha_1 + \alpha_2 = 1$. This is because $\alpha_1 x^1 + \alpha_2 x^2 \in X$ as X is convex.

Cartesian product sets. The concept of a cartesian product provides a useful procedure for combining given sets into a new set. Form an m-tuple $(x^1, x^2, \ldots, x^m)$ by taking element $x^i \in X_i$ at random and independently from each of a finite number of sets X_i $(i = 1, 2, \ldots, m)$. Then, the set of all m-tuples $(x^1, x^2, \ldots, x^m)$ is called a *cartesian product* of $X_1, X_2, \ldots, X_m$ and denoted by

$$X_1 \times X_2 \times \ldots \times X_m \quad \text{or} \quad \prod_{i=1}^{m} X_i \,.$$

If each X_i is a metric space in which a concept of convergence is defined, then one may introduce a concept of convergence, i.e. topology, into the cartesian product set in a straightforward manner by giving a definition that, for a sequence of points $(x^{1\nu}, x^{2\nu}, \ldots, x^{m\nu})$ in the cartesian product set,

$$\lim_{\nu \to \infty} (x^{1\nu}, x^{2\nu}, \ldots, x^{m\nu}) = (x^1, x^2, \ldots, x^m)$$

is equivalent to $\lim_{\nu \to \infty} x^{i\nu} = x^i$ for each i.

Example 28.2. A cartesian product $\underbrace{R^1 \times R^1 \times \ldots \times R^1}_{n}$ formed by combining n sets of all real numbers, i.e. one-dimensional R^1, is essentially identical with n-dimensional R^n **. More generally, one may consider

* See Section 10.

** See Theorem 11.1.

$R^{n_1} \times R^{n_2} \times \ldots \times R^{n_m}$ as $R^{n_1+n_2+\ldots+n_m}$. Therefore, linear operations are introduced straightforwardly into $R^{n_1} \times R^{n_2} \times \ldots \times R^{n_m}$ according to the rule

$$\alpha(x^1, x^2, \ldots, x^m) + \beta(y^1, y^2, \ldots, y^m)$$
$$= (\alpha x^1 + \beta y^1, \alpha x^2 + \beta y^2, \ldots, \alpha x^m + \beta y^m) \quad (\text{for } x^i, y^i \in R^{n_i}) .$$

THEOREM 28.3. (i) *If each* X_i *is a compact set, the cartesian product* $\prod_{i=1}^{m} X_i$ *is also compact.*

(ii) *If each* X_i *is a convex set in* R^{n_i}*, the cartesian product* $\prod_{i=1}^{m} X_i$ *is a convex set in* $R^{n_1+n_2+\ldots+n_m}$.

Proof. (i) Let a sequence of points $\{(x^{1\nu}, x^{2\nu}, \ldots, x^{m\nu})\}$, $x^{i\nu} \in X_i$ be given in the cartesian product. In the proof of Theorem 14.6, we extracted an appropriate subsequence from a given sequence of points $\{x^\nu\}$ in such a way that the numerical sequences of its components would converge. Following exactly the same procedure, we extract a subsequence of indexes $\{\nu'\}$ and make each $\{x^{i\nu'}\}$ converge within X_i. Needless to say, this procedure is made possible by the assumption that each X_i is compact.

(ii) Let $\prod_{i=1}^{m} X_i \ni x = (x^1, x^2, \ldots, x^m)$, $y = (y^1, y^2, \ldots, y^m)$, $\alpha \geqq 0$, $\beta \geqq 0$, $\alpha + \beta = 1$. The definition of linear operations shows that

$$\alpha x + \beta y = (\alpha x^1 + \beta y^1, \alpha x^2 + \beta y^2, \ldots, \alpha x^m + \beta y^m) .$$

As each X_i is a convex set, $\alpha x^i + \beta y^i \in X_i$. Thus, $\alpha x + \beta y \in \prod_{i=1}^{m} X_i$ by the definition of the cartesian product set.

Linear combination of sets. Let λ_i $(i = 1, 2, \ldots, m)$ be given real constants and X_i $(i = 1, 2, \ldots, m)$ subsets in the same R^n. Then, the set defined by

$$(28.3) \qquad \sum_{i=1}^{m} \lambda_i X_i = \{ \sum_{i=1}^{m} \lambda_i x^i | x^i \in X_i \ (i = 1, 2, \ldots, m)\}$$

is called a *linear combination* of X_i with λ_i as coefficients.

THEOREM 28.4. *Let* $X_i \subset R^n$ $(i = 1, 2, \ldots, m)$.

(i) *If each* X_i *is compact, the linear combination* (28.3) *is also compact.*
(ii) *If each* X_i *is convex, the linear combination* (28.3) *is also convex.*

Proof. Though a direct proof is possible, we make use of Theorems 28.2 and 28.3 here. The mapping defined by the formula

$$f((x^1, x^2, \ldots, x^m)) = \sum_{i=1}^{m} \lambda_i x^i ,$$

i.e.

$$f\colon R^n \times R^n \times \ldots \times R^n \to R^n \tag{28.4}$$

is apparently linear. The linear combination (28.3) is nothing but the image of the cartesian product set $\prod_{i=1}^{m} X_i$ under f, namely $f(\prod_{i=1}^{m} X_i)$. With this preliminary observation, let us prove (i) and (ii).

(i) As X_i is compact, (i) of Theorem 28.3 shows that $\prod_{i=1}^{m} X_i$ is compact. Now that the linear mapping (28.4) is a continuous mapping, Theorem 14.4 proves that $f(\prod_{i=1}^{m} X_i)$ is compact.

(ii) As X_i is convex, (ii) of Theorem 28.3 shows that $\prod_{i=1}^{m} X_i$ is convex. The linear mapping (28.4) is, of course, an affine mapping so that Theorem 28.2 proves that $f(\prod_{i=1}^{m} X_i)$ is a convex set. [Q.E.D.]

In the present theorem, (28.3) reduces to $\sum_{i=1}^{m} X_i$ if $\lambda_1 = \lambda_2 = \ldots = \lambda_m = 1$. This is called the *vectorial sum* of sets X_i's *. Similarly, the vectorial difference $X - Y$ of two sets X and Y may be considered a special case of (28.3).

* Not to be confused with the union $\bigcup_{i=1}^{m} X_i$.

29. Separation theorems

Following our study programme we now embark on an exposition of the separation theorems on convex sets that will replace differential calculus and prove as an effective tool of analysis of optimization problems.

In order to make a smooth transition from differential calculus to the separation theorems, let us note the following fact: Let $f(x)$ be a convex function defined on the entire domain of R^n and a a point in R^n. Then, as pointed out in Example 27.4, $X = \{x \mid f(x) \leqq f(a)\}$ forms a convex set in R^n. Further, let $f(x)$ have continuous partial derivatives $(\partial/\partial x_i)f(x)$ and assume that not all of partial derivatives $[\partial f/\partial x_i]_{x=a}$ $(i = 1, 2, \ldots, n)$ are zero at $x = a$. Then, as is well known in differential calculus, the hyperplane

$$(29.1) \qquad \sum_{i=1}^{n} \left[\frac{\partial f}{\partial x_i}\right]_{x=a} (x_i - a_i) = 0$$

is tangent at $x = a$ to the hypersurface $f(x) = f(a)$ in R^n. (Cf. fig. 29.1.)

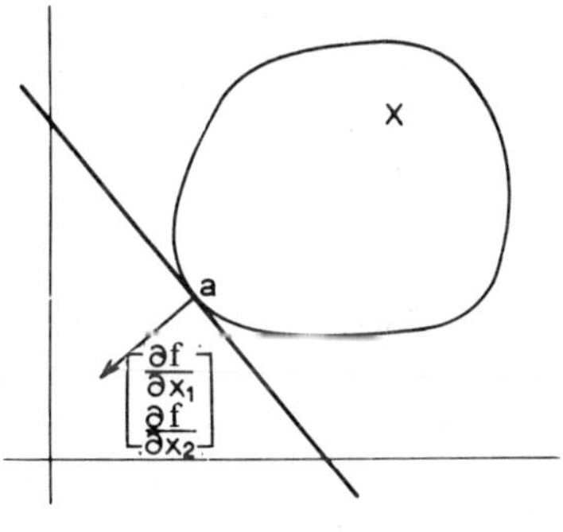

Fig. 29.1.

Now for any $x \in X$, we have $(1-t)a + tx \in X$ (for any $0 \leqq t \leqq 1$) because X is a convex set. Then, by definition of X,

$$f((1-t)a + tx) \leqq f(a) \qquad (0 \leqq t \leqq 1)\,.$$

We may transform this equation into

$$(29.2) \qquad \frac{f((1-t)a + tx) - f(a)}{t} \leqq 0 \qquad (0 < t \leqq 1)\,.$$

By putting

$$(29.3) \qquad F(t) = f((1-t)a + tx)$$

and noting that $F(0) = f(a)$, (29.2) is expressed as

$$(29.4) \qquad \frac{F(t) - F(0)}{t} \leqq 0 \quad (0 < t \leqq 1) \ .$$

(29.3) becomes differentiable with its derivative at $t = 0$ given by

$$(29.5) \qquad F'(0) = \sum_{i=1}^{n} \left[\frac{\partial f}{\partial x_i}\right]_{x=a} (x_i - a_i)$$

according to the rule on the derivative of a composed function. Letting $t \to 0$ in eq. (29.4), we get

$$(29.6) \qquad \sum_{i=1}^{n} \left[\frac{\partial f}{\partial x_i}\right]_{x=a} (x_i - a_i) \leqq 0 \, .$$

(29.6) shows that the set X is included in a half-space determined by the tangent hyperplane (29.1). When a hyperplane passes through a point a in a set X and the half-space determined by this hyperplane includes X, this hyperplane is called the *supporting hyperplane.* We have proved the existence of a supporting hyperplane for the convex set X by the help of differential calculus.

Now what about the proof when $[\partial f / \partial x_i]_{x=a} = 0$ $(i = 1, 2, ..., n)$ or when $f(x)$ does not have partial derivatives? We cannot expect a direct help from differential calculus in these cases. However, as shown in fig. 29.2, it is intuitively suggested that there exists a supporting hyperplane insofar as $\boldsymbol{a}$ is a boundary point of X. Going a step farther, we can anticipate that there must

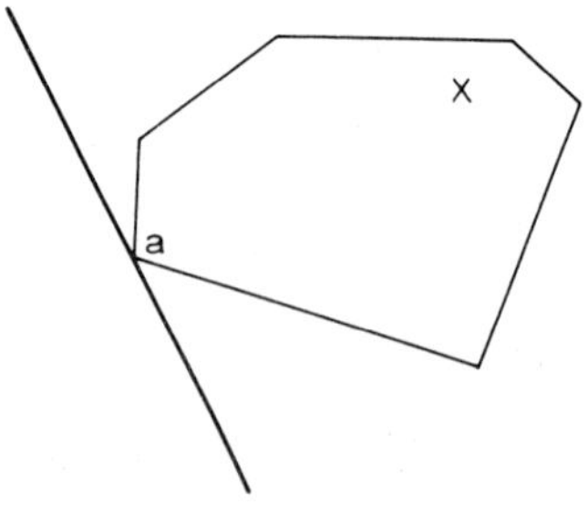

Fig. 29.2.

be supporting hyperplanes not only for convex sets of a special type like the one defined by the function $f(x)$ but also for convex sets in general. This anticipation is in fact correct. It is separation theorems to be discussed in this section that formulate this property in a clearcut way. In the differentiable case, the partial derivatives at $x = a$ are the coefficients of the supporting hyperplane (i.e. components of its normal vectors). Therefore, we can analogously regard the coefficients of the supporting hyperplane in the general case as substitutes for the non-existing partial derivatives.

THEOREM 29.1 * (*a separation theorem*). *Let a non-empty closed convex set X and a point a not contained in it, i.e. $a \notin X$, be given in R^n. Then, there exists a hyperplane that includes a in one of its half-spaces and X in the other of the half-spaces.*

Henceforth, to be brief, we may write that this hyperplane "separates a and X". Denote the normal vector of the hyperplane by $p \neq 0$. Represent the hyperplane by

$$(p, x) = \alpha .$$

Then, the theorem asserts that there exists p such that

(i) $(p, a) < \alpha$

and

(ii) $(p, x) \geqq \alpha$ (for all $x \in X$).

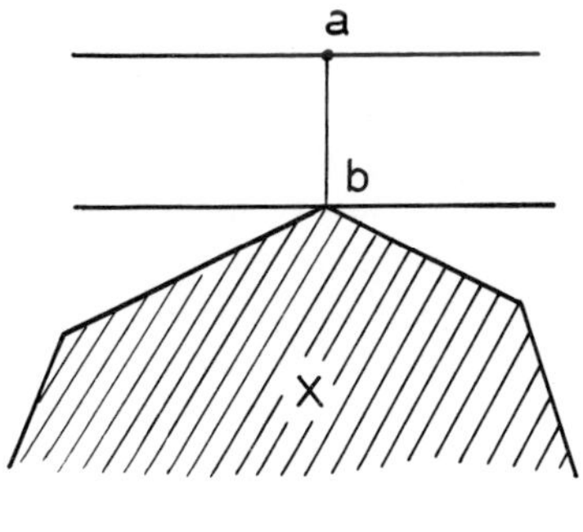

Fig. 29.3.

* The proof is due to von Neumann and Morgenstern [24].

Proof. A proof of this theorem can be derived by improving the essential part of the proof for the differentiable case. This fact alone suggests the affinity between differential calculus and the separation theorems.

Let us denote the distance between the point a and the set X by $d(a, X)$ as explained before. As X is a closed set, it coincides with its closure so that $\bar{X} = X$. $a \notin X$ then implies $a \notin \bar{X}$. As $\bar{X} = \{y \mid d(y, X) = 0\}$, we have $d(a,X) = \delta > 0$. On the other hand, by the definition of distance (12.1), there is a sequence of points $\{x^\nu\}$ in X such that $\lim_{\nu\to\infty} d(a, x^\nu) = \delta$. Then, by the definition of convergence of a sequence of numbers, $d(a, x^\nu) \leqq 2\delta$ for ν larger than a certain integer N, namely $x^\nu \in \bar{U}(a, 2\delta)$ $(\nu = N, N+1, \ldots)$. As $\bar{U}(a, 2\delta)$ is a compact set *, there is some subsequence of $\{x^\nu\}$ that converges. Thus, without loss of generality and according to the convention, we may assume that $\{x^\nu\}$ itself converges. Setting $\lim_{\nu\to\infty} x^\nu = b$, we have $b \in X$ because X is a closed set. As $d(a, x)$ is a continuous function of x,

$$d(a, b) = d(a, \lim_{\nu\to\infty} x^\nu) = \lim_{\nu\to\infty} d(a, x^\nu) = \delta\ ,$$

i.e.

(29.7) $$\delta = d(a, b) = \min d(a, x) \quad (\text{for all } x \in X).$$

After these preliminaries, let us prove that a hyperplane

(29.8) $$(p, x) = \alpha$$

where

(29.9) $$p = b - a, \quad \alpha = (p, b)$$

is a separating hyperplane that we are looking for.

(i) $$(p, a) = (b - a, a) = (b - a, a - b) + (b - a, b) = -\delta^2 + \alpha < \alpha\ ,$$

which demonstrates that the inequality (i) holds.

(ii) For any $x \in X$, the segment $[b, x] \subset X$ in view of $b \in X$. Now, the convex linear combination of b and x is given by $x(t) = (1 - t)b + tx$ $(0 \leqq t \leqq 1)$. As $x(t) \in X$, we have $d(a, b) \leqq d(a, x(t))$ so that we easily obtain

$$\|b - a\|^2 \leqq \|x(t) - a\|^2 = \|(1 - t)(b - a) + t(x - a)\|^2$$

$$= (1 - t)^2\|b - a\|^2 + 2t(1 - t)(b - a, x - a) + t^2\|x - a\|^2$$

* See Example 14.5.

by computations that make use of the relation between the inner product and norm $||x||^2 = (x, x)$, and the bilinearity of inner product. Rearranging terms of the above expression, we get

$$0 \leqq t(t-2)||b-a||^2 + 2t(1-t)(b-a, x-a) + t^2||x-a||^2 .$$

Dividing it through by t $(0 < t \leqq 1)$, we get

$$0 \leqq (t-2)||b-a||^2 + 2(1-t)(b-a, x-a) + t||x-a||^2 .$$

Letting $t \to 0$, we have in the limit

$$(29.10) \qquad (b-a, x-a) - ||b-a||^2 \geqq 0$$

(after dividing by 2). This is further reduced to

$$(b-a, x) \geqq (b-a, b) .$$

Thus, the inequality (ii) is obtained. [Q.E.D.]

Remark 1. In (ii) of the proof above, the conclusion may be obtained at once from $||b-a||^2 \leqq ||(1-t)(b-a) + t(x-a)||^2$ by applying exactly the same procedure as the one used after (29.2) in the differentiable case. Namely, put

$$F(t) = ||(1-t)(b-a) + t(x-a)||^2.$$

We have $F(t) \geqq F(0) = ||b-a||^2$. We may note that

$$F'(0) = 2\sum_{i=1}^{n}(b_i - a_i)(x_i - b_i)$$

as

$$F(t) = \sum_{i=1}^{n} [b_i - a_i + t(x_i - b_i)]^2 .$$

This helps us to understand that the proof following this procedure is permissible. The reader should try this approach.

The hyperplane that has been obtained here passes through b with its normal vector given by $p = b - a$. For another hyperplane that passes through

a with the same normal vector, (i) holds with an equality sign and (ii) with a strict inequality sign. For a hyperplane that passes through the mid-point of the segment joining a and b with the same normal vector, (i) and (ii) both hold with strict inequality signs; a and X are *strictly* separated. It is easily seen that this b is a boundary point of X. The hyperplane we have just obtained is nothing but a supporting hyperplane of X at b. However, as b is not an arbitrarily given boundary point, it is useful to prove a corollary below.

COROLLARY. *Let X be a non-empty convex set*. If a is a boundary point of X, then there exists a supporting hyperplane that passes through a.*

Proof. As X is a convex set, the closure $\bar{X}$ is a closed convex set by (i) of Theorem 28.1. Since a is a boundary point, we have $a \in \bar{X}$ and this excludes the foregoing separation theorem from being directly applied. However, because a is a boundary point of $\bar{X}$ as shall be explained at the end of this section, there is always a point in the neighborhood of a that is not contained in $\bar{X}$. In other words, we can select a sequence of points $\{a^\nu\}$ such that $a^\nu \notin \bar{X}$ and $\lim_{\nu\to\infty} a^\nu = a$. The application of the separation theorem to each a^ν reveals the existence of a separating hyperplane passing through a^ν, i.e. $(p^\nu, x) = (p^\nu, a^\nu)$, for which

$$(29.11) \qquad (p^\nu, x) > (p^\nu, a^\nu) \quad (x \in \bar{X}).$$

As each $p^\nu \neq 0$ and as (29.11) is homogeneous in p^ν, we can set $\|p^\nu\| = 1$ by putting the norms of the normal vectors equal to 1. We may therefore assume that $p^\nu \in C = \{x \mid \|x\| = 1\}$. As the unit sphere C is compact **, the sequence $\{p^\nu\}$ contains a convergent subsequence. Hence, as usual, we may as well assume that this sequence itself is convergent. Then, putting $\lim_{\nu\to\infty} p^\nu = p$, we see that $\|p\| = 1$ and $p \neq 0$. Because of the continuity of inner products, $\lim_{\nu\to\infty} (p^\nu, a^\nu) = (p, a)$. Therefore, setting $\nu \to \infty$ in eq. (29.11), we get in the limit

$$(p, x) \geqq (p, a) \quad (x \in \bar{X})$$

and we obtain a supporting hyperplane of $\bar{X}$ at a, i.e. $(p, x) = (p, a)$. As $X \subset \bar{X}$, X is contained in a half-space on one side of this hyperplane.

* Note that it is not assumed to be a closed set.
** See Example 14.5.

We now prove that a is a boundary point of $\bar{X}$. This property was used in the above proof. As $a \in \bar{X}$, a would be an interior point of $\bar{X}$ if this conclusion were not correct. Therefore, assuming the contrary, for an appropriate $\epsilon > 0$ we have

$$(29.12) \qquad U(a, \epsilon) \subset \bar{X}.$$

Because $X^{\mathrm{o}} \neq \phi$ on this assumption *, we have $a \in \overline{X^{\mathrm{o}}}$ by Corollary 3 of Theorem 28.1. Hence, one can choose c that satisfies

$$(29.13) \qquad U(a, \epsilon) \cap X^{\mathrm{o}} \ni c.$$

Let $d = 2a - c$. Then, by virtue of (29.12) and (29.13), we get

$$(29.14) \qquad d = a - (c - a) \in U(a, \epsilon) \subset \bar{X}.$$

It follows from (29.13) and (29.14) that

$$a = \frac{c+d}{2}, \quad c \in X^{\mathrm{o}}, \quad d \in \bar{X}.$$

We get $a \in X^{\mathrm{o}}$ from (ii) of Theorem 28.1. This contradicts the fact that a is a boundary point of X.

Remark 2. The theorem and corollary in this section may be summarized as follows: if a is not an interior point of a convex set X, there exists a hyperplane passing through a and including X in a half-space on one side of it.

30. Separation theorems in alternative forms

Separation theorems can be restated in various forms depending on the purposes of applications at hand. However, as we cannot cover all of them here, we restrict ourselves to introducing two important cases that we will make use of later on.

Separation by a hyperplane with a non-negative normal. Let X and Y be

* To prove this, we make use of Section 41 below. If the minimal affine subspace including X does not coincide with R^n, it is a k-dimensional plane ($n > k$). As it is a closed set, it contains $\bar{X}$ so that $a \in \overline{X^{\mathrm{o}}} = \phi$. This is a contradiction. Therefore, the minimal affine subspace including X is R^n and X contains an n-dimensional simplex. Hence, $X^{\mathrm{o}} \neq \phi$.

two sets in R^n. When X is contained in a half-space and Y in the other determined by a certain hyperplane $(p, x) = \alpha$, it is said that X and Y are separated by this hyperplane. Namely, when

$$(p, x) \geqq \alpha \quad (\text{for all } x \in X)$$

and

$$(p, y) \leqq \alpha \quad (\text{for all } y \in Y) ,$$

it is said that X and Y are separated by $(p, x) = \alpha$. (Cf. fig. 30.1.)

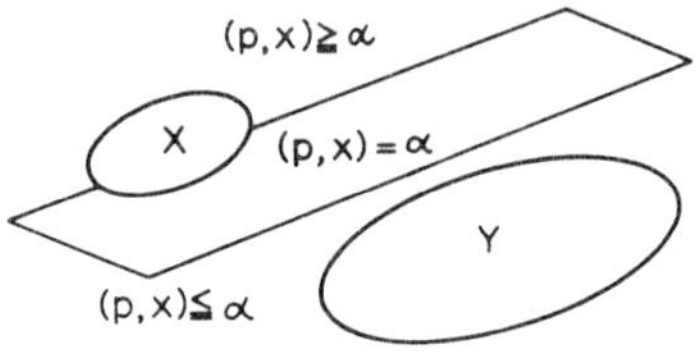

Fig. 30.1.

THEOREM 30.1. *If a convex set X contains no interior points of the positive orthant R^n_+, X and R^n_+ are separated by a hyperplane passing through the origin and with non-negative coefficients.*

Proof. X and R^n_+ are both convex so that their vectorial difference $R^n_+ - X$ is a convex set *. Designate this set as M. Then, the origin 0 cannot be an interior point of M. To prove this, suppose that 0 is an interior point of M so that some ϵ-neighborhood $U(0, \epsilon)$ is contained in M. $U(0, \epsilon)$ certainly contains an interior point $z > 0$ of R^n_+. Therefore, we also have $-z \in U(0, \epsilon) \subset M = R^n_+ - X$. Hence, we can write $-z = u - x$ $(u \in R^n_+, x \in X)$. Then, $z = x - u \leqq x$ ($\because u \geqq 0$). But as $z > 0$, we get $x > 0$. This result contradicts the assumption that X contains no interior points of R^n_+. This demonstrates that the origin 0 is not an interior point of M. Therefore, by Remark 2 of Section 29, there exists such a hyperplane $(p,x) = 0$ passing through the origin that M is included in a half-space on one side of it. I.e. for any $u \in R^n_+, x \in X$, we have $(p, u - x) \geqq 0$. This can be rewritten as

$$(30.1) \qquad (p, u) \geqq (p, x) \quad (\text{for all } u \in R^n_+,\ x \in X) .$$

* See Theorem 28.4.

As $0 \in R^n_+$, put $u = 0$ in (30.1) to get

(30.2) $\quad 0 = (p, 0) \geqq (p, x) \quad (\text{for all } x \in X)$.

(30.1) also shows that (p, u) is bounded from below on R^n_+. Denote one of the lower bounds by γ. Then, $(p, u) \geqq \gamma$. As $\lambda u \in R^n_+$ $(\lambda > 0)$, we have $(p, \lambda u) \geqq \gamma$. Thus, we see that $(p, u) \geqq \gamma/\lambda$ holds for any $\lambda > 0$. Letting $\lambda \to +\infty$, we obtain

(30.3) $\quad (p, u) \geqq 0 \quad (\text{for all } u \in R^n_+)$.

This proves that R^n_+ and X are separated by the hyperplane $(p, x) = 0$. Finally, it follows from (30.3) that $p \geqq 0$ because of (i) of Theorem 15.1. Combined with $p \neq 0$, we get $p \geq 0$. (Cf. fig. 30.2.)

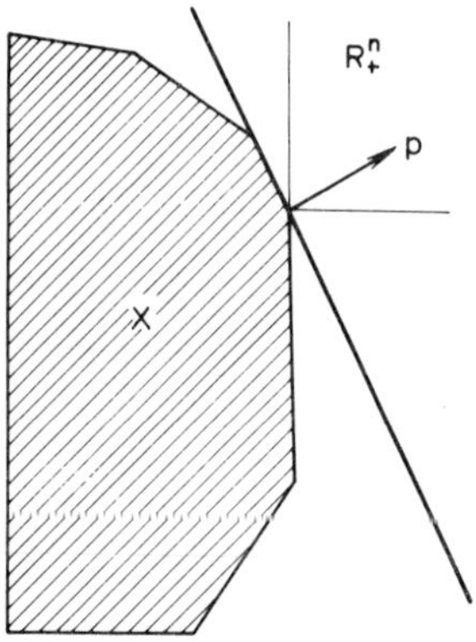

Fig. 30.2.

Remark 1. When a convex set X and the positive orthant R^n_+ do not intersect with each other or when they share only the origin, X and R^n_+ are separated by a hyperplane passing through the origin and with non-negative coefficients. This is a special case of the theorem above. (Cf. fig. 30.2.)

Convex cones and dual convex cones. For a convex cone K in R^n, consider a point whose inner product with each point of K is non-negative. Then, the collection of all such points

(30.4) $\quad K^* = \{y \mid (x, y) \geqq 0 \quad (\text{for all } x \in K)\}$

is called the *dual* or *polar convex cone* of K. As $0 \in K^*$, we see $K^* \neq \phi$. It is easily seen that K^* is a convex cone because it is defined by a system of linear inequalities. K need not be a closed set, but K^* is always a closed set. This is clear from the continuity of the inner product (x, y) and from the fact that the inequality defining K^*, $(x, y) \geqq 0$, includes the equality sign.

THEOREM 30.2. *Designate the dual convex cone of K^*, i.e. $(K^*)^*$, as K^{**}. Then,*

(i) $K \subset K^{**}$;

(ii) *If K is a closed convex cone, $K = K^{**}$ (duality of convex cones).*

Proof. (i) From the definition (30.4), it follows that $(x, y) \geqq 0$ for any $x \in K$, $y \in K^*$. This implies that a point x in K satisfies the condition by which K^{**} is defined as

(30.5) $$K^{**} = \{x \mid (x, y) \geqq 0 \quad (\text{for all } y \in K^*)\} .$$

Hence, $K \subset K^{**}$.

(ii) Because of (i), it suffices to show that $K^{**} \subset K$. To prove this, let us show that the contrapositive proposition, "$a \notin K \Rightarrow a \notin K^{**}$", holds. K is a closed convex cone and, therefore, a closed convex set. Hence, if $a \notin K$, there exists a hyperplane $(p, x) = \alpha$ separating a and K according to the separation theorem so that

(30.6) $$(p, a) < \alpha$$

and

(30.7) $$(p, x) \geqq \alpha \quad (\text{for } x \in K) .$$

Then, if $x \in K$, we have $\lambda x \in K$ $(\lambda > 0)$. Following exactly the same procedure as the derivation of (30.3) in the proof of Theorem 30.1, we obtain

(30.8) $$(p, x) \geqq 0 \quad (\text{for } x \in K) .$$

As (30.8) indicates that p satisfies the definitional relation in (30.4), we see $p \in K^*$.

On the other hand, as $0 \in K$, we get $0 \geqq \alpha$ by putting $x = 0$ in (30.7). Hence, $(p, a) < \alpha \leqq 0$ from (30.6). This means that a does not satisfy the definitional relation in (30.5). Therefore, $a \notin K^{**}$.

Remark 2. If a linear function $f(x) = (p, x)$ is bounded from below (or above) on a convex cone K, we in fact have $f(x) \geqq 0$ (or $f(x) \leqq 0$). An effective use was made of this fact in the proof of the two preceding theorems.

COROLLARY 1 (*the Minkowski-Farkas lemma*). *Let A be an (m, n) matrix and $b, x \in R^n$. Then, in order that $(b, x) \geqq 0$ for any x such that $Ax \geqq 0$, it is necessary and sufficient that b is a non-negative linear combination of column vectors of A', i.e.*

(30.9) $\quad b = A'u \quad (\textit{for some } u \geqq 0)\,.$

Proof. (i) *Sufficiency.* If (30.9) holds, we get $(b, x) = (A'u, x) = (u, Ax) \geqq 0$ for $Ax \geqq 0$.

(ii) *Necessity.* Let the m column vectors of A' be a^i $(i = 1, 2, ..., m)$ and the convex cone spanned by these m vectors (in R^n) be $K = K(a^1, a^2, ..., a^m)$. Then, K is a closed set because of Theorem 27.5 and $K^{**} = K$ by Theorem 30.2. If we show $b \in K^{**}$, then $b \in K$, i.e. b is a non-negative linear combination of a^i expressed in the form of (30.9).

$b \in K^{**}$ is proved as follows: if $y \in K^*$, then $(x, y) \geqq 0$ for all $x \in K$ by the definition (30.4). In particular, for $x = a^i$, we get $(a^i, y) \geqq 0$ $(i = 1, 2, ..., m)$. This means that $Ay \geqq 0$ holds. Therefore, $(b, y) \geqq 0$ by assumption. This proves that $(b, y) \geqq 0$ for all $y \in K^*$. Whence $b \in K^{**}$ follows from the definition (30.5). [Q.E.D.]

Remark 3. By the preceding remark, we see that if (b, x) is bounded from below, we have in fact $(b, x) \geqq 0$. Therefore, when we apply the Minkowski-Farkas lemma, we can conclude that (30.9) holds if we can confirm the lower boundedness of (b, x).

COROLLARY 2. (i) *If a closed convex cone K does not contain a point like $u \geq 0$, then $-K^*$ contains some $p > 0$.*

(ii) *Let A be an (m, n) matrix. For any $x \geqq 0$, if we do not have $Ax \geq 0$, we have $A'p \leqq 0$ for some $p > 0$.*

Proof. (i) If we deny the conclusion, the convex set $-K^*$ contains no $p > 0$ and, hence, no interior point of R^n_+. Therefore, by Theorem 30.1, $-K^*$ is separated from R^n_+ by a hyperplane passing through the origin and having non-negative coefficients $u \geq 0$, so that $(u, y) \leqq 0$ on $-K^*$. This means that

(30.10) $\quad (u, y) \geqq 0 \quad (\text{for all } y \in K^*)$

and that $u \in K^{**}$ by the definition (30.5). By assumption, K is a closed convex cone and $K^{**} = K$ by (ii) of Theorem 30.2. Thus, $u \in K$ and $u \geq 0$, which leads to a contradiction.

(ii) Let $K = \{y \mid y = Ax, x \geqq 0\}$. This is a closed convex cone spanned by the n column vectors of A. By assumption, K contains no $u \geq 0$ so that $-K^*$ contains some $p > 0$ according to (i) above. It follows from this that $(p, Ax) \leqq 0$ (for all $x \geqq 0$). As $(p, Ax) = (A'p, x)$, we see that $(A'p, x) \leqq 0$ for all $x \geqq 0$. Hence, $A'p \leqq 0$ by (i) of Theorem 15.1. [Q.E.D.]

We have completed introducing the apparatus necessary for the modern treatment of optimization and other related problems. The reader will see in Chapters 6 and 7 how these apparatus are to be used.

Chapter 6

OPTIMIZATION PROBLEMS (continued)

31. The proof of the duality theorems in linear programming

Duality theorems 25.1 and 25.2 in linear programming will now be given the most standard proof based on the separation theorems. For this purpose, it is convenient to make use of the Minkowski-Farkas lemma among the alternative forms presented in the last section. The reader should compare this proof with the direct proof based on differential calculus in Section 26. We make use of the notation and preliminary observations of Section 25. Therefore, what we are now required to do is to prove (ii) of Theorem 25.1 and (ii) of Theorem 25.2.

(a) *The proof of* (ii) *of Duality Theorem 25.1.* We start from a system of linear inequalities

$$(31.1)\qquad \begin{bmatrix} 0 & -A & b \\ A' & 0 & -c \\ 1 & & 0 \\ & \ddots & \\ 0 & & 1 \end{bmatrix} \begin{bmatrix} x_1 \\ x_2 \\ \vdots \\ x_m \\ y_1 \\ y_2 \\ \vdots \\ y_n \\ \rho \end{bmatrix} \geqq 0$$

in unknown vectors $x \in R^m$, $y \in R^n$ and an unknown scalar $\rho \in R$. The coefficient matrix of (31.1) is of $(2(m+n)+1, m+n+1)$ type, and the square in the lower part of the matrix is an identity matrix of the $(m+n+1)$st order.

Actual calculations show that

(31.2) $\quad Ay \leqq \rho b\,,$

(31.3) $\quad A'x \geqq \rho c\,,$

(31.4) $\quad x \geqq 0,\ \ y \geqq 0,\ \ \rho \geqq 0$

are just equivalent to (31.1).

X and Y, the sets of feasible points in (25.13) and (25.14), are not empty by assumption. Choose one $p \in X$ and one $q \in Y$ at random and keep them fixed. Then, one can readily see that

(31.5) $\quad Aq \leqq b\,,\quad A'p \geqq c$

and

(31.6) $\quad p \geqq 0\,,\quad q \geqq 0\,.$

Any solution x, y and ρ of (31.1) satisfies (31.2) ~ (31.4). By adding (31.5) and (31.6) to them respectively, we see

$$\frac{p+x}{1+\rho} \in X \quad \text{and} \quad \frac{q+y}{1+\rho} \in Y\,.$$

Then, (i) of Theorem 25.1 shows that

$$\left(b, \frac{p+x}{1+\rho}\right) \geqq \left(c, \frac{q+y}{1+\rho}\right).$$

Rewriting this, we get

$$(b, x) - (c, y) + 0 \cdot \rho \geqq (c, q) - (b, p) = \text{constant}\,,$$

i.e.

(31.7) $$\left(\begin{bmatrix} b \\ -c \\ 0 \end{bmatrix}, \begin{bmatrix} x \\ y \\ \rho \end{bmatrix}\right) \geqq \text{constant}\,.$$

This proves that $\begin{bmatrix} x \\ y \\ \rho \end{bmatrix}$ which satisfies (31.1) fulfils (31.7). Therefore, by the Minkowski-Farkas lemma, $\begin{bmatrix} b \\ -c \\ 0 \end{bmatrix}$ is a non-negative linear combination of the

$2(m+n)+1$ column vectors of the transpose of the coefficient matrix of (31.1). In other words, for appropriate values of

$$(31.8) \qquad s, u \in R_+^m, \quad t, v \in R_+^n, \quad \omega \geqq 0 \text{ (real number)},$$

we have

$$(31.9) \qquad \begin{bmatrix} b \\ -c \\ 0 \end{bmatrix} = \begin{bmatrix} 0 & A & \begin{matrix} 1 & & & 0 \\ & 1 & & \\ & & \ddots & \\ 0 & & & 1 \end{matrix} \\ -A' & 0 & \\ b' & -c' & \end{bmatrix} \begin{bmatrix} s \\ t \\ u \\ v \\ \omega \end{bmatrix}.$$

This is expanded into

$$(31.10) \qquad b = At + u, \quad -c = A's + v, \quad 0 = (b, s) - (c, t) + \omega.$$

As $u \geqq 0$, $v \geqq 0$, and $\omega \geqq 0$, it follows from (31.10) that

$$At \leqq b, \quad A's \geqq c, \quad (c, t) \geqq (b, s), \quad s \geqq 0, \quad t \geqq 0.$$

This proves that $s \in X$, $t \in Y$ and $(c, t) \geqq (b, s)$. [Q.E.D.]

(b) *The proof of* (ii) *of Duality Theorem 25.2.* For this, it suffices to prove its contraposition, "if (b,x) is bounded from below on $X(\neq \phi)$, then $Y \neq \phi$". Now choose one of the lower bounds γ so that

$$(b, x) \geqq \gamma \quad (\text{for all } x \in X).$$

Consider a system of linear inequalities

$$(31.11) \qquad \begin{bmatrix} A' \\ I_m \end{bmatrix} p \geqq 0,$$

where I_m is an identity matrix of the mth order. If it can be shown that (b, p) is bounded from below for any p satisfying (31.11), then the Minkowski-Farkas lemma demonstrates that there exist some $t \geqq 0$ and $v \geqq 0$ such that

$$(31.12) \qquad b = [A, I_m] \begin{bmatrix} t \\ v \end{bmatrix}.$$

Hence, we get $b = At + v$, $v \geqq 0$, which proves $t \in Y$ and $Y \neq \phi$. Therefore, what remains to be done is to prove the boundedness of (b, p). For this, we choose a point x in X and keep it fixed. For any p that satisfies (31.11), we can show that $p + x \in X$, just as in (a) above. Because of the nature of γ, we get

$$(b, p+x) \geqq \gamma ,$$

which is transformed into

$$(b, p) \geqq \gamma - (b, x) = \text{constant} .$$

The right-hand side of this inequality is a constant independent of p. This completes our proof.

32. Production processes in activity analysis

The critical review of difficulties involved in classical production functions and the attempt at a closer approach to realism focused our attention on linear processes of production with fixed input-output coefficients like (25.4). Typical examples are sectoral processes in input-output models and processes in linear programming models. A firm or an economy is in possession of a number of processes, on the basis of which it determines all technically feasible combinations of inputs and outputs. The collection of these combinations forms a set. In this section, we analyze the structure of this set and derive its economic implications.

Let there be n goods. If y_j'' units of the jth good are used as an input and y_j' units of the same good are produced as an output in a process, $y_j = y_j' - y_j''$ units of the jth good are its net output. The vector y, whose jth component is net output y_j of the jth good, represents a technical process of production. In what follows, we consider net flows. Then, in this process, the jth good is an output if $y_j > 0$, an input if $y_j < 0$, and a good essentially irrelevant to this process if $y_j = 0$.

If the fixity of input and output coefficients is presupposed, a process (or activity) is determined by n coefficients (where n is the number of goods) and its operation is indicated by the activity level as shown in Example 25.1. Suppose that there are s processes available to an economic unit like a firm (or an economy). Represent the jth process by

$$\text{(32.1)} \qquad a^j = \begin{bmatrix} a_{1j} \\ a_{2j} \\ \vdots \\ a_{nj} \end{bmatrix} \quad (j = 1, 2, \ldots, s) \ ,$$

and its activity level by $x_j \geqq 0$. Total outputs produced when all processes are simultaneously employed are given by

$$(32.2) \qquad y = \sum_{j=1}^{s} x_j a^j, \quad x_j \geqq 0 \quad (j = 1, 2, ..., s) .$$

Now define an (n, s) matrix

$$(32.3) \qquad A = [a^1, a^2, ..., a^s] = \begin{bmatrix} a_{11} & a_{12} & \cdots & a_{1s} \\ a_{21} & a_{22} & \cdots & a_{2s} \\ \cdots & \cdots & \cdots & \cdots \\ a_{n1} & a_{n2} & \cdots & a_{ns} \end{bmatrix}$$

and denote the vector of activity levels by x with x_j as its jth component. Then, (32.2) is given a concise expression

$$(32.4) \qquad y = Ax, \quad x \geqq 0 .$$

A is called the *input-output matrix* or *technology matrix.* All points y in R^n that can be expressed in the form (32.4) compose the collection of production possibilities technically available to the economic unit. This is designated as the set Y and called the *production possibility set.* Y is an example of the set Δ that was generally defined in Section 25. As it is a convex cone spanned by s points a^j ($j = 1, 2, ..., s$), it is a closed convex cone.

Remark 1. If $y_i = \sum_{j=1}^{s} a_{ij}x_j = 0$ for some activity levels $x \geqq 0$, then the ith good produced in all processes with $a_{ij}x_j \geqq 0$ is re-used as an input in all processes with $a_{ij}x_j \leqq 0$. In general cases where we do not have $y_i = 0$, we can also easily visualize that this sort of a phenomenon may take place somewhere in the system.

Remark 2. Let a non-negative matrix of the nth order A be an input-output matrix of an interindustry model. Then, the technology matrix (12.3), expressed in net terms, is not A but $I - A$. The relation (32.4) is represented by $y = (I - A)x$, $x \geqq 0$ in this case. By the definition of input coefficients, the activity level of the jth process, i.e. the jth sector, x_j, naturally coincides with the total output of the jth good.

Remark 3. Points of Y represent technically feasible methods of production. However, this does not mean that all of them are actually attainable.

The model, (32.2), that is to be discussed in this section, is called an open model. If we have $y_j < 0$ at a point $y \in Y$, i.e. if we require the jth good as an input, a certain amount of this good must flow into this system as a primary factor of production from outside the system. Land and labor are important examples of the factors of production that have been regarded as primary ever since economics was established as a discipline. A model that allows inflows from outside the system is called an *open model.* The existing amounts or feasible inflows of land and labor services within a given period of production have upper bounds. Let the nth good be labor and let $-\eta_n$ represent the upper bound of its feasible inflow (i.e. maximal inflow) in the period under study. Then, the nth component of feasible y must be subject to a condition

(32.5) $$y_n \geqq \eta_n \,.$$

As $y_n = \sum_{j=1}^{s} a_{nj} x_j$, (32.5) is a linear constraint on the activity levels x_j

(32.6) $$\sum_{j=1}^{s} a_{nj}\, x_j \geqq \eta_n \,.$$

If labor is indispensable as an input in every process, i.e. if $a_{nj} < 0$ ($j = 1, 2, ..., s$), then the attainable values of x are much more restricted than its technically feasible values. Production possibilities y that are attainable subject to the restrictions placed by the availabilities of bottleneck factors form a subset of Y. In addition to land and labor, capital facilities like plant and equipment may be treated as bottleneck factors, depending on what period of production is chosen (year, quarter, month, etc.) for our consideration. The constraints on the activity levels stemming from the availabilities of important bottleneck factors like land, labor and capital as well as from constant returns to scale and other premises of the model under study are in general represented by a system of linear inequalities like (32.6). This forces us to consider x to be subject to the same form of conditions as the constraints in linear programming problems. In other words, let B be an (m, s) matrix and $r \in R^m$, then the attainable activity levels x are presented by linear inequalities of the form

(32.7) $$Bx \leqq r, \quad x \geqq 0 \,.$$

Koopmans' postulates. From economic considerations, T.C.Koopmans proposed that the production possibility set Y satisfies all or one of the following two postulates *:

Postulate (I). Irreversibility of processes. For a production process $y \in Y$, $-y$ is a process that completely reverses inputs and outputs of y into outputs and inputs. Suppose now that, first, production is undertaken by y and then its resulting outputs used as inputs in $-y$. The final outputs should be identical with the initial inputs in y. In other words, y and $-y$ have turned over the input-output relations. If $y \in Y$ and $-y \in Y$, then y is technically reversible. However, when labor, land and other factors are regarded as non-producible primary factors of production, this reversibility of a production process fails. For instance, it would be impossible to reverse a process producing iron by using a number of goods including labor as inputs and to recoup labor and other inputs used up in the original process by using iron as an input. The *irreversibility* of a process implies that always $-y \notin Y$ for any process y except 0 in Y. This can be expressed set-theoretically as

(32.8) $$Y \cap (-Y) = \{0\} .$$

$-Y$ is the collection of all points that are multiples of y of Y by -1. It is a special case of linear combinations of sets that were explained in Section 27.

Postulate (II). The impossibility of the Land of Cockaigne. In the real world, labor and other sacrifices must be made if some returns are desired. At a point y in Y representing a technical input-output transformation, its positive components are outputs and negative ones inputs. Then, if Y contains a point $y \geq 0$, then at least one good is produced in a positive amount without using any goods as inputs. The present postulate on the impossibility of the Land of Cockaigne ** rejects this unrealistic situation. This postulate means that any point y of Y, except 0, always contains negative components. To represent this fact in terms of sets, we note that Y and the positive orthant R^n_+ share only 0 in common, i.e.

(32.9) $$Y \cap R^n_+ = \{0\} .$$

* He cites another postulate on the feasibility of processes due to the constraints placed by bottleneck factors. For the details, see ref. [26].

** Cockaigne is an imaginary Utopia in the medieval Western Europe where wine flowed in rivers, houses were made of candies, every good was free and people lived in utmost luxury.

Postulates (I) and (II) are mathematically independent of each other. A convex cone consists of a (in general, an infinite) number of rays issuing from the origin. Postulate (I) contends that no ray recrosses Y when it is extended beyond the origin in the opposite direction, i.e. that Y contains no complete straight line extending on both sides of the origin.

In contrast, Postulate (II) means, as we have seen above, that Y shares no point in common with R^n_+ except 0. The shaded parts in figs. 32.1 and 32.2 represent convex cones in R^2. Fig. 32.1 is the case where (I) and (II) are both satisfied, while fig. 32.2 is the case which does not satisfy (I) but satisfies (II). The reader should draw a figure representing the case that satisfies (I) but not (II).

Now denoting the price of the ith good by $p_i \geqq 0$, we can represent the price system by an n-dimensional vector p with p_i's as its components. Because of what is implied by the price system, not all prices must be zero so that we have $p \geq 0$. Then, for $y \in Y$, the inner product (p, y) is the difference of the total value of outputs and the total cost of production, i.e. the profit of the process y under the price system p. The theorem below indicates the interconnection between Postulate (II) and the price system.

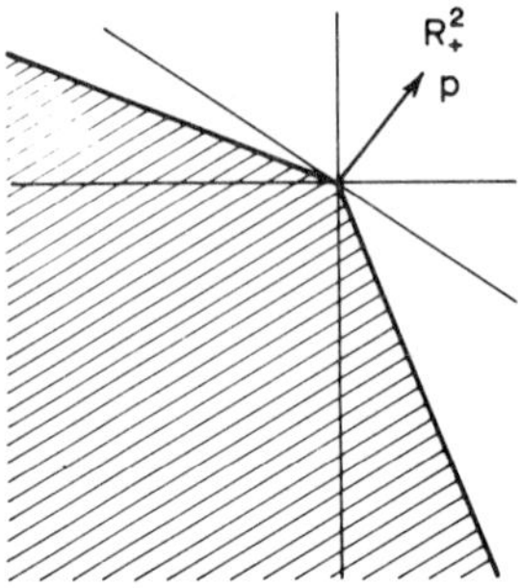

Fig. 32.1.

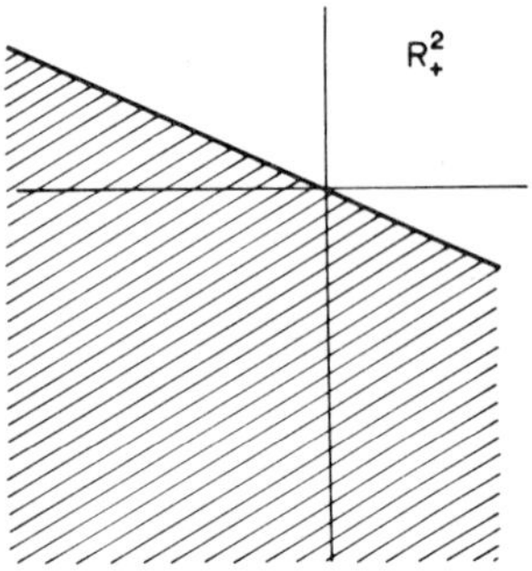

Fig. 32.2.

THEOREM 32.1. *Let the production possibility set Y be a set of processes represented in the form of* (32.4). *In order for Y to satisfy Postulate (II), it is necessary and sufficient that there exists a positive price vector $p > 0$ such that*

$$(32.10) \qquad (p, y) \leqq 0 \quad (\text{for all } y \in Y) .$$

This theorem holds in general if Y is a closed convex cone.

Proof. (i) *Necessity.* By applying (ii) of Corollary 2 of Theorem 30.2 to the (n, s) matrix A now under consideration, we see that Postulate (II) is exactly the assumption of the corollary. Therefore, there exists $p > 0$ such that $A'p \leqq 0$. (32.10) holds for the basic processes (column vectors of A). In general, for $y \in Y$, it follows from the expression (32.4) that $(p, y) = (p, Ax) = (A'p, x) \leqq 0$ ($\because x \geqq 0$).

(ii) *Sufficiency.* If there exists $p > 0$ like (32.10), we get $(p, y) > 0$ for $y \geq 0$. Therefore, this $y \notin Y$ and Postulate (II) holds.

(iii) For the proof for Y in general in the latter half of the theorem, we see that its necessity is merely a restatement of (i) of Corollary 2 of Theorem 30.2 and that its sufficiency can be demonstrated in the same way as the proof of sufficiency for the first half of the theorem. [Q.E.D.]

The general production possibility set. Postulates (I) and (II) still retain their economic and mathematical significance even if points of Y are not represented in the form of (32.4) or if Y is not a convex cone. Therefore, the two postulates are recognized by many theorists as an economic characterization of the general properties possessed by technical relationships between inputs and outputs and accepted as the basic postulates of production. In the general case, too, we regard Y as the set of all technically feasible processes y, though it is not required to be a convex polyhedral cone or even a convex cone. But it is usually assumed to be a closed convex set that contains 0. It is clear that it includes a convex cone as a special case. When Y is a convex cone, $y \in Y$ and $\lambda > 0$ imply $\lambda y \in Y$ and we have constant returns to scale. Let us now examine the properties of Y in the general case.

Let Y be a convex set containing the origin. Then, for $0 \leq \alpha \leq 1$, $y \in Y$, we get $\alpha y = \alpha y + (1 - \alpha)0 \in Y$, i.e. we have the *law of non-increasing returns to scale.* For $n = 2$, the set of processes Y as depicted in fig. 32.3 clearly satisfies this law. But let us make a further examination. Let $y = \begin{bmatrix} y_1 \\ y_2 \end{bmatrix}$, $y_1 < 0$, $y_2 > 0$. Then, y_2 units of the second good are produced with an input of $-y_1$ units of the first good. Draw a perpendicular line parallel to the y_2-axis and passing through αy and take its point of intersection with the boundary of Y. This is $z = \begin{bmatrix} z_1 \\ z_2 \end{bmatrix}$ where $z_1 = \alpha y_1$. In general, $z/\alpha \notin Y$. Hence, we have $y_2 < z_2/\alpha$ even for y, a process in Y, with the same amount of input of the first good as z/α and the maximal output of the second good. This case is described as *diminishing returns to scale.* This implies that it is technically infeasible to increase outputs at the same rate as inputs.

Efficient points and prices. If, for a point $y \in Y$ (the production possibility set), there exists a point $z \in Y$ such that $y \leq z$, then z is a production process

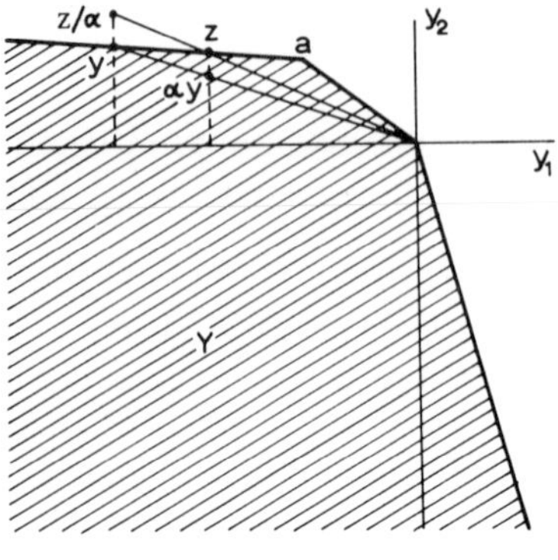

Fig. 32.3.

superior to y. For z produces at least the same outputs as y from at most the same inputs as y and requires less of an input or produces more of an output than y. However, for any y on the upper frontier of Y in fig. 32.3, we can see that there is no process superior to it in the sense we have described. When there is no $z \in Y$ such that $y \leq z$ for a point y in Y, the process y is said to be *efficient*. The collection of all efficient points of Y is, in general, a hypersurface in R^n. When this surface is round with a moderate degree of smoothness (i.e. continuously differentiable) with no cusps like the point a in fig. 32.3, we can apply the concept of a classical production function to give an exact formulation to it.

Efficient points themselves can no longer be compared with each other in the sense of partial ordering of vectors. The comparison of superiority of processes, including the comparison of efficient points, is made through the evaluation of profits under a given price vector.

THEOREM 32.2. Let *Y be a set. Then,* (i) *in order that $\hat{y} \in Y$ may be an efficient point of this set, it is necessary and sufficient that the vectorial difference $Y - \hat{y}$ shares no point in common with R^n_+ except* 0, *namely*

$$(32.11) \qquad (Y - \hat{y}) \cap R^n_+ = \{0\} .$$

(ii) *If Y is a convex set and $\hat{y} \in Y$ an efficient point, there exists a price vector $p \geq 0$ such that*

$$(32.12) \qquad (p, y) \leqq (p, \hat{y}) \quad (\text{for all } y \in Y) .$$

(iii) *If Y is a convex polyhedral cone, one can choose the price vector in* (ii) *as positive* $p > 0$.

(iv) *If there exists a positive price vector* $p > 0$ *such that* (32.12) *holds for* $\hat{y} \in Y$, *then* $\hat{y}$ *is efficient.*

Proof. All the propositions can be easily proved. (i) is evident. (ii) follows from the application of Theorem 30.1 because $X = Y - \hat{y}$ is a convex set and contains no interior points of R^n_+.

(iii) Let Y be the collection of all vectors y in the form of (32.4) and $\hat{y}$ an efficient point of Y. Denote the convex polyhedral cone spanned by the s column vectors of A and $-\hat{y}$ by $K(-\hat{y}, A)$. This satisfies Postulate (II). If, in fact, we assume that $K(-\hat{y}, A) \ni u \geq 0$, we get $u = -\lambda\hat{y} + Ax$ (for some $\lambda \geqq 0$, $x \geqq 0$). Then, rewrite this relation as $u + (1 + \lambda)\hat{y} = \hat{y} + Ax$ and divide it through by $1 + \lambda > 0$ to obtain $u/(1 + \lambda) + \hat{y} = (1/(1 + \lambda))(\hat{y} + Ax)$. Its right-hand side is contained in Y because $\hat{y}, Ax \in Y$ and Y is a convex cone. Hence, its left-hand side is contained in Y. At the same time, as $\hat{y} \leq u/(1 + \lambda) + \hat{y}$, there exists a point in Y superior to $\hat{y}$ and $\hat{y}$ is not efficient. Thus, $K(-\hat{y}, A)$ contains no points of R^n_+ except 0 so that it satisfies Postulate (II). Therefore, there exists $p > 0$ by Theorem 32.1 and $(p, y) \leqq 0$ (for all $y \in K(-\hat{y}, A)$). Rewriting this, we get $(p, y) \leqq 0$ (for all $y \in Y$) because $Y \subset K(-\hat{y}, A)$. Further, $(p, -\hat{y}) \leqq 0$ for $y = -\hat{y}$, i.e. $(p, \hat{y}) \geqq 0$. As $\hat{y} \in Y$, we get $(p, \hat{y}) \leqq 0$. Whence $(p, \hat{y}) = 0$.

(iv) If $y \geq \hat{y}$ for some y, its inner product with $p > 0$ is $(p, y) > (p, \hat{y})$. As (32.12) holds, this $y \notin Y$, i.e. $\hat{y}$ is efficient.

Remark 4. In the exposition above, we have considered efficient points for a production possibility set. The same argument can apply to an attainable possibility set that takes an account of the restrictions placed by the availabilities of bottleneck factors.

33. Preference ordering and demand functions

Preference fields. It is the traditional idea inherited from the marginal utility school founded by Jevons, Menger and Walras that economic units (chiefly households) as consumers have subjective value judgments on the wants satisfied by various goods. Psychological responses of consumers towards goods are theoretically formulated into the concept of utility or preference.

Let there be n goods. Given two baskets of goods

$$x = \begin{bmatrix} x_1 \\ x_2 \\ \vdots \\ x_n \end{bmatrix} \quad \text{and} \quad y = \begin{bmatrix} y_1 \\ y_2 \\ \vdots \\ y_n \end{bmatrix},$$

a consumer passes one of the following three judgments depending on his own tastes on goods:

(α) x is preferred to y;
(β) y is preferred to x;
(γ) x and y are equally preferred and the consumer is unable to decide which is more preferred. Therefore, when he is forced to make a selection between the two, he is entirely *indifferent* as to the choice.

In notation, (α) is denoted by $x \succ y$, (β) by $y \succ x$, "(α) or (γ)" by $x \succsim y$, and "(β) or (γ)" by $y \succsim x$.

A utility judgment $\succsim$ is a better-or-worse comparison between baskets of goods. It is known that $\succsim$ satisfies the following conditions of ordering according to the postulates of consumers' rational behavior:

reflexivity: $x \succsim x$

transitivity: $x \succsim y,\ y \succsim z \Rightarrow x \succsim z$.

We say that a preference field is given when there are criteria for judging preference according to $\succsim$ on X, a set of basket of goods for which utility judgments are possible. As the preference field represents a consumer's individual tastes, it is needless to say that it differs from one consumer to another.

What we should note here is that (γ) can hold even when $x \neq y$. For instance, a consumer may be indifferent to a basket of 3 kilograms of meat and 1 kilogram of fish and another of 2 kilograms of meat and 4 kilograms of fish. When a consumer is indifferent to x and y, we may express it as $x \sim y$ notationally. Then, $x \sim y$ is obviously equivalent to a system of conditions $x \succsim y$ and $y \succsim x$.

Points of X that are indifferent to x form a subset X_x in X. This is called an *indifference map*. Fig. 33.1 shows indifference curves for $n = 2$. This is a familiar diagram in economic textbooks.

Remark 1. $x \in X_x$.

Remark 2. $x \sim y$ is equivalent to $X_x = X_y$.

Remark 3. $x \nsim y$ is equivalent to $X_x \cap X_y = \phi$.

The reader should check for himself why these three properties hold. We may note that these are directly due to the fact that the indifference relation satisfies the three conditions of an equivalence relation:

(a) $x \sim x$,

(b) $x \sim y \Rightarrow y \sim x$,

(c) $x \sim y, y \sim z \Rightarrow x \sim z$.

The preference field that is depicted in fig. 33.1 implicitly contains many other conditions in addition to those already referred to. We may explain a few important ones among them.

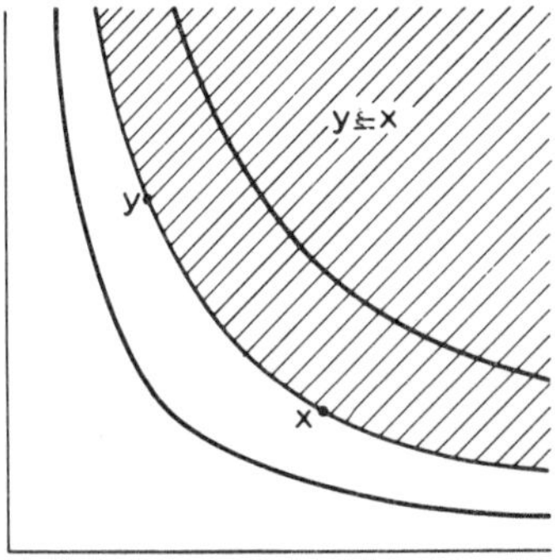

Fig. 33.1.

Convex preference ordering. In fig. 33.1, the set of all y such that $y \succeq x$ for a particular x (the shaded area in the figure) forms a convex set. In general, if $x, y \in X$, it is usually possible to pass a utility judgment on a convex linear combination of x and y. We make the following assumption on the preference ordering $\succeq$ in a convex set X:

If $x, y, w \in X$ and z lies on a segment $[x, y]$, then

(33.1) $\quad x \succeq w, \quad y \succeq w \quad$ implies $\quad z \succeq w$.

This property is equivalent to the fact that a set of all baskets which are indifferent or preferred to w is a convex set. It is said that the given preference ordering is *convex* when (33.1) is satisfied. The convexity of preference ordering is a premise traditionally recognized in economics. It plays a very important role in the more sophisticated analysis of mathematical economics.

Utility indicators. When a real value $u(x)$ is assigned to each point x in the preference field and when the preference ordering $\succeq$ among points of X completely corresponds to the ordering of the values $u(x)$, $u(x)$ is called a *utility indicator* of this preference ordering. In this case, for $x, y \in X$, $x \succeq y$ and $u(x) \geqq u(y)$ are mutually equivalent. There are interesting studies of the problem about what conditions the preference ordering must satisfy to ensure the existence of a utility indicator. However, space does not permit us to introduce them in this book. We limit ourselves to the preference ordering that is representable by a utility indicator in the traditional classical veins.

If u is a utility indicator and f a strictly increasing function, $v(x) = f(u(x))$ is obviously a utility indicator. Hence, a utility indicator is not uniquely determined.

When an indicator u is chosen, the indifference map is represented by $X_a = \{x \mid x \in X, u(x) = u(a)\}$. This is the contour formed by all points x with the height $u(a)$. (Cf. fig. 33.2.)

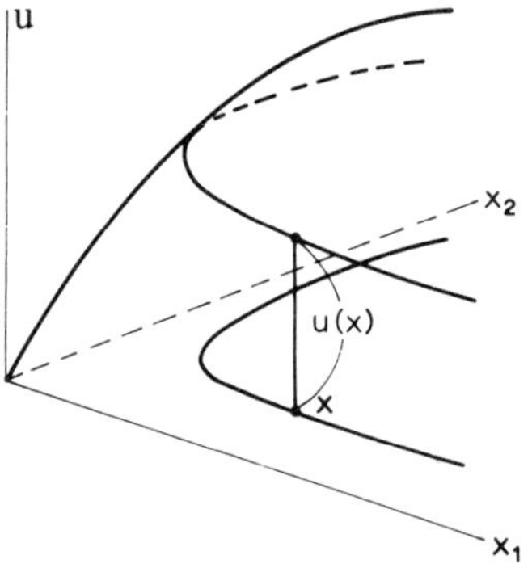

Fig. 33.2.

Classical studies assumed the differentiability of the utility indicator $u(x)$ and paid a great deal of attention on its partial derivatives $\partial u/\partial x_i$. The latter is called the marginal utility of the ith good. However, the concept of marginal utility itself is not particularly useful in advanced theoretical analysis such as given in a later chapter of this book. More attention is now directed to the continuity of the utility indicator.

If the given preference ordering is convex, a utility indicator associated with it obviously satisfies the following:

(33.2) if $z \in [x, y]$, $u(x)$, $u(y) \geqq \omega$, then $u(z) \geqq \omega$,

where ω is a real number. The converse is also true. A function that satisfies

(33.2) is called a *quasi-concave function* *.

Remark 4. Traditional discussions often considered the entire positive orthant R^n_+ as the preference field. When goods which are subjected to utility judgments are consumer goods alone, their amounts demanded are usually non-negative. This fact makes the above assumption reasonable. The consumer (household), however, serves as a supplier of labor in the capacity of an employee and of other primary factors of production. The supply of labor (acquisition of negative labor) yields *disutility* to the supplier. Therefore, it is more general to assume that utility judgments extend to baskets of goods including negative components. From this point of view, it is assumed nowadays that X is a convex set not necessarily included in the positive orthant. However, even in that case, X is often considered to be bounded from below. In other words, we have $b \leqq x$ for all $x \in X$ where b is a constant vector. This assumption is based, e.g., on the fact that there is a limit on the amount of labor suppliable within a year or that the amounts of consumer goods not sufficient to sustain life are outside of utility judgments.

Remark 5. Efficient points were defined in Section 32 in terms of the partial ordering $\geqq$ of vectors. A representative consumer is usually better off if consumer goods are acquired in greater quantities or if labor is offered in a smaller amount. Therefore, the following assumption of monotonicity on the preference ordering has sufficiently broad validity:

$u(x)$ is said to be *increasing* if $u(x) \geqq u(y)$ for $x, y \in X$ such that $x \geqq y$;

$u(x)$ is said to be *strictly increasing* if $u(x) > u(y)$ for $x, y \in X$ such that $x \geq y$.

In the increasing case, the following assumption on X is immediately suggested:

$$\text{(33.3)} \qquad \text{if} \quad y \geqq x \quad \text{and} \quad x \in X, \quad \text{then} \quad y \in X.$$

This may be expressed as follows:

$$\text{if} \quad x \in X, \quad \text{then} \quad x + R^n_+ \subset X.$$

Remark 6. If $u(x)$ has a maximal value on the whole range of X, the maximal point x is called a *saturation point.*

* This condition is less restrictive than that of a concave function discussed in Section 27.

Demand functions. Just like firms in Section 24, a consumer regards prices as given data on the competitive assumption. In other words, he behaves under prices taken as given constraints. While his wants for goods that underlie the preference ordering supply a psychological motive power, prices and income act as constraints on his behavior. The consumer's *demand* for goods is determined as the balance between the two forces. Let us examine in more details how demand is determined.

The basket $x \in X$ of goods that a consumer can purchase with a level of income $I > 0$ under a given price vector $p > 0$ is subject to a constraint

$$(33.4) \qquad (p, x) \leqq I\,.$$

This is called a budget constraint. There are, in general, many baskets $x \in X$ that satisfy (33.4). Which of the baskets is to be chosen is left to the consumer. If we accept the rationality of consumer behavior, this consumer would choose x that maximizes the utility indicator $u(x)$. This x is the volume of demand discussed by orthodox economists since Walras. Negative components of x, of course, represent goods like labor that are supplied by the consumer.

The demand x that is chosen in this fashion is an *ex ante schedule* or purchase plan of the consumer with prices and income given as data. It does not necessarily coincide with his actually realized *ex post* purchase. The demand x would in general be altered when prices and income change, i.e. as the constraints change. In other words, demand is determined as a schedule in response to various values of the price vector and income. This mapping from the price vector p and income I into a point x in X is called a *demand function.*

As stated above, the demand x subject to data $p > 0$ and $I > 0$ is obtained in the domain

$$(33.5) \qquad X \cap \{x \mid (p, x) \leqq I\}$$

as the solution of a maximization problem

$$(33.6) \qquad \max u(x)\,.$$

However, if the maximization problem as formulated here is mathematically nonsensical or lacks a solution, the concept of a demand function becomes an empty one. It is, therefore, necessary to examine whether the premises of the preference ordering are sufficient to ensure the construction of a demand function.

Suppose that X is a closed convex set that contains 0 and is bounded from below. Let one lower bound be b. Further, assume that the utility indicator $u(x)$ is a continuous, quasi-concave function on X. Then, the domain (33.5) always contains 0 and, therefore, is not empty. As X and $\{x \mid (p, x) \leqq I\}$ are both closed sets, (33.5) is also a closed set as their intersection. The domain (33.5) is also bounded because $b_j \leqq x_j \leqq I/p_j$ $(j = 1, 2, ..., n)$ if $x \in X \cap \{x \mid (p, x) \leqq I\}$. Thus, the domain (33.5) is compact by virtue of Theorem 14.6. The continuous function $u(x)$ attains a maximum on this set. Now denote the set of maximizing points by $\varphi(p, I)$ and the maximum of the utility indicator by ω. Then, if $x, y \in \varphi(p, I)$, we have $u(x) = u(y) = \omega$. Meanwhile, as the domain is obviously a convex set, it contains a segment $[x, y]$. By the quasi-concavity of u, $u(z) \geqq \omega$ if $z \in [x, y]$. Hence, from the definition of ω as a maximum, we get $\omega = u(z)$ and $z \in \varphi(p, I)$. In other words, $\varphi(p, I)$ is a convex set. As $\varphi(p, I)$ is a subset composed of points of (33.5) that satisfy an additional condition $u(x) = \omega$, it is a closed set. Thus, $\varphi(p, I)$ is a closed subset of a compact set (33.5) and is itself compact by virtue of Theorem 14.3. Therefore, we obtain the following conclusion: $\varphi(p, I)$ is a non-empty compact convex set for any $p > 0$ and $I > 0$. (Cf. fig. 33.3.)

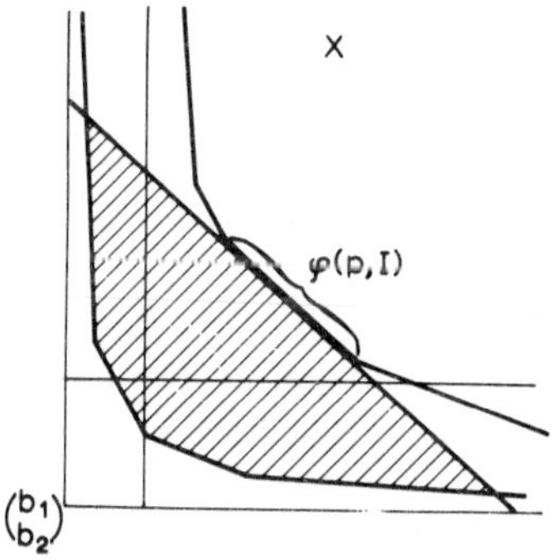

Fig. 33.3.

As the function value $\varphi(p, I)$ is a set, the demand function is in general a *multi-valued function* or *mapping*, or a point-to-set mapping that associates with each point (p, I) a set $\varphi(p, I)$. The classical analysis imposed very strict assumptions on the utility indicator $u(x)$ to make the demand function $\varphi(p, I)$ an ordinary single-valued function. It also assumed the partial differentiability of the function with respect to p_j and I. Nevertheless, one may note that these restrictive assumptions never facilitate elucidating the existence problem of equilibrium solutions that we are going to study later.

Chapter 7

SADDLE POINT PROBLEMS

34. The minimax theorem on zero-sum two-person games

Game theory. The late John von Neumann, who devoted his life to the studies of pure as well as applied mathematics and made brilliant achievements in many fields, published at the age of 25 a pathbreaking article [41] in a mathematical journal Mathematische Annalen that proposed the theory of games. The theory was popularized later through his famous book [24] written jointly with economist O.Morgenstern. It exerted a profound influence on economics. Though the original intention of revolutionizing the theory of imperfect competition was not met with success, it brought rigorous mathematical analytical methods for the first time into the studies of social phenomena. No one would deny the fact that it has been developed into one main stream of modern mathematical economics. The minimax theorem in the heading of this section is a basis of von Neumann's theory of n-person games. In our book, we treat it as part of the saddle point problems and do not embark on a full-fledged introduction of game theory because of the limitation of space.

Suppose that sets S and T are given. Two persons or *players* I and II, acting independently of each other, choose a point p in S and a point q in T respectively. When the choice $p \in S$ and $q \in T$ is made, Player I obtains a gain or payoff $K_1(p, q)$ and Player II another payoff $K_2(p, q)$. The payoffs $K_i(p, q)$ $(i = 1, 2)$ depend on the point chosen, (p, q), and as such are real-valued functions defined on the cartesian product $S \times T$. They are called *payoff functions.* Now Player I can freely control p but cannot intervene in II's choice of q. Moreover, I's payoff is not determined by his own choice of p alone. It is determined only after II has selected q and is thus subject to the influence of II's action. Similarly, II's payoff is not independent of I's action. What sort of a choice should the two players make in a situation like this game? This is the basic problem in game theory. Though the concept of games was fashioned after cards, chess and other games, the theory of games aims at an analysis of human behavior when subjects' interests are interdependent. It is intended as a contribution to social sciences.

We shall discuss the zero-sum game that is the simplest of two-person games, for which the authoritative theory was established. This is a game in which the two players' payoff functions are subject to an identity relation

$$K_1(p, q) + K_2(p, q) = 0$$

on $S \times T$. It is given a very important place in game theory because of its basic significance in game theory itself and of its close relation with various problems under study here (linear programming problems, the von Neumann balanced growth model, constrained optimum problems and the like).

The minimax principle and the saddle points. Taking I's payoff function as a basis, rewrite $K(p, q) = K_1(p, q)$. Then, we have $K_2(p, q) = -K(p, q)$ from the zero-sum identity. In a zero-sum two-person game, the two players have completely opposite interests. I's gain is immediately II's loss and I's loss is II's gain. Player I desires to make $K(p, q)$ as large as possible, while Player II wishes to make it as small as possible.

As we already noted, the competitive pattern of behavior of economic units (firms and households) are formulated as simple maximization (minimization) problems. Prices and income are given as data that are directly controlled by no economic units. They may be regarded as equivalent to the fixed environment in which the economic units are placed. Therefore, a consumer's demand determined by maximizing his utility subject to his budget constraint is obtained independently of other consumers' actions. In a game-theoretic environment, the variable q under II's control serves as a sort of a datum to I in the sense that q is beyond I's control. However, q is not fixed; it is varied by the opponent's action. Thus, I must always keep this in mind in selecting the value of the variable under his own control. Further, I has no prior information on what $q \in T$ would be chosen by his opponent II. Under such circumstances where one cannot anticipate the opponent's action, it would be wise for him to be pessimistic in his own action and to predict the most hostile action by his opponent. I's payoff $K(p, q)$ following from his choice of $p \in S$ depends also on II's choice of q. Therefore, the most hostile attitude of II is II's choice of q that minimizes I's gain. Then, the payoff that I can be absolutely certain of getting from his choice of p on the assumption that his opponent would take an action most unfavorable to him is

$$(34.1) \qquad F(p) = \min_{q \in T} K(p, q) \quad *.$$

$F(p)$ is the minimal payoff that Player I can secure under the least favorable situation to him. If II is not as belligerent as I's prediction, there is some room for a payoff above $F(p)$. The maximal payoff that I can safely obtain by his appropriate action is thus given by

$$(34.2) \qquad \nu_1 = \max_{p \in S} F(p) = \max_{p \in S} \min_{q \in T} K(p, q) .$$

This pattern of behavior on Player I's part is said to be based on the *maximin principle.* This is not a simple-minded maximization but a maximization of the minimum that can be secured in each instance.

Exactly the same behavior pattern can be envisioned for Player II. As we have noted, II's objective in this zero-sum two-person game is to minimize the opponent's gain. Hence,

$$(34.3) \qquad G(q) = \max_{p \in S} K(p, q)$$

represents the maximal payoff that II is deprived of by I in the worst situation (i.e. II's loss). By his appropriate action, II can minimize his maximal loss and keep his loss below

$$(34.4) \qquad \nu_2 = \min_{q \in T} G(q) = \min_{q \in T} \max_{p \in S} K(p, q) .$$

This pattern of behavior on II's part is said to be based on the *minimax principle.*

THEOREM 34.1. *There is an inequality*

$$(34.5) \qquad \nu_1 \leqq \nu_2$$

between the maximin payoff ν_1 *and the minimax loss* ν_2.

Proof. It follows from the definitions (34.1) and (34.3) that

$$F(p) \leqq K(p, q) \leqq G(q)$$

* For the time being, we assume that there exist the required maximum and minimum.

for any $p \in S$ and $q \in T$. Therefore, as $F(p) \leqq G(q)$ always,

$$\nu_1 = \max_{p \in S} F(p) \leqq \min_{q \in T} G(q) = \nu_2 . \qquad \text{[Q.E.D.]}$$

Let I's payoff be ν when I and II actually choose p and q. What is the value of ν? Insofar as I follows the maximin principle, I can secure at least ν_1 as his payoff so that ν should satisfy $\nu_1 \leqq \nu$. On the other hand, II can limit his loss below ν_2 whatever action I may take. Thus, we have $\nu \leqq \nu_2$ and ν must be determined in the interval

$$(34.6) \qquad \nu_1 \leqq \nu \leqq \nu_2 .$$

If the equality holds in (34.5), we get $\nu_1 = \nu = \nu_2$ in (34.6). I's maximin action and II's minimax action are both realized so that an equilibrium is established. ν is determined as the value of the game. In this sense, a zero-sum two-person game with $\nu_1 = \nu_2$ is said to be *strictly determined.*

Next, let us check in what way the strictly-determined game and the concept of a saddle point are related to each other. A point $(\hat{p}, \hat{q})$ in the cartesian product set $S \times T$ is called a *saddle point* of the payoff function $K(p, q)$ when it satisfies the following conditions:

(α) $K(p, \hat{q})$ as a function of p attains a maximum on S at $p = \hat{p}$;

(β) $K(\hat{p}, q)$ as a function of q attains a minimum on T at $q = \hat{q}$.

Combining (α) and (β), we get

$$(34.7) \qquad K(p, \hat{q}) \leqq K(\hat{p}, \hat{q}) \leqq K(\hat{p}, q) \quad (\text{for all } p \in S \text{ and } q \in T) .$$

This is called a saddle point because $(\hat{p}, \hat{q})$ corresponds to the saddle of the mountain in fig. 34.1 where $K(p, q)$ is the height of the mountain on $S \times T$ (see also fig. 34.2).

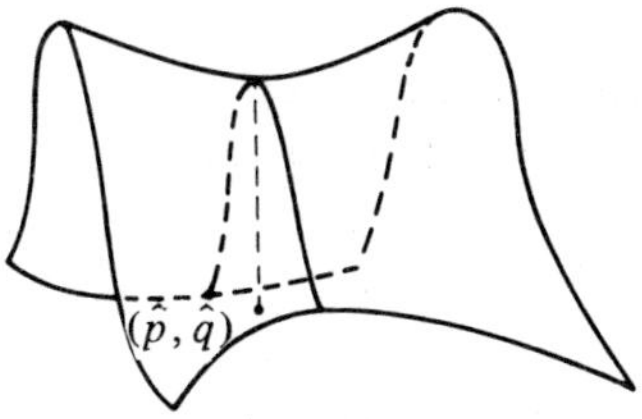

Fig. 34.1.

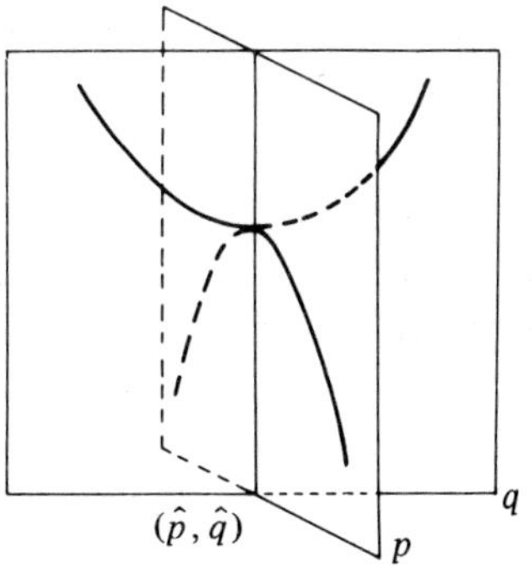

Fig. 34.2.

THEOREM 34.2. (i) *Let* $\hat{p}$ *be a point at which* $F(p)$ *is maximized and* $\hat{q}$ *a point at which* $G(q)$ *is minimized. If* $v_1 = v_2$, *then* $(\hat{p}, \hat{q})$ *is a saddle point of* $K(p, q)$ *and* $K(\hat{p}, \hat{q}) = v_1 = v_2$.

(ii) *If there exists a saddle point* $(\hat{p}, \hat{q})$ *of* $K(p, q)$, *there holds* $v_1 = v_2$.

Proof. (i) As $v_1 = F(\hat{p})$ and $v_2 = G(\hat{q})$, we have

$$\max_{p \in S} K(p, \hat{q}) = G(\hat{q}) = v_2 = v_1 = F(\hat{p}) = \min_{q \in T} K(\hat{p}, q)$$

if $v_1 = v_2$. In other words, for all p and q, we have $K(p, \hat{q}) \leqq v_1 = v_2 \leqq K(\hat{p}, q)$. Therefore, by substituting $q = \hat{q}$ in the right-hand side of this inequality, we obtain the left-hand inequality of (34.7), $K(p, \hat{q}) \leqq K(\hat{p}, \hat{q})$. Similarly, by substituting $p = \hat{p}$ in the left-hand side of the inequality, we obtain the other half of (34.7), $K(\hat{p}, \hat{q}) \leqq K(\hat{p}, q)$. At the same time, we get $K(\hat{p}, \hat{q}) = v_1 = v_2$.

(ii) If $(\hat{p}, \hat{q})$ is a saddle point and satisfies (34.7), then

$$\max_{p \in S} K(p, \hat{q}) = K(\hat{p}, \hat{q}) = \min_{q \in T} K(\hat{p}, q) ,$$

i.e.

$$G(\hat{q}) = F(\hat{p}) . \tag{34.8}$$

As

$$v_1 = \max_{p \in S} F(p) \geqq F(\hat{p})$$

and

$$v_2 = \min_{q \in T} G(q) \leqq G(\hat{q}) ,$$

we obtain $v_1 \geqq v_2$ from (34.8). When combined with Theorem 34.1, we get $v_1 = v_2$. It follows from this that $v_1 = F(\hat{p})$ and $v_2 = G(\hat{q})$ so that $\hat{p}$ is a maximizing point of $F(p)$ and $\hat{q}$ is a minimizing point of $G(q)$.

Rectangular games. For what sorts of sets and a function chosen for S, T and $K(p, q)$ could there be a saddle point? Many studies have been devoted to this *saddle point problem* ever since the original von Neumann paper was published. More elementary proofs were also introduced. It has been shown through von Neumann and other scholars' efforts that a wide range of games including rectangular games (to be discussed below) can be handled by the separation theorems. Now let

$$S = S_m = \{p \mid p \in R^m, \sum_{i=1}^{m} p_i = 1,\ p_i \geqq 0\ \ (i = 1, 2, ..., m)\},$$

and

$$T = T_n = \{q \mid q \in R^n, \sum_{j=1}^{n} q_j = 1,\ q_j \geqq 0\ (j = 1, 2, ..., n)\}\ .$$

Let $A = [a_{ij}]$ be an (m, n) matrix and define a payoff function on $S_m \times T_n$ as

$$K(p, q) = (p, Aq) = \sum_{i,j=1}^{m,n} a_{ij} p_i q_j\ . \tag{34.9}$$

This is called a *rectangular game* with A as its *payoff matrix.*

THEOREM 34.3 (*von Neumann's minimax theorem*). *A rectangular game is strictly determined.*

Proof. We first note that $F(p)$ of (34.1) and $G(q)$ of (34.3) can be actually defined for the payoff function in this theorem. We have

$$F(p) = \min_{1 \leqq j \leqq n} \sum_{i=1}^{m} a_{ij} p_i \tag{34.10}$$

and

$$G(q) = \max_{1 \leqq i \leqq m} \sum_{j=1}^{n} a_{ij} q_j\ . \tag{34.11}$$

If the right-hand value of (34.10) is attained in fact at $j = k$, we have

$$\sum_{i=1}^{m} a_{ij} p_i \geqq \sum_{i=1}^{m} a_{ik} p_i \quad (j = 1, 2, ..., n)\ . \tag{34.12}$$

Multiply (34.12) by $q_j \geqq 0$ and obtain the grand total as

$$\sum_{i,j=1}^{m,n} a_{ij} p_i q_j \geqq \sum_{i=1}^{m} a_{ik} p_i\ , \tag{34.13}$$

because q_j's sum up to 1. The left-hand side of (34.13) takes the value equal to its right-hand side for a specific q whose components are $q_j = 0$ $(j \neq k)$ and $q_k = 1$. This proves (34.10). (34.11) can be proved in exactly the same manner.

(34.10) and (34.11) show that $F(p)$ and $G(q)$ are continuous on S_m and T_n respectively. As S_m and T_n are compact *, $F(p)$ attains a maximum ν_1 on S_m and $G(q)$ a minimum ν_2 on T_n according to Theorem 14.2. As Theorem 34.1 shows that $\nu_1 \leqq \nu_2$, our proof is complete when we demonstrate $\nu_2 \leqq \nu_1$.

For any $p \in S_m$, we have $\nu_1 \geqq F(p)$. Hence, we never have $\nu_1 < F(p)$ for whatever $p \in S_m$. According to (34.10), this property is equivalent to the fact that the inequalities

$$(34.14) \qquad \nu_1 < \sum_{i=1}^{m} a_{ij} p_i \quad (j = 1, 2, \ldots, n)$$

have no solution p in S_m. Now take

$$e = \begin{bmatrix} 1 \\ 1 \\ \vdots \\ 1 \end{bmatrix} \in R^n ,$$

a vector whose components are all unity. Then, we see from the result given above that the set in R^n,

$$X = \{x \,|\, x = A'p - \nu_1 e,\ p \in S_m\} ,$$

contains no interior points of R^n_+. As X is apparently a convex set, X is separated from R^n_+ by a hyperplane with non-negative coefficients $(\hat{q}, x) = 0$, $\hat{q} \geq 0$ according to Theorem 30.1. We may assume that $\hat{q} \in T_n$ if we multiply it by some appropriate positive number when necessary. Hence, if $p \in S_m$, we have

$$\begin{aligned}(p, A\hat{q}) - \nu_1 &= (A\hat{q}, p) - \nu_1 \\ &= (\hat{q}, A'p) - (\hat{q}, \nu_1 e) \\ &= (\hat{q}, A'p - \nu_1 e) \leqq 0 ,\end{aligned}$$

* See Example 14.4.

so that

$$(34.15) \qquad (p, A\hat{q}) \leqq \nu_1 \quad (\text{for all } p \in S_m) .$$

Therefore, $G(\hat{q}) \leqq \nu_1$ holds. Together with $\nu_2 \leqq G(\hat{q})$, we get $\nu_2 \leqq \nu_1$.

Probability-theoretic interpretation. (34.9) is called a *bilinear form* of the variable (p, q). This is because (34.9) is linear in p if q is fixed and linear in q if p is fixed as explained in connection with the discussion of the properties of inner products *. A point p in S_m has non-negative components $p_i \geqq 0$, with their sum as

$$\sum_{i=1}^{m} p_i = 1$$

so that it can be regarded as a probability distribution on a finite set consisting of m elements, $\Gamma = \{s_1, s_2, ..., s_m\}$. Similarly, q can be considered as a probability distribution on a finite set with n elements, $\Delta = \{t_1, t_2, ..., t_n\}$. Let us examine a zero-sum two-person game in which player I selects s_i from Γ and player II chooses t_j from Δ. I's payoff is a_{ij} in this case. This game is not necessarily strictly determined. For instance, in

$$A = [a_{ij}] = \begin{bmatrix} 1 & 3 \\ 2 & 0 \end{bmatrix} ,$$

$\nu_1 = \max_i \min_j a_{ij} = 1$ and $\nu_2 = \min_j \max_i a_{ij} = 2$ so that $\nu_1 \neq \nu_2$. Thus, it is not strictly determined.

However, as Theorem 34.3 indicates, the bilinear form (34.9) with coefficients a_{ij}'s always has a saddle point on $S_m \times T_n$. I's selection of a probability distribution p implies that he behaves subject to a chance mechanism that generates a probability distribution $p_1, p_2, ..., p_m$ on the set Γ, e.g. a die with m faces numbered one to m and a probability of p_i for the coming up of the face i. He selects s_i by conforming to the random coming up of the face i effected by this mechanism. II takes a similar choice of the probability distribution q. Then, if I selects p and II q, I selects i and II j with a probability of $p_i q_j$. The payoff a_{ij} is realized with this probability. (34.9) is the expected value of I's payoff. This, however, is merely one interpretation. The reader should refrain from attaching himself to this interpretation alone. He should

* See Section 11, (11.19) ~ (11.22).

not reject other interpretations of Theorem 34.3 from alternative viewpoints nor block its free applications to other problems.

Remark 1. In game theory, the objects of choice (p, q) are called *strategies.* In a strictly determined game, I's best action is the choice of p such that $v = F(p)$ and II's best action is the choice of q such that $v = G(q)$ where v is the value of the game $(v = v_1 = v_2)$. These choices of p and q are called optimal strategies of I and II.

Remark 2. The collections of optimal strategies of I and II in a rectangular game are compact convex sets in S_m and T_n respectively. It is easy to verify this fact. It is left to the reader's examination. Optimal strategies are not necessarily unique but are in general multiple and form a set.

35. The von Neumann balanced growth model

Von Neumann reported on a balanced growth model in a paper [42] published in 1936. He applied a mathematical analysis with rigor unprecedented in the economic literature and made an invaluable pioneering contribution in examining the existence of economically meaningful solutions. This model is formulated in a very elegant form as two systems of linear inequalities that are dual to each other. Von Neumann's initial analysis was based on the fixed point theorem that is to be discussed later. It was found later that the major conclusion of the model could be obtained in a more elementary manner (namely by the application of the separation theorems) *. The present section is intended to introduce this model with an elementary proof of the existence of the solution.

The von Neumann model. Let the number of goods be n with indexes running $j = 1, 2, ..., n$. Assume that there are m linear processes available to the economy, numbered $i = 1, 2, ..., m$. In contrast to Section 32 that treated outputs as net flows, this model is formulated in terms of *stocks*. The ith process produces outputs of goods $b_{i1}, b_{i2}, ..., b_{in}$ by the end of a period by using as inputs the stocks of goods $a_{i1}, a_{i2}, ..., a_{in}$ existing at the beginning of the period (per unit of the activity levels). In other words, the ith process is

* N.Georgescu-Roegen, "The Aggregate Linear Production Function and its Applications to von Neumann's model", to be found in ref. [26], and NIkaido [44, 45]. The discussion below is based on the latter.

represented by the schema

$$(35.1) \qquad (a_{i1}, a_{i2}, ..., a_{in}) \to (b_{i1}, b_{i2}, ..., b_{in})\ * .$$

These outputs are carried over into the next period as the initial stocks. This model contains no primary factors of production. All goods are considered as outputs resulting from production activities in the preceding period. Labor is considered also as an output of a process that reproduces labor from the inputs of consumer goods. The model, therefore, has no inflow of goods from outside the system. It is a *closed model* in this sense. Let the activity level of the ith process in period t be $p_i(t) \geqq 0$ $(t = 1, 2, ...)$. As the input of any good in period $t + 1$ cannot exceed its output in period t, we have inequalities

$$(35.2) \qquad \sum_{i=1}^{m} a_{ij} p_i(t+1) \leqq \sum_{i=1}^{m} b_{ij} p_i(t) \quad (j = 1, 2, ..., n) .$$

Let the price of the jth good in period t be $q_j(t) \geqq 0$ and the interest factor (i.e. 1 + the rate of interest) in period t be $\beta(t)$ $(t = 1, 2, ...)$. Then, let the unit cost of production of each process including interest payments, evaluated at the prices of period t, be not less than the value of output evaluated in the prices of period $t + 1$. In other words, the rate of interest is high enough to absorb profits of each process. Thus,

$$(35.3) \qquad \beta(t) \sum_{j=1}^{n} a_{ij} q_j(t) \geqq \sum_{j=1}^{n} b_{ij} q_j(t+1) \quad (i = 1, 2, ..., m) .$$

Along with the model outlined in Section 22, von Neumann considered the state of balanced growth (or contraction), i.e. proportional growth of the activity levels with the prices and the rate of interest constant, in the model (35.2) and (35.3). This is given by

$$(35.4) \qquad \begin{aligned} & p_i(t+1) = \alpha p_i(t) \qquad (i = 1, 2, ..., m) , \\ & q_j(t+1) = q_j(t) \qquad (j = 1, 2, ..., n) , \\ & \beta(t+1) = \beta(t) . \end{aligned}$$

* Here, a process is denoted by a row vector.

Putting $\beta(t) = \beta$ and substituting (35.4) into (35.2) and (35.3), we get

$$\alpha \sum_{i=1}^{m} a_{ij} p_i(t) \leqq \sum_{i=1}^{m} b_{ij} p_i(t) \quad (j = 1, 2, ..., n) \tag{35.5}$$

and

$$\beta \sum_{j=1}^{n} a_{ij} q_j(t) \geqq \sum_{j=1}^{n} b_{ij} q_j(t) \quad (i = 1, 2, ..., m)\,. \tag{35.6}$$

Remark 1. α is 1 + the rate of growth.

We now add two subsidiary conditions according to von Neumann, namely

(35.7) the price of a free good: if the jth relation of (35.5) is a strict inequality, then $q_j(t) = 0$;

(35.8) the activity level of a process with loss: if the ith relation of (35.6) is a strict inequality, then $p_i(t) = 0$.

These two subsidiary conditions are similar to the conditions (α) and (β) in linear programming problems that were explained in connection with Example 25.2.

Now letting $p_i(0) = p_i$ and $q_j(0) = q_j$, we see that (35.5) ~ (35.8) subject to (35.4) are obviously equivalent to the following system of inequalities that are independent of time t:

$$\alpha \sum_{i=1}^{m} a_{ij} p_i \leqq \sum_{i=1}^{m} b_{ij} p_i \quad (j = 1, 2, ..., n)\,, \tag{35.9}$$

$$\beta \sum_{j=1}^{n} a_{ij} q_j \geqq \sum_{j=1}^{n} b_{ij} q_j \quad (i = 1, 2, ..., m)\,, \tag{35.10}$$

(35.11) $q_j = 0$ if the jth relation of (35.9) is a strict inequality,

(35.12) $p_i = 0$ if the ith relation of (35.10) is a strict inequality.

The input coefficients a_{ij} and output coefficients b_{ij} are assumed to satisfy the following assumptions (α) ~ (γ):

(α) $a_{ij} \geqq 0,\ b_{ij} \geqq 0$ (for all i and j) .

(β) Each process uses at least one good as an input, i.e. $\sum_{j=1}^{n} a_{ij} > 0$ (for all i).

(γ) In each process, any good appears as either an input or an output, i.e.

$$a_{ij} + b_{ij} > 0 \quad \text{(for all } i \text{ and } j) .$$

This is the von Neumann balanced growth model. Of our major concern here is the solution α and β of (35.9) ~ (35.12) together with the existence of

$$(35.9') \qquad p_i \geqq 0 \quad (i = 1, 2, ..., m) , \quad \sum_{i=1}^{m} p_i > 0$$

and

$$(35.10') \qquad q_j \geqq 0 \quad (j = 1, 2, ..., n) , \quad \sum_{j=1}^{n} q_j > 0 .$$

THEOREM 35.1. *If this model has a solution, then* $\alpha = \beta$, *whose value is uniquely determined. Moreover,* $\alpha, \beta \geqq 0$.

Proof. Multiplying the jth relation of (35.9) by q_j and summing them up, we get

$$(35.13) \qquad \alpha \sum_{i,j=1}^{m,n} a_{ij} p_i q_j = \sum_{i,j=1}^{m,n} b_{ij} p_i q_j$$

because of (35.11). Similarly, from (35.10) and (35.12), we get

$$(35.14) \qquad \beta \sum_{i,j=1}^{m,n} a_{ij} p_i q_j = \sum_{i,j=1}^{m,n} b_{ij} p_i q_j .$$

These two equations can be rewritten as

$$(35.15) \qquad (1 + \alpha) \sum_{i,j=1}^{m,n} a_{ij} p_i q_j = \sum_{i,j=1}^{m,n} (a_{ij} + b_{ij}) p_i q_j ,$$

and

$$(35.16) \qquad (1 + \beta) \sum_{i,j=1}^{m,n} a_{ij} p_i q_j = \sum_{i,j=1}^{m,n} (a_{ij} + b_{ij}) p_i q_j .$$

As the right-hand sides of these two equations are positive because of (35.9′), (35.10′) and (γ), we get

$$1+\alpha>0, \quad 1+\beta>0, \quad \sum_{i,j=1}^{m,n} a_{ij}p_iq_j>0\,.$$

Then, the left-hand sides of (35.15) and (35.16) are equal so that $1+\alpha=1+\beta$ and, hence, $\alpha=\beta$. Now let Γ represent the set of real numbers α that are solutions of (35.9) and (35.9′) and Δ the set of real numbers β that are solutions of (35.10) and (35.10′). Then, in the same way as the first half of this proof, we get

$$(1+\alpha)\sum_{i,j=1}^{m,n} a_{ij}p_iq_j \leqq \sum_{i,j=1}^{m,n} (a_{ij}+b_{ij})p_iq_j \leqq (1+\beta)\sum_{i,j=1}^{m,n} a_{ij}p_iq_j\;,$$

from which it follows that

$$\alpha \leqq \beta \quad (\alpha\in\Gamma,\ \beta\in\Delta)\,.$$

If α and β are solutions satisfying (35.9) ~ (35.12), (35.9′) and (35.10′), then $\alpha\in\Delta$, $\beta\in\Gamma$, and $\alpha=\beta$ so that we can uniquely determine $\alpha(=\beta)$ as the maximum of Γ and $\beta(=\alpha)$ as the minimum of Δ. As the right-hand side of (35.13) is non-negative and the coefficient of α on the left-hand side is positive, we have $\alpha \geqq 0$. [Q.E.D.]

This theorem suggests that we can proceed to the study of the solution on the premise of $\alpha=\beta$.

Now let p be an m-dimensional vector with p_i as components and q an n-dimensional vector with q_j as components. The solution consists of $p\geq 0$ and $q\geq 0$, and (35.9) ~ (35.12) are homogeneous relations in p and q. Hence, just as in the case of a rectangular game, we may assume that $p\in S_m$ and $q\in T_n$. In order to relate the problem to the findings of the preceding section, let A and B be (m, n) matrices with a_{ij} and b_{ij} as elements. For any real number ω, let

$$(35.17) \qquad C_\omega = B - \omega A\;,$$

which is an (m, n) matrix that depends on ω. Consider a rectangular game whose payoff matrix is C_ω. The results of the preceding section show that this game is strictly determined for any value of ω and has a saddle point. The value of the game is a function of ω, denoted by $\nu(\omega)$. The existence problem of the solution of the von Neumann model can be reduced to the minimax theorem on rectangular games by examining the properties of the function $\nu(\omega)$.

THEOREM 35.2. (i) $\alpha = \beta = \sigma, p \in S_m$ *and* $q \in T_n$ *form a solution of the von Neumann model if and only if*

(a) $\qquad \nu(\sigma) = 0$

and

(b) $\qquad$ *(p, q) is a saddle point of the payoff function* $(p, C_\sigma q)$.

(ii) *The equation* $\nu(\omega) = 0$ *has a solution* $\omega = \sigma$.

(iii) *The von Neumann model has a solution.*

Proof. (i) If $\alpha = \beta = \sigma$, $p \in S_m$, $q \in T_n$ are a solution of the model, we substitute σ into α and β in (35.9) and (35.10) and rearrange terms to get

$$(35.18) \qquad \sum_{j=1}^{n} (b_{ij} - \sigma a_{ij})\, q_j \leqq 0 \leqq \sum_{i=1}^{m} (b_{ij} - \sigma a_{ij}) p_i \quad \begin{pmatrix} i = 1, 2, \dots, m \\ j = 1, 2, \dots, n \end{pmatrix}$$

Then, putting $c_{ij}(\omega) = b_{ij} - \omega a_{ij}$, we have

$$(35.19) \qquad \nu(\sigma) \leqq \max_{1 \leqq i \leqq m} \sum_{j=1}^{n} c_{ij}(\sigma) q_j \leqq 0 \leqq \min_{1 \leqq j \leqq n} \sum_{i=1}^{m} c_{ij}(\sigma) p_i \leqq \nu(\sigma)\,,$$

so that (35.19) holds with all equality signs and $\nu(\sigma) = 0$. By virtue of (i) of Theorem 34.2, (p, q) is a saddle point. Conversely, if $\nu(\sigma) = 0$ and (p, q), $p \in S_m$, $q \in T_n$ is a saddle point, (35.19) holds with equality signs and (35.18) is obtained. Rearranging terms in (35.18), we get (35.9) and (35.10) with $\alpha = \beta = \sigma$ and (35.11) and (35.12).

(ii) Let us first show that $\nu(\omega)$ is a continuous function of ω. In fact, for any j and any $p \in S_m$, we have

$$\sum_{i=1}^{m} c_{ij}(\omega_1) p_i - \sum_{i=1}^{m} c_{ij}(\omega_2) p_i = (\omega_2 - \omega_1) \sum_{i=1}^{m} a_{ij} p_i\,.$$

Putting

$$\max_{i,j} \; a_{ij} = \delta\,,$$

we have $\delta > 0$ by (β) and if $\omega_1 \leqq \omega_2$, we have for any j and any p,

$$(35.20) \qquad 0 \leqq \sum_{i=1}^{m} c_{ij}(\omega_1)p_i - \sum_{i=1}^{m} c_{ij}(\omega_2)p_i \leqq \delta(\omega_2 - \omega_1)\,.$$

It follows from this that for any $p \in S_m$

$$(35.21) \qquad 0 \leqq \min_{1 \leqq j \leqq n} \sum_{i=1}^{m} c_{ij}(\omega_1)p_i - \min_{1 \leqq j \leqq n} \sum_{i=1}^{m} c_{ij}(\omega_2)p_i \leqq \delta(\omega_2 - \omega_1)$$

and from (35.21) in turn that

$$0 \leqq \max_{p \in S_m} \min_{1 \leqq j \leqq n} \sum_{i=1}^{m} c_{ij}(\omega_1)p_i - \max_{p \in S_m} \min_{1 \leqq j \leqq n} \sum_{i=1}^{m} c_{ij}(\omega_2)p_i$$

$$\leqq \delta(\omega_2 - \omega_1) \qquad (\text{when } \omega_1 \leqq \omega_2)\,.$$

This result is equivalent to

$$(35.22) \qquad 0 \leqq \nu(\omega_1) - \nu(\omega_2) \leqq \delta(\omega_2 - \omega_1) \quad (\text{when } \omega_1 \leqq \omega_2)$$

because of what is implied by the value of the game. Hence, $\nu(\omega)$ is continuous (and decreasing).

If $\nu(\omega) \leqq 0$ for some value of ω and $\nu(\omega) \geqq 0$ for another value of ω, then there exists σ such that $\nu(\sigma) = 0$ due to the theorem of intermediate values (Section 13). Therefore, it suffices to show that this function can take both non-negative and non-positive values.

Obviously, $\nu(0) \geqq 0$ because $c_{ij}(0) = b_{ij} \geqq 0$ (for all i and j) according to (α).

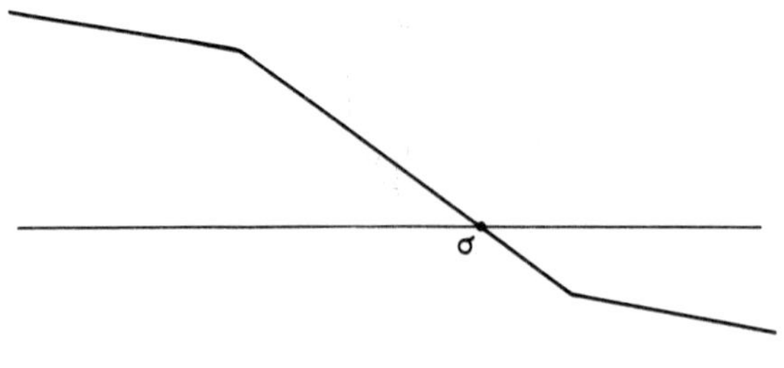

Fig. 35.1.

Next, put

$$\min_{1 \leqq i \leqq m} \frac{1}{n} \sum_{j=1}^{n} a_{ij} = L \quad \text{and} \quad \max_{1 \leqq i \leqq m} \frac{1}{n} \sum_{j=1}^{n} b_{ij} = M .$$

We see $L > 0$ from (β) and $M \geqq 0$ from (α). Then, for $\omega \geqq M/L$, we get $\nu(\omega) \leqq 0$. In fact, let $\hat{q}$ be a vector whose components are all equal to $1/n$. Then, $\hat{q} \in T_n$. If $\omega \geqq M/L$, we have

$$\sum_{j=1}^{n} c_{ij}(\omega)\hat{q}_j = \frac{1}{n} \sum_{j=1}^{n} b_{ij} - \frac{\omega}{n} \sum_{j=1}^{n} a_{ij} \leqq M - \omega L \leqq 0 \quad (i = 1, 2, ..., m)$$

for this $\hat{q}$. Hence,

$$\nu(\omega) \leqq \max_{1 \leqq i \leqq m} \sum_{j=1}^{n} c_{ij}(\omega)\hat{q}_j \leqq 0 .$$

(iii) It is shown in (ii) that there exists a solution $\omega = \sigma$ for $\nu(\omega) = 0$. Then, by Theorems 34.2 and 34.3, there exists a saddle point (p, q) of a rectangular game whose payoff matrix is C_σ. According to (i), $\alpha = \beta = \sigma$, p and q form a solution of the model [Q.E.D.]

Remark 2. $\alpha, \beta \geqq 0$ by Theorem 35.1, and $0 \leqq \alpha = \beta \leqq M/L$ by Theorem 35.2. As seen in the proof of Theorem 35.2, $\nu(M/L) \leqq 0 \leqq \nu(0)$ so that there exists a solution $\alpha = \beta = \sigma$ in the interval $[0, M/L]$ by virtue of the theorem of intermediate values. As the uniqueness of σ in Theorem 35.1 demonstrates that no other real number is a solution, the location of the solution in the interval is appropriate. It is also easy to see that $\alpha (= \beta) > 0$ if and only if $\nu(0) > 0$. It is similarly evident from the proof of Theorem 35.1 that $\alpha > 0$ is equivalent to

$$\sum_{i,j=1}^{m,n} b_{ij} p_i q_j > 0 .$$

To ensure $\nu(0) > 0$, it is sufficient if we assume a subsidiary condition, e.g.

$$\sum_{i=1}^{m} b_{ij} > 0 \quad (j = 1, 2, ..., m) ,$$

i.e. that each good is produced in some process. $\nu(0) > 0$ in this case because

$$\nu(0) \geqq \min_{1 \leqq j \leqq n} \frac{1}{m} \sum_{i=1}^{m} b_{ij} > 0 .$$

Remark 3. Von Neumann himself demonstrated the existence of the solution by making use of the relation between a zero-sum two-person game with a payoff function

$$K(p, q) = \sum_{i,j=1}^{m,n} b_{ij} p_i q_j \Big/ \sum_{i,j=1}^{m,n} a_{ij} p_i q_j \quad (p \in T_n)$$

and the model (35.9) ~ (35.12). If the value of this game is ν and its saddle point is (p, q), then $\alpha = \beta = \nu$, p and q are the solution of the model. The converse is also true. This relation can be checked without difficulty and is left to the interested reader. Von Neumann made use of a fixed point theorem to show the strict determinateness of this game. However, it was shown by Georgescu-Roegen (see his paper in ref. [26]) that this game could be handled by the separation theorem. It may be noted that the function $K(p, q)$ is not indeterminate because the numerator is positive when the denominator is 0 by the condition (γ).

36. Games and linear programming problems

There is an interesting close connection between rectangular games and linear programming problems. We shall show in this section that the two types of problems are equivalent and interchangeable in some sense.

The transformation of a rectangular game into a linear programming problem. We prove first a simple lemma.

LEMMA 1. *Let A be an (m, n) matrix and A_α a matrix obtained by adding the same real number α to every element a_{ij} of A. Let $\nu(A)$ and $\nu(A_\alpha)$ be the values of the rectangular games whose payoff matrices are A and A_α. Then, we get*

$$\nu(A_\alpha) = \nu(A) + \alpha .$$

The saddle points of the two games are identical.

Proof. Let the saddle point of A be (p, q), $p \in S_m$, $q \in T_n$. Then,

$$(36.1) \qquad \sum_{j=1}^{n} a_{ij} q_j \leqq \nu(A) \leqq \sum_{i=1}^{m} a_{ij} p_i \quad \text{(for all } i \text{ and } j\text{)} .$$

Adding

$$\alpha = \alpha \sum_{i=1}^{m} p_i = \alpha \sum_{j=1}^{n} q_j$$

to it, we obtain

$$\sum_{j=1}^{n} (a_{ij} + \alpha) q_j \leqq v(A) + \alpha \leqq \sum_{i=1}^{m} (a_{ij} + \alpha) p_i \quad \text{(for all } i \text{ and } j) .$$

It follows from this that $v(A_\alpha) = v(A) + \alpha$ in exactly the same way that (35.19) is obtained from (35.18) and that (p, q) is a saddle point of A_α. Now as A is the matrix with $-\alpha$ added to all elements of A_α, the saddle point of A_α is also a saddle point of A by the same token. [Q.E.D.]

By virtue of this lemma, we can make $v(A_\alpha) > 0$ by selecting an appropriate α when $v(A) \leqq 0$ and with no change in the essential structure of the game (i.e. the structure of the set of saddle points). Hence, we can assume $v(A) > 0$ without loss of generality.

THEOREM 36.1. *In a linear programming problem of type* (m), *i.e.*

$$\text{(36.2)} \qquad \min \sum_{i=1}^{m} x_i$$

subject to

$$\text{(36.3)} \qquad \sum_{i=1}^{m} a_{ij} x_i \geqq 1\,, \quad x_i \geqq 0 \quad (i = 1, 2, ..., m;\ \ j = 1, 2, ..., n)\,,$$

its objective functional has an optimal value equal to $1/v(A)$. *The optimal solution* x *of the linear programming problem and the optimal strategy* p *of Player I in the game are in one-to-one correspondence via the formula*

$$\text{(36.4)} \qquad p = v(A) x .$$

Proof. Let $F(p)$ represent the function of (34.10) in what follows. If x satisfies (36.3), we have obviously

$$\lambda = \sum_{i=1}^{m} x_i > 0 .$$

Dividing (36.3) through by λ, we get

$$x/\lambda \in S_m, \quad \sum_{i=1}^{m} a_{ij}(x_i/\lambda) \geqq 1/\lambda \quad (j = 1, 2, ..., n).$$

Hence, from

$$(36.5) \qquad v(A) = \max_{p \in S_m} F(p) \geqq F(x/\lambda) \geqq 1/\lambda ,$$

we obtain $\lambda \geqq 1/v(A)$.

Next, let p be an optimal strategy of Player I. Then,

$$\sum_{i=1}^{m} a_{ij} p_i \geqq F(p) = v(A) \quad (j = 1, 2, ..., n).$$

Dividing this by $v(A)$, we get

$$\sum_{i=1}^{m} a_{ij}(p_i/v(A)) \geqq 1, \quad p_i/v(A) \geqq 0 \quad \begin{pmatrix} i = 1, 2, ..., m \\ j = 1, 2, ..., n \end{pmatrix}.$$

The objective functional takes a value

$$\sum_{i=1}^{m} p_i/v(A) = \frac{1}{v(A)} \sum_{i=1}^{m} p_i = 1/v(A).$$

Hence, the minimum of the objective functional is equal to $1/v(A)$ and $x = p/v(A)$ is an optimal solution.

Finally, if x is an optimal solution of the linear programming problem, then $\lambda = 1/v(A)$ and (36.5) holds with all equality signs. Thus, $v(A) = F(v(A)x)$ and $p = v(A)x$ ($\in S_m$) is an optimal strategy of Player I. [Q.E.D.]

The next theorem is dual to the theorem above. Its proof follows exactly the same reasoning and is omitted here.

THEOREM 36.1d. *In a linear programming problem of type* (*M*): $\max \sum_{j=1}^{n} y_j$ subject to

$$\sum_{j=1}^{n} a_{ij} y_j \leqq 1, \quad y_j \geqq 0 \quad (i = 1, 2, ..., m;\ j = 1, 2, ..., n),$$

its objective functional has an optimal value equal to $1/\nu(A)$. The optimal solution y of the linear programming problem and the optimal strategy of II in the game are in one-to-one correspondence via the formula $q = \nu(A)y$.

The transformation of a linear programming problem into a rectangular game. If A, a square matrix of the nth order, is such that $A' = -A$, it is called a *skew-symmetric* or *alternating* matrix.

LEMMA 2. *If A is a skew-symmetric square matrix of the nth order, the value of a game whose payoff matrix is A is $\nu(A) = 0$.*

Proof. Let $(\hat{p}, \hat{q})$ be a saddle point of this game. Then, for any $p, q \in S_n$, we have

$$(36.6) \qquad (p, A\hat{q}) \leqq \nu(A) \leqq (\hat{p}, Aq)\,.$$

Hence, substituting $p = \hat{q}$ and $q = \hat{p}$ in particular, we have

$$(36.7) \qquad (\hat{q}, A\hat{q}) \leqq \nu(A) \leqq (\hat{p}, A\hat{p})\,.$$

But for any $p \in R^n$,

$$(p, Ap) = (A'p, p) = -(Ap, p) = -(p, Ap)$$

so that $2(p, Ap) = 0$. Thus, $(p, Ap) = 0$. Both sides of (36.7) are then 0 and $\nu(A) = 0$. [Q.E.D.]

LEMMA 3. *On the same assumptions as in Lemma 2, Player I's optimal strategy is equal to Player II's optimal strategy. $p \in S_n$ is an optimal strategy if and only if either*

$$\text{(a)} \qquad A\hat{p} \leqq 0 \quad \textit{or} \quad \text{(b)} \qquad A'\hat{p} \geqq 0\,.$$

Proof. Let any optimal strategies of I and II be $\hat{p}, \hat{q}$ respectively. Then, obviously, $A\hat{q} \leqq 0 \leqq A'\hat{p}$. Multiplying it by -1, we have $-A\hat{q} \geqq 0 \geqq -A'\hat{p}$. As $-A = A'$ and $-A' = A$, we get $A'\hat{q} \geqq 0 \geqq A\hat{p}$. In other words, $\hat{q}$ is an optimal strategy of I and $\hat{p}$ that of II. An almost identical reasoning is applied to prove the latter half of the lemma. [Q.E.D.]

For our convenience, let us restate the linear programming problem (M) and its dual (m):

Let A be an (m, n) matrix; $b, x \in R^m$; $c, y \in R^n$.

Then,

(M) $\max c'y$ subject to $Ay \leqq b,\ y \geqq 0$;

(m) $\min b'x$ subject to $A'x \geqq c,\ x \geqq 0$.

Now in connection with these problems, consider a game whose payoff matrix is a skew-symmetric matrix of the $(m+n+1)$st order

$$L = \begin{bmatrix} 0 & A & -b \\ -A' & 0 & c \\ b' & -c' & 0 \end{bmatrix} \begin{matrix} \}\, m \\ \}\, n \\ \}\, 1 \end{matrix}$$
$$\underbrace{}_{m} \quad \underbrace{}_{n} \quad \underbrace{}_{1}$$

Let us designate it as the game (L).

A strategy of the game (L) is written in the form of

$$(36.8) \qquad \begin{bmatrix} p \\ q \\ \rho \end{bmatrix} \begin{matrix} \}\, m \\ \}\, n \\ \}\, 1 \end{matrix}, \quad p \geqq 0,\ q \geqq 0,\ \rho \geqq 0,\ \sum_{i=1}^{m} p_i + \sum_{j=1}^{n} q_j + \rho = 1\,.$$

The game (L) is always strictly determined and its value is 0.

THEOREM 36.2. (i) *If the linear programming problem* (m) *and* (M) *both have optimal solutions* x *and* y,

$$(36.9) \qquad \begin{bmatrix} x/\lambda \\ y/\lambda \\ 1/\lambda \end{bmatrix}, \quad \text{where} \quad \lambda = 1 + \sum_{i=1}^{m} x_i + \sum_{i=1}^{n} y_j\,,$$

is an optimal strategy of the game (L).

(ii) *If* (36.8) *is an optimal strategy of the game* (L) *and if* $\rho > 0$, *then* p/ρ *is an optimal solution of* (m) *and* q/ρ *that of* (M).

Proof. (i) Let x and y be optimal solutions of (m) and (M). Then,

$$Ay - b \leqq 0\,, \quad -A'x + c \leqq 0\,, \quad b'x - c'y \leqq 0\,,$$

$$x \geqq 0\,, \quad y \geqq 0\,.$$

Hence, dividing these inequalities by $\lambda > 0$ that is referred to in the theorem, we have in a summary form

$$\begin{bmatrix} 0 & A & -b \\ -A' & 0 & c \\ b' & -c' & 0 \end{bmatrix} \begin{bmatrix} x/\lambda \\ y/\lambda \\ 1/\lambda \end{bmatrix} \leqq 0 .$$

By Lemma 3, (36.9) is an optimal solution of the game (L).

(ii) If (36.8) is an optimal solution of the game (L), we have

$$\begin{bmatrix} 0 & A & -b \\ -A' & 0 & c \\ b' & -c' & 0 \end{bmatrix} \begin{bmatrix} p \\ q \\ \rho \end{bmatrix} \leqq 0 ,$$

which is written piecemeal as

$$Aq - \rho b \leqq 0, \ -A'p + \rho c \leqq 0, \ b'p - c'q \leqq 0, \ p, q, \rho \geqq 0.$$

Now letting $\rho > 0$, dividing these inequalities by ρ and putting $x = p/\rho$ and $y = q/\rho$, we get

$$Ay - b \leqq 0 , \quad -A'x + c \leqq 0 , \ x \geqq 0 , \ y \geqq 0 .$$

Then, x and y satisfy the constraints of (m) and (M) respectively and

$$b'x - c'y \leqq 0.$$

Therefore, x and y are optimal solutions of (m) and (M) respectively.

37. Optimization problems and saddle point problems

The familiar and useful technique of transforming a constrained extremum problem into an unconstrained one through the introduction of Lagrangian multipliers has seen frequent applications in economics. Nevertheless, its true meaning seems not to be fully understood.

The reader must have learned from textbooks of calculus that an unconstrained extremum problem of the function $f(x_1, x_2)$ is reduced to solving a system of equations $\partial f/\partial x_1 = 0$ and $\partial f/\partial x_2 = 0$. Now, the problem of finding an extremum of $f(x_1, x_2)$ subject to a constraint

(37.1) $\quad g(x_1, x_2) = 0$

is handled by the method of Lagrangian multipliers. This treatment is discussed in textbooks of mathematical economics as follows: Multiply (37.1) by an unspecified multiplier λ and then subtract it from $f(x_1, x_2)$. This does not alter the value of $f(x_1, x_2)$ since (37.1) is kept equal to zero. Thus, $f(x_1, x_2) = f(x_1, x_2) - \lambda g(x_1, x_2)$. Differentiating it partially with respect to x_1 and x_2 and setting them equal to zero, we get $\partial f/\partial x_1 - \lambda(\partial g/\partial x_1) = 0$ and $\partial f/\partial x_2 - \lambda(\partial g/\partial x_2) = 0$. Our problem is now reduced to solving these two equations and (37.1) together.

The reader may have had serious qualm about this sort of exposition. According to it, differentiation is performed subject to (37.1) so that the problem is not transformed into an unconstrained extremum problem at all. This is the first question. Moreover, is it possible to differentiate g with respect to x_1 and x_2 subject to (37.1)? (37.1) represents in general a curve on the plane. $\partial g/\partial x_1$ is the limit of the rate of change of g with respect to x_1 while x_2 is held fixed, i.e. the limit of

$$\frac{1}{\Delta x_1}\,[g(x_1 + \Delta x_1, x_2) - g(x_1, x_2)]\,.$$

But $g(x_1 + \Delta x_1, x_2) \neq 0$ in general and the point $(x_1 + \Delta x_1, x_2)$ does not lie on this curve*.

The true meaning of the method of Lagrangian multipliers is as follows: Introduce an unconstrained, third variable λ and form a function of these real variables

$$F(x_1, x_2, \lambda) = f(x_1, x_2) - \lambda g(x_1, x_2)\,. \tag{37.2}$$

We can consider an unconstrained extremum problem of this function. Differentiate it partially with respect to the independent variables x_1, x_2, and λ (therefore, without regard to whether $g(x_1, x_2)$ is equal to 0 or not) and set the partial derivatives to be 0. Then, the extremum conditions are given by

$$\frac{\partial F}{\partial x_1} = \frac{\partial f}{\partial x_1} - \lambda\frac{\partial g}{\partial x_1} = 0\,,\quad \frac{\partial F}{\partial x_2} = \frac{\partial f}{\partial x_2} - \lambda\frac{\partial g}{\partial x_2} = 0\,,\quad \frac{\partial F}{\partial \lambda} = -g(x_1, x_2) = 0\,.$$

Hence, what the method of Lagrangian multipliers really means is the equivalence of the extremum problem of $f(x_1, x_2)$ subject to a constraint

* If (37.1) is solved for x_2, x_2 becomes a function of x_1, i.e. $x_2 = \varphi(x_1)$. Thus, identically, $g(x_1, \varphi(x_1)) = 0$. It is meaningful to differentiate this with respect to x_1. On the curve (37.1), we have $\partial g/\partial x_1 + \partial g/\partial x_2 \cdot \mathrm{d}\varphi/\mathrm{d}x_1 = 0$. The reader should fully understand the difference between the two modes of differentiation.

$g(x_1, x_2) = 0$ and the unconstrained extremum problem of $F(x_1, x_2, \lambda)$.

We have given our preliminary observation without specifying explicit assumptions. It must be noted that a clear understanding of this point is very useful in analyzing the problems of this section. We shall study how to transform an optimization problem subject to inequalities into an unconstrained non-negative saddle point problem through the introduction of Lagrangian multipliers.

Linear programming problems and non-negative saddle point problems. The linear programming minimization problem of type (m) (Section 36, (m)) is a minimization problem, namely

$$(37.3) \qquad \min \sum_{i=1}^{m} b_i x_i$$

subject to n linear constraints

$$(37.4) \qquad \sum_{i=1}^{m} a_{ij} x_i \geqq c_j \quad (j = 1, 2, ..., n) ,$$

for non-negative variables $x_i \geqq 0$. Corresponding to the jth constraint of (37.4), let us introduce a variable y_j $(j = 1, 2, ..., n)$ and form a *Lagrangian function*

$$(37.5) \qquad K(x, y) = \sum_{i=1}^{m} b_i x_i + \sum_{j=1}^{n} y_j \left(c_j - \sum_{i=1}^{m} a_{ij} x_i \right) .$$

Just as in differential calculus, $y_1, y_2, ..., y_n$ are called *Lagrangian multipliers.* (37.5) is easily rearranged as

$$(37.6) \qquad K(x, y) = \sum_{j=1}^{n} c_j y_j + \sum_{i=1}^{m} x_i \left(b_i - \sum_{j=1}^{n} a_{ij} y_j \right) .$$

We may readily note that (37.6) is the Lagrangian function with Lagrangian multipliers $x_1, x_2, ..., x_m$ in the linear programming problem of type (M) (Section 36, (M)), i.e. a maximization problem:

$$(37.7) \qquad \max \sum_{j=1}^{n} c_j y_j$$

subject to m linear constraints

$$(37.8) \qquad \sum_{j=1}^{n} a_{ij} y_j \leqq b_i \quad (i = 1, 2, \ldots, m)$$

for non-negative variables $y_j \geqq 0$.

We shall now examine how a saddle point $(\hat{x}, \hat{y})$ of the function $K(x, y)$ in the set of all non-negative points $x \geqq 0, y \geqq 0$, i.e.

$$(37.9) \qquad K(\hat{x}, y) \leqq K(\hat{x}, \hat{y}) \leqq K(x, \hat{y}) \quad (\text{for all } x \geqq 0,\ y \geqq 0)$$

is related to an optimal solution of the linear programming problem. In this game, Player I chooses x so as to minimize K, while Player II selects y so as to maximize K. In other words, the game is formulated on the basis of II's pay-off function.

THEOREM 37.1. (Goldman and Tucker [28]). *$\hat{x}$ is an optimal solution of the problem of type (m), (37.3) and (37.4), and $\hat{y}$ is an optimal solution of the problem of type (M), (37.7) and (37.8), if and only if $(\hat{x}, \hat{y})$ is a saddle point of $K(x, y)$ in $R_+^m \times R_+^n$.*

Proof. K of (37.5) and (37.6) may be expressed as

$$(37.10) \qquad K(x, y) = (b, x) + (c - A'x, y) = (c, y) + (x, b - Ay)\,.$$

(i) *Necessity.* If $\hat{x}$ is an optimal solution of (m) and $\hat{y}$ is that of (M), then

$$(b, \hat{x}) = (\hat{x}, A\hat{y}) = (A'\hat{x}, \hat{y}) = (c, \hat{y})$$

so that

$$(37.11) \qquad K(\hat{x}, \hat{y}) = (b, \hat{x}) = (c, \hat{y})\,.$$

Also for any $y \geqq 0$, its inner product with $c - A'\hat{x} \leqq 0$ is $(c - A'\hat{x}, y) \leqq 0$ so that

$$K(\hat{x}, y) = (b, \hat{x}) + (c - A'\hat{x}, y) \leqq (b, \hat{x}) = K(\hat{x}, \hat{y})\,.$$

On the other hand, for any $x \geqq 0$, its inner product with $b - A\hat{y} \geqq 0$ is $(x, b - A\hat{y}) \geqq 0$ so that

$$K(x, \hat{y}) = (c, \hat{y}) + (x, b - A\hat{y}) \geqq (c, \hat{y}) = K(\hat{x}, \hat{y})\,.$$

Thus, $(\hat{x}, \hat{y})$ is a saddle point of $K(x, y)$.

(ii) *Sufficiency*. Suppose that (37.9) holds for $\hat{x} \geqq 0, \hat{y} \geqq 0$. For $x = 0$ and $y = 0$, we have $K(\hat{x}, 0) \leqq K(\hat{x}, \hat{y}) \leqq K(0, \hat{y})$. Now from the expression (37.10), $K(\hat{x}, 0) = (b, \hat{x})$ and $K(0, \hat{y}) = (c, \hat{y})$ so that

$$(37.12) \qquad (b, \hat{x}) \leqq (c, \hat{y}) .$$

Then, from the left-hand inequality of (37.9) and (37.10), we get

$$(b, \hat{x}) + (c - A'\hat{x}, y) \leqq K(\hat{x}, \hat{y}) \quad (\text{for all } y \geqq 0) .$$

In other words, a linear function $(c - A'\hat{x}, y)$ is bounded from above on R^n_+ and, in fact, $(c - A'\hat{x}, y) \leqq 0$ (for all $y \in R^n_+$) because of Remark 2 in Section 30. Therefore, by virtue of (i) of Theorem 15.1, we get

$$(37.13) \qquad c - A'\hat{x} \leqq 0$$

and by the same token

$$(c, \hat{y}) + (b - A\hat{y}, x) \geqq K(\hat{x}, \hat{y}) \quad (\text{for all } x \geqq 0)$$

so that

$$(37.14) \qquad b - A\hat{y} \geqq 0 .$$

$\hat{x} \geqq 0, \hat{y} \geqq 0$, (37.12) ~ (37.14) demonstrate that $\hat{x}$ and $\hat{y}$ are respectively optimal solutions of (m) and (M). [Q.E.D.]

Remark 1. In the proof of the necessity given above, we employed the property that the duality theorem (Section 25), $(b, \hat{x}) \leqq (c, \hat{y})$, always holds for the optimal solutions $\hat{x}$ and $\hat{y}$.

Remark 2. To prove the duality theorem, it suffices to show that K has a saddle point according to this theorem. If $(\hat{x}, \hat{y})$ is a saddle point, $K(x, \hat{y})$ as a function of x attains a minimum at $x = \hat{x}$ on R^m_+. This K is a linear function of x as seen clearly from (37.6) and has a continuous partial derivative with respect to each x_i. Hence, by the lemma of Section 26, we see that

$$(\alpha) \qquad \left[\frac{\partial K}{\partial x_i}\right]_{\substack{x=\hat{x}\\ y=\hat{y}}} \geqq 0 \quad (i = 1, 2, \ldots, m) ,$$

and

$$(\beta) \qquad \sum_{i=1}^{m} \hat{x}_i \left[\frac{\partial K}{\partial x_i}\right]_{\substack{x=\hat{x}\\ y=\hat{y}}} = 0$$

must hold. Similarly, as $K(\hat{x}, y)$ attains a maximum at $y = \hat{y}$ on R^n_+,

$$(\gamma) \qquad \left[\frac{\partial K}{\partial y_j}\right]_{\substack{x=\hat{x}\\ y=\hat{y}}} \leqq 0 \quad (j = 1, 2, ..., n)$$

and

$$(\delta) \qquad \sum_{j=1}^{n} \hat{y}_j \left[\frac{\partial K}{\partial y_j}\right]_{\substack{x=\hat{x}\\ y=\hat{y}}} = 0 .$$

Thus, the saddle point whose existence we want to prove must be a solution of the system of inequalities $(\alpha) \sim (\delta)$. By performing differentiation, we see that $(\alpha) \sim (\delta)$ are reduced to

$$(\alpha') \qquad b_i - \sum_{j=1}^{n} a_{ij}\hat{y}_j \geqq 0 \quad (i = 1, 2, ..., m) ,$$

$$(\beta') \qquad \sum_{i=1}^{m} \hat{x}_i (b_i - \sum_{j=1}^{n} a_{ij}\hat{y}_j) = 0 ,$$

$$(\gamma') \qquad c_j - \sum_{i=1}^{m} a_{ij}\hat{x}_i \leqq 0 \quad (j = 1, 2, ..., n) ,$$

$$(\delta') \qquad \sum_{j=1}^{n} \hat{y}_j (c_j - \sum_{i=1}^{m} a_{ij}\hat{x}_i) = 0 .$$

We have been searching for a saddle point of K in order to prove the duality theorem and have found that the existence of such a saddle point is reduced to the existence of a solution of $(\alpha') \sim (\delta')$, which is nothing but the duality theorem itself that we wanted to prove. This shows that one might come back to the starting point after all the painstaking efforts to specify conditions through differential calculus. One must be wary of this pitfall.

Remark 3. Section 26 showed that a linear programming problem as a constrained optimum problem can be transformed into a problem of unconstrainedly minimizing $F(x, y)$ in (26.10) on the set of all non-negative points. We learned that this procedure provides an effective transformation for the proof of the duality theorems. The same procedure can be employed to prove the minimax theorem of a rectangular game. However, space does not permit to dwell on this point.

Non-linear optimum problems and saddle point problems. Take a constrained maximum problem for a function that is not necessarily linear, i.e.

$$(37.15) \qquad \max f(x)$$

subject to

$$(37.16) \qquad g_i(x) \geqq 0 \quad (i = 1, 2, ..., m),$$

where $f(x)$ and $g_i(x)$ are functions defined on a set M in R^n_+. Let us examine how this problem is related to a saddle point problem. If we form a Lagrangian function

$$(37.17) \qquad K(x, y) = f(x) + \sum_{i=1}^{m} g_i(x) y_i$$

by introducing m multipliers y_i's, we get the following theorem similarly as in a linear programming problem:

THEOREM 37.2. *If* $(\hat{x}, \hat{y})$ *is a saddle point of* (37.17) *on* $M \times R^m_+$. *i.e.*

$$(37.18) \qquad K(x, \hat{y}) \leqq K(\hat{x}, \hat{y}) \leqq K(\hat{x}, y) \quad (\textit{for all } x \in M,\ y \in R^m_+),$$

then

(i) $\hat{x}$ *is a solution of the maximum problem* (37.15) ~ (37.16);
(ii) $\hat{y}_i = 0$ *for an index i such that* $g_i(\hat{x}) > 0$.

Proof. The proof of this theorem is similar to that of sufficiency in Theorem 37.1. We outline the proof for the reader's benefit. From the right-hand inequality of (37.18), we get

$$\sum_{i=1}^{m} g_i(\hat{x}) \hat{y}_i \leqq \sum_{i=1}^{m} g_i(\hat{x}) y_i ,$$

for any $y \in R^m_+$. It follows from this that $g_i(\hat{x}) \geqq 0$ $(i = 1, 2, ..., m)$ and

$$\sum_{i=1}^{m} g_i(\hat{x})\, \hat{y}_i = 0$$

according to the procedure that we have repeatedly used. The reader should try it for himself. (ii) is a direct consequence of it. Next, from the left-hand inequality of (37.18) and the result above, we get

$$f(x) + \sum_{i=1}^{m} g_i(x)\hat{y}_i \leqq f(\hat{x}) + \sum_{i=1}^{m} g_i(\hat{x})\hat{y}_i = f(\hat{x})$$

for any $x \in M$. Thus, if x satisfies (37.16), we get, because of $\hat{y}_i \geqq 0$ $(i = 1, 2, ..., m)$,

$$f(x) \leqq f(x) + \sum_{i=1}^{m} g_i(x)\hat{y}_i \leqq f(\hat{x}),$$

from which follows (i). [Q.E.D.]

Theorem 37.2 holds whatever forms the functions $f(x)$ and $g_i(x)$ may take. We may next consider the converse problem, i.e. the reduction of the maximum problem (37.15) ~ (37.16) into the saddle point problem (37.17). This, however, is not always possible. The following is a sufficient condition for this:

THEOREM 37.3. (Uzawa [29] and Kuhn and Tucker [39])*. *Let M be a convex set and let $f(x)$ and $g_i(x)$ be concave functions ** on M. Assume that there is at least one point in M for which $g_i(x) > 0$ $(i = 1, 2, ..., m)$. If $f(\hat{x})$ is a maximum of $f(x)$ subject to* (37.16) *on these assumptions, there exists some $\hat{y} \in R^m_+$ such that $(\hat{x}, \hat{y})$ is a saddle point of* (37.17) *on $M \times R^m_+$.*

Proof. This theorem can be proved via the separation theorems almost in the same way as Theorem 34.3 was proved. For the sake of convenience, we define a mapping φ from M into R^{m+1} by the formula

$$(37.19)\qquad \begin{aligned} \varphi_0(x) &= f(x) - f(\hat{x}) \\ \varphi_i(x) &= g_i(x) \qquad (i = 1, 2, ..., m). \end{aligned}$$

* See Nikaido [44] in connection with its proof, especially the use of the separation theorems.

** See Example 27.4.

If $x \in M$ and $\varphi_i(x) \geqq 0$ $(i = 0, 1, 2, ..., m)$, we see that always $\varphi_0(x) = 0$ because of the assumption that $\hat{x}$ is a solution of the maximum problem (37.15) ~ (37.16). Thus, the image $\varphi(M)$ of M contains no interior points of R_+^{m+1}. Then, the convex hull $C(\varphi(M))$ of $\varphi(M)$ contains no interior point of R_+^{m+1} either. This can be seen as follows:

If

$$x^t \in M, \quad \alpha_t \geqq 0, \quad \sum_{t=1}^{s} \alpha_t = 1 \quad (t = 1, 2, ..., s) ,$$

then the convexity of M implies

$$\sum_{t=1}^{s} \alpha_t x^t \in M . \tag{37.20}$$

As it is assumed that each φ_i is a concave function,

$$\sum_{t=1}^{s} \alpha_t \varphi_i(x^t) \leqq \varphi_i \left(\sum_{t=1}^{s} \alpha_t x^t\right) \quad (i = 0, 1, 2, ..., m) . \tag{37.21}$$

Since $\varphi(M)$ contains no interior points of R_+^{m+1}, the right-hand side of (37.21) is 0 or negative at least for some index. Hence, by (37.21), at least one coordinate of each point of $C(\varphi(M))$ is 0 or negative so that $C(\varphi(M))$ contains no interior points of R_+^{m+1}.

Thus, by Theorem 30.1, $C(\varphi(M))$ is contained in a half-space

$$\sum_{i=0}^{m} \lambda_i z_i \leqq 0 \tag{37.22}$$

determined by a hyperplane through the origin and with non-negative coefficients

$$\lambda_i \geqq 0 \quad (i = 0, 1, 2, ..., m) , \quad \sum_{i=0}^{m} \lambda_i > 0 .$$

As $\varphi(M) \subset C(\varphi(M))$, we have

$$\sum_{i=0}^{m} \lambda_i \varphi_i(x) \leqq 0 \quad (\text{for any } x \in M) , \tag{37.23}$$

which is rewritten as an inequality

$$(37.24)\qquad \lambda_0(f(x)-f(\hat{x}))+\sum_{i=1}^{m}\lambda_i g_i(x)\leqq 0 \quad (\text{for any } x\in M)$$

by virtue of (37.19). The conclusion of the theorem is derived from (37.24) as follows:

Putting $x=\hat{x}$ in (37.24), we obtain

$$\sum_{i=1}^{m}\lambda_i g_i(\hat{x})\leqq 0\ ;$$

as $\lambda_i\geqq 0$ and $g_i(\hat{x})\geqq 0$ $(i=1, 2, ..., m)$, we get

$$(37.25)\qquad \sum_{i=1}^{m}\lambda_i g_i(\hat{x})=0\ .$$

We then show $\lambda_0>0$. If $\lambda_0=0$ is assumed, (37.24) is reduced to

$$(37.26)\qquad \sum_{i=1}^{m}\lambda_i g_i(x)\leqq 0 \quad (\text{for any } x\in M)\ .$$

Because of the assumption that there exists a point $x\in M$ such that $g_i(x)>0$ for all i, (37.26) implies $\lambda_1=\lambda_2=...=\lambda_m=0$. Thus, all the coefficients $\lambda_i=0$ $(i=0, 1, 2, ..., m)$. This is a contradiction. $\therefore \lambda_0>0$.

Dividing (37.24) through by λ_0 and putting

$$\hat{y}_i=\lambda_i/\lambda_0 \quad (i=1, 2, ..., m)\ ,$$

we get

$$K(x,\hat{y})=f(x)+\sum_{i=1}^{m}g_i(x)\hat{y}_i\leqq f(\hat{x})+\sum_{i=1}^{m}g_i(\hat{x})\hat{y}_i=K(\hat{x},\hat{y})$$

for all $x\in M$ after rearranging terms and considering (37.25).

On the other hand, as $g_i(\hat{x})\geqq 0$ $(i=1, 2, ..., m)$, we have

$$\sum_{i=1}^{m}g_i(\hat{x})\hat{y}_i=0\leqq\sum_{i=1}^{m}g_i(\hat{x})y_i\ ,$$

if $y \in R^m_+$. Adding $f(\hat{x})$ to both sides of it, we obtain

$$K(\hat{x}, \hat{y}) = f(\hat{x}) + \sum_{i=1}^{m} g_i(\hat{x})\hat{y}_i \leqq f(\hat{x}) + \sum_{i=1}^{m} g_i(\hat{x})y_i = K(\hat{x}, y)$$

for any $y \in R^m_+$.

Remark 4. In Theorem 37.2, assume that $M = R^n_+$ and that $f(x)$ and $g_i(x)$ all have continuous partial derivatives in R^n_+. Then, if $(\hat{x}, \hat{y})$ is a saddle point, $K(x, \hat{y})$ attains a maximum at $x = \hat{x}$ on R^n_+. Thus, by the lemma of Section 26, we get

$$\text{(37.27)} \quad \left[\frac{\partial K(x, \hat{y})}{\partial x_j}\right]_{x=\hat{x}} = \left[\frac{\partial f}{\partial x_j}\right]_{x=\hat{x}} + \sum_{i=1}^{m} \hat{y}_i \left[\frac{\partial g_i}{\partial x_j}\right]_{x=\hat{x}} \leqq 0 \quad (j = 1, 2, \ldots, n),$$

$$\text{(37.28)} \quad \sum_{j=1}^{n} \hat{x}_j \left[\frac{\partial K(x, \hat{y})}{\partial x_j}\right]_{x=\hat{x}} = \sum_{j=1}^{n} \hat{x}_j \left[\frac{\partial f}{\partial x_j}\right]_{x=\hat{x}}$$

$$+ \sum_{j=1}^{n} \sum_{i=1}^{m} \hat{x}_j \hat{y}_i \left[\frac{\partial g_i}{\partial x_j}\right]_{x=\hat{x}} = 0$$

for necessary conditions. Similarly, as $K(\hat{x}, y)$ attains a minimum at $y = \hat{y}$ on R^m_+, we get

$$\text{(37.29)} \quad \left[\frac{\partial K(\hat{x}, y)}{\partial y_i}\right]_{y=\hat{y}} = g_i(\hat{x}) \geqq 0 \quad (i = 1, 2, \ldots, m),$$

$$\text{(37.30)} \quad \sum_{i=1}^{m} \hat{y}_i \left[\frac{\partial K(\hat{x}, y)}{\partial y_i}\right]_{y=\hat{y}} = \sum_{i=1}^{m} g_i(\hat{x})\hat{y}_i = 0.$$

These are the necessary conditions for a saddle point, expressed in terms of Lagrangian multipliers, in general cases including the case of corner optima.

Remark 5. Let us introduce the converse case in which (37.27) ~ (37.30) are sufficient conditions for a saddle point. Assume, as in Remark 4, that $f(x)$ and $g_i(x)$ have continuous partial derivatives on R^n_+ and are concave functions. If $\hat{x} \in R^n_+$, $\hat{y} \in R^m_+$ satisfy (37.27) ~ (37.30) in this case, $(\hat{x}, \hat{y})$ is a saddle point of (37.17) on $R^n_+ \times R^m_+$. In fact, from (37.29) and (37.30), $K(\hat{x}, y)$

obviously attains a minimum on R_+^m at $y = \hat{y}$. Next, as $\hat{y}_i \geqq 0$, we can easily see that a non-negative linear combination of concave functions,

$$K(x, \hat{y}) = f(x) + \sum_{i=1}^{m} \hat{y}_i g_i(x) ,$$

is also a concave function. (The reader should verify this property as an exercise.) Hence, *

$$(37.31) \qquad \sum_{j=1}^{n} (\hat{x}_j - x_j) \left[\frac{\partial K(x, \hat{y})}{\partial x_j} \right]_{x=\hat{x}} \leqq K(\hat{x}, \hat{y}) - K(x, \hat{y}) .$$

The left-hand side of (37.31) is non-negative because of (37.27) and (37.28) so that its right-hand side is also non-negative and we get $K(x, \hat{y}) \leqq K(\hat{x}, \hat{y})$ (for any $x \in R_+^n$).

We conclude this section by presenting a theorem dealing with the case of linear constraints and a non-linear objective functional. Our objective is a maximum problem:

$$(37.32) \qquad \max f(x)$$

subject to

$$(37.33) \qquad \sum_{j=1}^{n} a_{ij} x_j \leqq b_i \quad (i = 1, 2, ..., m)$$

and

$$(37.34) \qquad x_j \geqq 0 \quad (j = 1, 2, ..., n) ,$$

where $f(x)$ is assumed to have continuous partial derivatives on R_+^n .

THEOREM 37.4. (i) *If* $f(x)$ *attains a maximum at* $x = \hat{x}$ *subject to the constraints* (37.33) *and* (37.34), *then a linear function*

$$(37.35) \qquad \sum_{j=1}^{n} c_j x_j \qquad \text{where} \quad c_j = \left[\frac{\partial f}{\partial x_j} \right]_{x=\hat{x}}$$

attains a maximum at $x = \hat{x}$ *subject to the same constraints.*

* As K is a concave function, $K((1-t)\hat{x} + tx, \hat{y}) \geqq (1-t) K(\hat{x}, \hat{y}) + tK(x, \hat{y})$ for $0 < t \leqq 1$ so that $-(1/t)[K(\hat{x} + t(x - \hat{x}), \hat{y}) - K(\hat{x}, \hat{y})] \leqq K(\hat{x}, \hat{y}) - K(x, \hat{y})$. Letting $t \to 0$, we get $-[(d/dt) K(\hat{x} + t(x - \hat{x}), \hat{y})]_{t=0} \leqq K(\hat{x}, \hat{y}) - K(x, \hat{y})$. Actual differentiation shows that this left-hand side is equal to the left-hand side of (37.31).

(ii) *There exist* $\hat{y}_i \geqq 0$ $(i = 1, 2, ..., m)$ *such that*

$$(37.36) \qquad \left[\frac{\partial f}{\partial x_j}\right]_{x=\hat{x}} \leqq \sum_{i=1}^{n} a_{ij}\hat{y}_i \quad (j = 1, 2, ..., n)$$

and

$$(37.37) \qquad \sum_{j=1}^{n} \hat{x}_j\left[\frac{\partial f}{\partial x_j}\right]_{x=\hat{x}} = \sum_{i,j=1}^{m,n} a_{ij}\hat{y}_i\hat{x}_j = \sum_{i=1}^{m} b_i\hat{y}_i \,.$$

(iii) *Assume in addition that* $f(x)$ *is a concave function. If* (37.33), (37.34), (37.36) *and* (37.37) *hold for* $x = \hat{x}$ *and* $y = \hat{y}$, $(\hat{x}, \hat{y})$ *is a saddle point of* $K(x, y)$ *on* $R_+^n \times R_+^m$, *with*

$$g_i(x) = b_i - \sum_{j=1}^{n} a_{ij}x_j \quad (i = 1, 2, ..., m)$$

in (37.17). *(Therefore, this* $\hat{x}$ *is a solution of the maximum problem* (37.32) ~ (37.34) *by virtue of* (i) *of Theorem 37.2.)*

Proof. (i) X denotes the convex set of points that satisfy (37.33) ~ (37.34). For any $x \in X$, we have $(1-t)\hat{x} + tx \in X$ $(0 \leqq t \leqq 1)$ so that $f((1-t)\hat{x} + tx) \leqq f(\hat{x})$. Thus, as usual, we rewrite it as

$$\frac{1}{t}(f(\hat{x} + t(x - \hat{x})) - f(\hat{x})) \leqq 0 \quad (0 < t \leqq 1)$$

and let $t \to 0$. Then, the left-hand side reduces to

$$\sum_{j=1}^{n} (x_j - \hat{x}_j)\left[\frac{\partial f}{\partial x_j}\right]_{x=\hat{x}} \leqq 0 \,,$$

which is rearranged as

$$\sum_{j=1}^{n} c_j x_j \leqq \sum_{j=1}^{n} c_j \hat{x}_j \,.$$

(ii) By virtue of (i), $\hat{x}$ is an optimal solution of the linear programming problem of maximizing (37.35) subject to (37.33) and (37.34). Hence, there exists a solution y for its dual problem by virtue of the duality theorems (Section 25) so that (ii) follows.

(iii) If (37.33), (37.34), (37.36) and (37.37) hold, $K(x, y)$ of this case satisfies conditions (37.27) ~ (37.30) given in Remark 4 at $x = \hat{x}$ and $y = \hat{y}$. $g_i(x)$'s are, of course, concave functions in view of their linearity and $f(x)$ is also a concave function by assumption. Hence, by Remark 5, (iii) holds.

PART 2

EXISTENCE OF EQUILIBRIUM

Chapter 8

THE THEORY OF GENERAL EQUILIBRIUM

38. Foundations of equilibrium analysis

Adam Smith as the author of *Wealth of Nations,* it is said, is the first to shape economics as a discipline of science. If he is to be compared to Galilei, it is Leon Walras who has a scholastic stature in theoretical economics comparable to that of Newton. In his *magnum opus* [53], he applied a deep, incisive analysis to the interdependence of economic variables and gave elaborate mathematical expressions to them. Economic variables are determined not by one-way causal relations running from causes to effects but simultaneously through interdependent relations among themselves. Their equilibrium values are understood as solutions of a system of equations. This idea lies in the core of general equilibrium theory that was systematized by Walras and elaborated further by his successor V.Pareto The theory provides even today the most important foundations of almost all theoretical and mathematical economic analysis.

However, even if we could represent interdependent relations among economic variables by a system of equations armored by formidable mathematical expressions according to the idea of general equilibrium theory, the system would be inconsistent if it lacks a solution. "The determination of equilibrium through interdependent relations" would degenerate into a method with no consequence. The situation may not be as bad as this, but if the existence of a solution is not positively demonstrated, it would remain a mere hypothesis or conjecture and the underpinnings of general equilibrium theory would still remain very fragile and insecure.

It is well known that Walras thought very highly of the logical power of mathematics. He tried to make positive use of mathematics and accomplished achievements unsurpassed at his time. But as for the basic proposition on the existence of equilibrium, not only Walras but also most later economists were satisfied for quite some time only with checking the numbers of equations and unknowns to be identical. This is a very naive and pre-mathematical reasoning and cannot provide any final word on the problem. A simple example suffices to demonstrate this. A system of equations

$$f(x,y) = x + y = 0 \quad \text{and} \quad g(x,y) = xy - 1 = 0$$

has a functional determinant

$$\begin{vmatrix} \dfrac{\partial f}{\partial x} & \dfrac{\partial f}{\partial y} \\ \\ \dfrac{\partial g}{\partial x} & \dfrac{\partial g}{\partial y} \end{vmatrix} = \begin{vmatrix} 1 & 1 \\ y & x \end{vmatrix} = x - y ,$$

which is not 0 in the open set G that is the entire plane less the line $x = y$. Hence, these equations form an independent system of equations in G. But it has no solutions in G and even on the entire plane.

The reader may entertain a doubt such as the following one: This counter-example is given a very arbitrary functional form with no economic considerations and may, therefore, lack special characteristics peculiar to economic equations; this may be responsible for this unreasonable situation with no solution. He is quite right, but the most important lesson that this counter-example gives us is the fact that a mere counting of the numbers of equations and unknowns fails to clarify the special characteristics of the general equilibrium system of equations and, therefore, does not come to full grips with the secret of the existence problem of solutions. Walras noted that ordinary reasoning would be powerless in elucidating the interdependent relations of economic variables and stressed that it is mathematics alone that would be able to do the job. There are few problems more appropriate than the existence problem of equilibrium that reconfirm Walras's emphasis of mathematics in the sense that the characterisitcs of equilibrium equations must be subjected to deep mathematical analysis. Though orthodox economists hanged on to tallying numbers of equations and unknowns for half a century since Walras, mathematicians and mathematical economists trained well in mathematics finally arrived at an almost complete solution of the problem after their intensive studies of the problem. Let us briefly review this history.

It is undoubtedly von Neumann's paper [41] on games that used for the first time full-fledged mathematical methods in studying social phenomena. We must then refer to the contributions, concerning the existence problem of equilibrium solutions in economic models, made by members of a group led by an Austrian mathematician Karl Menger *, in particular von Neumann and Abraham Wald. Von Neumann's balanced growth model was already introduced in Section 35. On the other hand, Wald proved the existence of solutions in an equilibrium model of a special form called the Walras-Cassel model. At about the same time, Leontief started the input-output analysis. As we introduced it at the beginning of the book, this is a highly simplified equilibrium model. The mechanism that guarantees the existence of an economically meaningful non-negative solution in this model is completely clarified by the Hawkins-Simon condition. These studies were undertaken in the nineteen-thirties.

Von Neumann's game theory was popularized after the publication of the 1944 book [24] by himself and Morgenstern. Along with this work, linear programming received a great deal of theoretical attention and practical applications and classical mathematical economics begun to be reformulated by the activity analysis approach.

Our book has covered almost all the problems mentioned above (except the work of Wald [51, 52]). These problems were formulated as problems of solvability of equations, optimum problems, and saddle point problems. They have their own proper significance, but at the same time we must emphasize their common character in the form of existence problems of equilibrium solutions, albeit in a very restricted sense. As for the interindustry analysis, we need not repeat noting that it is immediately given the property of the existence problem of an (economy-wide) equilibrium solution. Optimization problems are mostly thought of in terms of individual behaviors of economic units like firms and households. However, even in this case, one can observe the property of the eixstence problem of equilibrium in, e.g., the assertion of the duality theorems in linear programming (Example 25.2), though only in a very limited sense. Zero-sum two-person games, of course, have no direct economic meaning, but saddle point problems that deal with the equilibrium between two opponents have many points close to the existence problem of equilibrium solutions. Furthermore, we also learned the important role of game theory in the study of the von Neumann model.

After this development, the existence problem of equilibrium solutions for the original, orthodox Walrasian proposition was solved nearly completely by a group of mathematical economists and mathematicians such as K.J.Arrow and G.Debreu [33], D.Gale [35], L.McKenzie [40], and the present author

* Son of Carl Menger, the noted economist who along with Walras and Jevons was the originator of the marginal utility school.

[46]. Subsequent efforts were directed to generalizations of the results and elaborations of the proofs. But the crux of the matter is already sufficiently clarified. The remaining chapters of our book give an exposition of this problem based on the findings of these studies.

What sort of approach does general equilibrium theory take in the analysis of the "working" of an economy? We already outlined its important features in Section 23 above.

The "working" of an economy is recorded *ex post* as certain specific numbers assigned to economic variables like prices and outputs. It may be meaningful to accept these numerical values as describing economic realities. But we cannot consider it as a scientific analysis of economic phenomena unless we show why these variables do not take other values than those recorded. Thus, it is an important task of economic theory to explain economic phenomena by clarifying how and why economic variables are determined. General equilibrium theory initiated by Walras gives a superb answer to this problem and provides the foundations of modern economics.

It is quite natural to believe that realized values of prices and outputs are determined by the complex interactions of population, natural resource endowments, technology, capital equipment, consumer tastes, etc. General equilibrium theory is an analysis elaborated from this point of view. (a) and (b) in Section 23 are the analytical procedure for this. First in (a), schedules of competitive individual economic units subject to given prices are constructed on the basis of their individual preference orderings and profit motivation. (b) then analyzes the mutual restraining and coordination of actions of many individuals. Individual schedules planned under arbitrary prices are not necessarily attainable for all members of the economy. These schedules of economic behaviors are buying and selling plans of goods in response to given price situations. Unless desired sales and purchases are balanced for the economy as a whole, individual buying and selling plans are not fulfilled for all economic units. Now the aggregate gap of schedules of sales and purchases varies as the price situation changes. Under a certain price situation, this gap vanishes and the state of equilibrium is realized. This particular price system is called the equilibrium price system. General equilibrium theory identifies it with the actual price system. Thus, it is important for establishing general equilibrium theory to examine whether the procedure (b) is theoretically feasible.

39. A Walrasian equilibrium model

As the first step in studying the existence problem of an equilibrium solution, we shall give an exact formulation of a mathematical model that represents the equilibrium of the economy as a whole.

In order to come to full grips with the essence of the problem it is useful to begin with a very simple problem.

The pure exchange problem. Though dressed in a very simple garment, this problem is equipped with all essential features of the existence problem of an equilibrium solution. It is not too much to say that the general model to be analyzed later is only a sophisticated elaboration of this simple model.

Goods are numbered by j (= 1, 2, ..., n). Assume that there are l ($\geqq 2$) consumers, numbered by i (= 1, 2, ..., l). Let the amount of good j held by consumer i to be

$$a_j^i \geqq 0 \quad (j = 1, 2, ..., n) . \tag{39.1}$$

We further assume that each i holds at least one good in positive amount *. Hence, the vector a^i of consumer i's holdings with components (19.1) is

$$a^i \geq 0 \quad (i = 1, 2, ..., l) . \tag{39.2}$$

(39.2) represents consumer i's holdings of goods, e.g. produced directly by his labor or carried over from the preceding period. i may be a farmer or a village smith. The reader should visualize a small-scale pre-capitalistic exchange economy with divisions of labor.

Let us consider the problem of exchanging these holdings a^i in the market. In this case, we may assume that

$$a = \sum_{i=1}^{l} a^i > 0 \tag{39.3}$$

without loss of generality **.

Then, what motivates people to change their holdings of goods by exchange? Exchange takes place because people wish to increase the satisfaction of their wants by exchanging their current holdings for baskets of goods that stand higher in their preference orderings. If one's satisfaction of wants is re-

* It will be made clear later that demand and supply are both 0 for those consumers with 0 holdings as all equilibrium prices are positive. Therefore, we may disregard such consumers from the very beginning.

** From the beginning, we may confine our attention to only those goods whose total supplies are positive.

duced by exchange, he would not participate in the market transactions. For he can be better off simply by consuming his current holdings.

Let i's utility indicator be $u_i(x)$ that is defined on the positive orthant R^n_+. It is assumed to be continuous, quasi-concave and strictly increasing on R^n_+ *.

Let $\hat{x}^i$ be i's holdings after the market exchanges. Obviously, $u_i(\hat{x}^i) \geqq u_i(a^i)$. The larger $u_i(\hat{x}^i)$, the more i would gain from the exchanges.

The ratios of exchange among goods are determined as the inverses of the price ratios, once the prices are given. However, exchanges are not necessarily barter exchanges of one good for another and between one consumer and another **. Just as in our daily experiences, a consumer can first sell all his holdings in the market and then buy $\hat{x}^i$ in the market out of his proceeds.

Now let $p = (p_1, p_2, ..., p_n)' > 0$ be a given price vector. Then, the market value of consumer i's holdings is

$$(39.4) \qquad I_i(p) = (p, a^i) > 0 ,$$

which is his income if all his holdings are sold. He attempts to purchase $\hat{x}^i$ that will give him the highest utility out of his income. Thus, his most desired purchase $\hat{x}^i$ is such as, under the constraint

$$(39.5) \qquad (p, x) \leqq I_i(p) , \quad x \geqq 0 ,$$

maximizes his utility, i.e.

$$(39.6) \qquad \max u_i(x) = u_i(\hat{x}^i) .$$

Aggregate demand is the sum total of individual demands, i.e. $\sum_{i=1}^{l} \hat{x}^i$, while aggregate supply is the sum total of individual holdings, i.e. $\sum_{i=1}^{l} a^i$. Exchanges (the act of each consumer selling a^i and purchasing $\hat{x}^i$) are exactly carried out if and only if there is an equilibrium

$$(39.7) \qquad \sum_{i=1}^{l} \hat{x}^i = \sum_{i=1}^{l} a^i$$

* See Section 33.

** Even if these take place in the exchange transaction, we need only consider the result of the transaction without worrying about its actual features.

between aggregate demand and supply. The equilibrium equation (39.7) does not necessarily hold for an arbitrary price system p. For instance, if the price of good i is too low, consumers' demand for it would be so large that aggregate demand $\sum_{i=1}^{l} \hat{x}_1^i$ exceeds aggregate supply $\sum_{i=1}^{l} a_1^i$. It is only with an appropriate price vector $\hat{p}$ and appropriate demand vectors $\hat{x}^i$ associated with it that (39.5), (39.6), and (39.7) hold simultaneously. Every consumer's utility can then be maximized under the constraint of his initial holdings. Such a price system p is called an *equilibrium price system.* Whether there exists such a price system or not cannot be answered by appealing merely to our naive intuition. An unambiguous answer is possible only with detailed mathematical analysis.

A general equilibrium model involving production. A general equilibrium model is constructed by incorporating production possibilities into this model of pure exchanges.

Arrow and Debreu [33] constructed a model that is a typical modern version of the Walrasian general equilibrium system. They synthesized findings of mathematical formulations of the equilibrium system, ranging from Walras and Pareto to Hicks, eliminated classical assumptions inessential to the existence problem (differentiability of utility indicators and production functions) and modernized the system. In order to make it more easily understandable, the original Arrow-Debreu model is simplified in this book by adding partial modifications *. This model describes an economy consisting of households and firms.

In the model of pure exchanges, consumers' holdings of goods are redistributed among consumers without further processing. The model that is to be formulated below allows for the existence of various factors of production (in particular, labor), raw materials and semi-finished goods in addition to consumer goods in the initial holdings of goods.

Households purchase consumer goods out of their income acquired by selling their initial holdings of goods (and that part of income which is profits distributed by firms). Supplies for such consumers' purchases come partly from their own holdings and partly from firms' outputs.

Firms employ workers (i.e. purchase labor from households that hold labor) and purchase raw materials and semi-processed goods from households and firms. They carry out production with these goods as inputs, sell their

* For the original Arrow-Debreu model, see Arrow and Debreu [33] and Nikaido [55].

outputs, pay wages to workers and other expenses to other firms out of their total revenue, and disburse profits as dividends to households. Before giving an exact formulation to this model, let us schematize the exchange flows of goods in fig. 39.1. A thick clockwise arrow represents a flow of goods and a fine counterclockwise arrow denotes a flow of money.

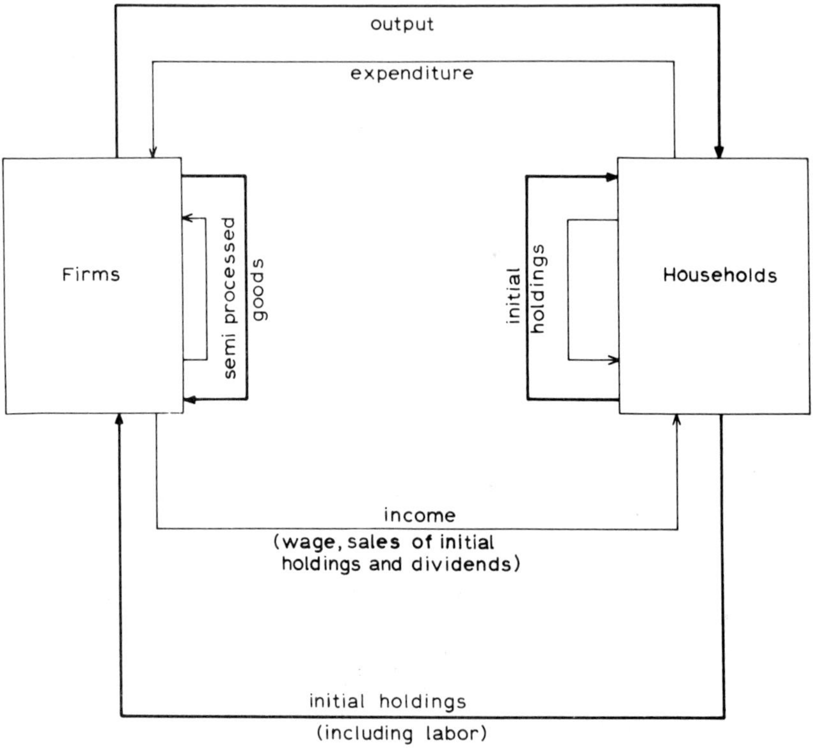

Fig. 39.1.

Let us construct our model in an exact way on the basis of our earlier examination of the production possibility set of a firm (Section 32) and of the preference field of a household (Section 33). In this model, households and firms are called consumer units and producer units respectively.

Suppose that the economy is composed of l consumer units, suffixed by i (= 1, 2, ..., l), and m producer units, suffixed by k (= 1, 2, ..., m). There are n goods, suffixed by j (= 1, 2, ..., n). We enumerate below the assumptions on production and consumption.

I. *Production.* Each production unit k has a set of processes Y_k, which satisfies the following conditions:

a. Y_k is a closed convex set containing 0.

b. $Y \cap R^n_+ = \{0\}$ for $Y = \sum_{k=1}^{m} Y_k$.

c. $Y \cap (-Y) = \{0\}$.

Positive and negative components of a process $y \in Y_k$ represent outputs and inputs respectively. This formulation of Y_k includes a special case where it is represented by an input-output matrix in the form of (32.4). Ia restricts Y_k to be merely a convex set, not necessarily a convex cone, in order to permit us to deal with the case of diminishing returns and the case where bottleneck factors constrain the production possibility set *. Y_k is thus formulated fairly loosely so that it can represent the production possibility set as well as its subsets determined by the constraints of bottleneck factors.

Y, of course, denotes the set of processes feasible in the economy as a whole. Ib indicates that this economy is not the land of Cockaigne *, while Ic shows that no process but for 0 is reversible * in this economy.

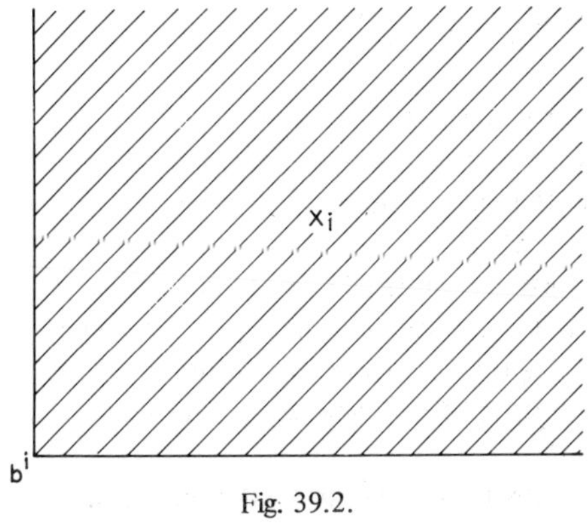

Fig. 39.2.

II. *Preference fields.* The preference field X_i of each consumer unit i and the utility indicator $u_i(x)$ defined thereon satisfy the following conditions:

a. $X_i = b^i + R^n_+$, i.e. X_i is a parallel translation of the positive orthant by b^i.

b. $u_i(x)$ is continuous.

c. $u_i(x)$ is quasi-concave.

d. $u_i(x)$ is strictly increasing.

* See Section 32.

III. *Distributive ratios of profits.* For each i and k, there is a given constant $\alpha_{ik} \geqq 0$ such that

$$(39.8) \qquad \sum_{i=1}^{l} \alpha_{ik} = 1 \quad (k = 1, 2, ..., m) .$$

When the producer unit k earns profits π_k, the consumer unit i receives a dividend $\alpha_{ik}\pi_k$. (39.8) shows that π_k is distributed completely among all consumer units.

IV. *Initial holdings.* Each consumer unit i holds a_j^i units of each good j $(= 1, 2, ..., n)$ as its initial holding. It is assumed that $a^i \geq b^i$ where a^i is a vector whose components are a_j^i. In this case, it is said, for simplicity, that initial holdings are non-negative. If $a^i > b^i$, initial holdings are said to be positive.

V. There exists $\bar{y}^k \in Y_k$ $(k = 1, 2, ..., m)$ such that

$$\sum_{i=1}^{l} b^i < \sum_{i=1}^{l} a^i + \sum_{k=1}^{m} \bar{y}^k .$$

This means that the economy as a whole is able to produce positive excess supplies for all goods if initial holdings and outputs are added together.

We now define the equilibrium conditions for this general equilibrium model. $[\hat{p}, \hat{x}^1, \hat{x}^2, ..., \hat{x}^l, \hat{y}^1, \hat{y}^2, ..., \hat{y}^m]$, composed of a price vector $\hat{p} > 0$, the demand of consumer units $\hat{x}^i \in X_i$, and the output of producer units $\hat{y}^k \in Y_k$, is called the equilibrium solution of the general equilibrium model I ~ IV when it satisfies the following conditions:

(i) *Profit maximization of producer units.* For each producer unit k,

$$(39.9) \qquad \pi_k(\hat{p}) = \max\,(\hat{p}, y) = (\hat{p}, \hat{y}^k) \;\; (\text{the maximum for all } y \in Y_k) .$$

(ii) *Utility maximization of consumer units.* For each consumer unit i,

$$(39.10) \qquad \max u_i(x) = u_i(\hat{x}^i)$$

subject to the budget constraint

$$(39.11) \qquad x \in X_i, \quad (\hat{p}, x) \leqq (\hat{p}, a^i) + \sum_{k=1}^{m} \alpha_{ik}\pi_k(\hat{p}) .$$

(iii) *Equilibrium of demand and supply.*

$$(39.12)\qquad \sum_{i=1}^{l} \hat{x}^i = \sum_{i=1}^{l} a^i + \sum_{k=1}^{m} \hat{y}^k .$$

What is implied by each of these conditions should be evident to the reader. Then, the following theorem holds for this model:

THEOREM 39.1. *The general equilibrium model* I ~ V *has an equilibrium solution.*

This theorem provides an affirmative answer to the existence problem of an equilibrium solution, which we have been seeking in this book. It will be proved in Chapter 10 after necessary mathematical preparations are completed.

We give two remarks before passing to the next section.

Remark 1. The general equilibrium model is reduced to the model of pure exchanges if we set $X_1 = X_2 = ... = X_l = R^n_+$ (i.e. $b^i = 0$ $(i = 1, 2, ..., l)$) and $Y_1 = Y_2 = ... = Y_k = \{0\}$. In this case, assumption V is equivalent to (39.3). Thus, the problem of pure exchanges can be solved as a corollary to this theorem.

Remark 2. If Y_k, the set of processes of the producer unit k, is a convex cone (so that it can be represented by (32.4) in a very special case), the profits of k must be $\pi_k(\hat{p}) = 0$ in equilibrium. In fact, if $\pi_k(\hat{p}) > 0$, we have for $\lambda > 1$, $\lambda\hat{y}^k \in Y_k$, $0 < \pi_k(\hat{p}) = (\hat{p}, \hat{y}^k) < \lambda(\hat{p}, \hat{y}^k) = (\hat{p}, \lambda\hat{y}^k)$. This contradicts the condition of profit maximization in (i). As $0 \in Y_k$, we have $\pi_k(\hat{p}) \geqq (\hat{p}, 0) = 0$. Combining these observations, we have $\pi_k(\hat{p}) = 0$. This represents the state of truly Walrasian equilibrium in the sense that the value of output coincides with its cost. On the other hand, under the law of diminishing returns to scale or the constraint of bottleneck factors (e.g. shortages of capital equipment), profits can accrue as surplus. In such a case, mathematics dictates that Y_k cannot be a convex cone, though it can be a convex set.

40. Demand and supply functions

In the preceding section, we gave an exact mathematical formulation to a Walrasian general equilibrium model and defined the state of equilibrium. We did not adhere to the formulation given by Walras himself. This is because

Walras did not formulate his model in a sufficiently rigorous mathematical way so that it could not be subjected to mathematical analysis in its original version.

Since the time of Walras, the problem of equilibrium has traditionally been discussed as that of solving a system of equations with prices as unknowns. These equations are obtained by equating demand and supply functions for individual goods. We shall follow this traditional approach as faithfully as possible in our subsequent analysis built on sufficiently strong mathematical grounds.

Demand and supply equations for the economy as a whole are derived as the aggregates of individual demand and supply functions of economic units (consumer and producer units). These individual demand and supply functions are obtained as solutions of individual optimization problems, as shown in Section 33. We must, however, raise a fundamental question as to whether the problem of maximizing utility or profit can be solved for any given price system. In the example shown in Section 33, the utility maximization problem certainly had a solution for any arbitrary positive price system so that demand functions could be constructed. Unfortunately, this is not always possible. For example, when Y_k, the set of processes available to the producer unit k, is a convex cone (in particular, represented by (32.4)), the profit maximization problem is solvable only for specific price vectors. If there is such $y \in Y_k$ for prices p that $(p, y) > 0$, then $\lambda y \in Y_k$ $(\lambda > 0)$ and profits $(p, \lambda y) = \lambda(p, y) \to +\infty$ as $\lambda \to \infty$ so that there is no maximum. This makes it mathematically impossible for us to be completely faithful to the traditional approach. In order to overcome this difficulty, it is necessary to add certain modifications to the utility and profit maximization problems conceived of on directly economic grounds. Demand and supply functions are to be derived from them. As will become clear, this procedure will prove very effective in our task at hand, i.e. that of presenting the existence proof of an equilibrium solution.

This difficulty stems from the fact that the domains of our maximum problems are not always bounded. It is very useful to recall the fact (Theorem 14.2) that "a continuous function always attains a maximum on a compact set". Thus, the next step that we must take is to restrict the domains of the maximum problems within bounded regions by some appropriate methods. For this purpose, let us first verify that, if there exist equilibrium solutions, all equilibrium demands x^i and equilibrium outputs y^k are located within a certain bounded domain.

Let $X = \sum_{i=1}^{l} X_i$ and $Y = \sum_{k=1}^{m} Y_k$. If there is an equilibrium solution

$[\hat{p}, \hat{x}^1, \hat{x}^2, ..., \hat{x}^l, \hat{y}^1, \hat{y}^2, ..., \hat{y}^m]$, it satisfies condition (iii) of (39.12) in the preceding section. Now we take a relation *

$$(40.1) \qquad a + \sum_{k=1}^{m} y^k \geqq \sum_{i=1}^{l} x^i \quad \text{where } a = \sum_{i=1}^{l} a^i ,$$

and consider all $(l+m)$-tuples that satisfy (40.1), i.e.

$$(40.2) \qquad [x^1, x^2, ..., x^l, y^1, y^2, ..., y^m] , \quad x^i \in X_i, \quad y^k \in Y_k .$$

Let $\widetilde{X}_i$ denote the set of those points in X_i that appear as x^i in any of the $(l+m)$-tuples (40.2). $\widetilde{Y}_k$ similarly represents the set of those points in Y_k that appear as y^k in any of the $(l+m)$-tuples (40.2). Thus, we have

$$(40.3) \qquad \widetilde{X}_i = X_i \cap (a + Y - \sum_{s \neq i} X_s - R^n_+) \quad (i = 1, 2, ..., l)$$

and

$$(40.4) \qquad \widetilde{Y}_k = Y_k \cap (X - a - \sum_{t \neq k} Y_t + R^n_+) \quad (k = 1, 2, ..., m) .$$

If there exists an equilibrium solution, then obviously we have

$$\widetilde{X}_i \ni \hat{x}^i \quad \text{and} \quad \widetilde{Y}_k \ni \hat{y}^k .$$

Let us now examine the properties of these sets.

LEMMA.

(i) *$\widetilde{X}_i$ and $\widetilde{Y}_k$ are non-empty sets.*
(ii) *$\widetilde{X}_i$ and $\widetilde{Y}_k$ are convex sets.*
(iii) *$\widetilde{X}_i$ and $\widetilde{Y}_k$ are bounded sets.*

Proof. (i) It may seem unnecessary to prove (i) because $\widetilde{X}_i \ni \hat{x}^i$ and $\widetilde{Y}_k \ni \hat{y}^k$. But this is a gross misunderstanding. Recall that we have not proved the existence of $\hat{x}^i$ and $\hat{y}^k$. Now (i) can be proved very simply. First, $a^i \in X_i$ by virtue of IIa and IV in Section 39, and $0 \in Y_k$ because of Ia in Section 39. Thus, the $(l+m)$-tuple $[a^1, a^2, ..., a^l, 0, 0, ..., 0]$ satisfies (40.1) with an equality sign so that $\widetilde{X}_i \ni a^i$ and $\widetilde{Y}_k \ni 0$. $\therefore \widetilde{X}_i \neq \phi$ and $\widetilde{Y}_k \neq \phi$.

* (40.1) is less restrictive than (39.12).

Remark. As the $(l+m)$-tuple $[b^1, b^2, ..., b^l, 0, 0, ..., 0]$ also satisfies (40.1), we see $\tilde{X}_i \ni b^i$. As the $(l+m)$-tuple $[b^1, b^2, ..., b^l, \bar{y}^1, \bar{y}^2, ..., \bar{y}^m]$ fulfils (40.2) because of Assumption V, we have $\tilde{Y}_k \ni \bar{y}^k$.

(ii) This is obvious from the expressions (40.3) and (40.4). As X_i, Y_k, R^n_+ and $\{a\}$ are all convex sets, $\tilde{X}_i$ and $\tilde{Y}_k$ are convex sets by virtue of Theorem 27.2 and (ii) of Theorem 28.4.

(iii) The proof is given in two parts.

(iii.a) The boundedness of $\tilde{Y}_k$. Reject the assertion and assume that $\tilde{Y}_k$ is unbounded. Then, there exists a sequence of points $\{y^{k\nu}\}$ in $\tilde{Y}_k$ such that

(40.5) $$\lim_{\nu\to\infty} \|y^{k\nu}\| = +\infty .$$

It follows from the definition (40.4) that there exist $y^{t\nu} \in Y_t$ and $x^{i\nu} \in X_i$ $(\nu = 1, 2, ...)$ such that

$$a + y^{k\nu} + \sum_{t\neq k} y^{t\nu} \geqq \sum_{i=1}^{l} x^{i\nu} .$$

Rearranging its terms and making use of the lower bound b^i of X_i in IIa, we get

(40.6) $$\sum_{t=1}^{m} y^{t\nu} \geqq \sum_{i=1}^{l} x^{i\nu} - a \geqq b - a \quad \text{where} \quad b = \sum_{i=1}^{l} b^i .$$

Putting

(40.7) $$\mu_\nu = \max_{1\leqq t\leqq m} \|y^{t\nu}\| ,$$

we find that $\mu_\nu \geqq 1$ for sufficiently large ν because $\mu_\nu \geqq \|y^{k\nu}\| \to +\infty$. Taking the convexity of Y_t into consideration, we have

(40.8) $$\frac{1}{\mu_\nu} y^{t\nu} = (\frac{1}{\mu_\nu}) y^{t\nu} + (1 - \frac{1}{\mu_\nu}) 0 \in Y_t \quad (t = 1, 2, ..., m) .$$

Dividing (40.6) through by μ_ν and letting $\nu \to +\infty$, we get

(40.9) $$\sum_{t=1}^{m} (y^{t\nu}/\mu_\nu) \geqq (b-a)/\mu_\nu \to 0 .$$

We also find that

(40.10) $$\|y^{t\nu}/\mu_\nu\| \leqq 1 \quad (t = 1, 2, ..., m)$$

for sufficiently large ν because of the definition (40.7) of μ_ν. This shows that $y^{t\nu}/\mu_\nu \in \bar{U}(0, 1)$ so that we may assume $\{y^{t\nu}/\mu_\nu\}$ to converge for each t and

$$\text{(40.11)} \qquad \lim_{\nu\to\infty} y^{t\nu}/\mu_\nu = y^{t0} ,$$

in view of the fact that $\bar{U}(0, 1)$ is compact (see Example 14.5). Now, Y_t is a closed set by virtue of Ia. As $\{y^{t\nu}/\mu_\nu\}$ is a sequence of points in Y_t because of (40.8), the closedness of Y_t implies

$$\text{(40.12)} \qquad y^{t0} \in Y_t \quad (t = 1, 2, ..., m).$$

(40.9) reveals that in the limit

$$\text{(40.13)} \qquad \sum_{t=1}^{m} y^{t0} \geqq 0 .$$

Hence,

$$\sum_{t=1}^{m} y^{t0} \in Y \cap R^n_+ .$$

By Assumption Ib, we get

$$\text{(40.14)} \qquad \sum_{t=1}^{m} y^{t0} = 0 .$$

Rearranging terms in (40.14), we rewrite it as

$$\text{(40.15)} \qquad -y^{t0} = \sum_{s\neq t} y^{s0} \in Y .$$

As $Y_t \subset Y$, we have

$$\text{(40.16)} \qquad y^{t0} \in Y .$$

It follows from (40.15), (40.16) and Assumption Ic, that

$$y^{t0} \in Y \cap (-Y) = \{0\} ,$$

i.e. that $y^{t0} = 0$ $(t = 1, 2, ..., m)$. Thus, for each t, $\lim_{\nu\to\infty} y^{t\nu}/\mu_\nu = y^{t0} = 0$ so that

$\lim_{\nu\to\infty} ||y^{t\nu}/\mu_\nu|| = 0$ and that $\max_{1\leqq t\leqq m} ||y^{t\nu}/\mu_\nu|| \to 0$ $(\nu \to \infty)$. On the other hand, the definition (40.7) of μ_ν leads to $\max_{1\leqq t\leqq m} ||y^{t\nu}/\mu_\nu|| = 1$ $(\nu = 1, 2, ...)$. This contradiction has arisen because the boundedness of $\widetilde{Y}_k$ was denied. This completes the proof of the first part.

(iii.b) The boundedness of $\widetilde{X}_i$. We make use of the result of (iii.a) in this proof. Let $x^i \in \widetilde{X}_i$. Then, there exists $x^s \in X_s$ and $y^k \in Y_k$ that, along with this x^i, form an $(l+m)$-tuple (40.2) satisfying (40.1). These vectors are thus

$$(40.17) \qquad y^k \in \widetilde{Y}_k \quad (k = 1, 2, ..., m)$$

so that we have

$$b^i \leqq x^i \leqq a + \sum_{k=1}^{m} y^k - \sum_{s\neq i} x^s \leqq a + \sum_{k=1}^{m} y^k - \sum_{s\neq i} b^s ,$$

which shows that x^i is bounded both from above and from below. The right-hand side is bounded from above because of (iii.a) and (40.17). [Q.E.D.]

It is clear from the definition that $\widetilde{X}_i \subset X_i$ and $\widetilde{Y}_k \subset Y_k$.

We are now well prepared to define demand and supply functions.

Construction of demand and supply functions. We introduce a set in R^n that is called a *hypercube.* This set is given by

$$(40.18) \qquad E = \{x | x \in R^n,\ c_j \leqq x_j \leqq d_j \quad (j = 1, 2, ..., n)\}$$

where c_j and d_j are constants subject to $c_j < d_j$. E is obviously a convex set. It is also compact as shown in the proof of Theorem 14.6. It is apparent that any bounded set can be included within the interior of a hypercube E if E is sufficiently large.

Now the lemma above has shown that $\widetilde{Y}_k$'s $(k = 1, 2, ..., m)$ are bounded. Select a hypercube E large enough to include all of them in its interior. In other words,

$$(40.19) \qquad E^{\mathrm{o}} \supset \widetilde{Y}_k \quad (k = 1, 2, ..., m) .$$

Form an intersection $Y_k \cap E$ for each k. It is not an empty set because of (40.19). It is a compact, convex set *

* As Y_k is closed and E is compact, their intersection is compact. As Y_k and E are convex, their intersection is convex.

We now define supply functions by restricting the domain Y_k of the profit maximization problem to be $Y_k \cap E$. This restriction enables us to relax the condition on the price vector from $p > 0$ to $p \geqq 0$. Unless otherwise noted, the price vector is assumed to be $p \geqq 0$ in what follows.

The supply function $\psi^k(p)$ and the profit function $\pi_k(p)$ of the producer unit k are defined as

$$(40.20) \qquad \psi^k(p) = \{y^k \mid \max(p, y) = (p, y^k) \text{ for } y \in Y_k \cap E\}$$

and

$$(40.21) \qquad \pi_k(p) = \max(p, y) \quad (\text{subject to } y \in Y_k \cap E)\,.$$

As $Y_k \cap E$ is compact and as the function (p, y) is continuous in y, we know that there always exists a maximum and that (40.20) and (40.21) are consistently defined for any p. $\pi_k(p)$ is an ordinary, single-valued function, but there are in general many maximizers y^k of (p, y) so that $\psi^k(p)$ is a set-valued function as explained in Section 33.

Form another hypercube in order to define demand functions. Let (40.18) be the hypercube E that was already selected. Let d be a vector whose components are d_j. Select a vector h^i that satisfies

$$(40.22) \qquad h^i > a^i + md$$

and *

$$(40.23) \qquad h^i > x \quad (\text{for any } x \in \tilde{X}_i)\,.$$

As the lemma shows that $\tilde{X}_i$ is bounded, this procedure is permissible.

We have $b^i \in \tilde{X}_i$ as noted in the proof of the lemma so that, of course, $b^i < h^i$ by (40.23). Take this h^i and form a hypercube

$$(40.24) \qquad E_i = \{x \mid x \in R^n,\ b^i \leqq x \leqq h^i\} \quad (i = 1, 2, \ldots, l)\,.$$

Thus, it immediately follows that

$$(40.25) \qquad X_i \supset E_i \supset \tilde{X}_i \quad (i = 1, 2, \ldots, l)\,.$$

* By md we mean $md = \underbrace{d + d + \ldots + d}_{m}$.

The demand function of the consumer unit i is defined by

(40.26)

$$\varphi^i(p) = \{x^i | \max u_i(x) = u_i(x^i) \text{ for } x \in E_i, (p, x) \leqq (p, a^i) + \sum_{k=1}^{m} \alpha_{ik}\pi_k(p)\}.$$

As $Y_k \cap E \ni 0$, we have $\pi_k(p) \geqq 0$. Further, $\alpha_{ik} \geqq 0$ by Assumption III so that

$$\sum_{k=1}^{m} \alpha_{ik}\pi_k(p) \geqq 0 .$$

Thus, by setting $x = a^i$, we see that the budget constraint

$$(p, x) \leqq (p, a^i) + \sum_{k=1}^{m} \alpha_{ik}\pi_k(p) \tag{40.27}$$

is fulfilled. On the other hand, as $a^i \in E_i$, the domain of this maximization problem is not an empty set. As this domain is an intersection of a hypercube and a half-space, it is compact. $u_i(x)$ is continuous and has always a maximum. (40.26) is defined consistently for any $p \geq 0$. (40.26) is, in general, a set-valued function.

Individual demand and supply functions have now been defined. By aggregating them, the aggregate demand and supply functions are defined. Thus, the aggregate demand function is given by

$$\varphi(p) = \sum_{i=1}^{l} \varphi^i(p) , \tag{40.28}$$

while the aggregate supply function is determined by

$$\psi(p) = a + \sum_{k=1}^{m} \psi^k(p) . \tag{40.29}$$

Both of them are in general set-valued functions.

Equilibrium of demand and supply functions. Demand and supply functions that have been defined here are, in general, set-valued functions. They reduce to ordinary, single-valued functions only under very special conditions. In such cases, the state of equilibrium in the system is expressed by equations "demand = supply":

$$(40.30)\qquad \varphi(p) = \psi(p)\,.$$

But in the general case of set-valued functions, the equilibrium is expressed not in the form of (40.30) *, but by

$$(40.31)\qquad \varphi(p) \cap \psi(p) \neq \phi\,,$$

which means that $\varphi(p)$ and $\psi(p)$ contain a common element for some price vector p. (40.31) is equivalent to

$$(40.32)\qquad \psi(p) - \varphi(p) \ni 0\,,$$

which states that the vectorial difference of $\psi(p)$ and $\varphi(p)$, i.e. the *excess supply function* $\psi(p) - \varphi(p)$, contains 0. In the case of single-valued functions, (40.31) and (40.32) obviously reduce to (40.30).

The Walras law. Individual demand and supply functions represent the schedules of economic units at given prices p. These schedules are based on individuals' decisions made independently of those of other economic units. But there are certain indirect mutual constraints on them. We now state this point in a clear-cut form.

The consumer unit i decides on his demand programme x^i so as to maximize $u_i(x)$ subject to the budget constraint (40.27) within the hypercube E_i. $\varphi^i(p)$ is the set of all demand programmes. Though (40.27) is an inequality constraint, the equality sign must hold for points x^i of $\varphi^i(p)$. To demonstrate this, assume that

$$(40.33)\qquad (p, x^i) < (p, a^i) + \sum_{k=1}^{m} \alpha_{ik}\pi_k(p)\,.$$

As

$$(40.34)\qquad \pi_k(p) = (p, y^k) \qquad (\text{for any } y^k \in \psi^k(p))\,,$$

we have

$$\sum_{k=1}^{m} \alpha_{ik}\pi_k(p) = \sum_{k=1}^{m} \alpha_{ik}(p, y^k) = \left(p, \sum_{k=1}^{m} \alpha_{ik}y^k\right).$$

* In the case of set-valued functions, (40.30) represents a very stringent situation where the sets on both sides of the equation completely coincide with each other.

As $y^k, 0 \in Y_k \cap E$ where $Y_k \cap E$ is a convex set and as $0 \leqq \alpha_{ik} \leqq 1$,

$$\alpha_{ik} y^k = (1 - \alpha_{ik})\, 0 + \alpha_{ik} y^k \in Y_k \cap E.$$

Hence, $\alpha_{ik} y^k \leqq d$ so that we get

$$a^i + \sum_{k=1}^{m} \alpha_{ik} y^k < h^i$$

because of (40.22). Taking its inner product with $p \geq 0$, we have

$$(p, a^i + \sum_{k=1}^{m} \alpha_{ik} y^k) < (p, h^i),$$

from which it follows that

$$(40.35) \qquad (p, a^i) + \sum_{k=1}^{m} \alpha_{ik} \pi_k(p) < (p, h^i).$$

Because $x^i \in E_i$, we have $h^i \geqq x^i$. As $h^i \neq x^i$ from (40.33) and (40.35), we see that $h^i \geq x^i$. It is easy to prove from this that points x ($\neq x^i$) on the segment $[x^i, h^i]$ all satisfy $x \geq x^i$. Hence, by the strict increasingness of the utility indicator in Assumption IId,

$$(40.36) \qquad u_i(x) > u_i(x^i)$$

holds for such x as those we have referred to above. On the other hand, if such x is sufficiently close to x^i, it satisfies the budget constraint (40.27) because of its continuity in view of (40.33) which is a strict inequality. This contradicts the fact that x^i maximizes utility. Hence, the equality sign must hold in (40.33) so that

$$(40.37) \qquad (p, x^i) = (p, a^i) + \sum_{k=1}^{m} \alpha_{ik} \pi_k(p) \quad (i = 1, 2, \ldots, l).$$

Now, aggregate (40.37) and take (40.34) into consideration. Then, because of

$$\sum_{i=1}^{l} \alpha_{ik} = 1,$$

we get

$$(p, \sum_{i=1}^{l} x^i) = (p, \sum_{i=1}^{l} a^i) + \sum_{k=1}^{m} \pi_k(p)$$

$$= (p, \sum_{i=1}^{l} a^i) + (p, \sum_{k=1}^{m} y^k) = (p, \sum_{i=1}^{l} a^i + \sum_{k=1}^{m} y^k) .$$

From this, we observe that

(40.38) $\quad (p, x) = (p, y)$ (for any $p \geq 0$, $x \in \varphi(p)$, $y \in \psi(p)$) .

(40.38) reveals the identity of revenue and expenditure and is called the *Walras law.* This shows that revenue arising from the supply of goods (production and sales of initial holdings) is entirely spent on purchases of goods. It is an important relation representing complete circular flows of income. It should particularly be noted that (40.38) is an identity holding for any p. When the demand and supply functions are single-valued, it reduces to an identity

$$(p, \varphi(p)) = (p, \psi(p))$$

for $p \geq 0$. As will be made clear, the Walras law is one of the important keys for solving the existence problem of an equilibrium solution.

Relation with the equilibrium in the original model. The demand and supply functions as defined in this section are constructed by modifying some what the utility and profit maximization problems in the original model. Therefore, it is necessary to clarify what it implies for the study of the existence problem of an equilibrium solution in the original model to discuss the equilibrium (40.31) of these demand and supply functions. We prove the theorem below for this purpose.

THEOREM 40.1. (i) *If* $[\hat{p}, \hat{x}^1, \hat{x}^2, ..., \hat{x}^l, \hat{y}^1, \hat{y}^2, ..., \hat{y}^m]$ *is an equilibrium solution of the original model, then*

$$\varphi(\hat{p}) \cap \psi(\hat{p}) \ni \sum_{i=1}^{l} \hat{x}^i = a + \sum_{k=1}^{m} \hat{y}^k ,$$

which shows that the equilibrium of the demand and supply functions (40.31) *holds at* $p = \hat{p}$.

(ii) *If $\hat{p}$ is an equilibrium price vector of the demand and supply functions, the* $(l + m + 1)$-tuple $[\hat{p}, \hat{x}^1, \hat{x}^2, \ldots, \hat{x}^l, \hat{y}^1, \hat{y}^2, \ldots, \hat{y}^m]$ *that is derived by decomposing any point of* $\varphi(\hat{p}) \cap \psi(\hat{p})$ *into the sum*

$$\sum_{i=1}^{l} \hat{x}^i = a + \sum_{k=1}^{m} \hat{y}^k$$

(for appropriate $\hat{x}^i \in \varphi^i(\hat{p})$, $\hat{y}^k \in \psi^k(\hat{p})$*) is an equilibrium solution of the model.*

Proof. (i) The solutions of the maximization problems modified by restricting the domains of the original maximization problems are $\varphi^i(p)$ and $\psi^k(p)$. $\hat{x}^i$ and $\hat{y}^k$ are contained in these restricted domains. Thus, obviously $\hat{x}^i \in \varphi^i(\hat{p})$ and $\hat{y}^k \in \psi^k(\hat{p})$. On the other hand, as (39.12) holds,

$$\varphi(\hat{p}) \ni \sum_{i=1}^{l} \hat{x}^i = a + \sum_{k=1}^{m} \hat{y}^k \in \psi(\hat{p})\ .$$

(ii) (39.12) undoubtedly holds because of the way the $(l + m + 1)$-tuple is constructed. Hence, it suffices to show that $\hat{x}^i$ and $\hat{y}^k$ are solutions of the original maximization problems.

(ii.a) Let us first show that $\hat{y}^k$ maximizes $(\hat{p}, y)$ in Y_k. When the conclusion is denied, we have $(\hat{p}, z) > (\hat{p}, \hat{y}^k)$ for some $z \in Y_k$. Then, points y $(\neq y^k)$ on the segment $[\hat{y}^k, z]$ all satisfy $(\hat{p}, y) > (\hat{p}, \hat{y}^k)$. But we get $\hat{y}^k \in \tilde{Y}_k$ in view of (39.12) that holds. $\hat{y}^k$ is an interior point of E because of (40.19). Hence, we have $y \in Y_k \cap E$ for such y as those mentioned above that are close enough to $\hat{y}^k$. Moreover, $(\hat{p}, y) > (\hat{p}, \hat{y}^k)$, which contradicts what $\hat{y}^k \in \psi^k(\hat{p})$ implies.

(ii.b) Let us first show that $\hat{p} > 0$. Suppose that $\hat{p} \ngtr 0$ and set $\hat{p}_j = 0$ for some j. Let x^i be a vector formed by substituting h^i_j for the jth component of $\hat{x}^i$ *. Then, $x^i \in E_i, x^i \geqq \hat{x}^i$. As $\hat{x}^i \in \tilde{X}_i$ because of (39.12), the jth component h^i_j of x^i is larger than that of $\hat{x}^i$ due to (40.23) so that we have $x^i \geq \hat{x}^i$. It, therefore, follows from Assumption IId that $u_i(x^i) > u_i(\hat{x}^i)$. But we get $(\hat{p}, x^i) = (\hat{p}, \hat{x}^i)$ because $\hat{p}_j = 0$ and because all components except the jth one are identical in x^i and $\hat{x}^i$. x^i also satisfies the budget constraint. This contradicts what $\hat{x}^i \in \varphi^i(\hat{p})$ implies. Hence, $\hat{p} > 0$.

We now prove that $\hat{x}^i$ maximizes $u_i(x)$ subject to (39.10). Suppose that a point $w \in X_i = b^i + R^n_+$ outside of E_i satisfies the budget constraint (40.27)

* h^i_j is the jth component of h^i that was defined in (40.22) and (40.23).

and that $u_i(w) > u_i(\hat{x}^i)$. A point x on the segment $[b^i, w]$ satisfies $w \geq x$ if $x \neq w$. If it is taken sufficiently close to w, we get

$$u_i(x) > u_i(\hat{x}^i) \tag{40.39}$$

because of the continuity of u_i. Setting

$$x(t) = (1-t)\hat{x}^i + tx \quad (0 \leqq t \leqq 1)\,, \tag{40.40}$$

we find

$$u_i(x(t)) \geqq u_i(\hat{x}^i) \tag{40.41}$$

from (40.39) and (40.40) because of the quasi-concavity of u_i (Assumption IIc). On the other hand, as $\hat{p} > 0$ and $w \geq x$, we have $(\hat{p}, x) < (\hat{p}, w) \leqq (\hat{p}, \hat{x}^i)$ *. Therefore, we get

$$(\hat{p}, x(t)) < (\hat{p}, \hat{x}^i) \quad (0 < t \leqq 1) \tag{40.42}$$

for (40.40).

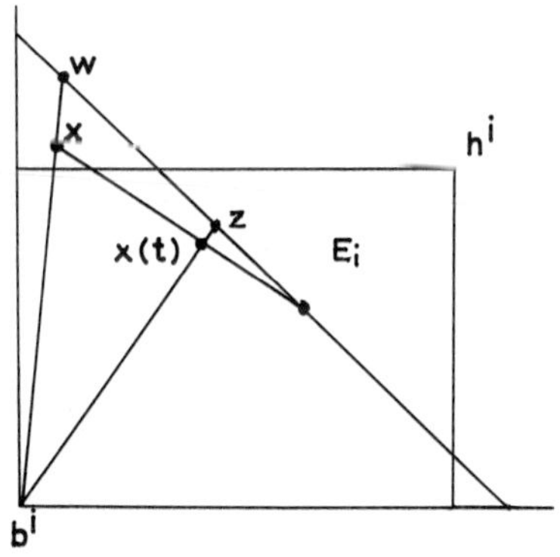

Fig. 40.1.

* As we have already noted, $\hat{x}^i \in \varphi^i(\hat{p})$ satisfies the budget constraint with the equality sign, i.e. $(\hat{p}, \hat{x}^i) = (\hat{p}, a) + \sum_{k=1}^{m} \alpha_{ik}\pi_k(\hat{p})$. On the other hand, $(\hat{p}, w) \leqq (\hat{p}, a) + \sum_{k=1}^{m} \alpha_{ik}\pi_k(\hat{p})$ so that $(\hat{p}, w) \leqq (\hat{p}, \hat{x}^i)$.

As $\hat{x}^i \in \tilde{X}_i$, we get $\hat{x}^i < h^i$. By taking $t > 0$ sufficiently close to 0, we see that

(40.43) $\quad x(t) < h^i$

holds. Then, the strict inequalities (40.42) and (40.43) enable us to choose z that satisfies

(40.44) $\quad (\hat{p}, z) \leqq (\hat{p}, \hat{x}^i)$

and

(40.45) $\quad x(t) < z \leqq h^i.$

This z is obviously such that $z \in E_i$ and satisfies the budget constraint. Because of (40.41) and the strict increasingness of u_i (Assumption IId), we get

$$u_i(z) > u_i(\hat{x}^i)\,,$$

which contradicts what $\hat{x}^i \in \varphi^i(\hat{p})$ implies. Hence, $\hat{x}^i$ maximizes utility in the entire domain of X_i under the budget constraint. [Q.E.D.]

Now it is clear that the existence problem of an equilibrium solution in the original model is completely translated into that of demand-and-supply equilibrium. We are thus led to the study of properties of demand and supply functions. This requires us to go beyond the separation theorems. In the next chapter, we shall describe the fixed point theorems that illuminate properties of convex sets more clearly.

Chapter 9

INTRODUCTION TO MATHEMATICS (III) FIXED POINT THEOREMS

In this chapter, we shall first fill in gaps in Mathematical Introductions (I) and (II) and then give an exposition of the fixed point theorems that are indispensable in elucidating the existence problem of an equilibrium solution so as to prepare ourselves for the final solution of this problem.

41. Simplexes

In Section 27, we introduced the convex hull $C(X)$ of a set X in R^n. $C(X)$ is the minimal convex set that includes X. As we saw there, it may be regarded as the set of all convex linear combinations of points of X. In this section, we give more detailed observations on $C(X)$ where X is a finite set.

Consider points in R^{n+1}

(41.1) $$\underline{x}^i = \begin{bmatrix} x^i \\ 1 \end{bmatrix} \quad (i = 0, 1, ..., k)$$

corresponding to $k + 1$ points x^i $(i = 0, 1, ..., k)$ in R^n. The procedure of associating a point with another one in a space of a dimension higher by one by giving an additional component to the former was already employed in our exposition of the convex hull in Section 27.

When the points (41.1) are linearly independent, the points x^i $(i = 0, 1, ..., k)$ are said to be *affinely independent.* It is readily seen from this definition that points x^i $(i = 0, 1, ..., k)$ are affinely independent if $\alpha_0 = \alpha_1 = \alpha_2 = ...$

$= \alpha_k = 0$ follows from two linear relations

$$\sum_{i=0}^{k} \alpha_i x^i = 0 , \tag{41.2}$$

$$\sum_{i=0}^{k} \alpha_i = 0 . \tag{41.3}$$

LEMMA. *Points x^i $(i = 0, 1, ..., k)$ in R^n are affinely independent if and only if the k points*

$$x^i - x^0 \quad (i = 1, 2, ..., k) \tag{41.4}$$

are linearly independent.

Proof. (i) *Necessity.* Let x^i $(i = 0, 1, ..., k)$ be affinely independent. If

$$\sum_{i=1}^{k} \alpha_i (x^i - x^o) = 0 , \tag{41.5}$$

it is reduced to (41.2) and (41.3) by setting

$$\alpha_0 = -\sum_{i=1}^{k} \alpha_i .$$

Then, $\alpha_0 = \alpha_1 = ... = \alpha_k = 0$ by the assumed affine independence. Hence, $x^i - x^0$ $(i = 1, 2, ..., k)$ are linearly independent.

(ii) *Sufficiency*. Conversely, let $x^i - x^0$ $(i = 1, 2, ..., k)$ be linearly independent. We can derive $\alpha_0 = \alpha_1 = ... = \alpha_k = 0$ from (41.2) and (41.3) under this assumption. By subtracting

$$(\sum_{i=0}^{k} \alpha_i)\, x^0 = 0$$

from both sides of (41.2), we get (41.5). Therefore, $\alpha_1 = \alpha_2 = ... = \alpha_k = 0$ by the assumed linear independence. Finally again from (41.3), it follows that $\alpha_0 = 0$. Hence, x^i $(i = 0, 1, ..., k)$ are affinely independent. [Q.E.D.]

Remark 1. It is immediately clear from the definition that $k \leqq n$ if x^i $(i = 0, 1, ..., k)$ are affinely independent points in R^n.

The convex hull $C(X)$ of a finite set X composed of $k+1$ affinely independent points $x^i \in R^n$ $(i = 0, 1, ..., k)$ is called a *k-dimensional simplex* generated by vertices $x^0, x^1, ..., x^k$. It is denoted by $\overline{x^0 x^1 ... x^k}$. Thus, the simplex $\overline{x^0 x^1 ... x^k}$ is a set of all points representable as

$$(41.6) \qquad \sum_{i=0}^{k} \alpha_i x^i, \quad \alpha_i \geqq 0, \quad \sum_{i=0}^{k} \alpha_i = 1 \quad (i = 0, 1, ..., k).$$

Example 41.1. A point x^0, a segment with two points x^0 and x^1 as its end points, a triangle with three points x^0, x^1 and x^2 as vertices, and a tetrahedron with four points x^0, x^1, x^2 and x^3 as vertices are simplexes of 0, 1, 2 and 3 dimensions. k-dimensional simplexes generalize these well-known concepts to higher dimensions.

Example 41.2. We made frequent use of the compactness of the set

$$S_n = \{x \mid x \geqq 0, \sum_{j=1}^{n} x_j = 1\}.$$

This set is an $(n-1)$-dimensional simplex $\overline{e^1 e^2 ... e^n}$, whose vertices are n unit vectors e^i (e^i is a vector whose components are all 0 except the ith one that is unity). Fig. 41.2 represents the case of $n = 3$.

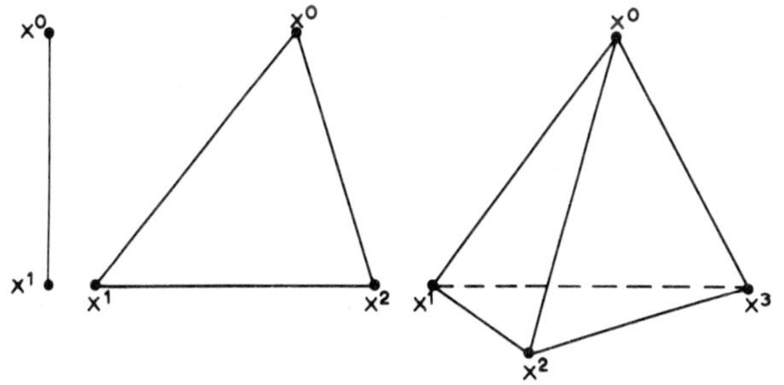

Fig. 41.1.

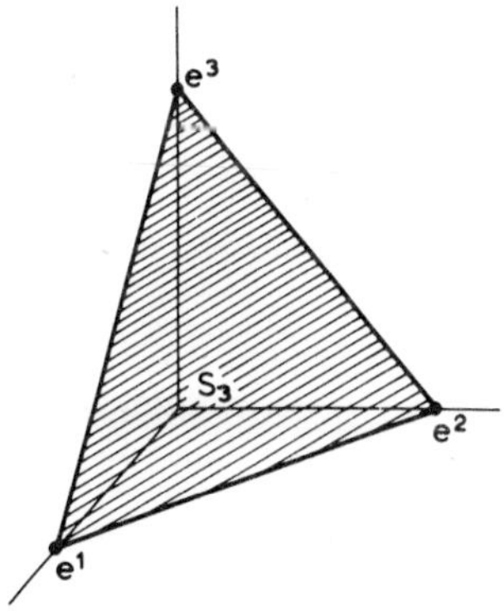

Fig. 41.2.

The straight line passing through two distinct points x^0 and x^1 is represented by $x = x^0 + \alpha(x^1 - x^0)$ where α is a real-valued parameter. It can be rewritten as $x = (1 - \alpha)x^0 + \alpha x^1$. In other words, this straight line is representable as

$$x = \alpha_0 x^0 + \alpha_1 x^1, \quad \alpha_0 + \alpha_1 = 1 .$$

The simplex $\overline{x^0 x^1}$ is the set of all points on this straight line with non-negative parameter values $\alpha_0 \geqq 0$ and $\alpha_1 \geqq 0$. Similarly, the plane determined by three affinely independent points x^0, x^1 and x^2 is represented by $x = x^0 + \alpha_1(x^1 - x^0) + \alpha_2(x^2 - x^0)$, ($\alpha_1$ and α_2 are parameters), i.e. by

$$x = \alpha_0 x^0 + \alpha_1 x^1 + \alpha_2 x^2, \quad \alpha_0 + \alpha_1 + \alpha_2 = 1.$$

The simplex $\overline{x^0 x^1 x^2}$ is a subset of this plane that is characterized by the non-negative parameters $\alpha_0 \geqq 0$, $\alpha_1 \geqq 0$ and $\alpha_2 \geqq 0$. We may now generalize this property.

The *k-dimensional plane* determined by $k + 1$ affinely independent points x^i ($i = 0, 1, ..., k$) is given by

$$x = x^0 + \sum_{i=1}^{k} \alpha_i (x^i - x^0)$$

($\alpha_1, \alpha_2, ..., \alpha_k$ are parameters) or

$$(41.7) \qquad x = \sum_{i=0}^{k} \alpha_i x^i , \quad \sum_{i=0}^{k} \alpha_i = 1 .$$

It includes the simplex $\overline{x^0 x^1 ... x^k}$ as its subset. This plane is called the *k-dimensional plane generated by the simplex* $\overline{x^0 x^1 ... x^k}$.

Remark 2. (41.7) implies that $\begin{bmatrix} x \\ 1 \end{bmatrix}$ is a linear combination of $k + 1$ points $\begin{bmatrix} x^i \\ 1 \end{bmatrix}$. Theorem 9.3 shows that the $(n - 1)$-dimensional plane (41.7) for $k = n - 1$ is represented by a linear equation *

$$\begin{vmatrix} x_1^0 & x_1^1 & \cdots & x_1^{n-1} & x_1 \\ x_2^0 & x_2^1 & \cdots & x_2^{n-1} & x_2 \\ \vdots & \vdots & & \vdots & \vdots \\ x_n^0 & x_n^1 & \cdots & x_n^{n-1} & x_n \\ 1 & 1 & \cdots & 1 & 1 \end{vmatrix} = 0 .$$

* Expanding the determinant on the left-hand side along its $(n + 1)$st column, we get a linear equation in $x_1, x_2, ..., x_n$.

In other words, an $(n-1)$-dimensional plane is a hyperplane. Conversely, it can be shown that a hyperplane is an $(n-1)$-dimensional plane. This is left as an exercise to the reader.

Remark 3. As can easily be verified, a k-dimensional plane (41.7) is an affine subspace that was defined in Section 27. Conversely, any affine subspace L in R^n is a k-dimensional plane. We first note that, for any finite number of $x^i \in L$, we can follow the procedure adopted in the proof of Theorem 27.1 to prove that x in the form of (41.7) is contained in L. Now consider the number of elements of a set of affinely independent points in L. It cannot exceed $n+1$ because of Remark 1 above. Its maximum $k+1$ is attained by a certain set $\{x^0, x^1, ..., x^k\}$. The collection of all points x that are represented by the points in this set in the form of (41.7) is exactly L. It is obvious from this that the former is contained in L. Therefore, it suffices to show that any $x \in L$ can be expressed in the form of (41.7). Because of the way k was chosen, $\{x, x^0, x^1, ..., x^k\}$ is not affinely independent so that we can find coefficients $\beta, \beta_0, \beta_1, ..., \beta_k$, not all of which are 0, such that

$$\beta x + \sum_{i=0}^{k} \beta_i x^i = 0\,, \quad \beta + \sum_{i=0}^{k} \beta_i = 0\,.$$

If $\beta = 0$, we get $\beta_0 = \beta_1 = ... = \beta_k = 0$ because of the assumption of affine independence of $\{x^0, x^1, ..., x^k\}$. This is not consistent with the choice of the coefficients. Hence, $\beta \neq 0$. Divide both sides of the equations above by β and set $\alpha_i = -\beta_i/\beta$ $(i = 0, 1, ..., k)$ to get the expression (41.7).

Let $k+1$ be the maximum number of elements in sets of affinely independent points in a convex set $X\,(\neq \phi)$ in R^n. k is called the dimension of X and denoted by $\dim(X) = k$. Let a set of $k+1$ affinely independent points of X be $\{x^0, x^1, ..., x^k\}$. Then, we have the following theorem:

THEOREM 41.1. (i) *The k-dimensional plane $L(x^0, x^1, ..., x^k)$ generated by the simplex $\overline{x^0 x^1 ... x^k}$ includes X. It is the smallest affine subspace that includes X.*

(ii) *If X is compact, X and the simplex $\overline{x^0 x^1 ... x^k}$ are homeomorphic *. In this case, the topology of these two sets is considered in the relative topology ** that is induced in a natural manner by the topology of R^n*

Proof. (i) For any $x \in X$, the set $\{x, x^0, x^1, ..., x^k\}$ is not affinely independent by virtue of the definition of k. Following Remark 3 above, we see that

* See Section 13

** See Section 12.

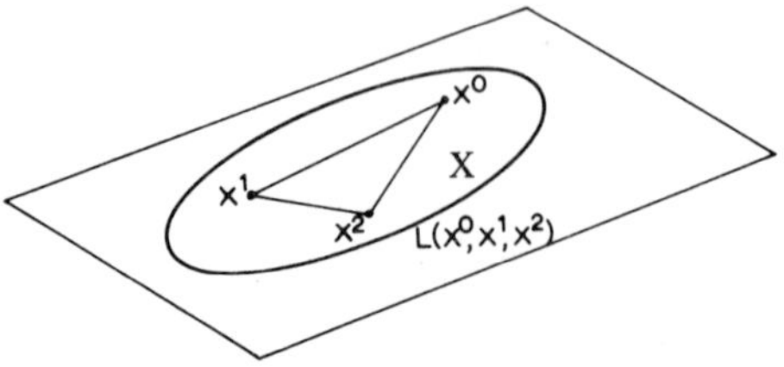

Fig. 41.3.

x can be expressed in the form of (41.7) so that $x \in L(x^0, x^1, ..., x^k)$, i.e. $X \subset L(x^0, x^1, ..., x^k)$. Now suppose that L is any affine subspace that includes X. As $L \ni x^i$ $(i = 0, 1, ..., k)$, L contains all points expressed in the form of (41.7) so that $L \supset L(x^0, x^1, ..., x^k)$. Hence, $L(x^0, x^1, ..., x^k)$ is the smallest affine subspace that includes X.

(ii) The proof is given in three steps.

(ii.a) Denote by α_i $(i = 1, 2, ..., k)$ the components of a point p in R^k. Consider a mapping

$$(41.8) \qquad p \to \varphi(p) = (1 - \sum_{i=1}^{k} \alpha_i) x^0 + \sum_{i=1}^{k} \alpha_i x^i : R^k \to L(x^0, x^1, ..., x^k) .$$

This mapping is obviously an affine mapping from R^k onto $L(x^0, x^1, ..., x^k)$. It is also continuous. As $x^0, x^1, ..., x^k$ are affinely independent, the lemma shows that $y^1, y^2, ..., y^k$ are linearly independent where $y^i = x^i - x^0$ $(i = 1, 2, ..., k)$. Therefore, they are extended to a basis of R^n, $\{y^1, y^2, ..., y^k, y^{k+1}, ..., y^n\}$ by virtue of Theorem 9.2. A point x in R^n is uniquely expanded into a linear combination of vectors of this basis. The coefficients of expansion $\alpha_i(x)$ $(i = 1, 2, ..., n)$ are continuous functions of x as we saw in Section 13, (2). Hence, we can write

$$(41.9) \qquad x - x^0 = \sum_{i=1}^{n} \alpha_i(x - x^0) y^i \quad (\text{for any } x \in R^n) .$$

Rearranging x^0 and recalling $y^i = x^i - x^0$ $(i = 1, 2, ..., k)$, we rewrite it as

$$(41.10) \qquad x = (1 - \sum_{i=1}^{k} \alpha_i(x - x^0))x^0 + \sum_{i=1}^{k} \alpha_i(x - x^0)x^i + \sum_{i=k+1}^{n} \alpha_i(x - x^0)y^i \, .$$

Noting that

$$x \in L(x^0, x^1, ..., x^k) \Leftrightarrow \alpha_i(x - x^0) = 0 \quad (i = k + 1, ..., n) \, ,$$

we find that a mapping

$$(41.11) \qquad x \to \psi(x) = \begin{bmatrix} \alpha_1(x - x^0) \\ \alpha_2(x - x^0) \\ \vdots \\ \alpha_k(x - x^0) \end{bmatrix} : L(x^0, x^1, ..., x^k) \to R^k$$

is a continuous inverse mapping of φ in (41.8).

Let the k unit points of R^k be

$$e^i = \begin{bmatrix} 0 \\ \vdots \\ 0 \\ 1 \\ 0 \\ \vdots \\ 0 \end{bmatrix} \quad (i = 1, 2, ..., k)$$

(where the first i entries, up to and including the 1, are marked by a brace labelled i)

and consider the k-dimensional simplex * $\overline{0e^1e^2...e^k}$. It is apparent that the two simplexes $\overline{0e^1e^2...e^k}$ and $\overline{x^0x^1..x^k}$ and the two sets $\varphi^{-1}(X)$ and X are both associated with each other under the mapping φ in a one-to-one way and continuously in both directions, and are homeomorphic. Thus, if it is demonstrated that $\varphi^{-1}(X)$ and $\overline{0e^1e^2...e^k}$ are homeomorphic by a homeomorphism θ, then X and $\overline{x^0x^1...x^k}$ are homeomorphic by the homeomorphism $\varphi\theta\varphi^{-1}: X \to \overline{x^0x^1...x^k}$.

(ii.b) In the second step, we investigate the properties of $\overline{0e^1e^2... e^k}$ and $\varphi^{-1}(X)$. We can easily see

$$\overline{0e^1e^2... e^k} = \{p | 1 \geqq \sum_{i=1}^{k} \alpha_i, \; \alpha_i \geqq 0 \quad (i = 1, 2, ..., k)\} \, .$$

* 0, e^1, e^2, ..., e^k are affinely independent.

It is a bounded closed set, i.e. a compact set *. We also have

$$(41.12)\qquad \overline{0e^1e^2...e^k} \supset \{p \mid 1 > \sum_{i=1}^{k} \alpha_i,\ \alpha_i > 0\ \ (i = 1, 2, ..., k)\},$$

whose right-hand side is a non-empty open set (in R^k). This is demonstrated as follows:

$k+1$ sets

$$G_0 = \{p \mid 1 > \sum_{i=1}^{k} \alpha_i\},\quad G_i = \{p \mid \alpha_i > 0\}\quad (i = 1, 2, ..., k)$$

are open sets ** so that

$$\bigcap_{i=0}^{k} G_i$$

is an open set by (ii) of Theorem 12.2. Obviously, this set is identical with the right-hand side of (41.12). It is not empty because it contains

$$p = \left(\frac{1}{k+1}, \frac{1}{k+1}, ..., \frac{1}{k+1}\right)'.$$

In other words, it has been shown that $\overline{0e^1e^2... e^k}$ is a compact convex set and contains an interior point (in R^k).

We now show that $\varphi^{-1}(X)$ has exactly the same properties. First, $\varphi^{-1}(X)$ is compact because X is compact and φ is a homeomorphism. As $X \supset \overline{x^0x^1...x^k}$, we get $\varphi^{-1}(X) \supset \varphi^{-1}(\overline{x^0x^1...x^k}) = \overline{0e^1e^2...e^k}$. Because $\overline{0e^1e^2...e^k}$ contains an interior point as we have seen above, $\varphi^{-1}(X)$ contains an interior point. It remains to prove that $\varphi^{-1}(X)$ is a convex set.

φ is an affine mapping so that

$$(41.13)\qquad \varphi(\lambda p + \mu q) = \lambda\varphi(p) + \mu\varphi(q)$$

where $p, q \in \varphi^{-1}(X)$, $\lambda \geqq 0$, $\mu \geqq 0$, $\lambda + \mu = 1$. Because $p, q \in \varphi^{-1}(X)$, we have $\varphi(p), \varphi(q) \in X$ so that $\lambda\varphi(p) + \mu\varphi(q) \in X$ because X is a convex set. By virtue of (41.13), $\varphi(\lambda p + \mu q) \in X$, i.e. $\lambda p + \mu q \in \varphi^{-1}(X)$. Thus, $\varphi^{-1}(X)$ is a convex set.

* See Theorem 14.6.

** $f_0(p) = \sum_{i=1}^{k} \alpha_i$, $f_i(p) = \alpha_i$ are continuous functions. We get $G_0 = \{p \mid f_0(p) < 1\}$, $G_i = \{p \mid f_i(p) > 0\}$. Therefore, G_i's are open sets as shown in Example 13.5.

(ii.c) A compact convex set in R^k that contains an interior point (in R^k) is called a *convex body*. The results of (ii.a) and (ii.b) show that (ii) can be proved by demonstrating that any pair of convex bodies in R^k are homeomorphic. All subsequent discussion refers to R^k.

Consider a sphere with its center at 0 and with a radius of one. The closed spherical neighborhood $\bar{U}(0, 1) = \{p \mid \|p\| \leqq 1\}$ is a convex body. Take it as the standard of reference. We now prove that any convex body Y and $\bar{U}(0, 1)$ are homeomorphic. Then, any pair of convex bodies are homeomorphic via $\bar{U}(0, 1)$. Select an interior point a of Y and keep it fixed. There always exists a boundary point of Y on any ray l starting from a. To see this, note that as l is a closed set and Y is compact, $l \cap Y$ is also compact so that the continuous function $l(y) = \|y - a\|$ attains a maximum on a certain point b in this set. Any point y satisfying $\|y - a\| > \|b - a\|$ is $y \notin Y$, however close it may be to b on l. Thus, b is a boundary point of Y. This demonstrates the existence of a boundary point on l, while Corollary 1 of Theorem 28.1 shows that there is no other boundary point on l.

Let Y^b represent the set of all boundary points of Y. Then, the result above indicates that $Y^b \neq \phi$ and $Y^b \not\ni a$. For any ray issuing at a, $Y^b \cap l \neq \phi$. Since we have $\|y - a\| > 0$ for any point y of Y^b, the mapping

$$g(y) = (y - a)/\|y - a\|$$

is a continuous mapping from Y^b into the boundary of $\bar{U}(0, 1)$, i.e. the sphere $C(0, 1) = \{p \mid \|p\| = 1\}$. Now it can be shown that this g is a one-to-one and bicontinuous mapping onto $C(0, 1)$. This can be seen as follows: for any $p \in C(0, 1)$, there exists one and only one point of Y^b on a ray l: $y = a + \lambda p$ $(\lambda \geqq 0)$ issuing at a, and it is mapped to p under g. There is no inverse image of p except on this ray. Hence, g: $Y^b \to C(0, 1)$ maps Y^b onto $C(0, 1)$ in a one-to-one way and continuously. We already learned in Section 28 that the boundary of any set is a closed set. Thus, Y^b is a closed set. As $Y^b \subset Y$ and Y is compact, we see that Y^b is compact. Then, from Theorem 14.5, we find that g is a homeomorphism. Take an inverse mapping of g, i.e. g^{-1}: $C(0, 1) \to Y^b$. g^{-1} maps homeomorphically the sphere $C(0, 1)$ that is the boundary of $\bar{U}(0. 1)$ onto the boundary Y^b of Y.

Next, we extend this g^{-1} from a boundary homeomorphism to a homeomorphism between $\bar{U}(0, 1)$ and Y. For this purpose, consider a mapping f: $\bar{U}(0, 1) \to Y$ defined by

$$f(p) = \begin{cases} a & (\text{for } p = 0) \\ (1 - \|p\|)\, a + \|p\|\, g^{-1}(p/\|p\|) & (\text{for } p \neq 0)\,. \end{cases} \tag{41.14}$$

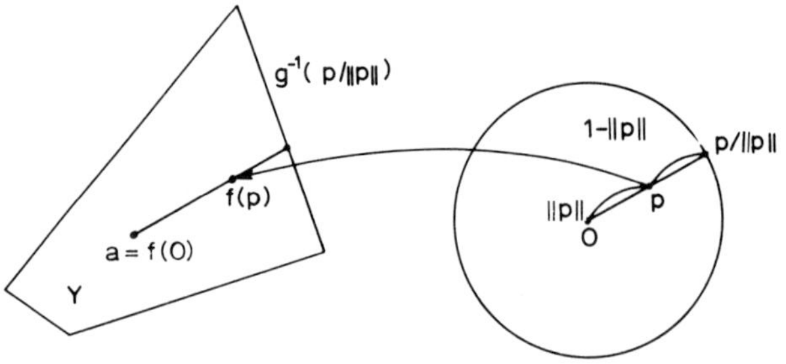

Fig. 41.4.

We can interprete $f(p)$ for $p \neq 0$ as follows: The segment connecting 0 and p meets the sphere at $p/\|p\|$ if extended in the direction of p, $f(p)$ is a convex linear combination of the images of 0 and $p/\|p\|$, i.e. the average of $f(0)$ and $g^{-1}(p/\|p\|)$ weighted by $1-\|p\| \geqq 0$ and $\|p\| > 0$ respectively. On the other hand, as Y is a convex set, we have $f(p) \in Y$. It is certainly continuous at $p \neq 0$ as (41.14) is composed of continuous mappings. If $\{p^\nu\}$ converges to 0, then $\|p^\nu\| \to 0$. Moreover, because $g^{-1}(p/\|p\|)$ is bounded, $f(p^\nu) \to a$ $(p^\nu \to 0)$. Thus, $f(p)$ is continuous at $p = 0$, too. Now it can be shown that the mapping (41.14) is a one-to-one mapping onto Y just like g^{-1} and that its inverse mapping, too, is continuous. It is very easy to see that the union of all segments $[a, y]$ with a and y as end points $(y \in Y^b)$ coincides with Y. It can also be easily verified that, for any $y \in Y^b$, $[a, y]$ and a segment $[0, g(y)]$ (in $\bar{U}(0, 1)$) are associated with each other in a one-to-one way under f. If $p \in C(0, 1)$ is $p \neq g(y)$, then $f([0, p])$ and $[a, y]$ share only a. This argument shows that the continuous mapping f is a one-to-one mapping from $\bar{U}(0, 1)$ onto Y. As $\bar{U}(0, 1)$ is compact, Theorem 14.5 again shows that f is a homeomorphism between $\bar{U}(0, 1)$ and Y. [Q.E.D.]

Remark 4. Let O be the set of those points for which the coefficients α_i (which are called *barycentric coordinates*) in a k-dimensional simplex (41.6) in R^n are all positive $\alpha_i > 0$ $(i = 0, 1, \ldots, k)$. O is the interior in $L(x^0, x^1, \ldots, x^k)$ of the simplex (41.6). Borrowing the tools used in the proof (ii.a) and (ii.b) of Theorem 41.1, we may clarify this property. R^k and $L(x^0, x^1, \ldots, x^k)$ are exactly associated with each other by the affine homeomorphism (41.8) so that the topological properties in $L(x^0, x^1, \ldots, x^k)$ are precisely transferred to R^k. It can easily be verified that the set $\varphi^{-1}(O)$ in R^k associated with O is nothing but the set on the right-hand side of (41.12) and that the latter is the interior of the simplex $0e^1e^2 \ldots e^k$.

Example 41.3. As we showed in Example 41.2, S_n is a simplex. We henceforth call it the *standard simplex.* The $(n-1)$-dimensional plane generated by S_n is the hyperplane

$$\sum_{j=1}^{n} x_j = 1 .$$

As S_n is included in this hyperplane, the interior of S_n (in R^n) is an empty set. However, the set

$$\{x \mid \sum_{j=1}^{n} x_j = 1,\ x_j > 0\ \ (j = 1, 2, \ldots, n)\} \neq \phi$$

is the interior of S_n in the relative topology of this hyperplane. We denote it by $S_n^{\square}$.

42. Simplicial subdivision

A simplex $x^{i_0}x^{i_1}\ldots x^{i_m}$ that is formed by some of the vertices $x^0, x^1, \ldots, x^k$ of a k-dimensional simplex (41.6) is called an m-dimensional *face simplex.* The number of such m-dimensional face simplexes is given by $\binom{k+1}{m+1}$, i.e. the number of combinations of $m+1$ vertices from a total of $k+1$ vertices.

A point in a k-dimensional simplex (41.6) whose barycentric coordinates are $\alpha_0 = \alpha_1 = \ldots = \alpha_k = 1/(k+1)$ is called the *barycenter.* In this section, we explain how to subdivide a simplex into a number of smaller simplexes by adding the barycenter as a new vertex. This is the method of *barycentric subdivision.*

(0) *0-dimensional simplexes.* A point x^0 cannot be subdivided any further. We consider that the barycentric subdivision has been completed as it is.

(1) *1-dimensional simplexes.* Take the barycenter y of $\overline{x^0x^1}$ as shown in fig. 42.1 and subdivide it into two 1-dimensional simplexes $\overline{x^0y}$ and $\overline{x^1y}$. In this case, it can be seen that 0-dimensional face simplexes x^0, y, x^1 (i.e. vertices) are face simplexes of one or two 1-dimensional derived simplexes (i.e. new simplexes created by the subdivision) $\overline{x^0y}$, $\overline{x^1y}$ depending on whether x^0, y and x^1 are on the boundary of $\overline{x^0x^1}$.

Now assume that the subdivision of $(k-1)$-dimensional simplexes has been completed in a manner, and proceed to that of k-dimensional simplexes.

(k) *k-dimensional simplexes.* Note that $k+1$ $(k-1)$-dimensional face simplexes of $S=\overline{x^0 x^1 \ldots x^k}$ have been subdivided into $k!$ $(k-1)$-dimensional derived simplexes by the inductive hypothesis. Take the barycenter y of S and form the convex hulls of these $(k-1)$-dimensional derived simplexes T and y. They are k-dimensional simplexes *. S can be subdivided into a total of $(k+1)!$ such k-dimensional derived simplexes. If a $(k-1)$-dimensional derived simplex of S lies completely on the boundary of S, then it forms a face simplex of exactly one k-dimensional derived simplex. Otherwise, it forms a face simplex of exactly two k-dimensional derived simplexes. To verify this fact, assume that it holds for $(k-1)$-dimensional simplexes. (Note that it holds for 0- and 1-dimensional simplexes). First, if a $(k-1)$-dimensional derived simplex T lies on the boundary of S, it is clear from the method of subdivision that only a k-dimensional derived simplex that forms the convex hull of the barycenter y and T has T as a face simplex. Other k-dimensional derived simplexes are not given this property.

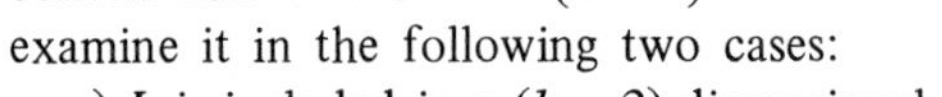

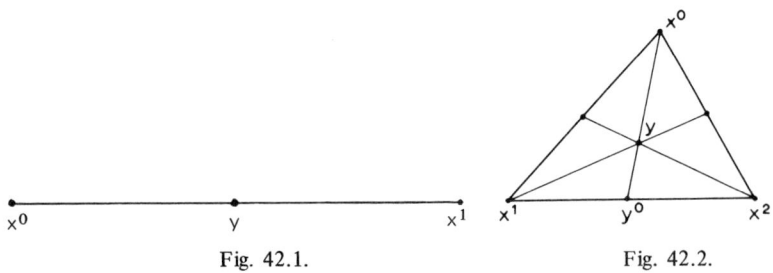

Fig. 42.1.

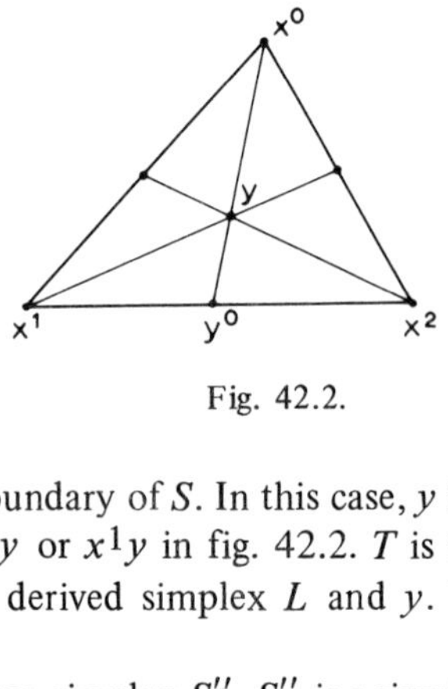

Fig. 42.2.

Next, suppose that T does not lie on the boundary of S. In this case, y is a vertex of T. It is illustrated by cases like $y^0 y$ or $x^1 y$ in fig. 42.2. T is the convex hull of a certain $(k-2)$-dimensional derived simplex L and y. We examine it in the following two cases:

a) L is included in a $(k-2)$-dimensional face simplex S''. S'' is a simplex generated by the $k-1$ vertices that are obtained by eliminating two vertices x^i and x^j from the $k+1$ vertices of S. Hence, S'' is included in exactly two $(k-1)$-dimensional face simplexes $C(S'', x^i)$ and $C(S'', x^j)$ and L lies on the respective boundaries of $C(S'', x^i)$ and $C(S'', x^j)$. Therefore, there exist exactly one derived simplex T_i of $C(S'', x^i)$ and another T_j of $C(S'', x^j)$ that include L in their face simplexes. (This is due to the inductive hypothesis.) $C(T_i, y)$ and $C(T_j, y)$ are the two k-dimensional derived simplexes that have T as a face simplex.

* y is not contained in the affine subspace generated by T.

b) L is included in no $(k-2)$-dimensional face simplex. In this case, L is included in a unique $(k-1)$-dimensional face simplex S' and yet does not lie on the boundary of S'. Hence, by the inductive hypothesis, just two $(k-1)$-dimensional derived simplexes T_i and T_j of S' have L as their face simplex. $C(T_i, y)$ and $C(T_j, y)$ are the two k-dimensional derived simplexes that have T as a face simplex.

νth barycentric subdivision. Each of the derived simplexes resulting from the barycentric subdivision of a k-dimensional simplex can again be barycentrically subdivided. The operation of repeating the barycentric subdivision ν times on a simplex is called the *νth barycentric subdivision.* Resulting derived simplexes are called *νth derived simplexes.*

THEOREM 42.1. *Suppose that the νth barycentric subdivision has been performed on a k-dimensional simplex S. A $(k-1)$-dimensional νth derived simplex, if it lies on the boundary of S, is a face simplex of exactly one k-dimensional νth derived simplex. If it does not lie on the boundary of S, it is a face simplex of exactly two k-dimensional νth derived simplexes.*

Proof. It was already demonstrated for $\nu = 1$. Suppose that the theorem holds for ν. We then prove it for $\nu + 1$.

Let $T^{(\nu+1)}$ be a $(k-1)$-dimensional $(\nu+1)$st derived simplex. We consider two cases.

a) $T^{(\nu+1)}$ is obtained as a subdivision of a $(k-1)$-dimensional νth derived simplex $T^{(\nu)}$. If $T^{(\nu+1)}$ lies on the boundary of S, so is $T^{(\nu)}$. By the inductive hypothesis, $T^{(\nu)}$ is a face simplex of exactly one k-dimensional νth derived simplex $S^{(\nu)}$. Let y be the barycenter of $S^{(\nu)}$. The simplex $C(T^{(\nu+1)}, y)$ is a unique k-dimensional $(\nu+1)$st derived simplex that has $T^{(\nu+1)}$ as a face simplex. On the other hand, if $T^{(\nu+1)}$ is not on the boundary of S, the same is true of $T^{(\nu)}$. By the inductive hypothesis, $T^{(\nu)}$ is a face simplex of exactly two k-dimensional νth derived simplexes $S_1^{(\nu)}$ and $S_2^{(\nu)}$. Let y^1 and y^2 be the barycenters of $S_1^{(\nu)}$ and $S_2^{(\nu)}$. Then, the simplexes $C(T^{(\nu+1)}, y^1)$ and $C(T^{(\nu+1)}, y^2)$ are exactly two k-dimensional $(\nu+1)$st derived simplexes that have $T^{(\nu+1)}$ as face simplexes.

b) When a) does not hold, $T^{(\nu+1)}$ is obtained by a subdivision of a k-dimensional νth derived simplex $S^{(\nu)}$. It contains the barycenter y of $S^{(\nu)}$ as a vertex. Hence, $T^{(\nu+1)}$ is not on the boundary of $S^{(\nu)}$ (nor on that of S) and exactly two k-dimensional derived simplexes of $S^{(\nu)}$, i.e. k-dimensional $(\nu+1)$st derived simplexes of S, have $T^{(\nu+1)}$ as a face simplex.

We define the *diameter* of a set X in R^n by

$$(42.1)\qquad \delta(X) = \sup d(x, y) \quad (\text{the supremum for all } x, y \in X)\,.$$

It is easily seen that the boundedness of X is equivalent to $\delta(X) < +\infty$. It is also clear from the definition that $X \supset Y$ implies $\delta(X) \geqq \delta(Y)$.

THEOREM 42.2. *The νth barycentric subdivision has been performed on a k-dimensional simplex S. Then, for any νth derived simplex $S^{(\nu)}$,*

$$(42.2)\qquad \delta(S^{(\nu)}) \leqq \left(\frac{k}{k+1}\right)^{\nu} \delta(S)\,.$$

Proof. It suffices to show that

$$(42.3)\qquad \delta(S^{(\nu+1)}) \leqq \frac{k}{k+1}\,\delta(S^{(\nu)}) \quad (\text{where } S^{(\nu+1)} \subset S^{(\nu)})$$

when ν is raised to $\nu+1$. (42.2) follows from (42.3). To prove (42.3), we need only to show that

$$(42.4)\qquad \delta(S^{(1)}) \leqq \frac{k}{k+1}\,\delta(S)$$

holds when a barycentric subdivision is performed once on any k-dimensional simplex.

(a) We begin our proof with demonstrating a formula

$$(42.5)\qquad \delta(\overline{x^{0}x^{1}\ldots x^{m}}) = \max_{0 \leqq i,j \leqq m} d(x^i, x^j)\,.$$

It is clear in (42.5) that the left-hand side $\geqq$ the right-hand side. As any a, $b \in \overline{x^{0}x^{1}\ldots x^{m}}$ are convex linear combinations of x^i, we get (α_i and β_j are coefficients of the convex linear combinations)

$$d(a, b) = \left\| \sum_{i=0}^{m} \alpha_i x^i - \sum_{j=0}^{m} \beta_j x^j \right\| = \left\| \sum_{i=0}^{m}\sum_{j=0}^{m} \alpha_i\beta_j x^i - \sum_{i=0}^{m}\sum_{j=0}^{m} \alpha_i\beta_j x^j \right\|$$

$$= \left\| \sum_{i,j=0}^{m} \alpha_i\beta_j (x^i - x^j) \right\| \leqq \sum_{i,j=0}^{m} \alpha_i\beta_j \|x^i - x^j\|$$

$$\leqq \max_{0 \leqq i,j \leqq m} d(x^i, x^j) \sum_{i,j=0}^{m} \alpha_i\beta_j = \max_{0 \leqq i,j \leqq m} d(x^i, x^j)\,.$$

Hence, the left-hand side $\leqq$ the right-hand side also holds in (42.5).

(b) We prove (42.4) by induction on k. For $k = 0$, it is clear from the definition of the barycentric subdivision of 0-dimensional simplexes that (42.4) holds. Now assume that (42.4) holds for simplexes of dimensions up to $k - 1$.

One of the vertices of $S^{(1)}$ is the barycenter

$$y = \frac{1}{k+1} \sum_{i=0}^{k} x^i$$

of S. Denote the remaining vertices by $y^1, y^2, \ldots, y^k$. Then, $S^{(1)} = \overline{yy^1y^2 \ldots y^k}$. $\overline{y^1y^2 \ldots y^k}$ is a simplex obtained by a barycentric subdivision of a $(k-1)$-dimensional face simplex T of S. Hence, by the inductive hypothesis, we get

$$\text{(42.6)} \qquad \max_{1 \leqq i,j \leqq k} d(y^i, y^j) = \delta(\overline{y^1y^2 \ldots y^k}) \leqq \frac{k-1}{k} \delta(T) \leqq \frac{k}{k+1} \delta(S) .$$

We also have

$$d(y, x^j) = \left\| \frac{1}{k+1} \sum_{i=0}^{k} x^i - x^j \right\| = \left\| \frac{1}{k+1} \sum_{i \neq j} (x^i - x^j) \right\|$$

$$\leqq \frac{1}{k+1} \sum_{i \neq j} \| x^i - x^j \| \leqq \frac{k}{k+1} \delta(S) .$$

Therefore, for any point a of S, i.e. for any convex linear combination of $x^0, x^1, \ldots, x^k$, we have $d(y, a) \leqq (k/(k+1))\delta(S)$ *. In particular, for $a = y^j$ $(j = 1, 2, \ldots, k)$, we have

$$\text{(42.7)} \qquad d(y, y^j) \leqq \frac{k}{k+1} \delta(S) .$$

Combining (42.6) and (42.7), we get (42.4).

43. Brouwer's fixed point theorem

As one of the important properties of convex sets, we now proceed to prove Brouwer's fixed point theorem given below **.

* As y is fixed, $d(y, x)$ is a convex function of x, which proves this statement.
** L.E.J.Brouwer (1881–1966): a Dutch mathematician.

THEOREM 43.1 (*Brouwer's fixed point theorem*). *Let X be a compact convex set in R^n. $f: X \to X$ is a continuous mapping that associates a point $f(x)$ of X with a point x of X. Then, there exists a fixed point $\hat{x} = f(\hat{x})$.*

This theorem may be proved on an advanced level of topology, but we introduce here an elementary and well-known proof by Knaster, Kuratowski and Mazurkiewicz. Their proof makes use of Sperner's lemma that is to be given below. Let us first give a preliminary observation.

Let $\dim(X) = k$. Then, X and a k-dimensional simplex S are homeomorphic by virtue of (ii) of Theorem 41.1. Further, S and the standard simplex S_{k+1} in R^{k+1} are homeomorphic. X and S_{k+1} are, therefore, homeomorphic by a homeomorphism $g: S_{k+1} \to X$. Suppose the theorem holds in S_{k+1}. Then, as the composed mapping $g^{-1}fg$ continuously sends points p of S_{k+1} to points $g^{-1}[f\{g(p)\}]$ of S_{k+1}, there exists a fixed point $\hat{p} \in S_{k+1}$ such that $\hat{p} = g^{-1}[f\{g(\hat{p})\}]$. From this, we get $g(\hat{p}) = f\{g(\hat{p})\}$ so that $\hat{x} = g(\hat{p}) \in X$ is a fixed point of f, i.e. $\hat{x} = f(\hat{x})$. Hence, it suffices to prove the theorem for the standard simplex.

We now show Sperner's lemma that is required for the proof of the theorem above.

LEMMA (*Sperner's lemma*). *The νth barycentric subdivision has been performed on a simplex $S = \overline{x^0 x^1 ... x^k}$. Assign to each vertex y of this simplicial subdivision one of the vertices $x^0, x^1, ..., x^k$ of S, which is denoted by $\sigma(y)$, in such a way that $\sigma(y)$ is a vertex of a face simplex including y and of the lowest dimension (of the original S). Then, for a k-dimensional νth derived simplex $S^{(\nu)} = \overline{y^0 y^1 ... y^k}$ in general, not all of $\sigma(y^o), \sigma(y^1), ..., \sigma(y^k)$ may be different from each other. But there exists at least one and, more exactly, an odd number of νth derived simplexes such that in particular $\sigma(y^i) \neq \sigma(y^j)$ $(i \neq j)$.*

Proof. The proof is by induction on k. It is obvious for $k = 0$. Therefore, we can proceed to proving the general case. But to illuminate a crucial point of the proof, let us examine the case of $k = 1$.

When $k = 1$, $S = \overline{x^0 x^1}$ is a segment $[x^0, x^1]$. The subdivision is equivalent to setting up dividing points on this segment. Because of the assumed assignment of vertices $y \to \sigma(y)$, we have $\sigma(x^o) = x^o$ and $\sigma(x^1) = x^1$. This is due to the fact that the face simplexes of S including x^0 and x^1 and of the lowest dimension are respectively x^0 and x^1 themselves. On the other hand, the face simplex of S including a new vertex y created by the subdivision (like the point y in fig. 43.2) and of the lowest dimension is S itself. Hence, $\sigma(y)$ is either x^0 or x^1. Now suppose we check the value of $\sigma(y)$ while moving from

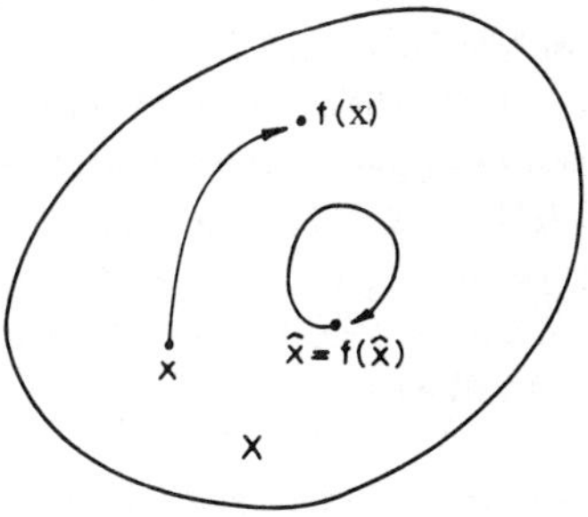

Fig. 43.1.

Fig. 43.2.

left to right in fig. 43.2. We keep on moving so long as $\sigma(y) = x^{0}$. As $\sigma(x^1) = x^1$ eventually, we come across a vertex at which $\sigma(y) = x^1$ for the first time. Denote this vertex by b and its closest left-hand vertex by a. Then, the derived simplex $\overline{ab}$ is what we have been looking for. The number of such derived simplexes as this one is equal to the number of times that the value of $\sigma(y)$ changes from x^{0} to x^1 or x^1 to x^{0}. The number is obviously odd.

Now suppose that the theorem holds for all dimensions lower than k. We shall prove that it holds for k. For the sake of simplicity, let us call a νth derived simplex a d-simplex. Unless otherwise noted in what follows, simplexes and d-simplexes are all k-dimensional and face simplexes and derived face simplexes are all $(k-1)$-dimensional.

When $\sigma(y^i) \neq \sigma(y^j)$ $(i \neq j)$, the d-simplex $S' = \overline{y^{0}y^{1}...y^{k}}$ is called a regular d-simplex. When $\sigma(z^i) \neq x^k$ $(i = 0, 1, ..., k-1)$ and $\sigma(z^i) \neq \sigma(z^j)$ $(i \neq j)$, the $(k-1)$-dimensional d-simplex $T' = \overline{z^{0}z^{1}...z^{k-1}}$ is called a regular face d-simplex. Let

λ = the number of regular d-simplexes,

μ = the number of regular face d-simplexes on the boundary of S,

$\mu(S')$ = the number of regular face d-simplexes that are face simplexes of the d-simplex S'.

Then, what we have to prove is that λ is an odd number.

First, check the value of $\mu(S')$. If S' is regular, the vertices of a unique face simplex of S' are mapped by σ to $x^{0}, x^1, ..., x^{k-1}$. This is because vertices of other face simplexes include some vertex associated with x^k. Hence, $\mu(S') = 1$

in this case. If S' is not regular, there is a vertex among the $k+1$ vertices $x^0, x^1, \ldots, x^k$ that is not the image of the vertices of S'. If such a vertex is found among $x^0, x^1, \ldots, x^{k-1}$, then obviously $\mu(S') = 0$. In other cases, renumbering the vertices of S' in an appropriate manner, we can let $S' = \overline{y^0 y^1 \ldots y^k}$, $\sigma(y^i) = x^i$ $(i = 0, 1, \ldots, k-1)$, $\sigma(y^k) = x^j$ (for some j, $0 \leqq j \leqq k-1$). Hence, there are a total of two regular face d-simplexes, i.e. $\overline{y^0 y^1 \ldots y^{k-1}}$ and the one that replaces the vertex y^j of this simplex by y^k. Then, $\mu(S') = 2$. We summarize these results as follows:

(43.1) $\qquad \lambda \equiv \sum \mu(S') \pmod 2$ (the sum over all d-simplexes S') *.

(43.1) is the sum of the numbers of regular face d-simplexes, but there is a double counting. Theorem 42.1 shows that a regular face d-simplex is a face simplex of a unique d-simplex if it lies on the boundary of S and that of two d-simplexes if it does not. Hence,

(43.2) $\qquad \mu \equiv \sum \mu(S') \pmod 2$ (the sum over all d-simplexes S') .

Then, from (43.1) and (43.2), we get

(43.3) $\qquad \lambda \equiv \mu \pmod 2$.

If T' is a regular face d-simplex and if it is on the boundary of S, then it must be on $T = \overline{x^0 x^1 \ldots x^{k-1}}$, a face simplex of S. This is because at least one of $x^0, x^1, \ldots, x^{k-1}$ is not included in the images of the vertices of T' if T' lies on another face simplex. In short, a regular face d-simplex of S on the boundary is identical with a $(k-1)$-dimensional regular d-simplex of the $(k-1)$-dimensional simplex T. Thus, by restricting the correspondence $y \to \sigma(y)$ on T, we see that it satisfies the correspondence rule given earlier. Hence, the number of regular d-simplexes of T, i.e. μ, is seen to be odd by the inductive hypothesis. Thus, λ is an odd number because of (43.3).

The proof of the fixed point theorem. As we already noted, it suffices to prove the theorem when X is a standard simplex

$$S_{k+1} = \{p \mid p \geqq 0, \sum_{i=0}^{k} p_i = 1\}.$$

* $\alpha \equiv \beta \pmod 2$ means that $\alpha - \beta$ is an even number.

Let f be a continuous mapping that sends each point p of S_{k+1} to a point $f(p) = (f_0(p), f_1(p), ..., f_k(p))' \geqq 0$,

$$\sum_{i=0}^{k} f_i(p) = 1$$

of S_{k+1}. Now form $k+1$ closed sets

$$F_i = \{ p \mid p \in S_{k+1},\ p_i \geqq f_i(p)\} \quad (i = 0, 1, ..., k) . \tag{43.4}$$

As f_i's are continuous functions, F_i's in (43.4) are closed sets.

For this family of closed set $\{F_i\}$, we have

$$T \subset F_{i_0} \cup F_{i_1} \cup ... \cup F_{i_m} \tag{43.5}$$

where T is any face simplex $\overline{e^{i_0}e^{i_1}...e^{i_m}}$ of S_{k+1}, which is the simplex $\overline{e^0e^1...e^k}$ with unit vectors e^i as its vertices. This can be seen as follows: points p of T always satisfy $p_{i_0} + p_{i_1} + ... + p_{i_m} = 1$. If $p \notin F_{i_t}$ $(t = 0, 1, ..., m)$, we get $p_{i_t} < f_{i_t}(p)$ for all t so that, summing up, we have

$$1 < \sum_{t=0}^{m} f_{i_t}(p) \leqq \sum_{i=0}^{k} f_i(p) ,$$

which is a contradiction. Hence, (43.5) holds.

Now perform a νth barycentric subdivision on S_{k+1} and cover it with a mesh of d-simplexes. Let $T = \overline{e^{i_0}e^{i_1}...e^{i_m}}$ be the face simplex of the lowest dimension including a vertex y of a νth d-simplex. Then, as (43.5) holds, there always exists one F_{i_t} among $F_{i_0}, F_{i_1}, ..., F_{i_m}$ that contains y. Choosing such an F_{i_t}, define $\sigma(y) = e^{i_t}$ by assigning e^{i_t} with y. This assignment $y \to \sigma(y)$ obviously satisfies the conditions of the lemma because of the way it was formulated, so that there exists a regular νth d-simplex $S^{(\nu)}$. Renumbering the vertices of $S^{(\nu)}$ in an appropriate manner, we may put $S^{(\nu)} = \overline{y^0y^1...y^k}$, $y^i \in F_i$ $(i = 0, 1, ..., k)$.

Let

$$S^{(\nu)} = \overline{y^{0\nu}y^{1\nu}...y^{k\nu}},\ y^{i\nu} \in F_i \quad (i = 0, 1, ..., k) \tag{43.6}$$

represent such a νth regular d-simplex as the above one that corresponds to the νth barycentric subdivision ($\nu = 1, 2, ...$). Then, by Theorem 42.2, we get

$$\max_{0 \leqq i,j \leqq k} d(y^{i\nu}, y^{j\nu}) = \delta(S^{(\nu)}) \leqq \left(\frac{k}{k+1}\right)^{\nu} \delta(S_{k+1}) . \tag{43.7}$$

Its right-hand side converges to 0 as $\nu \to \infty$ so that its left-hand side converges to 0, too. Because S_{k+1} is compact, appropriate subsequences $\{y^{i\nu'}\}$ (ν' represents a subsequence of integers that is common to all i) of $k + 1$ sequences of points $\{y^{i\nu}\}$ ($i = 0, 1, \ldots, k$) converge to p^i respectively. As F_i is a closed set and $\{y^{i\nu'}\}$ converges to p^i in F_i. we have $p^i \in F_i$. On the other hand,

$$\max_{0 \leqq i,j \leqq k} d(y^{i\nu}, y^{j\nu}) \to 0 \quad (\nu \to \infty),$$

the limits p^i must be a common $\hat{p}$. Hence, $\hat{p} = p^i \in F_i$ ($i = 0, 1, \ldots, k$). By definition, $\hat{p}_i \geqq f_i(\hat{p})$ ($i = 0, 1, \ldots, k$). Hence, we have $\hat{p}_i = f_i(\hat{p})$ for all i because of

$$\sum_{i=0}^{k} \hat{p}_i = \sum_{i=0}^{k} f_i(\hat{p}) = 1.$$

Namely, $\hat{p}$ is a fixed point of f. [Q.E.D.]

Brouwer's fixed point theorem is very important and useful. In direct or extended forms, it has been applied to prove many existence theorems in mathematics. Our major objective in this book is to apply this theorem to the existence problem of a competitive equilibrium. However, before closing this section, we give an illustration of its direct application.

Application to the existence proof of the Frobenius root *. Let A be a non-negative square matrix of the nth order. Suppose we have come to the second step in the proof as outlined in Remark 2 in Section 17. Let S_n be the standard simplex and $\Omega = \{x \mid x \in S_n, Ax \geqq \lambda x\}$, $\lambda = \lambda(A)$. Then, Ω is a non-empty compact convex subset of S_n. Form a continuous mapping f: $\Omega \to S_n$ according to a formula $f(x) = \rho(x)(I + A)x$,

$$\rho(x) = 1 / \left(1 + \sum_{i,j=1}^{n} a_{ij} x_j\right)$$

(where I is the unit matrix of the nth order). If $x \in \Omega$, then $Af(x) = \rho(x)(I + A)Ax \geqq \rho(x)(I + A)\lambda x = \lambda\rho(x)(I + A)x = \lambda f(x)$ so that $f(x) \in \Omega$. Hence, by Brouwer's fixed point theorem, there exists a fixed point $\hat{x} = f(\hat{x}) = \rho(\hat{x})(I + A)\hat{x}$. Considering how the value of $\rho(x)$ is defined, we get $\lambda\hat{x} = A\hat{x}$,

$$\lambda = \sum_{i,j=1}^{n} a_{ij} \hat{x}_j$$

* See ref. [4], pp. 480–481.

after simple calculations. It may be noted that $\rho(x)$ appears in the definition of the mapping f in order to ensure $f(x) \in S_n$.

44. Kakutani's fixed point theorem

When extended to multi-valued or point-to-set mappings, Brouwer's theorem is generalized into a form very convenient for applications. This is Kakutani's theorem *, the essence of which was discovered by von Neumann **.

Closed mappings. We begin with explaining the concept of continuity of a point-to-set mapping. Let X and Y be two sets in (identical or different) R^n. Y is assumed to be compact. Of course, $X, Y \neq \phi$. Suppose that there is a point-to-set mapping $f: X \to Y$ that associates a non-empty subset $f(x)$ of Y with a point x of X. The subset in the cartesian product $X \times Y$

$$(44.1) \qquad G_f = \{(x, y) \mid y \in f(x),\ x \in X,\ y \in Y\}$$

is called the *graph* of the mapping f. This is a natural extension of the ordinary concept of the graph of a single-valued mapping.

When G_f is a closed set in $X \times Y$, i.e. when $y \in f(x)$ if $\lim\limits_{\nu\to\infty} x^\nu = x$, $\lim\limits_{\nu\to\infty} y^\nu = y$, $y^\nu \in f(x^\nu)$ $(\nu = 1, 2, ...)$ ***, the mapping $f: X \to Y$ is called a *closed mapping.*

We noted earlier in Section 12 that the concept of a closed set is a concept relative to the topological space that includes this set. Thus, the concept of a closed mapping is one relative to the sets X and Y because it is defined in reference to the fact that its graph is a closed set. Therefore, for a precise statement, we must say that "the point-to-set mapping $f: X \to Y$ is closed". But when the domain X and the range Y are self-evident, we need not be so precise.

If f is closed, then the image $f(x)$ of each point x is compact. To see this, it suffices to show that $f(x)$ is a closed set in Y because Y is compact †. Let $y^\nu \in f(x)$, $\lim\limits_{\nu\to\infty} y^\nu = y \in Y$. Take a sequence of points $x^\nu = x$ $(\nu = 1, 2, ...)$. Of course, $\lim\limits_{\nu\to\infty} x^\nu = x$. By the definition of a closed mapping, we get $y \in f(x)$ so that $f(x)$ is a closed set.

* See Kakutani [37].

** See von Neumann [42].

*** See Section 28 for the definition of convergence in cartesian products.

† See Theorem 14.3.

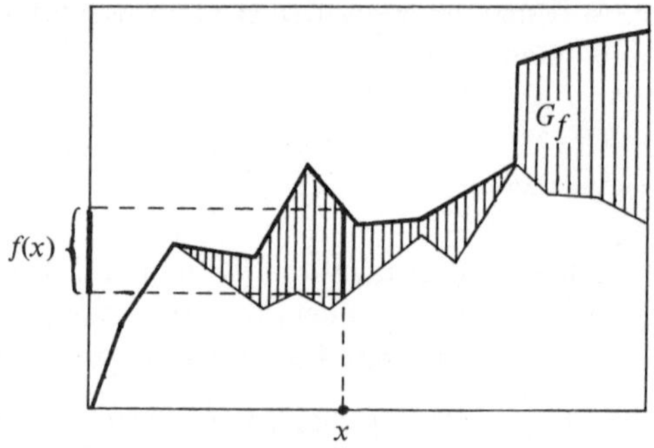

Fig. 44.1.

Now let us recall the Cauchy condition on the continuity of a single-valued mapping in Theorem 13.1. We now give a broader interpretation to the Cauchy condition in order to apply it to a point-to-set mapping. For this purpose, define the ϵ-neighborhood $U(A, \epsilon)$ of a set A by

$$(44.2) \qquad U(A, \epsilon) = \{x \mid d(x, A) < \epsilon\}$$

in a manner analogous to the ϵ-neighborhood of a point. Here, $d(x, A)$ represents the distance of the point x and the set A. As $U(A, \epsilon) = \bigcup_{a \in A} U(a, \epsilon)$, (44.2) is an open set.

Let a point-to-set mapping be given by $f: X \to Y$. If, for any ϵ-neighborhood $U(f(a), \epsilon)$ of the image $f(a)$ of $a \in X$, such an appropriate δ-neighborhood $U(a, \delta)$ of a is determined that $f(x) \subset U(f(a), \epsilon)$ for $x \in U(a, \delta)$, the mapping f is said to be *upper semi-continuous* at $x = a$.

LEMMA 1. *On this assumption, if $f: X \to Y$ is a closed mapping, it is upper semi-continuous at every point $a \in X$.*

Proof. We show that a contradiction results from the assumption that there exists no such δ-neighborhood of a in the definition of upper semi-continuity. Then, there exists x^ν in the $1/\nu$-neighborhood $U(a, 1/\nu)$ ($\nu = 1, 2, 3, \ldots$) of a such that $f(x^\nu) \not\subset U(f(a), \epsilon)$. One can select points $y^\nu \in Y$ such that $y^\nu \in f(x^\nu)$, $y^\nu \notin U(f(a), \epsilon)$. As Y is compact, some subsequence $\{y^{\nu'}\}$ of the sequence of points $\{y^\nu\}$ converges. Denote its limit by b. Then, as $\lim_{\nu' \to \infty} x^{\nu'} = a$, $\lim_{\nu' \to \infty} y^{\nu'} = b$, $y^{\nu'} \in f(x^{\nu'})$, we must have $b \in f(a)$ by the definition of a closed mapping. On the other hand, as $y^{\nu'} \notin U(f(a), \epsilon)$, we see $d(b, y^{\nu'}) \geqq$

ϵ (for all ν'). Thus, letting $\nu' \to \infty$, we get $d(b, b) \geqq \epsilon$ by the continuity property. This is a contradiction. [Q.E.D.]

A set of a finite number of points $\{a^i | i = 1, 2, ..., s\}$ in a metric space X is called an *ϵ-net* if the union of the ϵ-neighborhoods $U(a^i, \epsilon)$ of a^i includes X, i.e.

$$(44.3) \quad X \subset U(a^1, \epsilon) \cup U(a^2, \epsilon) \cup ... \cup U(a^s, \epsilon) .$$

LEMMA 2. *If X is compact, there exists an ϵ-net for any $\epsilon > 0$.*

Proof. We derive a contradiction by denying the existence of an ϵ-net. Form a sequence of points $\{a^\nu\}$ according to the following procedure: Choose $a^1 \in X$ arbitrarily. Then, as no ϵ-net is assumed to exist, $X \subset U(a^1, \epsilon)$ does not hold. Therefore, there exists a point a^2 in X such that $a^2 \notin U(a^1, \epsilon)$. Again as $X \subset U(a^1, \epsilon) \cup U(a^2, \epsilon)$ does not hold, there exists a point a^3 in X such that $a^3 \notin U(a^1, \epsilon) \cup U(a^2, \epsilon)$. Repeating this procedure and keeping the assumption that no ϵ-net exists, we get a sequence of points $\{a^\nu\}$ such that

$$(44.4) \quad a^{\nu+1} \notin U(a^1, \epsilon) \cup U(a^2, \epsilon) \cup ... \cup U(a^\nu, \epsilon) \quad (\nu = 1, 2, ...) ,$$

which shows that this sequence of points satisfies $d(a^\mu, a^\nu) \geqq \epsilon$ (for any μ and ν $(\mu \neq \nu)$). Then, no subsequence of the sequence $\{a^\nu\}$ converges. This is in contradiction with the compactness of X. [Q.E.D.]

With these preliminary observations, we now introduce Kakutani's theorem.

THEOREM 44.1 *(Kakutani's fixed point theorem). Let X be a compact, convex set in R^n and f: $X \to X$ a closed mapping that associates a non-empty convex subset $f(x)$ in X with a point x in X. Then, there exists a fixed point $\hat{x} \in f(\hat{x})$* *.

Proof **. As X is compact, there exists a δ-net $\{a^{\delta i} | i = 1, 2, ..., s_\delta\}$ for any $\delta > 0$ (due to Lemma 2). The number s_δ depends on δ. Now define s_δ continuous functions

$$(44.5) \quad \theta_i^\delta(x) = \max\,[0, \delta - d(x, a^{\delta i})] \quad (i = 1, 2, ..., s_\delta)$$

* A fixed point is defined in this manner because $f(x)$ is a set.

** Based on Nikaido [43] that made more concise the logic given in von Neumann [42].

on X. Then, $\theta_i^\delta(x) \geqq 0$. By the definition of the δ-net for each $x \in X$, we always have $d(x, a^{\delta i}) < \delta$ for some i, i.e. $\theta_i^\delta(x) > 0$. Hence,

$$\sum_{i=1}^{s_\delta} \theta_i^\delta(x) > 0$$

everywhere. Thus, we get s_δ continuous functions

$$(44.6) \qquad w_i^\delta(x) = \theta_i^\delta(x) \bigg/ \sum_{j=1}^{s_\delta} \theta_j^\delta(x) \quad (i = 1, 2, \ldots, s_\delta)\,.$$

As $w_i^\delta(x) \geqq 0$ and

$$\sum_{i=1}^{s_\delta} w_i^\delta(x) = 1\,,$$

we can use them as the coefficients of a convex linear combination. Then, we can form a single-valued continuous mapping

$$(44.7) \qquad g_\delta(x) = \sum_{i=1}^{s_\delta} w_i^\delta(x)\, b^{\delta i}$$

that maps a point x in X to a point $g_\delta(x)$ in X, where $b^{\delta i}$ is a point arbitrarily chosen from among points in $f(a^{\delta i})$. As $g_\delta(x)$ is a convex linear combination of $b^{\delta i}$ with the weights $w_i^\delta(x)$, we have $g_\delta(x) \in X$. (44.7) is called a *Kuratowski-type mapping.* g_δ continuously maps each point of X to a point of X, and X is a compact, convex set. Hence, by Brouwer's theorem, there exists a fixed point

$$(44.8) \qquad x^\delta = g_\delta(x^\delta)\,.$$

As X is compact, points x^{δ_ν} that satisfy (44.8) for an appropriate sequence of positive numbers $\{\delta_\nu\}$ fulfilling $\lim_{\nu\to\infty} \delta_\nu = 0$ converge to a point $\hat{x}$ in X. We shall demonstrate that this $\hat{x}$ is a fixed point $\hat{x} \in f(\hat{x})$.

As f is a closed mapping, it is upper semi-continuous at $\hat{x}$ by Lemma 1. In other words, for any ϵ-neighborhood $U(f(\hat{x}), \epsilon)$ of $f(\hat{x})$ there exists such a δ-neighborhood $U(\hat{x}, \delta)$ that $f(x) \subset U(f(\hat{x}), \epsilon)$ for $x \in U(\hat{x}, \delta)$.

After these preliminary observations, we set $\delta_\nu < \delta/2$ and $d(\hat{x}, x^{\delta_\nu}) < \delta/2$ by letting ν sufficiently large. In view of the way of choosing x^{δ_ν} according

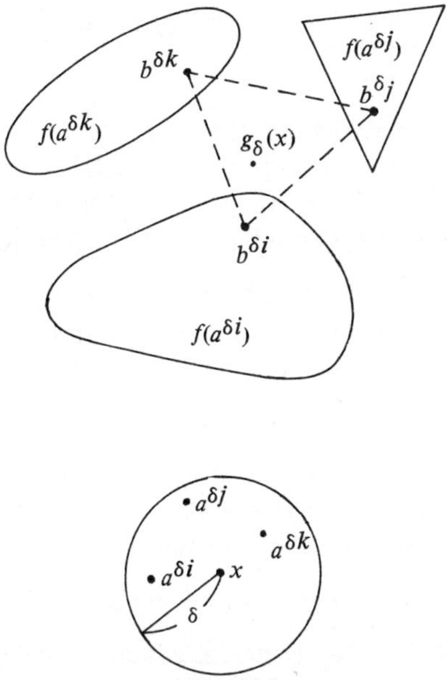

Fig. 44.2

to (44.8), we get

(44.9) $$x^{\delta_\nu} = g_{\delta_\nu}(x^{\delta_\nu}) = \sum_{i-1}^{s_{\delta_\nu}} w_i^{\delta_\nu}(x^{\delta_\nu})\, b^{\delta_\nu i}\,.$$

If $w_i^{\delta_\nu}(x^{\delta_\nu}) > 0$, then $d(x^{\delta_\nu}, a^{\delta_\nu i}) < \delta_\nu < \delta/2$ so that

$$d(\hat{x}, a^{\delta_\nu i}) \leqq d(\hat{x}, x^{\delta_\nu}) + d(x^{\delta_\nu}, a^{\delta_\nu i}) < \delta/2 + \delta/2 = \delta.$$

I.e., if $w_i^{\delta_\nu}(x^{\delta_\nu}) > 0$, then $a^{\delta_\nu i} \in U(\hat{x}, \delta)$. For such an index i, we have $b^{\delta_\nu i} \in f(a^{\delta_\nu i}) \subset U(f(\hat{x}), \epsilon)$ so that x^{δ_ν} is a convex linear combination of points in the convex set* $U(f(\hat{x}), \epsilon)$, i.e. $x^{\delta_\nu} \in U(f(\hat{x}), \epsilon)$. Letting $\nu \to \infty$, $\hat{x} = \lim_{\nu\to\infty} x^{\delta_\nu} \in \overline{U(f(\hat{x}), \epsilon)}$, which holds for any $\epsilon > 0$. Therefore,

(44.10) $$d(\hat{x}, U(f(\hat{x}), \epsilon)) = 0 \quad \text{(for any } \epsilon > 0) \,.$$

* If A is convex, $U(A, \epsilon)$ is convex. For we can write $U(A, \epsilon) = A + U(0, \epsilon)$ (vectorial sum) where A and $U(0, \epsilon)$ are both convex.

(44.10) implies that for any $\epsilon > 0$, $\epsilon' > 0$ there exists z that satisfies $d(\hat{x}, z) < \epsilon'$, $d(z, f(\hat{x})) < \epsilon$. Thus *,

$$d(\hat{x}, f(\hat{x})) \leqq d(\hat{x}, z) + d(z, f(\hat{x})) < \epsilon' + \epsilon .$$

As ϵ' and ϵ are arbitrary, $d(\hat{x}, f(\hat{x})) = 0$, i.e. $\hat{x} \in \overline{f(\hat{x})}$. We saw that $f(\hat{x})$ is a closed set in X. Hence, $\overline{f(\hat{x})} = f(\hat{x})$ so that $\hat{x} \in \overline{f(\hat{x})} = f(\hat{x})$. [Q.E.D.]

Operations on mappings. It often becomes necessary in actual applications of Kakutani's theorem to compound a number of given mappings into a new mapping. What follows gives some useful methods for this purpose.

(1) *Composition of mappings*

(i) Let $x \to f(x): X \to Y$ be a single-valued continuous mapping and $y \to g(y): Y \to Z$ a point-to-set mapping that is closed. Then, the composed mapping $x \to g(f(x)): X \to Z$ is a closed mapping.

Proof. Let $\lim_{\nu\to\infty} x^\nu = x$, $\lim_{\nu\to\infty} z^\nu = z$, $z^\nu \in g(f(x^\nu))$. Then, by virtue of the continuity of f, $\lim_{\nu\to\infty} f(x^\nu) = f(x)$. Hence, as g is closed, $z \in g(f(x))$. [Q.E.D.]

(ii) Let $x \to f(x): X \to Y$ (Y is compact) be a closed point-to-set mapping and $y \to g(y): Y \to Z$ a single-valued continuous mapping. Then, the composed mapping $x \to g(f(x)): X \to Z$ is a closed mapping.

Proof. Let $\lim_{\nu\to\infty} x^\nu = x$, $\lim_{\nu\to\infty} z^\nu = z$, $z^\nu \in g(f(x^\nu))$. There exists some $y^\nu \in f(x^\nu)$ such that $z^\nu = g(y^\nu)$. As Y is compact, we can assume that $\{y^\nu\}$ converges and $\lim_{\nu\to\infty} y^\nu = y$ as usual. Then, first, we have $z = g(y)$ because of the continuity of g. On the other hand, $y \in f(x)$ as f is a closed mapping. Combining all these together, we see $z \in g(f(x))$ and $x \to g(f(x))$ is a closed mapping. [Q.E.D.]

(2) *Cartesian product of mappings.* Construct a *cartesian product*

$$f(x) = f^1(x) \times f^2(x) \times \ldots \times f^s(x) ,$$

$$x \to f(x): X \to Y_1 \times Y_2 \times \ldots \times Y_s \equiv Y$$

* For a set A and any two points a and b, we have $d(a, A) \leqq d(a, b) + d(b, A)$. $\because$ For any $\epsilon > 0$ there exists $x \in A$ that satisfies $d(b, x) < d(b, A) + \epsilon$ so that $d(a, A) \leqq d(a, x) \leqq d(a, b) + d(b, x) \leqq d(a, b) + d(b, A) + \epsilon$. The arbitrariness of ϵ yields the result above.

out of s closed point-to-set mappings $x \to f^i(x)$: $X \to Y_i$ $(i = 1, 2, ..., s)$. This is also a closed mapping.

Proof. Let $y, y^\nu \in Y$, $\lim_{\nu\to\infty} y^\nu = y$, $x, x^\nu \in X$, $\lim_{\nu\to\infty} x^\nu = x$, $y^\nu \in f(x^\nu)$. Then, $y = (y^1, y^2, ..., y^s)$, $y^\nu = (y^{1\nu}, y^{2\nu}, ..., y^{s\nu})$, y^i, $y^{i\nu} \in Y_i$, $\lim_{\nu\to\infty} y^{i\nu} = y^i$, $y^{i\nu} \in f^i(x^\nu)$. As each f^i is a closed mapping, we have $y^i \in f^i(x)$, i.e. $y \in f(x)$. Thus, $x \to f(x)$ is closed. [Q.E.D.]

(3) *Linear combination of mappings.* Given closed point-to-set mappings: $x \to f^i(x)$: $X \to Y_i$ (Y_i are compact sets in the same R^n) and real numbers λ_i, the mapping

$$x \to h(x) = \sum_{i=1}^{s} \lambda_i f^i(x):\ X \to \sum_{i=1}^{s} \lambda_i Y_i$$

that is a *linear combination* of them is closed.

Proof. The cartesian product mapping of f^i,

$$x \to f(x) = f^1(x) \times f^2(x) \times ... \times f^s(x):\ X \to \prod_{i=1}^{s} Y_i$$

(cartesian product of Y_i) is a closed mapping as shown in (2) above. On the other hand, the linear mapping

$$g(y^1, y^2, ..., y^s) = \sum_{i=1}^{s} \lambda_i y^i:\ \prod_{i=1}^{s} Y_i \to \sum_{i=1}^{s} \lambda_i Y_i$$

is single-valued and continuous. Now we note that $h(x) = g(f(x))$ and that the range of f, i.e.

$$\prod_{i=1}^{s} Y_i\,,$$

is compact *. Because of (ii) in (1) above, one sees that $x \to h(x)$ is a closed mapping. [Q.E.D.]

* See Theorem 28.3, (i).

We give below an application that illustrates how useful Kakutani's theorem is and how to apply it. This is its application to the proof of the minimax theorem on rectangular games. Kakutani's theorem was originally inspired by this.

Application to the minimax theorem. We employ Kakutani's fixed point theorem to prove that the payoff function $K(p, q) = (p, Aq)$ of (34.9) has a saddle point $(\hat{p}, \hat{q})$ on $S_m \times T_n$. For any $q \in T_n$, $K(p, q)$ is a continuous function in p and has a maximum on S_m. Hence,

$$\varphi(q) = \{p \mid p \in S_m,\ K(p, q) = \max_{x \in S_m} K(x, q)\} \neq \phi .$$

As $K(p, q)$ is linear in p, $\varphi(q)$ is a closed convex set, i.e. a compact convex set. Similarly,

$$\psi(p) = \{q \mid q \in T_n,\ K(p, q) = \min_{y \in T_n} K(p, y)\}$$

is a non-empty compact convex set for any $p \in S_m$. Now consider

$$(p, q) \to f(p, q) = \varphi(q) \times \psi(p)\colon S_m \times T_n \to S_m \times T_n .$$

If this mapping f has a fixed point $(\hat{p}, \hat{q}) \in f(\hat{p}, \hat{q})$, then $\hat{p} \in \varphi(\hat{q})$, $\hat{q} \in \psi(\hat{p})$. By definition of φ and ψ, $K(p, \hat{q})$ takes a maximum on S_m at $p = \hat{p}$ and $K(\hat{p}, q)$ a minimum on T_n at $q = \hat{q}$. Thus, $(\hat{p}, \hat{q})$ is a saddle point. Hence, it suffices to demonstrate that this mapping f satisfies the assumptions of Kakutani's theorem. In fact, S_m and T_n are standard simplexes so that they are compact convex sets in R^m and R^n. Hence, the cartesian product $S_m \times T_n$ is a compact convex set in R^{m+n} (by virtue of Theorem 28.3). Similarly, the image $f(p, q) = \varphi(q) \times \psi(p)$ is a compact convex set in $S_m \times T_n$. Therefore, it suffices in the final analysis to verify that f is a closed mapping. To show this, let us put $q, q^\nu \in T_n$, $\lim_{\nu\to\infty} q^\nu = q$, $p, p^\nu \in S_m$, $\lim_{\nu\to\infty} p^\nu = p$, $p^\nu \in \varphi(q^\nu)$. Then, because of $p^\nu \in \varphi(q^\nu)$, we get $K(p^\nu, q^\nu) \geqq K(x, q^\nu)$ ($\nu = 1, 2, \ldots$) for any $x \in S_m$ that is kept fixed. Letting $\nu \to \infty$ here, we find $K(p, q) \geqq K(x, q)$ because of the continuity of K. Thus, $p \in \varphi(q)$ and φ is a closed mapping. Similarly, we see that ψ is a closed mapping. As $(p, q) \to q\colon S_m \times T_n \to T_n$ is single-valued and continuous, $(p, q) \to \varphi(q)\colon S_m \times T_n \to S_m$ is a closed mapping by (i) in (1) above. Similarly, we see that $(p, q) \to \psi(p)\colon S_m \times T_n \to T_n$ is a closed mapping. Then, by virtue of (2) above, the cartesian product mapping $(p, q) \to f(p, q) = \varphi(q) \times \psi(p)$ is a closed mapping.

Extension of mappings. Consider two point-to-set mappings $x \to f(x)$: $X \to Y$ and $x \to g(x)$: $\tilde{X} \to Y$ (where Y is compact). When $X \subset \tilde{X}$ and $f(x) = g(x)$ for $x \in X$, it is said that g is an *extension* of f. Let us examine an extension of a closed mapping.

We defined the closedness of a point-to-set mapping f: $X \to Y$ by the closedness of its graph G_f as a set. Conversely, given a closed set G in the cartesian product $X \times Y$, for any x if there always exists $y \in Y$ such that $(x, y) \in G$, then a point-to-set mapping of X into Y, $f(x) = \{y \mid y \in Y, (x, y) \in G\}$, is defined. f is a closed mapping because the graph of f is exactly G. This operation is a convenient method of producing a closed mapping. We can establish a closed extension of a mapping according to this method.

X is siad to be *dense* in $\tilde{X}$ when X is a subset of $\tilde{X}$ and $\bar{X} = \tilde{X}$ (the closure of X is identical with $\tilde{X}$).

(a) f: $X \to Y$ (Y is compact) is a closed point-to-set mapping and X is dense in $\tilde{X}$. Then, f can be extended to a closed mapping $g(g(x) \neq \phi)$ from $\tilde{X}$ into Y.

Proof. G_f, the graph of f, is a closed set in $X \times Y$ but not necessarily so in $\tilde{X} \times Y$. Its closure $\bar{G}_f$, however, is a closed set in $\tilde{X} \times Y$. Now as X is dense in $\tilde{X}$, for any $x \in \tilde{X}$ we can select a sequence of points $\{x^\nu\}$ such that $x^\nu \in X$, $\lim_{\nu \to \infty} x^\nu = x$. Select a point y^ν from $f(x^\nu)$. As Y is compact, we may as usual assume that $y^\nu \to y \in Y$ $(\nu \to \infty)$. Thus, $(x^\nu, y^\nu) \in G_f$ and $(x^\nu, y^\nu) \to (x, y)$ (in $X \times Y$) so that $(x, y) \in \bar{G}_f$. Hence, according to the method described above, we can define a closed mapping $g(x) = \{y \mid y \in Y, (x, y) \in \bar{G}_f\}$.

Let us now show that g is an extension of f. If $x \in X$ and $y \in f(x)$, then $f(x) \subset g(x)$ because $(x, y) \in G_f \subset \bar{G}_f$. On the other hand, $g(x) \subset f(x)$ also holds. In fact, if $y \in g(x)$, then $(x, y) \in \bar{G}_f$. Hence, there must exist a sequence of points (x^ν, y^ν) of G_f such that $\lim_{\nu \to \infty} (x^\nu, y^\nu) = (x, y)$. As $(x, y) \in X \times Y$ and G_f is a closed set in $X \times Y$, we must have $(x, y) \in G_f$. Hence, $y \in f(x)$, which demonstrates $g(x) \subset f(x)$. Thus, $f(x) = g(x)$ on X.

(b) f: $X \to Y$ is a closed mapping. Y is a compact convex set in R^n. Then, a mapping that associates the convex hull $C(f(x))$ of $f(x)$ with each $x \in X$ is also closed.

Proof. The corollary of Theorem 27.4 shows that points of $C(f(x))$ are convex linear combinations of at most $n+1$ points of $f(x)$. Let $\lim_{\nu \to \infty} x^\nu = x$, $\lim_{\nu \to \infty} z^\nu = z$, $z^\nu \in C(f(x^\nu))$. Now we have for some $y^{s\nu} \in f(x^\nu)$ and coefficients

$\lambda_{s\nu}$,

$$(44.11)\qquad z^\nu = \sum_{s=1}^{n+1} \lambda_{s\nu} y^{s\nu}, \quad \lambda_{s\nu} \geqq 0, \quad \sum_{s=1}^{n+1} \lambda_{s\nu} = 1 \quad (\nu = 1, 2, \ldots).$$

As $y^{s\nu} \in Y$, $(\lambda_{1\nu}, \lambda_{2\nu}, \ldots, \lambda_{n+1\nu})' \in S_{n+1}$, and Y and S_{n+1} are both compact, we may as usual assume that

$$\lim_{\nu\to\infty} (\lambda_{1\nu}, \lambda_{2\nu}, \ldots, \lambda_{n+1\nu})' = (\lambda_1, \lambda_2, \ldots, \lambda_{n+1})' \in S_{n+1}$$

and

$$\lim_{\nu\to\infty} y^{s\nu} = y^s \in Y \quad (s = 1, 2, \ldots, n+1).$$

Then, $y^s \in f(x)$ because f is closed and $y^{s\nu} \in f(x^\nu)$. In view of these, we get

$$z = \sum_{s=1}^{n+1} \lambda_s y^s, \quad \lambda_s \geqq 0, \quad \sum_{s=1}^{n+1} \lambda_s = 1 \quad (\nu = 1, 2, \ldots)$$

by letting $\nu \to \infty$ in (44.11) so that $z \in C(f(x))$. This demonstrates that $x \to C(f(x))$ is closed.

(c), (a) and (b) together yield the theorem below.

THEOREM 44.2. *X, $\tilde{X}$ and Y are sets in (identical or different) R^n. X is dense in $\tilde{X}$ and Y is a compact convex set. f: $X \to Y$ is a closed point-to-set mapping and $f(x) \neq 0$. $f(x)$ is always a convex set. On these assumptions, one can extend f to a closed mapping h from $\tilde{X}$ into Y such that $h(x) \neq \phi$ is always a convex set.*

Proof. Extend f to g: $\tilde{X} \to Y$, a closed mapping on $\tilde{X}$, according to the operation (a) above. Form $h(x) = C(g(x)) \neq \phi$ according to the operation (b). Then, h: $\tilde{X} \to Y$ is a closed mapping and the image $h(x)$ is a convex set. Also for $x \in X$, we have $g(x) = f(x)$. Further, as $f(x)$ is convex, $C(f(x)) = f(x)$. Thus, $h(x) = f(x)$ on X. $h(x)$ is, therefore, the desired extension. [Q.E.D.]

Now we have completed our mathematical preparations. The next chapter will present a final solution to the existence problem of a competitive equilibrium by means of the fixed point theorems.

Chapter 10

THE EXISTENCE OF COMPETITIVE EQUILIBRIUM

45. The Walras law and economic equilibrium

In Section 39 we have discussed a modern version of the general equilibrium model in detail. There are alternative models of the same type. But they differ very little in basic structure in spite of minor variations in formulation. The essential mechanism that yields the existence of competitive equilibrium remains the same for all such models. Thus, we shall formulate an *abstract economic model* that is basically characterized by those properties that are shared by all these models and play decisive roles in the existence problem of equilibrium, while permitting completely free interpretations in all other respects. We shall then establish, as a theorem, the existence of an equilibrium solution in this model. This approach will clarify the ground for and give a unified proof to the existence of an equilibrium solution in all models. Arrow and Debreu [33] achieved this objective by constructing a generalized game-theoretic abstract model. In contrast to and independently of them, Gale [35] and Nikaido [46] formulated abstract models along lines more faithful to traditional economic thought in order to solve the problem. We shall follow the latter approach in this chapter.

In formulating the general equilibrium model in Section 39, we took prices p as a positive vector. In Section 40, we constructed demand and supply functions that are defined for non-negative price vectors excluding 0 and demonstrated that the solution of the original problem is equivalent to that of the existence problem of demand-and-supply equilibrium.

In order to demonstrate the existence of equilibrium prices $\hat{p} \geq 0$, it suffices to show that there exist equilibrium prices in S_n, as will be explained in the next section. Therefore, we assume $p \in S_n$ in our abstract economic model to be given below. This procedure is effective because of the mathematically convenient properties that S_n is endowed with (e.g., compactness). We have often taken advantage of them in the present book.

What are the important conditions that guarantee the existence of an equilibrium solution in a Walrasian model? The basic theorem below clearly shows that they are nothing but the Walras law and the continuity of demand and supply functions.

THEOREM 45.1 *(Gale [35], Nikaido [46]). There are n goods, and an excess supply function $\chi(p)$ of prices $p \in S_n$ is given. Excess supply is the vectorial difference of supply and demand. $\chi(p)$ satisfies the following conditions:*

(i) *$p \to \chi(p)$ is a closed mapping that associates convex subsets $\chi(p) \neq \phi$ of Γ with points p of S_n where Γ is a hypercube in R^n.*

(ii) *The Walras law in the general sense holds, that is, if $x \in \chi(p)$, then the inner product $(p, x) \geqq$ holds at every point $p \in S_n$.* *

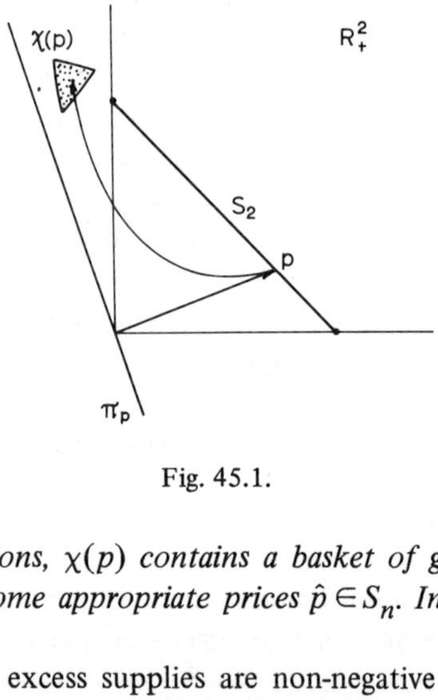

Fig. 45.1.

On these assumptions, $\chi(p)$ contains a basket of goods in non-negative amounts, $\hat{x} \geqq 0$, at some appropriate prices $\hat{p} \in S_n$. In other words, $\chi(\hat{p}) \cap R^n_+ \neq \phi$.

The situation that excess supplies are non-negative for all goods may be considered as a state of economic equilibrium in the most general sense. Before proceeding to the proof of the theorem, we may describe what the theorem means geometrically. The hyperplane π_p that passes through the

* In Section 40, the Walras law represented an identity $(p,x) = 0$ (for $x \in \chi(p)$). The Walras law in the general sense substitutes an inequality sign for the equality sign. The former is, if necessary, called the Walras law in the narrow sense.

origin with a normal vector $p \in S_n$ is represented by the equation $(p, x) = 0$. The Walras law in the general sense implies that the image set $\chi(p)$ always lies on the non-negative side of π_p. Fig. 45.1 shows the case of $n = 2$. We may note that the non-negative half-space determined by π_p changes as p changes. The set $\chi(p)$ moves around in this half-space while changing its shape. If $\chi(p)$ does not intersect with R_+^n, its movement is restricted in the area sandwiched between π_p and R_+^n. Intuition suggests that, in the case of $n = 2$, $\chi(p)$ cannot help intersecting with R_+^n at some time. However, it must be noted that the conclusion of the theorem itself is not self-evident even by intuition for the general case $n \geqq 3$.

Proof. We may first introduce a price response function which associates certain prices $q = \theta(p, x)$ with pairs $[p, x]$ of any point x in R_n and arbitrarily given prices $p \in S_n$. Its components are defined by

$$(45.1) \qquad \theta_j(p, x) = \frac{p_j + \max(-x_j, 0)}{1 + \sum_{s=1}^{n} \max(-x_s, 0)} \qquad (j = 1, 2, \ldots, n)\,.$$

We have $\theta_j(p, x) \geqq 0$ $(j = 1, 2, \ldots, n)$ and $\sum_{j=1}^{n} \theta_j(p, x) = 1$ identically so that the image $\theta(p, x)$ is always a point in S_n. It is also easily seen that the functions (45.1) are continuous functions of $[p, x]$. Hence, by restricting the variation of x within the hypercube Γ, we get a single-valued continuous mapping that is defined on the cartesian product $S_n \times \Gamma$ and takes values of S_n:

$$(45.2) \qquad [p, x] \to \theta(p, x): S_n \times \Gamma \to S_n\,.$$

Though $\theta(p, x)$ is introduced to facilitate the proof, it can be given an economic interpretation. Goods are exchanged in the market according to their prices (namely, exchange ratios). If their demand and supply are not equal, current prices are induced to change under the influence of the "Invisible Hand". * If new prices do not equate demand and supply, another

* Adam Smith noted that pursuits of maximal individual interests by members of society would lead to a natural economic harmony in society as a whole. He called this the Invisible Hand of God.

round of price changes follows. Successive changes in prices which induce alterations in demand and supply continue until demand and supply are equated for all goods. In place of the Invisible Hand, we may suppose a fictitious auctioneer who declares prices p in the market. Participants in the market then cry out quantities they buy and sell. If their demand and supply do not match, the auctioneer declares a new set of prices p. $\theta(p, x)$ defined above may be interpreted as an adjustment mechanism of demand and supply that associates new prices with current prices p and excess supply x.

Now combine the given excess supply function $\chi(p)$: $S_n \to \Gamma$ and the price response function (45.2). Define an equation

$$(45.3) \qquad f(p, x) = \{\theta(p, x)\} \times \chi(p)$$

and form a mapping

$$(45.4) \qquad [p, x] \to f(p, x): S_n \times \Gamma \to S_n \times \Gamma\,,$$

that associates a set $f(p, x)$ in the cartesian product $S_n \times \Gamma$ with a point $[p, x]$ in $S_n \times \Gamma$. Then, as we shall see later, the mapping (45.4) satisfies the assumptions of Kakutani's fixed point theorem so that there exists a fixed point $[\hat{p}, x] \in f(\hat{p}, \hat{x})$ in $S_n \times \Gamma$. This implies that

$$(45.5) \qquad \hat{p} = \theta(\hat{p}, \hat{x})$$

and

$$(45.6) \qquad \hat{x} \in \chi(\hat{p})\,,$$

for $\hat{p} \in S_n$ and $\hat{x} \in \Gamma$.

Next let us show that $\hat{x} \geqq 0$. As (45.5) holds, the definition (45.1) gives

$$\hat{p}_j = \frac{\hat{p}_j + \max(-\hat{x}_j, 0)}{1 + \sum_{s=1}^{n} \max(-\hat{x}_s, 0)} \qquad (j = 1, 2, \ldots, n)\,.$$

Putting $\sum_{s=1}^{n} \max(-\hat{x}_s, 0) = \lambda$, we get

(45.7) $\lambda\hat{p}_j = \max(-\hat{x}_j, 0) \qquad (j = 1, 2, ..., n)$.

Multiplying the jth equation of (45.7) by $\hat{x}_j$ and summing up produce *

$$\lambda \sum_{j=1}^{n} \hat{p}_j\hat{x}_j = \sum_{j=1}^{n} \hat{x}_j \max(-\hat{x}_j, 0)$$

$$= -\sum_{j=1}^{n} -\hat{x}_j \max(-\hat{x}_j, 0)$$

$$= -\sum_{j=1}^{n} [\max(-\hat{x}_j, 0)]^2 .$$

Thus,

(45.8) $$0 \leqq \sum_{j=1}^{n} [\max(-\hat{x}_j, 0)]^2 = -\lambda(\hat{p}, \hat{x}) .$$

Considering (45.6), we have $(\hat{p}, \hat{x}) \geqq 0$ by virtue of the Walras law in the general sense. Also it follows from the definition that $\lambda \geqq 0$. Thus, the right-hand side of (45.8) is non-positive so that

$$\sum_{j=1}^{n} [\max(-\hat{x}_j, 0)]^2 = 0 ,$$

from which we get $-\hat{x}_j \leqq \max(-\hat{x}_j, 0) = 0$ for each j, i.e. $\hat{x}_j \geqq 0$ $(j = 1, 2, ..., n)$.

Finally in order to show that the mapping (45.4) satisfies the assumptions of Kakutani's theorem, consider the following:

(a) As S_n and Γ are both compact convex sets in R^n, $S_n \times \Gamma$ is a compact convex set in R^{2n} by virtue of Theorem 28.3.

(b) As $[p, x] \to p$: $S_n \times \Gamma \to S_n$ is a single-valued continuous mapping and as the mapping $p \to \chi(p)$: $S_n \to \Gamma$ is a closed one by assumption, the com-

* We use the formula (26.17) $[\max(t, 0)]^2 = t \max(t, 0)$.

posed mapping

$$(45.9) \qquad [p, x] \to \chi(p)\colon S_n \times \Gamma \to \Gamma$$

is closed. On the other hand, because (45.2) is single-valued and continuous, the mapping (45.4) that is the cartesian product of (45.2) and (45.9) is a closed mapping by virtue of (2) of the preceding section.

(c) The image (45.3) of each $[p, x]$ under the mapping (45.4) is a convex set because $\theta(p, x)$ is a point and $\chi(p)$ is a convex set. [Q.E.D.]

Remark 1. Simplification of the proof for a single-valued $\chi(p)$. In this theorem, if $\chi(p)$ is an ordinary single-valued continuous function, the image (45.3) is always a single point and the mapping (45.4) is single-valued. Thus, the existence of a fixed point $[\hat{p}, \hat{x}] = f(\hat{p}, \hat{x})$ can be directly demonstrated by means of Brouwer's fixed point theorem (Theorem 43.1).

Alternatively, we may make a direct substitution of $\chi(p)$ into x of $\theta(p, x)$ in (45.2) and form a single-valued continuous mapping that associates with points p in S_n points $f(p) = \theta(p, \chi(p))$ in S_n. Then, we apply Brouwer's theorem to prove the existence of a fixed point $\hat{p} = f(\hat{p}) = \theta(\hat{p}, \chi(\hat{p}))$ and to show $\chi(\hat{p}) \geqq 0$ in exactly the same way as the preceding proof.

In either case, Brouwer's theorem is sufficient when $\chi(p)$ is a single-valued continuous mapping. In general, however, when $\chi(p)$ is set-valued, $f(p) = \theta(p, \chi(p))$ is a mapping too complicated to be handled even by Kakutani's theorem.

Remark 2. If the Walras law in the narrow sense is assumed, $(\hat{p}, \hat{x}) = 0$ at the equilibrium point $\hat{x}$ in the theorem above. Combined with $\hat{x} \geqq 0$, we see that $\hat{p}_j = 0$ for components $\hat{x}_j > 0$, i.e. the price of a free good is 0.

Remark 3. $\chi(p)$ is often assumed to be such that the demand for the jth good is at least equal to its supply, i.e. $x_j \leqq 0$ if $p_j = 0$ and $x \in \chi(p)$. If the Walras law in the general sense is assumed in addition, we get $\hat{x}_j = 0$ for all goods in equilibrium so that demand and supply are completely equated.

Remark 4. For $\chi(p)$ such that $x_j < 0$ always if $x \in \chi(p)$ and $p_j = 0$, the equilibrium prices $\hat{p}$ are obviously positive, $\hat{p} > 0$.

46. The existence of an equilibrium solution

We now prove the existence of an equilibrium solution in our general equilibrium model by means of Theorem 45.1.

Normalization of prices. We explained in the last section why it is mathematically convenient to restrict prices within S_n. We now examine its economic meaning.

Demand and supply functions, $\varphi(p)$ and $\psi(p)$, in the general equilibrium model are defined for any $p \geq 0$. As their definition readily suggests, we have $\varphi(\lambda p) = \varphi(p)$ and $\psi(\lambda p) = \psi(p)$ for any positive number $\lambda > 0$. In other words, these functions are positively homogeneous functions of the 0th order. Hence, what matters in the general equilibrium model is not prices themselves but their ratios $p_1 : p_2 : ... : p_n$. Take a specific commodity (say, gold) as a standard of measurement and obtain the ratios at which it is exchanged with all other goods. This essentially determines the price system. The good used as the standard of measurement is called a *numéraire.* Traditional theory often confines its attention to the price system in which the price of the numéraire is always unity. This is the *normalized* price system. Though the normalization of prices on the basis of a numéraire is sufficiently meaningful in the real economic world, it proves to be not too convenient for our own theoretical analysis. This is because the price of the numéraire is always unity without any possibility of ever becoming 0. All this leads to a great deal of mathematical difficulty.

Therefore, recent theoretical analysis employs an alternative and ingenious method of normalization. A single good that is taken as a numéraire by the traditional method may be replaced by a basket of one unit each of all goods $u = [1, 1, ..., 1]'$ which now serves as a standard of measurement. The price system is normalized in such a way that its value is unity, i.e.

$$(p, u) = \sum_{j=1}^{n} p_j = 1 \ .$$

In this system, $p \geq 0$ and yet any price can become 0. This property is theoretically very convenient. Any price system $p \geq 0$ can be normalized when it is divided by the sum of all components. The ratios of the components of p remain unchanged in this normalization. As before, the totality of normalized prices p is denoted by S_n and the set of all points p in S_n such that $p > 0$ is denoted by $S_n^{\square}$.

The orientation of the proof. In order to prove the existence of an equilibrium solution in a Walrasian model, * it suffices to demonstrate the exist-

* Section 39, I–V.

ence of the equilibrium (40.31) for demand and supply functions (40.28) and (40.29). This was established in Section 40. *

Denote the vectorial difference of supply and demand functions $\psi(p)$ and $\varphi(p)$, i.e. the excess supply function, by

$$(46.1) \qquad \chi(p) = \psi(p) - \varphi(p) \,,$$

which is a point-to-set mapping that associates a subset $\chi(p)$ in R^n with a point p in S_n. Now let us enumerate some important properties of this function.

For the hypercubes E in (40.18) and E_i in (40.24) that were used to define demand and supply functions in Section 40, we always have $\psi^k(p) \subset E$ and $\varphi^i(p) \subset E_i$. Thus,

$$(46.2) \qquad \chi(p) = a + \sum_{k=1}^{m} \psi^k(p) - \sum_{i=1}^{l} \varphi^i(p)$$

$$\subset a + \underbrace{E + E + \ldots + E}_{m} - (E_1 + E_2 + \ldots + E_l) \,.$$

Let Γ be a hypercube large enough to include the set on the right-hand side above. Then

(a) $\qquad \chi(p) \subset \Gamma$

holds for any $p \in S_n$.

As $\{a\}$, $\psi^k(p)$ and $\varphi^i(p)$ are nonempty convex sets for all $p \in S_n$ (see Section 33), we see from (ii) of Theorem 28.4 that

(b) $\qquad \chi(p)$ is a nonempty convex subset of Γ.

As the demand and supply functions satisfy the Walras law (in the narrow sense) (40.38) as shown in Section 40, the excess supply function $\chi(p)$ is such that

(c) $\qquad (p, x) = 0$ (at each point $p \in S_n$) if $x \in \chi(p)$.

* See Theorem 40.1.

If the mapping $p \to \chi(p)$: $S_n \to \Gamma$ is a closed mapping in the entire domain of S_n, then (*a*), (*b*) and (*c*) imply that $\chi(p)$ satisfies the conditions of Theorem 45.1. Hence, $\chi(p)$ contains a non-negative basket of goods $\hat{x} \geqq 0$ at some $\hat{p} \in S_n$. We can easily find from this that $\hat{p} > 0$, $\hat{x} = 0$. Unfortunately, the proof cannot be straightforward. This is because the closedness of $\chi(p)$ is not ensured all over S_n. By considering the summand mappings that compose (46.2), we can find out that this property is due to the fact that the closedness of individual demand functions $\varphi^i(p)$ does not hold all over S_n. It is therefore necessary to modify somewhat the method of directly constructing $\chi(p)$. We make Theorem 45.1 applicable to $\chi(p)$ by reconstructing it according to the method to be described below.

(α) *individual supply functions.* Each individual supply function (40.20) $\psi^k(p)$: $S_n \to E$ is a closed mapping.

In fact, if $\lim_{\nu\to\infty} p^\nu = p$ (in S_n), $\lim_{\nu\to\infty} y^{k\nu} = y^k$ (in E) and $y^{k\nu} \in \psi^k(p^\nu)$ ($\nu = 1, 2, \ldots$), then $y^k \in Y_k \cap E$ and

$$(46.3) \qquad (p^\nu, y) \leqq (p^\nu, y^{k\nu}) \qquad (\text{for any } y \in Y_k \cap E)\,.$$

By letting $\nu \to \infty$ in (46.3), the continuity of the inner product leads to

$$(p, y) \leqq (p, y^k) \qquad (\text{for any } y \in Y_k \cap E)\,,$$

from which we get $y^k \in \psi^k(p)$ so that ψ^k is closed on S_n.

(β) *individual demand functions.* We construct a modified individual demand function which is a closed mapping all over S_n and by which the image of each point p is a convex subset of E_i.

Though the income of the consumer unit i is $(p, a^i) + \sum_{k=1}^{m} \alpha_{ik}\pi_k(p)$, we make use of b^i that appears in the preference field of i, $X_i = b^i + R^n_+$ * and define, for convenience,

$$(46.4) \qquad I_i(p) = (p, a^i - b^i) + \sum_{k=1}^{m} \alpha_{ik}\pi_k(p) \qquad (i = 1, 2, \ldots, l)\,.$$

We observe $(p, a^i - b^i) \geqq 0$, $\pi_k(p) \geqq 0$, $\alpha_{ik} \geqq 0$. As those functions are con-

* Section 39, Assumption II.a.

tinuous functions of p, * $I_i(p)$ is a continuous function whose value is always non-negative. Using this $I_i(p)$, we may rewrite $\varphi^i(p)$ as

$$(46.5) \qquad \varphi^i(p) = \{x^i \mid \max u_i(x) = u_i(x^i) \text{ subject to } x \in E_i\,, \\ (p, x - b^i) \leqq I_i(p)\}\,.$$

As we have already noted, $I_i(p) \geqq 0$ always holds on S_n but not necessarily $I_i(p) > 0$. This is due to the fact that we have employed the assumption $a^i \geq b^i$ that is more realistic than that of positive initial holdings $a^i > b^i$. This less restrictive assumption is responsible for making it complicated to examine the closedness of individual demand functions.

Now set

$$(46.6) \qquad S_n^i = \{p \mid p \in S_n, I_i(p) > 0\} \qquad (i = 1, 2, ..., l)\,,$$

for each i. As $a^i \geq b^i$, $(p, a^i - b^i) > 0$ for $p > 0$ (i.e. $p \in S_n^{\square}$) so that $I_i(p) > 0$ (for $p > 0$). Thus, we get the relation

$$(46.7) \qquad S_n^{\square} \subset S_n^i \subset S_n\,.$$

Then

β.1 $\varphi^i(p)$ is closed on S_n^i, i.e. the mapping $\varphi^i(p)$: $S_n^i \to E_i$ is closed. In fact, if $\lim_{\nu\to\infty} p^\nu = p$ (in S_n^i), $\lim_{\nu\to\infty} x^\nu = x$ (in E_i) and $x^\nu \in \varphi^i(p^\nu)$, then we get $(p, x - b^i) \leqq I_i(p)$ by virtue of the continuity property by putting $\nu \to \infty$ in $(p^\nu, x^\nu - b^i) \leqq I_i(p^\nu)$. This implies that x satisfies, at any rate, the budget constraint at p. Next, let us prove that $u_i(x) \geqq u_i(y)$ for any $y \in E_i$ such that $(p, y - b^i) \leqq I_i(p)$. As $p, p^\nu \in S_n^i$, we have $I_i(p) > 0$ and $I_i(p^\nu) > 0$. In view of this fact, we let

$$(46.8) \qquad \lambda_\nu = I_i(p^\nu)/\max\,[I_i(p^\nu), (p^\nu, y - b^i)]$$

for this y. As $I_i(p^\nu) > 0$, the ratio (46.8) is determinate and we have clearly

$$(46.9) \qquad 0 < \lambda_\nu \leqq 1 \qquad (\nu = 1, 2, ...)$$

because of the definition. Now construct a convex linear combination

* The continuity of $\pi_k(p)$ can be demonstrated in a manner similar to (α).

(46.10) $\quad y^\nu = (1-\lambda_\nu)b^i + \lambda_\nu y \qquad (\nu = 1, 2, \ldots)$.

Then, as $b^i, y \in E_i$, we get

(46.11) $\quad y^\nu \in E_i \qquad (\nu = 1, 2, \ldots)$.

By (46.8) that defines λ_ν, we have

$$\begin{aligned}(p^\nu, y^\nu - b^i) &= (p^\nu, \lambda_\nu(y - b^i)) = \lambda_\nu(p^\nu, y - b^i)\\ &= I_i(p^\nu)(p^\nu, y - b^i)/\max\,[I_i(p^\nu), (p^\nu, y - b^i)]\\ &\leqq I_i(p^\nu)\,,\end{aligned}$$

because

$$(p^\nu, y - b^i)/\max\,[I_i(p^\nu), (p^\nu, y - b^i)] \leqq 1\,.$$

Hence,

(46.12) $\quad (p^\nu, y^\nu - b^i) \leqq I_i(p^\nu) \qquad (\nu = 1, 2, \ldots)$.

y^ν satisfies the budget constraint for p^ν because of (46.11) and (46.12) so that

(46.13) $\quad u_i(x^\nu) \geqq u_i(y^\nu) \qquad (\nu = 1, 2, \ldots)$

due to what is implied by $x^\nu \in \varphi^i(p^\nu)$. Now letting $\nu \to \infty$, we get

$$\lim_{\nu\to\infty} \lambda_\nu = I_i(p)/\max\,[I_i(p), (p, y - b^i)]$$

because of the continuity of (46.8). As $(p, y - b^i) \leqq I_i(p)$, we have

(46.14) $\quad \lim_{\nu\to\infty} \lambda_\nu = 1\,,$

so that

(46.15) $\quad \lim_{\nu\to\infty} y^\nu = y$

by letting $\nu \to \infty$ in (46.10). Hence, $\nu \to \infty$ in (46.13) leads to

$$(46.16) \qquad u_i(x) \geqq u_i(y)$$

by virtue of the continuity of u_i. This demonstrates that $x \in \varphi^i(p)$. In other words, φ^i is a closed mapping on S_n^i.

$\boxed{\beta.2}$ Each $\varphi^i(p)$: $S_n^i \to E_i$ can be extended to $\tilde{\varphi}^i(p)$ defined on S_n in such a way that $\tilde{\varphi}^i(p)$: $S_n \to E_i$ is a closed mapping and that the image $\tilde{\varphi}^i(p)$ of every point is a convex subset in E_i.

In fact, $\varphi^i(p)$: $S_n^i \to E_i$ is closed by virtue of $\boxed{\beta.1}$. The image $\varphi^i(p)$ of every point in S_n is convex as noted earlier in this section. It is *a fortiori* convex for every point in S_n^i. Now as the inclusion (46.7) holds and as $S_n^{\square}$ is dense in S_n, S_n^i is also dense in S_n. Therefore, the application of Theorem 44.2 provides the required extension.

(γ) *modified excess supply function.* Let Γ be the hypercube defined earlier in this section. Then, the functions $\psi^k(p)$ and $\tilde{\varphi}^i(p)$ associate non-empty convex subsets in E and E_i respectively with points p in S_n. Moreover, these mappings are closed. Thus, by (ii) of Theorem 28.4 and the result (3) in Section 40 on linear combinations of mappings, we find that the modified excess supply function

$$(46.17) \qquad \tilde{\chi}(p) = a + \sum_{k=1}^{m} \psi^k(p) - \sum_{i=1}^{l} \tilde{\varphi}^i(p)$$

is a closed mapping that associates a convex subset of Γ with a point p in S_n.

(δ) *the Walras law.* $\tilde{\chi}(p)$ satisfies the Walras law in the narrow sense all over S_n.

To verify this property, let us recall the proof given in Section 40 on the Walras law with respect to the original excess supply function $\chi(p)$. We see that the proof was reduced to demonstrating that the budget constraint holds with an equality sign at any point x^i in the image $\varphi^i(p)$ of individual demand functions so that (40.37) holds. To prove the Walras law for $\tilde{\chi}(p)$, we can see that it suffices to show the same property with respect to the modified individual demand functions $\tilde{\varphi}^i(p)$.

As $\tilde{\varphi}^i(p) = \varphi^i(p)$ on S_n^i, all that has to be demonstrated here is that the budget constraint holds with an equality sign at a point $p \in S_n$ such that $p \notin S_n^i$.

If $x \in \tilde{\varphi}^i(p)$ for this point p, then we can write

$$x = \sum_{s=1}^{n+1} \lambda_s y^s , \quad \lambda_s \geqq 0 , \quad \sum_{s=1}^{n+1} \lambda_s = 1 ,$$

$$y^s = \lim_{\nu \to \infty} y^{s\nu} , \quad p = \lim_{\nu \to \infty} p^{s\nu}, \quad p^{s\nu} \in S_n^i , \quad y^{s\nu} \in \varphi^i(p^{s\nu})$$

in view of the way $\tilde{\varphi}^i$ is constructed. As we have already noted, $(p^\nu, y^{s\nu} - b^i) = I_i(p^{s\nu})$ holds on S_n^i so that

$$(p, x - b^i) = \sum_{s=1}^{n+1} \lambda_s \lim_{\nu \to \infty} (p^\nu, y^{s\nu} - b^i)$$

$$= \sum_{s=1}^{n+1} \lambda_s \lim_{\nu \to \infty} I_i(p^{s\nu})$$

$$= \sum_{s=1}^{n+1} \lambda_s I_i(p)$$

$$= I_i(p) .$$

The existence of an equilibrium solution. $(\alpha) \sim (\delta)$ above ensure that $\tilde{\chi}(p)$: $S_n \to \Gamma$ satisfies all the assumptions of Theorem 45.1. Hence, $\tilde{\chi}(p)$ includes a non-negative vector $\hat{u} \geqq 0$ at some $\hat{p} \in S_n$. Thus $\hat{u} \in \tilde{\chi}(\hat{p})$ can be decomposed into a vectorial sum

$$(46.18) \qquad 0 \leqq \hat{u} = \sum_{i=1}^{l} a^i + \sum_{k=1}^{m} \hat{y}^k - \sum_{i=1}^{l} \hat{x}^i , \quad \hat{y}^k \in \psi^k(\hat{p}) , \quad \hat{x}^i \in \tilde{\varphi}^i(\hat{p})$$

because of the definition of $\tilde{\chi}(\hat{p})$. The proof is completed by demonstrating that in fact

(A) $\quad \hat{p} > 0$ so that $\tilde{\varphi}^i(\hat{p}) = \varphi^i(\hat{p})$, $\quad \tilde{\chi}(\hat{p}) = \chi(\hat{p})$, $\quad (i = 1, 2, ..., l)$

and

(B) $\quad \hat{u} = 0$.

The proof of (A). We already noted that $I_i(p) \geqq 0$ everywhere in S_n but not necessarily $I_i(p) > 0$. But let us now note that

$$\sum_{i=1}^{l} I_i(p) > 0 \tag{46.19}$$

everywhere in S_n. We shall now prove (46.19).

Taking note of $\bar{y}^k$ ($k = 1, 2, ..., m$) in Assumption V in the equilibrium model given in Section 39, we find

$$0 < \sum_{i=1}^{l} (a^i - b^i) + \sum_{k=1}^{m} \bar{y}^k . \tag{46.20}$$

Because of the way the hypercube E is constructed, we have $\bar{y}^k \in E$. While keeping in mind the definition (40.21) of $\pi_k(p)$, we take an inner product of (46.20) and any $p \in S_n$

$$0 < \sum_{i=1}^{l} (p, a^i - b^i) + \sum_{k=1}^{m} (p, \bar{y}^k)$$

$$\leqq \sum_{i=1}^{l} (p, a^i - b^i) + \sum_{k=1}^{m} \pi_k(p)$$

$$= \sum_{i=1}^{l} (p, a^i - b^i) + \sum_{k=1}^{m} \sum_{i=1}^{l} \alpha_{ik}\pi_k(p)$$

$$= \sum_{i=1}^{l} \left[(p, a^i - b^i) + \sum_{k=1}^{m} \alpha_{ik}\pi_k(p) \right]$$

$$= \sum_{i=1}^{l} I_i(p) \qquad \left(\because \sum_{i=1}^{l} \alpha_{ik} = 1 \right) .$$

Hence, we get (46.19).

(46.19) assures that for each $p \in S_n$ the income is positive, i.e. $I_i(p) > 0$, for some consumer unit. * This property also applies to $\hat{p}$ above. Now let the consumer unit with positive income be t. As $I_t(\hat{p}) > 0, \hat{p} \in S_n^t$ so that, for this t, we have in fact

$$(46.21) \qquad \tilde{\varphi}^t(\hat{p}) = \varphi^t(\hat{p}) .$$

As (46.18) holds, we see $\hat{x}^t \in \tilde{X}^t$. We can show that the assumption of $\hat{p} \not> 0$ leads to a contradiction by following the argument employed in the first half of (b) in the proof of (ii) of Theorem 40.1. Hence, we must have $\hat{p} > 0$. For any i, we therefore have $\hat{p} \in S_n^i$ so that $\tilde{\varphi}^i(\hat{p}) = \varphi^i(\hat{p})$ and $\tilde{\chi}(\hat{p}) = \chi(\hat{p})$.

The proof of (B). As $\tilde{\chi}(p)$ satisfies the Walras law in the narrow sense, we have

$$(46.22) \qquad (\hat{p}, \hat{u}) = 0 .$$

We get $\hat{u} = 0$ from this and from $\hat{p} > 0, \hat{u} \geqq 0$.

* The value of i depends on p.

BIBLIOGRAPHY AND REFERENCES

Bibliography

Books listed below are introductory ones that are easily accessible to the reader. (Japanese books cited in the original edition of this book are replaced by comparable English books that were available at the time this English edition was under preparation. These are denoted by * below.)

On point set theory and elementary topology:

[1] * J.Dieudonné, *Foundations of Modern Analysis* (Academic Press, 1960).

[2] * E.M.Patterson, *Topology* (Oliver and Boyd, 1956).

[3] * J.L.Kelley, *General Topology* (D.van Nostrand, 1955).

[4] P.Alexandroff and H.Hopf, *Topologie I* (Springer, 1935).

[5] S.Lefschetz, *Introduction to Topology* (Princeton University Press, 1949).

[6] M.H.A.Newman, *Elements of the Topology of Plane Sets of Points* (Cambridge University Press, 1939).

[7] L.S.Pontryagin, *Foundations of Combinatorial Topology* (English translation: Graylock Press, 1952).

On linear algebra:

[8] * G.Hadley, *Linear Algebra* (Addison-Wesley, 1961).

[9] * R.Bellman, *Introduction to Matrix Analysis* (McGraw-Hill, 1960).

[10] * H.L.Hamburger and M.E.Grimshaw, *Linear Transformations in n-dimensional Vector Space, An Introduction to the Theory of Hilbert Space* (Cambridge University Press, 1951).

[11] G.Birkhoff and S.MacLane, *Survey of Modern Algebra* (Macmillan, 1951).

[12] P.R.Halmos, *Finite Dimensional Vector Spaces* (Princeton University Press, 1948).

On modern economics in general:

[13] * J.M.Henderson and R.E.Quandt, *Microeconomic Theory, A Mathematical Approach* (McGraw-Hill, 1958).

[14] * T.C.Koopmans, *Three Essays on the State of Economic Science* (McGraw-Hill, 1959).

[15] R.G.D.Allen, *Mathematical Economics* (Macmillan, 1957).

[16] R.Dorfman, P.A.Samuelson and R.M.Solow, *Linear Programming and Economic Analysis* (McGraw-Hill, 1958).

On interindustry analysis and the Frobenius root:

[17] * M.Morishima, *Equilibrium, Stability, and Growth, A Multi-sectoral Analysis* (Oxford University Press, 1964).
[18] * D.Gale, *The Theory of Linear Economic Models* (McGraw-Hill, 1960).
[19] W.W.Leontief, *The Structure of American Economy 1919–39* (Oxford University Press, 1951).

On linear programming, see [16] for a detailed exposition. For a more mathematical treatment:

[20] * G.Hadley, *Linear Programming* (Addison-Wesley, 1960).
[21] W.W.Cooper, A.Henderson and A.Charnes, *An Introduction to Linear Programming* (John Wiley and Sons, 1953).

On game theory:

[22] * J.C.McKinsey, *Introduction to the Theory of Games* (McGraw-Hill, 1952).
[23] * S.Karlin, *Mathematical Methods and Theory in Games, Programming and Economics, I, II* (Addison-Wesley, 1959).
[24] J.von Neumann and O.Morgenstern, *Theory of Games and Economic Behavior* (Princeton University Press, 1944).

On the existence problem of equilibrium:

[25] * G.Debreu, *Theory of Value* (John Wiley and Sons, 1959).

As collected papers on some of these subjects:

[26] T.C.Koopmans, ed., *Activity Analysis of Production and Allocation* (John Wiley and Sons, 1951).
[27] *Contributions to the Theory of Games, I–IV* (Princeton University Press, 1950–1959). Vols. I and II (H.W.Kuhn and A.W.Tucker, eds.), Vol. III (M.Drescher and P.Wolfe, eds.), Vol. IV (A.W.Tucker and R.D.Luce, eds.).
[28] H.W.Kuhn and A.W.Tucker, eds., *Linear Inequalities and Related Systems* (Princeton University Press, 1956).
[29] K.J.Arrow, L.Hurwicz and H.Uzawa, eds., *Studies in Linear and Non-linear Programming* (Stanford University Press, 1958).

As introduction to economics:

[30] J.R.Hicks, *The Social Framework* (Oxford University Press, 1952).
[31] J.R.Hicks, *Value and Capital* (Oxford University Press, 2nd ed., 1946).
[32] P.A.Samuelson, *Economics* (McGraw-Hill, 1st ed., 1948; 7th ed., 1967).

References

Articles and books that were consulted in writing this book are listed below.

[33] K.J.Arrow and G.Debreu, Existence of an equilibrium for a competitive economy, *Econometrica* 22 (1954).

[34] G.Debreu and I.N.Herstein, Non-negative square matrices, *Econometrica* 21 (1953).

[35] D.Gale, The law of supply and demand, *Mathematica Scandinavica* 3 (1955).

[36] D.Hawkins and H.A.Simon, Some conditions on macroeconomic stability, *Econometrica* 17 (1949).

[37] S.Kakutani, A generalization of Brouwer's fixed point theorem, *Duke Mathematical Journal* 8 (1941).

[38] H.W.Kuhn, On a theorem of Wald, in [28].

[39] H.W.Kuhn and A.W.Tucker, Nonlinear programming, *Proceedings of the Second Berkeley Symposium on Mathematical Statistics and Probability* (University of California Press, 1951).

[40] L.McKenzie, On equilibrium in Graham's model of world trade and other competitive systems, *Econometrica* 22 (1954).

[41] J. von Neumann, Zur Theorie der Gesellschaftsspiele, *Mathematische Annalen* 100 (1928).

[42] J.von Neumann, Über ein ökonomisches Gleichungssystem und eine Verallgemeinerung des Brouwerschen Fixpunktsatzes, *Ergebnisse eines Mathematischen Kolloquiums* 8 (1935–36); English translation, A model of general economic equilibrium, *The Review of Economic Studies* 13 (1945–46).

[43] H.Nikaido, Zusatz und Berichtigung für meine Mitteilung 'Zum Beweis der Verallgemeinerung des Fixpunktsatzes', *Kodai Mathematical Seminar Reports* 6 (1954).

[44] H.Nikaido, Note on the general economic equilibrium for nonlinear production functions, *Econometrica* 22 (1954).

[45] H.Nikaido, New aspects of von Neumann's model with special regard to computational problems, *Annals of the Institute of Mathematical Statistics* 6 (1955).

[46] H.Nikaido, On the classical multilateral exchange problem, *Metroeconomica* 8 (1956); A supplementary note to [46], *Metroeconomica* 9 (1957).

[47] H.Nikaido, On some recent topics in mathematical economics (in Japanese), *Sugaku* 8 (Iwanami Shoten, 1956).

[48] H.Nikaido, On a proof of the minimax theorem (in Japanese), *Sugaku* 10 (Iwanami Shoten, 1958).

[49] H.Nikaido, On a method of proof for the minimax theorem, *Proceedings of American Mathematical Society* 10 (1959).

[50] R.M.Solow and P.A.Samuelson, Balanced growth under constant returns to scale, *Econometrica* 21 (1953).

[51] A.Wald, Uber die eindeutige positive Lösbarkeit der neuen Produktionsgleichungen, *Ergebnisse eines Mathematischen Kolloquiums* 6 (1933–34).

[52] A.Wald, Über die Produktionsgleichungen der ökonomischen Wertlehre, *Ergebnisse eines Mathematischen Kolloquiums* 7 (1934–35).

[53] M.E.L.Walras, *Eléments d'économie politique pure* (Paris, 1900); English translation by W.Jaffé, *Elements of pure economics* (George Allen and Unwin, 1954 and Richard D.Irwin, 1954).

[54] H.Wielandt, Unzerlegbare, nicht negative Matrizen, *Mathematische Zeitschrift* 52 (1950).

For the treatment of the problems in the present book on a more comprehensive and advanced level, the reader may consult:

[55] H.Nikaido, *Convex Structures and Economic Theory* (Academic Press, 1968).

[34], [35], [36], [37], [38], [39] and [46] are included in Vol. I of [56], and the English translation of [42] is included in vol. II of [56].

[56] P.Newman, ed., *Readings in Mathematical Economics,* Vol. I, II (The Johns Hopkins Press, 1968).

INDEX

activity analysis 158, 214
activity level 165
affine
  mapping 195
  subspace 183
affinely independent 289
Arrow, K.J. 267
Arrow-Debreu model 271
average value added 21

balanced growth 127
  model (of von Neumann) 239
  solution 149
barycenter 299
barycentric coordinate 298
barycentric subdivision 299
  νth 301
basis 55
bilinear form 235
bilinearity 77
bottleneck factor 216
bound
  lower 40
  upper 40
boundary 193
  point 193
bounded
  from above 40
  from below 40
  (for a set) 101
Brauer-Solow criteria 18
Brouwer, L.E.J. 303
budget constraint 226

Cantor, G. 2
cartesian product 196
  (of mappings) 314
Cassel-Wald model 3
Cauchy criterion of continuity 90
characteristic equation 115
closure 82
Cockaigne, Land of 217
column sum criteria 18
compact 101
competitive 160
complement 30
completeness of the real number
  system 38
composition of mappings 35
concave function 183
  quasi 225
consumer behavior, theory of 156
consumer unit 272
continuity
  (of a mapping) 88
  axiom of 39
convergence
  (of a sequence of numbers) 41
  (of a sequence of points) 72
convex cone 188
  dual 208
  polar 208
convex
  function 183
  hull 185
  linear combination 181
  polyhedral cone 189

convex (continued)
preference ordering 223
set 181
Cournot, A.A. 1
Cramer's rule 17, 69

data 160
Debreu, G. 267
decreasing
sequence of numbers 42
sequence of points 112
demand
final 12
function 226
individual d.f. 282
dense 317
densely distributed 38
De Morgan's rule 31
diameter (of a set) 302
distance
(between two points) 72, 73
(between a point and a set) 82
disutility 225
dollar's worth unit 22
domain 33
dual
equation 19
problem 168
duality 19
(in linear programming) 167
(for convex cones) 208
theorem 170

efficient 220
eigenvalue 115
eigenvalue problem 114
non-negative 113
eigenvector 115
ϵ-net 311
equilibrium
conditions 274
price system 271
equivalence relation 223
ex ante 226
ex post 226
excess supply function 283
expected value 235
extension (of mappings) 317

factor of production 166
primary 216
feasible 170
fixed point 304, 311
theorem (Kakutani's) 311
(Brouwer's) 304
free good 173
Frobenius, G. 118
Frobenius root 118
successive approximation of, 152
Frobenius theorem 118

Gale, D. 267, 320
Galilei, G. 265
game
rectangular 233
theory of 228
zero-sum 229
general equilibrium
model 271
theory 265
Goldman, A.J. 252
graph (of a point-to-set mapping) 309

half-space 183
Harvey, W. 7
Hawkins-Simon condition 13
Hicks, J.R. 159
homeomorphism 94
hypercube 280
hyperplane 183
separating 202
supporting 200

image
(of a point) 33
(of a set) 33
increasing
sequence of numbers 42
sequence of points 112
utility indicator 224
indifference map 222
infimum 41
initial holding 274
inner product 71
input coefficient 11
input-output analysis 9
input-output matrix 215

interior 193
point 193
intermediate value, theorem of 97
intersection 28
inverse image
(of a point) 34
(of a set) 34
iterative method (for a non-negative inverse matrix) 130
irreversibility 217

Jevons, S. 155

Koopmans' postulates 216
Kuhn, H.W. 256

Lagrangian function 251
Lagrangian multiplier 251
Leontief, W.W. 10
limit 42
linear combination 55
of mappings 315
of sets 197
non-negative 186
positive 186
linear
mapping 60
programming 163
space 48
subspace 183
linearly
dependent 50
independent 50

McKenzie, L. 267
Marx, K. 10
mapping 33
affine 195
closed 309
constant 90
continuous 88
identity 93
inverse 35
Kuratowski-type 312
linear 60
one-to-one 34
onto 35
point-to-set 227
topological 94
matrix 58, 59
alternating 247
completely decomposable 132
decomposable 132
imprimitive 139
indecomposable 132
inverse 67
non-negative 108
payoff 233
primitive 140
skew-symmetric 247
technology 215
transposed 65
maximin principle 230
Menger, C. 155
Menger, K. 267
metric space 78
microeconomics 157
minimax
principle 230
theorem (of von Neumann) 233
Minkowski-Farkas' lemma 209
minimum point
corner 162
interior 162
model
abstract economic 319
Arrow-Debreu 271
balanced growth (of von Neumann) 239
closed 237
general equilibrium 271
open 216
Walrasian equilibrium 268
Morgenstern, O. 3, 228

national income 21
distributed 166
earned 166
produced 166
national product 21
neighborhood
spherical ϵ- 85
closed spherical ϵ- 106
Neumann, J. von 3, 228
model 239
Neumann, C. 129
series 129
Newton, I. 265

Nikaido, H. 320
non-negative
  eigenvalue problem 113
  matrix 108
  saddle point problem 251
  vector 108
norm 70
normalization (of prices) 325
numéraire 325

objective functional 168
off-diagonal element 112
open model 216
ordering
  partial 110
  semi- 110

Pareto, V. 1, 265
payoff function 228
plane
  k-dimensional 292
  k-dimensional plane generated by a simplex 292
Poincaré, H. 2
positive orthant 182
positive linear homogeneity 122
preference
  field 222
preference ordering
  convex 223
price response function 321
process 164, 214
production
  function 159
  possibility set 215
  unit 272
profit maximization principle 156
pure exchange problem 269

Quesnay, F. 7

range 33
reflexivity 222
relative topology 86
returns to scale
  constant 164
  diminishing 219
  non-increasing 219
row sum criteria 18

saddle point 231
saturation point 225
Schwarz's inequality 71
sector
  endogenous 10
  exogenous 10
segment 181
separating hyperplane 202
separation theorem 201
set 25
  closed 78
  convex 181
  embracing 30
  open 80
simplex 291
  face 299
  regular derived 305
  standard 299
simplicial subdivision 299
slack variable 190
Smith, Adam 155, 265
solvability
  strong 13
  weak 13
Sperner's lemma 304
stability
  relative 154
strategy 236
  optimal 236
strictly determined 231
supremum 41
surplus 275

tableau économique 8
topological space 86
topology 86
  relative 86
transitivity 222
Tucker, A.W. 252, 256

union 29
upper semi-continuity 310
utility 157, 221
  indicator 223
  marginal 224
  maximization principle 157

Uzawa, H. 256

vector 48
column 57
non-negative 108
row 57
vector space 48
vectorial sum (of sets) 198

Wald, A. 3, 267
Walras, M.E.L. 1, 155, 265, 266
Walras law 285
(in the general sense) 320
Walrasian equilibrium model 268
Weierstrass, K. 2